The Generals of Saratoga

The Generals

Max M. Mintz

YALE UNIVERSITY PRESS   NEW HAVEN & LONDON

John Burgoyne & Horatio Gates

# of Saratoga

Published with assistance from the
foundation established in memory of
William McKean Brown.

Designed by James J. Johnson and set in
Monticello Roman type by The Composing Room of
Michigan, Inc.
Printed in the United States of America by Vail-Ballou Press,
Binghamton, New York.

Library of Congress Cataloging-in-Publication Data
Mintz, Max M., 1919–
    The generals of Saratoga : John Burgoyne and Horatio
        Gates / Max M. Mintz.
           p. cm.
    Includes bibliographical references.
    ISBN 0–300–04778–9 (alk. paper)
    1. Saratoga Campaign, 1777. 2. Burgoyne, John,
1722–1792. 3. Gates, Horatio, 1728–1806. I. Title.
      E241.S2M56   1990
    973.3'33—dc20   90–34052
                  CIP

*The paper in this book meets the
guidelines for permanence and
durability of the Committee on
Production Guidelines for Book Longevity
of the Council on
Library Resources.*

1 3 5 7 9 10 8 6 4 2

8378505

Rco

To my wife, Pat,
and my son, Ken

Contents

Illustrations

MAPS

Acknowledgments

Portions of this book were read in manuscript by Edmund S. Morgan, Jonathan R. Dull, and John F. Burke, and I am most grateful for their criticisms and suggestions. The maps were drawn by Lynn Ohlsen and James J. Johnson. Meighan Pritchard did superb copyediting.

Grants from the National Endowment for the Humanities and the American Philosophical Society and two sabbatical leaves and a Presidential Fellowship from Southern Connecticut State University gave me undivided time and facilitated travel. At Saratoga National Historical Park, Chief Historian S. Paul Okey permitted me to borrow valuable staff research reports.

Many correspondents took the trouble to answer my queries. In America, these included Philander D. Chase, associate editor of The Papers of George Washington, and Harmon Cook Leonard, a direct descendant of Colonel Thaddeus Cook. In Canada, these included Norman M. Willis, archivist at the National Archives of Canada. In England, these included H. Davis, borough librarian of Greenwich; Richard Green, curator of the York City Art Gallery; Margaret Holmes, Dorset County archivist; E. D. Mercer, head archivist of the Greater London Record Office; Heather E. Peek, keeper of the archives of the University of Cambridge; W. A. L. Seaman, Durham County archivist; Alastair Smart, professor emeritus of art history at the University of Nottingham; and J. V. Stacey, verger of St. Alfege Church in Greenwich.

The staffs of the libraries whose manuscripts I have cited in my notes were uniformly helpful, as were those in my home base libraries at Southern Connecticut State and Yale universities, and I am in their debt.

A section of chapter 20 was previously published in *History Today* and is reproduced here with the kind permission of the editor.

Charles Grench, executive editor of Yale University Press, gave encouragement when it was needed during the writing of this book, and he has been its staunch advocate in the program of publication.

Prologue:
Appointment at Saratoga

THE GUNS WERE SILENT AT SARA-toga, and October 17, 1777, dawned clear after nine days of mist and rain. John Burgoyne, exhausted but defiant, rose early to prepare for his surrender to Horatio Gates. In place of the clothes he had slept in without change for sixteen nerve-racking days, he donned full regimentals. Rich plumes waved from his braided, well-brushed hat. In a face roughened by exposure and hard living, his frank, hazel eyes and jutting jaw marked him a man of action. He was enough above average in height to be considered tall, and still, at fifty-four, a man of imposing figure.[1]

Gates's aide-de-camp, twenty-year-old Colonel James Wilkinson, his youth accentuated by his slight build, arrived to conduct the British commander and his staff to the American headquarters. First they rode east to the junction of Fish Creek and the Hudson to inspect the meadow where the British troops were to lay down their arms and artillery later that morning. Then they forded the swollen creek over a slender connector thrown across the sleepers of the broken bridge. On the opposite bank they turned west, past the charred remains of General Philip Schuyler's house and mills that Burgoyne had ordered put to the torch a week earlier. A mile further along the shore of the creek, they arrived at the breastworks ringing the American camp. Sentries, relieved of the strain of sniper fire, allowed them through.

From a crude cabin partially dug out of the bank on the side of the road, a solitary, unimpressive figure emerged on horseback. Horatio Gates was dressed only in a plain blue coat, with scarcely any sign of his rank as major general. His thinning gray hair was unpowdered and cut close to his round head. He peered from behind spectacles that his shortsightedness seldom

I

permitted him to do without. At fifty, he looked older than his years. Although slightly above average in height, his stooped shoulders and beefy build made him appear short. But if, as was said, Burgoyne had dubbed him an "old midwife," the put-down had clearly been a costly miscalculation. There was a worldly-wise, mildly disillusioned air about his sharp eyes and long nose with its tilted tip, and a homey friendliness that had won him popularity with his troops.

Burgoyne spurred forward to meet him, flanked by his aides and followed by his generals. They reined up at a sword's length from each other. Wilkinson performed the introductions. The formalities were unnecessary; the two men had known each other for thirty-two years.

"I am glad to see you," said Gates.

"I am not glad to see you," was Burgoyne's tight-lipped reply. "It is my fortune, sir, and not my fault that I am here."[2]

Thirty-two years before, in England, they had started out as lieutenants in the same regiment. But Burgoyne was the son of an army captain and grandson of a baronet, or better yet, if rumor was true, the bastard son of Lord Bingley. Gates was the son of a lowly customs official who had begun life as a Thames River boatman. Who then would have believed that the skipjack would dare to challenge the aristocrat? Who now could resist believing that destiny had reunited them in the New World to reverse the order of the Old?

❦ 1 ❦

Privilege

THE KNOWLEDGEABLE WORLD OF London did not believe that the son born to Anna Maria Burgoyne on February 4, 1723, had been fathered by her husband, ex-Captain John Burgoyne, Sr.

It was common talk that Lord Bingley, a wealthy Yorkshire politician who had been rewarded with a baronage for serving as Chancellor of the Exchequer, was taken with Anna Maria. He was the owner of the row house in which the Burgoynes lived, on Park Prospect, a terrace at the southeast end of St. James's Park. Anna Maria was lovely and charming. Bingley's wife, whom he had married for her money, was plain and unpleasant. He maintained a small residence in the street behind the Burgoynes, and he found Anna Maria a delight and a refuge from the gloom of his great house in Cavendish Square. For her sake he lent Captain Burgoyne, a compulsive gambler, large sums and never demanded payment. The day after the birth of her boy, named John, Bingley stood as godfather at the christening in nearby St. Margaret's. When he died in 1731, he left Anna Maria an annuity of four hundred pounds, ownership of the row house, lease rent-free for life of an estate, "The Nunnery," in Cheshunt, and forgiveness of her husband's debts. In the event of the deaths of his one legitimate daughter and another natural one without issue (the legitimate daughter did produce a son), young John Burgoyne was to become his residual heir, on condition that he take Bingley's name, Robert Benson.[1]

The legacy provided the tuition for John's education, which his father of record could never have afforded. Captain Burgoyne ran hopelessly into debt. He was the second son of Sir John Burgoyne, third baronet of Sutton, in Bedfordshire, and received from him a small inheritance. With his wife, the daughter of a wealthy Hackney merchant, he received a generous dowry.

He spent it all at cards, defaulted on his debts, and ended in King's Bench Prison.

At the age of ten, John was enrolled at Westminster School, the foremost hatchery for England's political, military, and ecclesiastical establishment, and a two minute walk south of the Burgoyne home. Westminster alumni included the philosopher John Locke, the poet John Dryden, and future prime ministers Henry Pelham and the duke of Newcastle. Lord George Sackville, the future colonial secretary during the American Revolution, had just left when John entered, and among John's contemporaries was the future commanding general in America, Thomas Gage. The school was located between St. Margaret's and Westminster Abbey, near the houses of Parliament, and the students had the privilege of attending debates and coronations. Members of both houses frequently stopped to chat with the boys about affairs of state.

The headmaster was John Nicoll, who was beginning his tenure in 1733, the year Burgoyne entered. A kindly man, he instituted the honor system, preferring that students be disciplined by peer pressure rather than physical chastisement. Confessions softened him to lenience. He sometimes waived tuition for needy students. He was "a master," an acquaintance observed, "not only of the dead languages, but also of the living manners." Westminster instruction centered on Latin and Greek, with the usual emphasis on memorization. There was a distinctive Westminster Latin enunciation. Each year a play of Terence was produced two weeks before the Christmas holiday. Even mathematics was taught in Latin. All classes were held in one large, Norman-style schoolroom, ninety-six by thirty-four feet, of bare stone covered with names gouged or painted through the ages. The high, exposed roof of ancient chestnut was supported by arched iron rafters. Six round-headed windows on each side provided light, and in the center was an open hearth for a warming fire. A curtain separated the upper from the lower forms. Senior students tutored the juniors; the honor system enforced obedience under pain of public contempt. Hours were from eight to six. Sports included boxing, wrestling, and cricket. Little of this differed from the training provided in other reputable schools.

What set Westminster apart was its social selectivity and school spirit. Schoolboy friendships continued through life. Horseplay, practical jokes, juvenile brutality, touchiness on points of honor, tests of endurance, and pride of belonging generated a camaraderie that defied erosion. A withdrawn, sensitive boy might find this experience a torment. Lord Chesterfield, whose son left the school, wrote that it was "the scene of illiberal manners and brutal

4

behaviour."[2] An outgoing, athletic lad would relish the game. John Burgoyne fitted in. Well built, bright, pleasure loving, he inspired lasting affection. There was about him a touch of romance and an air of abandon. He had a flair for words and colored his conversation and writing with imagery and an aura of adventure. Among the friends he made was Lord James Strange, only son of the enormously wealthy earl of Derby. Although Strange was five years older than John, a close bond sprang up between them. For the younger lad it was to prove Westminster's greatest boon.

At the age of fifteen, John decided on an army career. There was hardly any other option open to a youth of his class. Yet he may have been expressing a love-hate relationship with his scapegrace father—emulating his profession on the one hand and determining to surpass and eclipse it on the other. Military commissions were then usually obtained by paying an official purchase price to the incumbent. Restrictive and inefficient though the system was, it at least in its day opened opportunity to those who could not expect preference through birth, and it provided a retirement income for the seller. On August 9, 1737, the Burgoynes scraped together the purchase price, probably twelve hundred pounds, for a commission as sub-brigadier in the Third Troop of Horse Guards. The Guards served at home, so young Burgoyne had only light duties of ceremonial parade and police patrol on the roads. He had the time to cut a figure in society. He had style and spirit. He womanized. Like his father, he gambled. Perhaps it was gambling debts that forced him to resign his commission in November 1741. The pattern was forming for the ultimate gamble at Saratoga.

His friendship with Strange deepened. The world of the Derbys meant lavish country estates, the company of beautiful, clever women, the excitement of politics and power. The Derby ancestral seat was Knowsley Hall, in Lancashire, eight miles northeast of Liverpool. Although Liverpool was then the third seaport of England, the rest of the county was still predominantly rural, a fertile land of undulating valleys just south of the mountains that were to be known as Wordsworth Lake Country. Knowsley was a regal domain, ten to twelve miles in circumference, with forests of oak, fields of rhododendron, a splendid, three-mile-long lake, and a lovely park that Benjamin Disraeli, when he visited Knowsley in 1853, pronounced "almost as large as Windsor." The great house consisted of a Tudor-style dark brown stone castle and a Georgian red brick wing with two stories of nineteen tall sash windows surmounted by a central section of seven shorter windows; the whole was embellished with stone dressings, quoins, and balustrades. The royal family addressed the Stanleys (the Derby family name) as "cousin" and regularly came for informal visits, often unannounced. Politically, the Stanleys generally supported the Crown but steered a sufficiently middle-of-the-road course to keep on good terms with the Whigs. In 1852, Edward Stanley, the fifteenth earl of Derby, became prime minister.

Strange was model as well as sponsor for Burgoyne. He had studied, after Westminster, at the University of Leyden, and was now a member of Parliament for the traditional Derby family seat of Lancaster. Respected for his independence, industry, and intelligence, he was, according to Horace Walpole, a speaker of "spirit, quickness and fire" and a master of timed humor. He read widely and among friends delighted to contradict for the fun of the dispute. He was an ardent and fearless huntsman. He lived in Patten House, the family town residence in Preston, a cotton manufacturing village about twenty-five miles north of Knowsley. Seen through its wrought-iron fence with an ornate gateway topped by the Derby coronet, on the north side of Church Street at its junction with Derby Street, Patten House dominated the town just as Knowsley Hall dominated the countryside. It was a three-storied brick mansion with twenty-four fronting windows, a projecting central pediment three windows wide, and a railed stairway leading to the doorway flanked with Corinthian pillars. The Stanleys were all devoted track fans, and when they came to attend the races on Preston Moor, or to share in local festivities, they were guests of Strange. The wine flowed, conversation sparkled; Strange was at his entertaining best.[3]

In April 1744 Burgoyne was able to rejoin the army as a coronet in the First Royal Dragoons, a commission he did not have to pay for, as it was newly created and therefore exempt from the requirement. In the Royals he had his first experience of action abroad, in the War of the Austrian Succession (known in America as King George's War), the latest contest in the century-old struggle for supremacy between Britain and France. He must have acquitted himself creditably, for on February 23, 1745, he was promoted to lieutenant, a position also exempt from the purchase requirement because its incumbent had obtained it through seniority. Eight months later he was appointed to a new regiment recruited by the duke of Bolton, where he served uneventfully until 1747, when he managed somehow to obtain two thousand pounds to purchase a captaincy back in the Royals. Perhaps he had a run of luck at the gaming tables—his winnings in later years were good enough to provoke the snide remark that he was a cardsharp.[4]

By 1751, at twenty-eight, he was ready to settle down. He had been infatuated with Frances Poole, a baronet's daughter, but now he discovered that Strange's sister, Charlotte, had grown to womanhood. Twenty-three years old, slender and sensitive but not a striking beauty, she succumbed to the charm of her brother's landless friend. When Lord Derby positively refused to sanction such an unequal match, they eloped and on April 14, 1751, were secretly married in London's St. George's Chapel, in Curzon Street, Mayfair. Derby cut them off without a penny, and they soon found life on a low-paid officer's salary intolerable for an earl's daughter. They chose a drastic recourse. In October of that year, Burgoyne sold his commission and they departed for France, where expenses were lower and the twenty-six hundred pounds he had received might keep them going.[5] If driven, they could resort to selling Charlotte's jewels.

In France, the Burgoynes met the Comte de Stainville and his wife, a couple their own age. Stainville was to become duc de Choiseul in 1758 and minister for foreign affairs under Louis XV. While Burgoyne was learning French and trading pleasantries, he could sense in his friends the roots of the Anglophobia that helped provoke the Seven Years' War with Britain in 1756 and later was to bring France into the American Revolution in the wake of Saratoga. The Burgoynes remained abroad for four years, traveling to the south of France and to Italy. At Aix, they dined with the Scottish architect, Robert Adam, and gamed half the day. In Rome they again met Stainville, now French ambassador to the Vatican, and the painter, Allan Ramsay, who did a vivid portrait of Burgoyne, the first we have. In October or November of 1754, Charlotte gave birth to a daughter, Charlotte Elizabeth, the Burgoynes' only child. Probably in hope of the softening effect a granddaughter might have on Lord Derby, they returned to England in 1755.[6]

Derby surrendered. Strange had helped, and soon Burgoyne became the family favorite. With Derby influence behind him, there seemed no limit now to the heights to which he might aspire. He decided to reenter the army. On June 14, 1756, he purchased a captaincy in the Eleventh Dragoons, with the understanding that he would not have to wait long for promotion.

The Seven Years' War had broken out on May 15. If he was avid for rank, he was equally eager to face danger. His chance came when William Pitt came to power as prime minister in May of the following year. Part of Pitt's plan of operations was to conduct raids on the French coast in order to relieve French pressure on Germany and America. Late in May 1758, Burgoyne's regiment was ordered to join an amphibious force of 10,450 troops under the titular leadership of the third duke of Marlborough. The real commander was Lord George Sackville, who was later to become first a friend of Burgoyne and then, after Saratoga, his enemy. Also in the expedition was William Howe, the man who was to abandon Burgoyne to his fate at Saratoga.

The armada made a successful landing near Saint-Malo. French merchantmen and naval stores were destroyed. The French fort, however, proved too strong to attempt, and the expedition returned to Spithead. British politicians were unenthusiastic about such inconclusive ventures, which a pamphleteer declared would alarm no one but "a few peasants and few old women for fear they should not be ravished." Pitt nevertheless persisted, and a month later the armada, under the new leadership of Lieutenant General Thomas Bligh, landed on the Normandy coast and looted and destroyed Cherbourg. Another landing was made near Saint-Malo, but this time the French arrived with overwhelming reinforcements. The British fled during the night to their ships at Saint-Cast, where the French caught up with them, killed 750, and captured 400 before the British could reembark for England. The casualties would have been greater had not Burgoyne and another officer launched a decisive counterattack against a French flanking force. For this, when the army returned home, he was rewarded with a transfer to the elite Second, or Coldstream, Regiment of Foot Guards.[7]

Pitt, on the alert for enterprising officers, kept his eye on him. On August 4, 1759, Burgoyne was named lieutenant colonel to recruit a new regiment, the Sixteenth Light Dragoons. Inevitably, in such a meteoric rise, some toes were stepped on. Lord Barrington, the secretary at war, bluntly told him that the command of a regiment was a prize to which, with all his "amiable and valuable qualities as a man," he had "not the least claim as a soldier."[8] The quality Barrington grudgingly acknowledged was in fact a commanding personality, which had been strikingly captured three years before in the painting done by Ramsay in Rome. The hand on the right hip appears vigorously to have swept aside the gold-brocaded red coat to uncover a snug, buff waistcoat. The other arm, with tricornered, gold-bordered hat in hand, leans with imperious assurance on a remnant of Roman statuary. The face, with its generous, straight nose, full lips firmly drawn over slightly buck teeth, and large, well shaped jaw, wears an expression that is serious and decisive, yet open and instantly intimate. The hazel eyes, somewhat protruding, are pensive but not inhibited and convey confidence mingled with understanding. Reddish brown hair and clear skin complete the impression of a sunny disposition. It is a portrait not of a classically handsome man but of a vigorous, magnetic one with the determination and dash, even brashness, to undertake great enterprises.[9]

The Sixteenth Light Dragoons quickly demonstrated that its lieutenant colonel was a talented regimental organizer. Well within the four months he had been given, he had his full complement of enlisted men. "Young men out of employment or uncomfortable," his posters exhorted, "Nick in instantly and enlist." Splendid horses, colorful uniforms, and pay and privileges of two guineas a week awaited. "You are admired by the fair, which, together with the chance of getting switched to a buxom widow, or of brushing a rich heiress, renders the situation truly enviable and desirable." What country lad of sixteen could resist such blandishments? Next, Burgoyne drew up a personnel guidebook for his officers, with the startling proposal that, instead of training men, like the Prussians, as "spaniels, by the stick," or like the French, merely by "the point of honor," soldiers should be treated as "thinking beings." The Englishman, he observed, "will not bear beating so well as the foreigners." He must not be sworn at, and there were "occasions, such as during stable or fatigue duty," when an officer might "slacken the reins so far as to talk with soldiers; nay, even a joke may be used." Among themselves, officers were encouraged to cultivate off-duty camaraderie regardless of rank; to learn personally to saddle a horse; and to study military science, mathematics, French, and the writing of English "with swiftness and accuracy." The response was predictable: "Burgoyne's Light Horse" became a model corps, regularly called out for the king's reviewing pleasure. Its first battle assignment was to another of Pitt's maritime raids, this time to capture an island off the coast of Brittany in the Bay of Biscay, Belle-Ile, which might be exchanged for Minorca. Only two hundred of the regiment's men were needed, however, requiring no more than a captain to command them. Burgoyne appointed his friend Sir William Williams and went along himself as a volunteer observer. The island was conquered in two costly assaults. Williams was killed on a reconnaissance mission. Burgoyne, with his knowledge of French, conducted negotiations for improved treatment of prisoners. He returned to England chafing for a full-scale challenge.[10]

The moment arrived in May 1762. Spain had entered the war on the side of France and had invaded Portugal, England's ally. The Portuguese king, Joseph I, called upon England for help, and the earl of Bute, who had succeeded Pitt as prime minister, responded with an army of seven thousand under Lord Loudon. Burgoyne's Sixteenth Light Dragoons was the only cavalry assigned to the expedition; it would be in the van of any operation.

The allied commander of the Portuguese-British troops was Count Wilhelm von der Schaumberg-Lippe-Bückeburg, son of a bastard of George I by the Duchess of Kendall and princeling of a tiny northwest German principality. Better known to the English as Count La Lippe, he had earned a reputation as Europe's top artillerist under Prince Ferdinand of Brunswick. He was said to be a double for Sweden's intrepid Charles XI, with moustache and goatee, flowing hair, and piercing eyes. He wore a long, caped coat, buttoned from top to bottom. In private, he could be "silently supercilious" (Thomas Carlyle's description). Before his troops he acted the forbidding disciplinarian, but they knew him for a compassionate advocate and affectionately nicknamed him "The thundering black Prince." He had a genius for selecting subordinates and knowing when to give them freedom of movement. He quickly spotted Burgoyne and gave him, as the senior cavalry officer present, local rank as brigadier general in command of a three-thousand-man force, two-thirds of it ill-trained and -equipped Portuguese. Burgoyne exulted. His zest and self-confidence communicated themselves to the men. To appeal to his Portuguese recruits, he grew a moustache and goatee.

A Spanish army of fourteen thousand under the Count de Aranda was then heading down the Tagus River and threatening Lisbon. Burgoyne was assigned the mission of stopping it, with La Lippe's assurance of his personal "defence and protection" for whatever action he took. He chose, as his first target, the Spanish troop and supply center at Valencia de Alcántara, a walled frontier town sixteen miles south of the Tagus, just across the border in Spain. After a forced march of five days across the Castel da Vida Mountains, he neared his goal on the night of August 27. He had planned a surprise attack, but four miles from the town he realized that his guides had deceived him about the distance. His infantry could not make it there before daybreak. Determined not to lose his opportunity, he galloped ahead with his dragoons. They found the town gate open and charged through, killing or taking prisoner the guards and securing the street arteries. A few squads of Spaniards attempted counterattacks, but all organized resistance soon ceased. To flush out snipers, he forced the priests to announce that the town would be burned unless all doors and windows were instantly thrown open. All firing promptly ended. Large caches of arms and ammunition were confiscated or destroyed. Captured, Burgoyne reported, were a major general, a colonel, two captains, seventeen subalterns, hostages for the return of British wounded, "a year's king's revenue for sparing the convents and town," and, a vital point of prestige, three Spanish flags.

The victory slowed the Spanish, but they continued down the Tagus into

Portuguese territory, seizing a Moorish castle at Vila Velha. Probing for a weak spot, Burgoyne noticed that the Spaniards had reduced their garrison in order to pursue a retreating Portuguese brigade, and he dispatched a force of 250 grenadiers and 50 light dragoons under Lieutenant Colonel Charles Lee for a surprise attack on Vila Velha. Lee crossed the Tagus on the night of October 5 and struck swiftly, inflicting huge casualties, spiking six guns, destroying supplies, and escaping with a herd of horses and mules. After that, desertion, disease, and November's torrential rains forced Aranda back across the border to Albuquerque. Lisbon had been saved. King Joseph presented Burgoyne with a diamond ring, and in Paris peace negotiations brought an end to the war and permanent delivery from the Spanish menace.[11]

The experience under La Lippe had been profound. Burgoyne venerated him as a man who "united the deepest political reasoning with exquisite military address." Under him he had been entrusted with a crucial mission and given wide latitude in discharging it. He had succeeded in managing a multinational army, switching plans in the face of an emergency, and obtaining obedience from a civilian population. Yet, ultimately, this experience proved an equal liability. His intimidation of impoverished and oppressed Spanish peasants was not to be an adequate guide for dealing with a free, self-reliant American populace and citizen-army. He could not, in America, take for granted that he would receive support at home for decisions in the field. "This prepossession," he ruefully admitted after Saratoga, "may in some measure account for and excuse my imprudence."[12]

2

The Skipjack

FOR HORATIO GATES IT ALL BEGAN with the birth of a star on the London stage in 1728. In a moment of inspiration, John Rich, manager of the Theatre Royal, chose an unknown young actress named Lavinia Fenton to play the lead role of Polly Peacham, a highwayman's mistress, in John Gay's *The Beggar's Opera*. The opera was a lampoon of contemporary politics, likening Newgate jailbirds to Whitehall ministers, and Lavinia seemed bred for her part. She had grown up in the Old Bailey, where her stepfather was an imprisoned debtor (her natural father, a naval lieutenant, had absconded), and she had learned her manners from the noblemen she met through Mother Needham, one of London's most notorious madams. At seventeen Lavinia had eloped with a Portuguese nobleman; when he wound up in debtors' prison, she had cheerfully taken up with a formidable string of lovers. "Polly" was an instant success. The London *Daily Journal* announced that "most of the boxes are taken to the 25th Night," and Gay wondered whether her fame did not eclipse that of the opera. Hogarth painted her, street singers serenaded her, a duel was even fought over her, and a wag remarked that she "has raised her Price from one Guinea to 100, tho she cannot be a greater whore than she was before." Her supreme conquest was the duke of Bolton, known as a gambler and a rake. At the June 19 performance of the *Opera,* a surprised audience learned that Lavinia had been replaced by another "Polly." She was never to return. She had run off with Bolton, who, Gay informed Jonathan Swift, "settled £400 upon her during pleasure, and upon disagreement £200."[1]

Unfortunately, there was already a duchess of Bolton. Well educated but homely and "Cram'd with virtue," as Lady Mary Montague reported, the duchess had "fail'd to give Passion." Rumor had it the marriage was never consummated. She lived apart from her husband on her own estate in

Ireland. Bolton's intentions toward Lavinia were honorable, and years later, when his wife died, he made the former actress a duchess. But for now he settled Lavinia at Greenwich in Westcombe House, a sumptuous villa overlooking the winding Thames at what a guidebook described as "one of the most desirable spots in England."[2] They conducted themselves in all respects as man and wife, living quietly, traveling abroad, eventually raising three children. Of course, some circumspection was required to shield Lavinia from coarse comment and to prevent the children from growing up with any sense of inferiority. The first essential was a capable housekeeper, skilled in setting up the new establishment and discreet enough to put off inquisitive guests and impertinent tradespeople. Such a one might be difficult to find and once obtained would have to be well rewarded.

Bolton made a momentous choice. In 1729, he engaged Robert and Dorothy Gates, parents of an infant son named Horatio. Dorothy had served for many years as housekeeper for the duke of Leeds, who had just died. Robert was a Thames River boatman who had been scraping together a precarious living by ferrying and bartering produce among the ships in the crowded Pool of London. The Pool in those days had no modern docks, so that ships had to anchor in the river and load and unload their cargoes by means of lighters that plied to and from the quays and wharves where duties were collected. Robert had followed his family into this milieu—his father was a victualler and an elder brother a waterman. "I row up to Greenwich and buy fresh meat there," says a waterman in Daniel Defoe's *Journal of the Plague Year,* "and sometimes I row down the river to Woolwich and buy there, then I go to single farm-houses on the Kentish side, where I am known, and buy fowls and eggs and butter, and bring to the ships, as they direct me, sometimes one, sometimes the other." Sometimes Robert Gates smuggled cargo from the ships, as when he rowed nine hogsheads of French wine for importer David Boyes in 1724 and was caught. Arraigned in court, he pleaded that he was only Boyes's hireling and was destitute. The immovable judges fined him £104 5s., treble the value of the contraband. That impossible sum was still waiting to be paid when Robert entered Bolton's service.[3]

Servants in eighteenth-century England were the fortunate poor. From several in a small household, there were as many as fifty or more on a large estate. Their wages were low and their time was their masters', but they had their perquisites. They were frequently supplied with board, lodging, and livery. They sold off candle ends, used livery, and worn carriage parts. They could be insistent. Visitors to great houses have left pained testimony to servants' demands for "vails." The servants formed two lines on both sides of the front door, and the departing guest did not escape without giving each his appropriate gratuity. Daniel Defoe complained that "there is not one Servant in twenty now, that will take a Blow from a Master, but with their Tongues will insult them." Noblemen's servants also received reflected prestige. If they gave satisfaction, their patron might help them to set up independently in business or to obtain government employment. Retired servants frequently became tavern keepers. Some won distinction in the professions. Robert Dodsley, a footman, attracted attention as a poet and playwright and with a hundred-pound donation from Alexander Pope became a bookseller and publisher. Adam Charles, the duke of Chandos's valet, became a surgeon. Lancelot Brown, a gardener, became the country's most eminent landscapist. Some servants received positions in the customs service, and some, like the valet of army Commander in Chief Sir John Ligonier, were even given military commissions. These were significant precedents for the Gateses.

Greenwich was a mile east of Deptford, the easternmost limit of the expanding city of London. It lay south of a bend of the Thames, across from which was the Isle of Dogs. Still bucolic, it was a favored location for noblemen's summer estates. It had a popularly frequented park, the Royal Hospital for seamen designed by Christopher Wren, and the famed National Observatory. Westcombe House, on the eastern outskirt, stood on a commanding elevation overlooking Shooter's Hill, with a fine view of London and its adjacent hills of Highgate and Hampstead. Built for Alfridus Walpole, brother of the prime minister, by John Vanbrugh, architect of Blenheim palace, it was a square two-story brick mansion with single-story wings at both sides and a low, tiled, four-sided roof, with chimneys at each corner and a cupola at the apex. The Gateses probably "lived in" at first. In time, they fared well enough to afford a place of their own on Crane Street, a small leader off the shore of the Thames, just east of the Royal Hospital. The Woolwich Road extended west to Crane Street. Westcombe House was a short walk away.[4]

The Gateses did give satisfaction. Dorothy, no doubt, managed the household with assurance, bullied the townspeople, and placated the guests (although Lavinia proved able enough to take good care of herself). Dorothy was a native of Durham, and her father, John Hubbock, a vintner, had served as the city postmaster. The family came of a line of clergymen, and one of her nephews, another John Hubbock, later received bachelor's and master's degrees from St. John's College, Oxford, and became rector of Holy Trinity and St. Peter's churches in Dorset. She had some schooling, enough to write a well-constructed letter. She was an ambitious woman, eager to ingratiate herself with her employer. Married once before, she had named one of her children Peregrine, after the duke of Leeds. When her first husband died, she had sensed potential in Robert Gates, a rough and ready unlettered but intelligent waterman much younger than herself, whom she may have met when he came to peddle his produce at the Leeds estate in Wimbledon. Robert, one suspects, rendered an out-of-house service to Bolton more in line with his former calling. Bolton was deep in army contract profiteering on a scale large enough to provoke public comment. "Now Bolton comes with beat of drums," ran a current verse of political doggerel,

> though fighting be his loathing,
> He much dislikes both guns and pikes,
> But relishes the *clothing*.

Robert's reward was not long in coming. Within the year he paid his smuggling fine. On July 10, 1729, he was appointed tidesman in the customs service.[5]

Horatio Gates probably was born July 26, 1727, at Old Malden, near Wimbledon, in Surrey. No record of his birth has survived, and presumably none was made, as was then not uncommon. The only testimony we have, other than his own contradictory remarks, is a letter from Horace Walpole:

> Gates was a son of a housekeeper of the second Duke of Leeds, who marrying a young husband when she was very old had this son by him. That Duke of Leeds had been saved, when guilty of a Jacobite plot, by my father, Sir Robert Walpole, and the Duke was very grateful, and took great notice of me when I was quite a boy. My mother's woman was intimate with that housekeeper and thence I was godfather to her son, though, I believe, not then ten years old myself.

As Walpole was born September 24, 1717, that would identify the year of Horatio's birth as 1727. Tradition speaks of the place as Maldon, Essex, but because Dorothy Gates was employed at the Leeds estate at Wimbledon, the more likely location is at nearby Old Malden.

Enemies and detractors of Gates, skeptical that the son of servants should receive a commission in the British army, have alleged that he was Leeds's illegitimate son. It was not impossible, although Leeds was sixty-eight at the time of conception. An engraving reveals features similar to those of Gates:

long rounded chin and long nose with tilted tip. One wonders, after all, what could have induced young Robert Gates to take aging Dorothy Reeve, with her brood of children by a first husband, as his wife. Undoubtedly, he hoped that her high connections would improve his fortunes. But could it have been that she was already pregnant by Leeds, and that Gates was offered a special compensation, such as an extension of time to pay his smuggling fine? The naming of the child raises still another suspicion. Why the name Horatio? Horace's uncle was Horatio Walpole. Was there a link there?

The unanswered questions haunted Horatio all his life. When he aspired to advancement, he was accused of illegitimate pretensions. If he earned a promotion, it was ascribed to his birth. The result was an intense desire for approval and an acute susceptibility to flattery. The contradictory dates he gave at various times for his birth suggest a youthful attempt to silence gossip. As an infantry captain he gave the year as 1729, the year of Leeds's death, when presumably the duke was too old and too infirm to father a child. But in America, where the slurs might be forgotten, and when the issue had become inconsequential—he had no surviving children—he reverted at first to the birth year of 1728 and finally to 1727.[6]

Young Horatio preferred his untutored, self-made father to his domineering, status-conscious mother. He loved his cousins by his father's elder brother, Thomas, and afterward kept in contact with them when he had become famous and they remained obscure. He never cared to cultivate relationships with relatives on his mother's side. Long after her death, her second cousin wrote to invite a correspondence, but he let the letter go unanswered.[7] His ambition for rank may have stemmed from a desire to outdo the Hubbocks.

If ever a boy grew up amid physical surroundings that spoke daily of ambition and grandeur, it was in Greenwich, close to the most magnificent assemblage of classical architecture in England. The grounds of the majestic Royal Navy Hospital were one block away from the Gates home on Crane Street. Surrounding a great courtyard were colonnaded palaces built by four of England's monarchs over a period of three-quarters of a century, and Horatio saw the last palace completed in 1735. Still used as a lodging for diplomats was the Queen's Castle, and their mysterious arrivals and departures breathed of bold designs and dangerous intrigues.[8]

Horatio walked past these sights to school every day. Just behind the hospital, the lovely Greenwich Park, which included the observatory that dictated the world's time, had special allurements—two of its diagonally opposite paths were named Love Walk and Brazen Face Walk. West of the Queen's House, in the area of the present King William Street and Trafalgar

Road, stood three schools side by side, a comprehensive system for all the common children of the community. The Green Coat School accommodated the sons of watermen, fishermen, and mariners; the Grey Coat School enrolled boys of other modest families; and the Blue Coat School admitted girls. Horatio, presumably a Green Coat boy, in round hat, green coat, knee breeches, and buckle shoes, would walk south from Crane Street into East Lane and cross westward between the hospital and the Queen's House to his school on London Street. The curriculum of the Green Coat School can only be inferred from what we know of Horatio's accomplishments. In later years Dr. Benjamin Rush said that he "possessed some learning."[9] He wrote English in a clear, smooth style. His letters show some knowledge of Latin and Greek and the classics. He had a good command of French, which may have been acquired at this time, as there was a Huguenot colony in Greenwich. He developed steady work habits and attention to detail.

Personality traits emerged. He learned, probably from Horatio, Charles, and Percy Paulet (Lavinia's children), to mingle with aristocracy on terms of easy familiarity. He exuded a sense of competence and dependability. Acquaintances felt at home with him and gave him their trust. He put a high value on friendship, he always remained loyal, and he could be counted on in an emergency. He conveyed the feeling that he not only gave but needed friendship, and he had a comforting look of maturity that made him seem older than his age. He tried, perhaps too hard, to please.

The fortunes of the Gates family took a sharp turn upward in 1741. The post of surveyor of customs at Greenwich fell vacant—the incumbent had requested a transfer to a position as river inspector. Again Bolton used his influence, and on August 21 Robert Gates was appointed.[10] The new position meant security and status. Now the Gateses might dare to hope for prospects for Horatio. He might be a gentleman, as good as those Hubbocks.

Horatio's chance came with the Rising of 1745, "Bonnie" Prince Charles Edward's quixotic attempt to reestablish the Stuart family on the throne of England. Suppression of the rising required new troops. Bolton, who had been out of royal favor for some years because of his Whig attachments and had been dismissed from a number of sinecures, saw this as an opportunity to affirm his loyalty. He volunteered to raise an infantry regiment for service in the Highlands and was named lieutenant general. Because this was to be a new unit, the appointment of officers did not fall under the elitist system that applied to existing regiments, in which the award of each commission required the recipient to pay an official purchase price to the officer resigning it. A critic carped that a "thick and thin" patron might reward a favorite servant with a commission. The Gateses were quick to see this opportunity for Horatio. They had given Bolton loyal service for fifteen years. Robert Gates had risen to a respectable position, Horatio was a promising lad, and a commission for him would be the ultimate prize of the family's rise on the social ladder. Bolton proved to be that "thick and thin" patron. Undoubtedly through his influence, Horatio was commissioned an ensign in Colonel Thomas Bligh's Twentieth Regiment of Foot. This was to give him the entry rank from which he was then promoted to Bolton's own regiment. On October 14, 1745, the clerk in the War Office wrote down, "Horatio Gates, Gentleman to be Lieutenant," the fifteenth entry on the roster of Bolton's officers. Astoundingly, the sixteenth name was "John Burgoyne," likewise "Gentleman to be Lieutenant."[11]

Horatio's elevation, although unusual, was not unique. Henry Fielding's villainous Lieutenant Northerton, in *Tom Jones,* was the son of a nobleman's butler. But the Northertons were expected to know their place and aspire no further. Fielding's characterization of Northerton as "ignorant of the Greeks and Trojans, profane, immoral, and dishonest," was in itself a sign of the aristocrat's disdain of an upstart's presumptuousness. What distinguished Horatio was that he refused to be either a second-class officer or a second-class gentleman. He was not prepared, like Tobias Smollett's Obadiah Lismahago in *Humphrey Clinker,* to serve thirty years and suffer wounding, maiming, and mutilation without ever rising above the rank of lieutenant.[12] He was willing to work hard and to learn his trade. He was a good hand at cards, a jolly drinking partner, and an adept at barrack ribaldry. He found that he was equally popular with aristocrats and commoners. He expected to be rewarded.

3

Luster

Burgoyne returned to England to a triumphal reception. All London read La Lippe's tribute in the *Gentleman's Magazine* to "the glorious conduct of Brigadier Burgoyne, who having marched fifteen leagues without halting, had taken Valencia d'Alcantara sword in hand."[1] How exhilarating the image of the debonair colonel fulfilling in the field the promise of his performance on the parade ground! For a full colonel he soon became. La Lippe had also written Lord Bute glowingly of Burgoyne's "remarkable valour, conduct, and presence of mind." This, and as always the influence of Strange, procured the promotion Burgoyne had unabashedly pursued with his usual persistence. The new rank carried with it tenure as commandant of the Sixteenth Light Dragoons and an annual income of approximately £650. Lady Charlotte was already receiving a yearly stipend of about four hundred pounds from her family, and her father had willed her twenty-five thousand pounds. Now they could live in the mode.

The indispensable ingredient of arrival was a seat in Parliament. In Georgian England, where suffrage was tied to property, large property owners virtually dictated the choice of members for their districts. Before Burgoyne left for the campaign in Portugal, his regimental friend, Captain Williams, owner of a substantial number of burgages (enfranchised property units) in Midhurst, Sussex, offered to sponsor him for one of the borough's two seats. Williams could also control many of the borough's 217 voters, as he was their employer. Additional support came through Hans Stanley, one of the Derby clan and a member of the Admiralty Board, who won over the duke of Newcastle with the promise that "Col. Burgoyne will honourably and steadily adhere to every assurance he gives your Grace." The other major local burgage owner in Midhurst was Viscount Montagu, a Catholic and therefore by law ineligible for office. A deal was concluded whereby Montagu would name his candidate, William Hamilton, for one of the seats, and Williams would name Burgoyne for the other. They were elected without opposition on March 30, 1761, while Burgoyne was in Portugal.[2]

On his return, he took his seat November 25, 1762, when the Seven Years' War was drawing to a close and Parliament was about to face the challenge of administering an expanded empire. In April 1763, the colorless George Grenville succeeded Bute as prime minister, and, with little thought to the consequences, acquiesced to a plan proposed by the king and amplified by the Tories to station fifteen infantry battalions of ten thousand men in North America. Subsistence of the troops, it was assumed, would be paid for by the colonists. The Americans, however, denied that there was any need for the soldiers, and an attempt to tax colonial imports of molasses in 1764 provoked colonial boycotts of British goods. Grenville was determined, and the following year he returned with the Stamp Act. The American response this time was not only nonimportation but riots fomented by newly sprung up Sons of Liberty organizations, and a Stamp Act Congress, meeting in New York, that took the first step toward intercolonial resistance.

The position that Burgoyne took on the Stamp Act determined the direction of the part he was to play in the American contest. He did not question that the rulers of England had an inherent right to legislate for the colonies in America. His own career was dependent on those rulers. Yet, in supporting the Stamp Act, he voted also from sincere conviction, a deep-rooted reverence for the British Empire. He had fought in a war that enlarged that empire. He saw it as a benevolent, enlightened institution that provided for all its subjects the basic human freedoms of the British Constitution. But Parliament must retain the central authority to knit the whole together, or there would be no empire. Grenville's tax did not interfere with liberties of speech, religion, or the person. It merely required the colonies to contribute to their own defense.[3]

Reverence for the Constitution did not resolve itself so easily for Burgoyne in another controversy that surfaced at the same time. John Wilkes, in his newspaper the *North Briton*, issue number 45, attacked the king as a liar for his terms of praise for the Peace of Paris that ended the Seven Years' War. He also published a parody of Alexander Pope, *An Essay on Woman*, which was accused of being blasphemous and obscene. Grenville instituted court proceedings against him for false and seditious libel. Because number 45 had been published anonymously, however, Wilkes was arrested on the doubtful legal authority of a general warrant. He became a cause célèbre; court circles despised him and the common people idolized him. "I hate the very name of

Wilkes," Charlotte Burgoyne wrote to Lord Palmerston, and no doubt she echoed her husband's sentiments. But Burgoyne was concerned with the threat to civil liberty that the use of general warrants posed, and he requested floor time to state his objections. In the end, though, he voted for the warrants on February 18, 1764. Interest triumphed over principle. He had the previous month requested appointment as secretary to Lord Northumberland, lord lieutenant of Ireland, and he needed Grenville's support. Unfortunately, as it turned out, he could not also win over Northumberland.[4]

The Stamp Act aroused opposition in England as well as the colonies. British merchants, hurt by the colonies' retaliation of nonimportation, clamored for repeal. Pitt thundered against the act, and Benjamin Franklin, agent for Pennsylvania, testified before a Commons committee that any attempt to collect the tax in America by force would provoke rebellion. A new prime minister, the marquess of Rockingham, now replaced Grenville, who had a falling out with the king over patronage. A seemingly insignificant politician, Rockingham undertook the thankless task of repealing the Stamp Act. He could not hope to succeed without the support of the country members and the "King's Friends," and to placate them he proposed the Declaratory Act, asserting Parliament's authority in principle to legislate for the colonies. Burgoyne spoke strongly for it, reaffirming his vote for the Stamp Act. The bill passed easily, but Rockingham still needed the approval of the king to overcome the opposition of Bute, Grenville, and the faction led by the duke of Bedford. On February 3, 1766, he had an interview with the king, after which he reported that he had received royal endorsement for repeal of the Stamp Act. Here Burgoyne's brother-in-law, Strange, who had led an unsuccessful attempt to enforce the act, stepped in to block Rockingham. He had his own interview in the royal "Closet" seven days later, and reported that the king actually was "for a modification of the Act, but not for the repeal of it." The result was a meeting of the king with Rockingham and Strange "to reconcile this seeming contradiction," followed by an announcement, with suitable face saving, that "his Majesty was for the Repeal." The balloting took place in a crowded house at 1:30 in the morning on February 22. Burgoyne, adamant as ever, voted against repeal, as did Strange. Repeal nevertheless carried, 275 to 167.[5]

In his hesitating, undramatic way, Rockingham was proving himself a conciliator. He repealed the obnoxious search provisions of the cider tax. He reduced the duty of the Sugar Act from 3d. per gallon to 1d., thereby obtaining more revenue from the colonies than from any previous levy. But while these measures defused the blunders of the Grenville administration, Rockingham had no clear-cut program and his cabinet had no outstanding talents. He was accused of that cardinal sin of the eighteenth century—organizing a political party. His loyal secretary, Edmund Burke, afterward pronounced this his achievement. Modern historians maintain that the "Rockinghams" were too amorphous for that, but they do not deny that the Rockingham measures constituted the kinds of compromises that parties typically produce. Perhaps more of such compromises would have averted the American Revolution. Nothing that Rockingham might propose, however, could satisfy as long as the towering figure of Pitt dominated the political scene. Rockingham tried in vain to entice him into the cabinet. Pitt magisterially replied that he was above party, although he did, in fact, have the unbidden backing of a group of approximately seventy-five King's Friends. And the king, who resented Pitt's arrogance, found it expedient to call him to form a cabinet in order to rid himself of the Rockingham Whigs.

Burgoyne was elated at Pitt's return to power. True, they had differed on the Stamp Act, but Pitt was out of office when it was repealed, so there was no implication of disloyalty. Burgoyne never forgot that he owed his regiment to Pitt. And Pitt (now Lord Chatham) had the vision of empire Burgoyne admired. He understood that Burgoyne's quondam friend, Choiseul, now French foreign minister, was an unrelenting foe of England, and he did not shrink from the prospect of another war. If war with France was imminent, how might Burgoyne contribute? Burgoyne decided to embark on a scouting tour of Europe's armies. The information he gathered would give him a platform from which to advocate preparedness. The expertise he acquired would give him a claim to promotion. The trip would certainly be more congenial than the precarious jockeyings in Parliament. Also, unhappily, the Burgoynes' daughter had died on March 7, 1764, at the age of ten, and a trip abroad might be a good cathartic. Charlotte was never to have any other children. Her letters show her still delighting in banter and gossip, but her health began to decline.[6]

Chatham gave the trip his blessing with a letter of introduction to Prince Ferdinand of Brunswick and a hint of things to come—a flattering recollection of the éclat of the late exploits of "General" Burgoyne. The Burgoynes visited Dresden, Prague, Brunswick, Vienna, and Flanders. "I move not a step upon the Continent," Burgoyne dutifully reported to Chatham, "without seeing the impression your Lordship's name makes." He journeyed to the battlefields, inspected the armies in their camps, and conferred with their commanders. Everywhere he observed the character of the leaders, the spirit of the common soldier, the details of organization, training, and dress. He drew up for Chatham a lengthy position paper, warning that war was imminent and urging an immediate arms buildup. Austria was determined to recover Silesia from Prussia. France, under the direction of Choiseul, was modernizing her army—her cavalry was now superior to any in Europe—and clearly preparing for an invasion of England or Ireland. England must develop a cavalry second to none.

The Burgoynes arrived home by the end of 1766. Chatham wrote to say "how much pleasure and how much instruction" he had received from the report. The invasion, however, did not come. Choiseul chose to challenge British strength obliquely by fomenting disaffection in the colonies. Chatham suffered a complete mental and physical breakdown in January of 1767. Tormented by manic depression, gout, and probably kidney disease, he closeted himself away from society and concentrated obsessively on ruinously expensive renovations of his residences. Had Chatham held out, Burgoyne might have served in America far sooner than eventually happened. The previous August, news had arrived of the refusal of the New York Assembly to vote provisions and barracks for British troops, as required by the Quartering Act of 1765. Chatham, despite his opposition to the Stamp Act, believed that New York should be pressured to obey. His secretary of state for the Southern Department, Lord Shelburne, advocated coercion and proposed that Burgoyne be appointed military governor of New York in place of the sitting civilian, Sir Henry Moore.[7] Chatham was already incapacitated, and nothing came of the recommendation.

There was no other military employment in sight for Burgoyne.

Parliament's allotted life of seven years was due to expire on March 11, 1768, and in 1767 the constituencies geared up for the coming general election. Burgoyne could not expect to be returned for Midhurst, now that his patron, Williams, was dead. Lord Derby came to his rescue. The Stanleys regarded the borough of Preston as their political preserve, and Derby nominated him for one of the two seats, on the Whig ticket. It was, however, far from a sure thing. Preston's government was in the hands of the borough's corporation, which was traditionally Tory, and it nominated Sir Peter Leicester, an incumbent, and Sir Frank Standish, a native of Lancashire with deep roots in his Duxbury barony. Compared to them, Burgoyne could be tagged an outsider. Strange, who managed the campaign for the Stanleys, moved to bolster Burgoyne's chances by putting forward as his running mate Sir Henry Hoghton, a wealthy Lancashire landowner who would give the ticket local weight, and who, as a staunch Presbyterian, would also attract the support of dissenters. The contest revolved around the interpretation of the suffrage. At first, only town freemen were allowed to vote. Then, when Burgoyne and Hoghton began to fall behind, they demanded the franchise for all townsmen, citing a House of Commons resolution in 1661 in support of their claim. Violence erupted. The corporation's supporters sported dark blue cockades; Burgoyne's, orange ones. Both sides imported toughs from neighboring towns. Partisans were beaten in the streets. The Tory mayor at Fishergate was thrown under the pump in the cold of February, and when an elderly bystander intervened he was also doused and died of exposure.

A month before the election, Burgoyne, on the advice of friends, decided to campaign in person. On the road to town his carriage was pelted with stones. A mob assaulted a house where he was dining. He proposed a meeting with the opposition to negotiate restoration of order, but the street rioting at the meeting houses required the calling of the militia. He was warned to "quit the Town or probably Die in it."

Defiantly, he walked the streets with a pistol under one arm and another in his pocket. He refused to call off his out-of-town supporters. The polls opened on March 21, 1768. Burgoyne arrived with a pistol in each hand and an armed guard. The violence continued all during the two-week polling period. Homes were destroyed and Catholic chapels looted. "There wasn't a how [whole] winda in t'tawn," a resident afterward recalled. Mayor Robert Moss, acting as Returning Officer, disqualified more than six hundred of the Burgoyne-Hoghton ballots, one because the man "laid many wagers that Colonel Burgoyne will be chose." He accepted nonresident and Catholic votes for Leicester and Standish and on April 2 declared them elected by narrow margins. Burgoyne and Hoghton angrily protested that a Commons resolution of 1661 vested the vote in "all the inhabitants." According to their tally, Burgoyne led with 589 votes, Hoghton was next with 558, and Standish and Leicester trailed with 277 and 276 respectively. They appealed, through Strange, to Parliament, where the Whigs, under the duke of Grafton, in the absence of Chatham, were in control. Burgoyne and Hoghton were seated.

The aftermath was ugly. The corporation hailed Burgoyne before King's

Bench court and charged him with "brutal violence." He pleaded self-protection. A crown's witness testified that Burgoyne had exhorted his supporters to "level the town before you." He denied that he had ever, even against a wartime enemy, proposed such a barbarity; he wished to be considered an "unconscious offender." Judge Sir Joseph Yates "laid on very hard" with a long reprimand and imposed a fine of a thousand pounds. There were complaints that Burgoyne should have been sent "to keep Mr. Wilkes company" in jail, like poorer offenders convicted of the same crime and not let off so lightly. It was, nevertheless, a stiff price to pay for carrying the Whig banner, and Grafton acknowledged it. Burgoyne was granted a three-hundred-pounds a year sinecure, the governorship of the obsolete Fort William in Scotland. In the press, the anonymous "Junius" labeled it a kickback "to defray the extensive bribery of a contested election," alleging that Grafton also rewarded Burgoyne with thirty-five hundred pounds obtained from the sale of a customs-house post at Exeter; and, for good measure, pictured Burgoyne as a cardsharp who made a practice of victimizing drunken young noblemen.[8]

Yet none of this could obscure the fact that Burgoyne had won a remarkable victory. The Commons election decision, in the judgment of historian Sir Lewis Namier, had granted Preston the widest male franchise anywhere in the British Isles. Burgoyne's election gave him a more direct mandate than any other member of Parliament could claim. Now he established himself as a Lancaster squire. He built a three-story mansion, Cooper Hill, at Walton-le-Dale, about a mile from Strange's Patten House. Designed by himself and said to include lightning rods donated by Benjamin Franklin, it was situated on a hill with a sweeping view of the surrounding country. In London in 1769, he purchased a terrace house in Mayfair, at 10 Hertford Street, still standing, just east of Hyde Park and two blocks north of Hyde Park Corner. He commissioned his friend Robert Adam to design all the decorations. He also owned or rented a shooting lodge, The Oaks, at Banstead Downs (now Epsom Downs), about fifteen miles south of London, where he and Charlotte could escape from the city to attend the races and bathe in the mineral waters.[9]

His acquaintance with Adam and Ramsay opened the London world of painters and dramatists to him. It was an age when the open camaraderie of the coffeehouse was yielding to the exclusive decorum of the club. He gamed at Brooks's and dined at the Thursday Night Club. He met Sir Joshua Reynolds, with his hearing horn and snuff box, and the idolized actor and producer, David Garrick. He was himself a budding author. He composed poems to Charlotte and to friends, contributed prologues and epilogues, in the custom of the day, to his friends' plays, and even performed in one for a charity at Preston. The content was the standard eulogy, the style stiffly classical, but the tone was tripping and the repartee in the best high fashion. Reynolds painted him in 1766, as vivid as in life, in the pink-cheeked prime of health—confident, perhaps a trifle too well fed, hair barely beginning to turn gray, elegant in his Sixteenth Light Dragoons colonel's crimson coat with black cravat, white lace ruffles, and dun-colored waistband.

He began to assert himself. He ventured to vote against Strange. Domestic matters did not much interest him, but on "great national points," he declared, involving "the interest or honour of the State," he held himself "at liberty to maintain my own opinion." The field of arms was still his absorbing concern; he still believed a war with France inevitable, even desirable; his imagination was fired with the glory of empire. But where was the political leadership to pursue these aims? Grafton was well meaning but ineffectual and absorbed with his mistress, Fanny Parsons, and the track at Newmarket. "He thought," an opponent taunted, "the World should be postponed to a Whore and a Horse-race."[10] Chatham lived isolated in a world of unreality at his Kent country house, Hayes Place. And Lord North, who replaced Grafton in 1770, was only the unenterprising tool of the shortsighted George III.

Miraculously, Chatham achieved a complete recovery and in January 1770 returned to Parliament. Five months later, on June 10, a crisis erupted in the Falkland Islands, off the tip of South America. A Spanish expedition, apparently with French encouragement, seized the British naval station at Fort Egremont. North demanded restitution. Chatham, convinced more than ever of France's hostility, welcomed the prospect of war. Spain yielded at the last minute, but Chatham scorned the concession. Melodramatically, in the House of Lords, he invoked the memory of the Spanish Armada and demanded assurances so drastic as to invite confrontation. Burgoyne, in the Commons, applauded: Spain was not to be trusted. Britain must not sleep, lest Spain, "perhaps on the morrow of your disarming," think herself encouraged "again to take the vanguard of the family compact [the Franco-Spanish alliance in 1761]." And, while disclaiming saber rattling, he pointedly declared himself ready to support words with arms:

The man who would wantonly promote bloodshed, who upon private views of advantage or ambition would involve Europe in war, would be a promoter of ferocity—a disgrace to his profession, to his country, and to human nature. But there are motives for which a soldier may wish for war; these are a sense of satisfaction due for an injury inflicted; a desire to make a return to our country for the honours and rewards we receive at her hands: a zeal to be the forward instrument to battle for the honour of the Crown, and the rights of the people of Great Britain.[11]

Chatham and Burgoyne lost. Parliament preferred peace, by a vote of 271 to 157. In France, Louis XV refused to fight a war with an empty treasury, and Choiseul, having incurred the displeasure of the king's new mistress, Madame du Barry, resigned.

Burgoyne in the opposition? "The seeing Colonel Burgoyne's name on the side of the minority appears so extraordinary," George III observed, "that I almost imagine it was a mistake."[12] The consequences could be serious. In 1764, Henry Seymour Conway had been dismissed as colonel of the First Dragoons for voting against general warrants. So were two lieutenant colonels—Isaac Barré and William Ashe A'Court. At the very least, insurgency might cut off promotion. Fortunately, George did not consider the Falklands crisis a fundamental test of loyalty.

On a major issue of the king's prerogative, the Royal Marriages Bill of March 1772, Burgoyne remained orthodox. The measure gave the king control over the marriage choices of all his family under the age of twenty-six. It was inspired by the imprudent matches of two of his brothers, the dukes of Gloucester and Cumberland. Cumberland had married Ann Horton, a widowed sister of Henry Luttrell, a captain and friend of Burgoyne in the Portugal campaign. The king refused to countenance the marriage of any of his family to a subject, still less to one whose father, Simon Luttrell (Lord Irnham), was known as "the greatest reprobate in England" (the stricture of Lord Bute's daughter, Lady Louisa Stuart). If Burgoyne had not voted correctly, the king dryly remarked to Lord North, his new prime minister, he would have been "obliged to have named a new governor [of Fort William]."[13] On May 25, Burgoyne received his reward: he was promoted by seniority to major general.

Yet there was a spark of independence on an issue involving religious toleration. Earlier that year, on February 6, his Parliamentary mate from Preston, Sir Henry Hoghton, introduced a petition containing some 250 signatures, including some of Anglican clergymen, asking that dissenters at

Oxford and Cambridge universities be exempted from subscribing to the thirty-nine articles of faith. The king and North both opposed it and Parliament overwhelmingly rejected it, 217 to 71, but Burgoyne voted for it. He was himself a believer in "the merits and the oblation of Jesus Christ, as understood by the Church of England, as the only means of salvation," but he was dependent on dissenters in Preston for reelection to Parliament, and he knew that the duke of Grafton, who had supported him in his contested election, was a champion of the dissenters.[14] Interest, this time, was on the side of principle.

4

Merit

WITH HIS WHOLE PATRIMONY IN-
vested in "a suit of regimentals, a few camp equipments and a pair of colors in
a marching regiment," Lieutenant Gates set out for his corps. He was sent
not to Scotland, as originally planned, but to Germany, to serve in the
campaigns of the War of the Austrian Succession. He soon became "the pet of
the mess and the favorite of the Colonel." His forte became staff work. It was a
time of rigid rules and draconian punishments. There were no military
schools, and officers acquired expertise only by experience. The British common soldiers were a motley lot of released debtors, pardoned criminals, and
naive farm boys recruited with delusions of glamor or under the befuddle-
ment of drink. Poorly paid and fed and sent into battle in lockstep linear
formation under the fearful strain of close-range volleys, they could be kept in
line only by frequent use of the lash. Young Gates made himself an expert in
organizational minutiae and parade-ground technique. Regiments depended
on the few such officers who applied themselves to detail. When the regimental adjutant died, Gates was named to take his place.[1] For an aspiring officer
without fortune, this proved the channel for advancement. It could also be a
handicap. Was he a planner, not a leader, as his detractors were to ask? At
Saratoga was the victory really won by his battlefield subordinates while he
wrote directives in the command tent?

A disconnected, faraway aspect of the war determined the subsequent
direction of Gates's life. On June 16, 1745, on Cape Breton Island off the
northwest tip of Nova Scotia, the French Fort Louisbourg surrendered to a
four-thousand-man force of New England militia led by William Pepperrell
of Kittery Point, Maine, and supported by a British squadron from the
Leeward Islands under the command of Sir Peter Warren, who had married
one of the wealthy New York DeLanceys. An eternity, declared a New

England divine, would be necessary to give thanks. But only three years later, when the war ended, the outraged New Englanders learned that the Treaty of Aix-la-Chapelle had handed the conquest back to France in exchange for Madras, "a petty factory in India." In French hands, Louisbourg threatened American fisheries and the security of New England seaports. To silence Yankee fears and to plant a staging place for a future invasion of Canada, the Henry Pelham ministry decided to establish a naval base at Halifax, Nova Scotia. On March 7, 1749, the Board of Trade and Plantations advertised in the London *Gazette,* inviting applications from "officers and private men lately dismissed from His Majesty's land and sea service as are willing to accept grants of land and to settle with or without families in Nova Scotia." Among the inducements were three hundred acres of land for lieutenants, plus farm equipment, munitions, and rations for one year.[2] Gates had returned from Germany. His regiment had been disbanded and he was among the thousands disgorged into civilian life with no prospect of employment. The Halifax settlement was a possibility. It would still not be full reinstatement in the army; he would have to go as a volunteer without pay. But he might find opportunities in the New World. He was now twenty-two, confident, and unattached.

His application came when the expedition's commander, Colonel Edward Cornwallis, was looking for an aide-de-camp. Cornwallis was a friend of Horace Walpole, and it may be that Gates included a recommendation from his godfather. The young man that Cornwallis interviewed had grown to a stocky five feet seven inches. His brown eyes had a penetrating, canny look. Ruddy and sandy haired, he exuded a worldly wise affability, but in the changing expression of the eyes decisiveness alternated with defensiveness.

Cornwallis liked what he saw, and he was impressed with Gates's record of staff experience. He appointed him to his "family" and to additional duties that would net him about two hundred pounds a year. In time, Cornwallis became for Gates another "thick and thin" friend, the patron who started him on his upward climb in the army. The son of a baron and the twin brother of a future archbishop of Canterbury, Cornwallis was a veteran of the Battle of Fontenoy in Flanders and of the 'Forty-five in Scotland. (He was the uncle of Charles Cornwallis, who was later defeated at the Battle of Yorktown.) Still a bachelor at thirty-six, he was slender and somewhat above middle height, with black hair, steady blue eyes, a straight, prominent nose, a resolute jaw, and a resonant voice. A sufferer from debilitating rheumatism, he was a cool and ceremonious man. Perhaps it was the attraction of opposites that drew him to the gregarious, informal Gates.

Fifty or sixty former army and navy officers, a few hundred discharged soldiers and sailors, and an outpouring of cockneys desperate to escape the poverty and filth of London flocked to register at Whitehall for the expedition. There were a few Irish, Scottish, and Germans. The turnout was so great that it delayed departure by more than a month while additional vessels and supplies were obtained. Ventilators with pumps were installed below decks to provide circulation of air in the crowded quarters. A fleet of thirteen transports was assembled in the Thames, to be joined by a hospital ship outfitted at Liverpool. Cornwallis and his staff were to sail aboard the sloop-of-war, *Sphinx*. All told, there were about three thousand persons bound for Nova Scotia.

The *Sphinx* set out on May 14, 1749, and steered for Cape Race at the southeastern tip of Newfoundland. It met head winds, but on June 14 it safely sighted Nova Scotia, where it stood offshore until a Yankee vessel chanced by with two pilots to guide it to Chebucto. On June 21 it landed at a marshy cove on the western shore where a brook emptied into the harbor. "It was that time of year in Nova Scotia," writes Halifax's historian-novelist, Thomas H. Raddall, "when after the bleak east winds of April and May the sun breaks forth with almost tropical heat, when trees, shrubs and grasses have a lush green only to be matched in Ireland." Cornwallis wrote home that "all the officers agree the harbor is the finest they have ever seen." The soil looked fertile, the fish were plentiful. A site for the settlement was chosen on a wooded slope at the water's edge, shielded from the winter's northwest winds. The town was laid out in a grid pattern around a small square, with 33 blocks, each containing 16 house lots 40 feet wide and 60 feet deep. Each settler was alotted five acres and a bounty of five shillings was offered for every acre fenced and cleared. A wooden barricade and five blockhouses were planned to surround the whole. Cornwallis called a conference with three chiefs of the local Micmac and Malicete Indian tribes, and with due solemnity, aboard the transport *Beaufort,* they signed a treaty of friendship.

But problems quickly arose. The felled trees and dry moss rapidly caught fire. The uncovered soil turned out to be a thin, clayey layer spread over a plateau of slate rock. The colonists proved so shiftless that by mid-September Cornwallis reported that one-half of them were still being victualed and housed aboard the transports. The Indians became hostile, and the colony's council was driven to offer ten guineas for each Indian scalp. When Louisbourg had been transferred back to French control, the two British regiments that had garrisoned the fort moved down to Halifax, bringing their camp followers with them and spawning bars and brothels along Water

Street. Uncleanliness brought a typhoid epidemic that claimed a thousand victims.

Cornwallis himself was seized with a crippling attack of rheumatism that incapacitated him for fully half his stay in Halifax. The burden of administration fell on his aides, Captain Richard Bulkely and Gates. Bulkely was a tall, handsome Irishman in his early thirties, of good family, who had served under Cornwallis in previous campaigns, returned to Dublin, and then, restless in retirement, joined the Halifax expedition in search of new experience. Surrounded by nine thousand unruly Acadians, the two aides fended off French and Indian encroachments. They set up governmental machinery, supervised the construction of streets and housing, and, when typhoid struck, personally helped bury the dead.

The best that Cornwallis could do for Gates, within the confines of the army purchase system, was to appoint him to the temporary rank of captain lieutenant (lieutenant, acting as captain) in one of the regiments that had arrived from Louisbourg, Colonel Hugh Warburton's famous Forty-fifth. Then a full captaincy became vacant in the same unit; Cornwallis offered him the company at the bargain price of four hundred pounds and wrote to Robert Gates to urge him to advance the money to his son. Horatio could pay it back from his yearly income of two hundred pounds. Apparently, four hundred pounds was more than the father could manage, and the opening was allowed to slip by.[3]

Bulkely and Gates became boon companions. Bulkely could spend freely, and he built a luxurious house in Halifax, on the east side of Argyle Street between Prince and Sackville. He employed a valet, butler, and groom, entertained lavishly, maintained an extensive library, and rode regularly to hounds. Gates lived in modest quarters but dressed in style and kept his table well supplied with select wines—claret was his favorite. A circle of friends formed, among whom was a lusty Hertfordshireman, Lieutenant John Hale, who became a lasting friend of Gates. On one of their boat trips, with an officer's daughter in the party, he bragged of "feeling Miss Greens Bubbies between decks and some attempts to get a little Farther." Gates, for his part, had a married mistress whom he generously passed on to Hale, but who, Hale discovered, was pregnant, "whether by you or her husband is more than I or you either perhaps can determine."[4] The most exalted member of the circle was Lieutenant Colonel Robert Monckton, son of Viscount Galway and of the daughter of the duke of Rutland. An imperious yet clubbable man, a year older than Gates, he was clearly destined for high position in the colonial service. Here was distinctly another good thick-and-thin friend to have.

In October of 1752, Cornwallis was replaced by Peregrine Thomas Hopson, a slight man with a booming voice who promptly followed his predecessor's example by contracting rheumatism a week after his arrival. Bulkely and Gates carried on, contending now with an influx of New England traders who threatened to demoralize the settlement with a flood of imported rum. Fires were a daily occurrence. By then, Gates's commitment to the problems of Halifax was wearing thin. He had begun to court pretty Elizabeth Phillips of nearby Annapolis Royale, whose father was fort major and commissary and a nephew of the colony's former governor, Colonel Richard Phillips. Oval faced, with light brown hair and dark brown eyes, she had a straight nose, a small mouth drawn up in a confident half moon, a chin that was a little long yet alluring, a graceful neck, and white, well-shaped shoulders. English born and related through her mother to the earl of Thanet, she was a strong-willed girl, sensitive to status and ambitious to rise. A "Medusa who governs with a rod of scorpions," Charles Lee later called her.[5] She was a big step up the social ladder for Gates and more than an answer to his mother's pretensions.

Under Betsy's prodding, Gates developed a new drive. He was no longer content with the reflected power of a governor's aide and the carefree evenings with Dick Bulkely and Jack Hale, waiting for a promotion to a permanent captaincy that never came. He realized what a golden opportunity had been lost when Cornwallis made his offer of a company. Hopson, though a kindly man, did nothing to advance Gates's prospects. He was replaced on November 1, 1753, by Charles Lawrence, but there was no reason to expect any more from Lawrence. Gates decided that the only hope was to return to England to see what could be done in person. Cornwallis had just been elected to Parliament for Westminster, and he might help. Also, in London, Gates would be on the spot to search for vacancies elsewhere.

Gates sailed from Halifax in November and was in London by January. He took lodgings in Southampton Street, just north of the busy Strand, which led directly southwest, along the Thames, to the army offices at Whitehall. As soon as he was settled, he made the rounds of the officials who had power over commissions. He found that he could expect little help. Among his friends, Bolton had disappeared from the political scene. Married now to his "Polly" after his first wife's death in 1751, he spent much of his time at the resort of Tunbridge Wells. Horace Walpole's godfatherly connection was too tenuous to draw upon. There was only Cornwallis, and he was on bad terms with the Pelham ministry. In March, however, Pelham died, and Cornwallis's position might improve with the next ministry. Gates could only hope and wait, for influence as well as the purchase price was necessary in order to obtain a commission. James Boswell, also hunting an army commission in his first visit to London, encountered similar disappointment. He went to the duke of Queensberry and then to the duke of Northumberland without success.[6]

Gates waited six long, discouraging months. To pass the time, he could indulge his pleasure-loving inclinations at nearby Covent Garden, with its theatres, taverns, and coffeehouses, and one wonders whether he patronized the Blue Periwig near his lodgings on Southampton Street, at the corner of the Strand, where visiting young Boswell six years later "first experienced the melting and transporting rites of love."[7] But his hopes of a commission were getting nowhere. In despair, late in June, he booked return passage to Halifax. Then came a sudden turn of events. Startling news arrived from America that a four-hundred-man force of regulars and colonials at Great Meadows, in the Ohio territory, under the command of a young Virginia lieutenant colonel of militia named George Washington, had been captured by a French force based at Fort Duquesne, at the junction of the Ohio and Allegheny rivers. The news was not so startling to Gates. Franco-British relations, he knew from hard experience, had not cooled off with the Peace of Aix-la-Chapelle. The French had been strengthening their garrison at Louisbourg and inciting the Acadians in Nova Scotia to revolt. In Massachusetts, Governor William Shirley had been forced to raise eleven hundred troops and build two new forts to resist encroachments from Quebec. In Virginia, Governor Robert Dinwiddie had been sending urgent requests for troops from home to drive the French out of the Ohio valley.

In the face of the Ohio crisis, the duke of Newcastle, who had succeeded his late brother, Pelham, as prime minister, wished to avoid an all-out war with France. He had plans for financial retrenchment that would be destroyed by military expenditures, and a war would be risky when Austria and Holland could not be counted on as allies. Rather than hazard a large-scale offensive against the French in America with regular troops, he preferred a limited response with colonial militia. He was opposed by the "war party," led by Henry Fox, secretary at war, and the duke of Cumberland, captain general (commander in chief) of the army, who demanded the dispatch of regular troops from the United Kingdom. Cornwallis supported Fox, and it may have been through him that the war party attempted to persuade Gates, as a veteran fresh from America, to give advice to justify strong measures.

Gates was too cautious to antagonize Newcastle. He replied that his entire experience in America had been in Nova Scotia, and he could not advise on the situation in the Ohio territory.[8]

His prudence paid off. A captaincy became vacant for the Fourth Independent Company of Foot, based at New York and then on duty in Maryland. The incumbent, Thomas Clarke, had fallen ill at Alexandria and had not followed orders to join Washington's expedition to the Ohio. Washington blamed him bitterly for the defeat at Fort Necessity. This would be no soft berth for Gates; it looked as though the war party was going to succeed in launching a major attack on the French in the Ohio territory. Undeterred, he was eager, and Cornwallis lost no time in recommending him. But he was short of cash, and Clarke's London agent, Thomas Calcraft, was asking a bottom purchase price of fourteen hundred pounds. Gates importuned. At last Calcraft relented and accepted part of the payment on credit. On September 13, Gates received his commission.[9] He promptly took ship for Halifax.

⁀⧰ 5 ⧰⁀

"The Hard Hand of Power"

T HE VOYAGE WAS SMOOTH AND
swift, and the proud new captain hurried north across the island to present
himself to the girl at Annapolis Royale. On October 20, 1754, they were
married by Halifax's Anglican minister, Jonathan Breynton. For four months
they honeymooned, arranged their affairs, and paid last visits to Betsy's
parents and brother and sister. As expected, news arrived that regular troops
had been sent to America for an expedition against Fort Duquesne—two
regiments from Ireland under Major General Edward Braddock that landed
at Hampton, Virginia, on February 20. Braddock carried instructions to
organize a force that included Gates's company. Did Horatio and Betsy have
forebodings? The two regiments were under strength, manned with "Justice Fielding's recruits" (the novel-writing judge's criminal wards), and in
bad odor for having run from the field at the Battle of Prestonpans in 1745.
Braddock, it was said, had never in his long career been known to "do
anything but swear." Before leaving England, he told his closest friend that
he did not expect to see her again.[1]

In March, the Gateses left for New York City, where they had decided
Betsy would stay while Horatio was away in the field. They arranged for her
to live at the home of Francis Lewis, a well-to-do merchant on Broadway.
New York appealed instantly to the Gateses. It was both a reminder of
London and a gateway to the spirit of the New World. Restricted as yet to the
southern tip of Manhattan Island, it was already polyglot and expansive. The
Dutch influence was evident in language and customs and in the three-story,
wall-to-wall houses with gable ends facing the street. The brick mansions
were in the Georgian style, with pillared doorways and semicircular fan-
lights. New Yorkers dressed in the London vogue, if a year late. They had
their servants and carriages, their plays, concerts, dancing assemblies, cof-

feehouses, and social clubs. There was Old World poverty, too. A year before the Gateses arrived, the New York *Independent Reflector* had complained the poor were denied handouts while the city's thousand-odd canine population, "Towser, Tray and Mopsy," was "gorged with the Fat of the Land."[2]

Near the Lewises, at 5 Broadway, lived William Smith, Jr., a shrewd, disputatious, Yale-bred lawyer, son of a magistrate, and a Presbyterian Whig. He and Gates became friends. He was one of a triumvirate, including William Livingston and John Morin Scott, who were leading the "Presbyterian party" in a struggle with acting governor James DeLancey over the issue of whether the proposed King's College (now Columbia) should be chartered as an Anglican or a nonsectarian institution.[3] Until then, Gates had associated primarily with military men. Now he was meeting politicians and hearing oppositionist talk. For the moment, he had his army assignment mainly to think about, but Smith's ideas were not uncongenial to a young man recently emerged from a hard struggle to win a captain's commission from a reluctant officialdom, a young man with roots in the British working masses who were traditionally distrustful and scornful of the establishment.

At the end of March, Gates left to join Braddock's army in Maryland. He found it encamped at Frederick, a town of two hundred houses ten miles north of the Potomac, on the Monacacy River east of Catoctin Mountain. Clarke's men had pitched their tents on a hill to the north. They were in wretched shape, overaged, low in morale, and poorly provisioned. Braddock, when he inspected the company, had pronounced it "good for nothing." The transfer of command proved not a smooth matter. Clarke refused to accept the fourteen-hundred-pound purchase price Gates had contracted for with Calcraft in London, pointing out that Captain James Mackay had received fifteen hundred pounds for his smaller company of sixty men; perquisites per enlisted man, a part of a captain's income, had to be figured into the price. He demanded sixteen hundred pounds, and Gates had no choice but to agree.[4]

On May 1, George Washington rode into camp. The Virginian, whose report of his experience at Fort Necessity had been retailed about London with delight—"I heard the bullets whistle, and, believe me, there is something charming in the sound"—was as striking in person as in story. In the saddle, he rode with superb grace and assurance. On the ground, he stood six feet two inches, well muscled at a spare 175 pounds, broad shouldered, and long armed, and long legged. He walked with perfectly coordinated precision: straight legs moving in parallel lines, feet placed with the care of a cat in the forest. His head was long, his hair brown and worn in a cue. He had blue-gray eyes, pale skin that burned and peeled in the sun, a large nose, high cheekbones, a firm mouth, and a solid jaw. Incongruously, as a result of a pulmonary infection, he spoke in a weak voice that became labored when he was excited.[5]

He was a type unfamiliar to Gates. In one sense an English squire, he was in the other a unique Virginia breed. He was not only a landowner but a land speculator, eager to acquire thousands of acres of wilderness. A slave owner accustomed to the habit of absolute command, he aspired to leadership in his colony's affairs without preferment from the lords overseas. With no contacts in England, he claimed the right to convert his provincial colonelcy into a regular army commission. Now he was serving as a volunteer aide to Braddock without rank or pay, asking only the opportunity to demonstrate his valor.

Washington was glad to find Clarke replaced by a new, hopefully more forceful captain of the New York Independent Company. Gates, however, was similarly unfamiliar to him. Unlike the other Englishmen Washington had met, Gates was a salty product of London port, an officer who could justify his commission with no claims of family or property. He cared little for exercise, was inclined to overweight, liked a ribald jest and a bout of drinking, and made a point of cultivating friendships with his superiors. He was not the sort with which Washington instinctively felt at home. Twenty years later, the incongruity of these two men was to pose a national problem when they met again in a war neither of them now anticipated.

Braddock stayed at Frederick only long enough to deal with a crisis in supply. Benjamin Franklin came from Philadelphia and promised to procure wagons and pack horses—he advanced his own bond for part of the payment. On May 2, the troops left for Fort Cumberland, at the junction of the Potomac River and Wills Creek, traveling by way of Winchester through rugged mountains along miserable roads and twisting river channels. There the irascible Braddock's difficulties mounted: discipline worsened, the "bloody flux" spread, and men slept with the Indian squaws (Bright Lightning, a chief's daughter, was equally popular with the officers), while futile orders continued to call for full-dress parades with marching bands. Braddock ridiculed provincials and offended Indians. When Washington presumed to contradict, he snapped, "What think you of this, from a young hand—from a beardless boy!"[6] Before the 110-mile trek from Fort Cumberland to the forks of the Ohio River could begin, a road had to be cleared out of camp over an almost perpendicular mountain two miles away. Three hundred men, after four days of work, failed to reduce the grade enough for the wagons and howitzers to pass. Then a lieutenant Charles Spendelow discovered an overlooked bypass west of the fort. On June 7, Colonel Sir Peter Halkett's brigade moved out, and the next day Lieutenant Colonel Ralph Burton followed with his brigade and Gates's Independent Company.

It was an unwieldy conglomeration. Sometimes it stretched out three to four miles in a thin, vulnerable line. The heat set in, and the horses proved so feeble that the officers had to volunteer some of their mounts as pack carriers. They were covering little more than two miles a day; at that rate the future of the whole enterprise was in doubt. By June 16, Braddock acknowledged that he needed expert advice, and he called Washington to his tent for a conference. His aide had a detailed plan worked out: divide the expedition in two; send a lightly equipped detachment, with artillery support, ahead to seize Fort Duquesne before the French could bring up reinforcements; let the second half of the British forces follow with the wagons. Braddock agreed and chose Halkett's brigade, with Gates's company, to lead the advance. By July 8, the army had progressed to within two miles east of the Monongahela River and only twelve miles south of Fort Duquesne. The plan of march, dictated by the obstacles of terrain, was to cross to the west bank of the river at a shallow ford at Crooked Run, proceed a couple of miles downstream to another ford at Turtle Creek, and recross to the east bank. From there the way would be unobstructed for the remaining seven miles to Duquesne. Washington suggested that the Virginia rangers be thrown into the advance to cope with Indian attacks, but Braddock brusquely rejected any more advice.

The next day the army struggled awake in the dark, early hours of the morning. At 2:00 A.M., the advance party of 350 redcoated regulars under Lieutenant Colonel Thomas Gage broke camp and headed for the river. Gage's force consisted of two companies of grenadiers (the elite of the Forty-fourth) and Gates's Independent Company of Foot. A short distance out of camp, they ran into a band of about 30 Indians who quickly disappeared. Unconcerned, the British continued forward and crossed easily at Crooked Run. At the Turtle Creek recrossing, muddied water and many footprints on the river bank suggested that many more Indians were nearby, but again Gage showed no concern. Back at the main encampment, a second party of 250 carpenters and woodsmen and their wagons, under Lieutenant Colonel Sir John St. Clair, set out at 4:00 A.M. By 8:00 A.M., both Gage's and St. Clair's men were safely across the river and entrenched in their covering positions; "men hugg'd themselves with joy." Then the main force under Braddock himself, with band playing and ranks precise, began to move. The operation was flawless, and by 3:00 P.M. the last of the 1,459 men and 50-odd soldiers' wives and camp followers were on the opposite bank.

Up ahead the guides and engineers, marking out the twelve-foot-wide road to be cut by workmen, now moved forward again, followed by Gage's men in files four feet deep: first the grenadiers, then Gates's company a hundred yards behind. In view of Gates's newness in the command, Captain Robert Cholmley was assigned to ride with him and make the combat decisions. At 2:30 in the afternoon, when the engineers had progressed a half mile past the river bank, the guides reported that a force of about three hundred Indians had been sighted two hundred yards ahead. The scouts opened fire on the Indians but were repulsed with a volley that drove them back to Gage's party. Gage, having already made the mistake of failing to secure a dominating hill to the right, now sealed his fate by retreating between flanking ravines into which shrieking Indians had poured.

Gates afterward bitterly recalled that it took Braddock "near ten minutes" to come to Gage's assistance, "of which time the enemy made so good use that fifteen out of eighteen Officers were kill'd and wounded and half of the 300 men." Among the wounded was Gates himself. "I cannot say," he wrote, "how I was shot through the left breast." One of his men, a private, Francis Penfold, although himself wounded, carried him off somehow to safety. When Braddock did arrive, it was only to collide with Gage's men and produce complete confusion. "So great was the disorder," said Gates, "that there was no setting it to rights and from the instant all was lost."

Few of the Indians or their French officers were even visible as their war whoops and shooting spread terror. Washington later said that the Virginians "behaved like men, and died like soldiers," while the English proved "cowardly dogs of soldiers" who fired on their own comrades. Officers, futilely attempting to rally their men, were cut down as easy marks on their horses. Braddock charged among the demoralized redcoats, vainly exhorting them to stand and fight. There was a brief lull as the troops gathered around their wagons. Soon heavier fire opened again from the front and rear. It was the last straw: utter panic took over as the desperate men streamed back, choking through a narrow ravine in a mad rush to escape across the river. Braddock's horses had been struck five times, and now he himself was shot through the right arm and lung. Reluctantly, he ordered a retreat. Four days later he died, murmuring, "Who would have thought it?" The remnant of his army fled back to Fort Cumberland.

Gates's wound had paralyzed his left arm, "the ball," he thought, "having cut some string."[7] First he was taken to Fort Cumberland, then to Lancaster and Philadelphia. By January 1756 he had recovered sufficiently to rejoin Betsy in New York. Feeling returned to the arm. Now what reward might he expect for his sacrifice, when he had no money to purchase a promotion? None, it appeared, unless Cornwallis could come once more to his rescue and find a loophole.

Cornwallis, unfortunately, was embroiled in extreme difficulties because of having been too loyal to another friend. In London, he had been a member of a fast bachelor set, "The Corinthians," one of whom was Admiral John Byng. In November 1756, Cornwallis was assigned to an expedition under Byng for the relief of the British garrison at Minorca. There Byng encountered a French fleet but sailed away after a brief engagement, abandoning the garrison to casualties of seven hundred and eventual surrender. In this he was supported by his council of war, including Cornwallis and two other colonels, all Corinthians. The news was met in England with outrage. When the officers arrived at Portsmouth a crowd almost tore them to pieces. All four were courtmartialed, and Byng was shot before a firing squad. Although the colonels were exonerated, two of them resigned. Cornwallis later received promotions to lieutenant general and governor of Gibraltar, but his prestige was irreparably damaged.

Gates could only wait for him to recoup. He returned to duty at frontier posts at Fort Oswego on Lake Erie, Fort Herkimer on the Mohawk River, and Fort Edward on the Hudson River, southeast of Lake George. From Fort Edward, in 1757, he moved down the river's west bank, past the village of Saratoga (now Schuylerville), to a fort at Stillwater, where the Hoosic River joins the Hudson. Whenever possible, he spent the winters with Betsy in New York. "New York," said William Smith, Jr., "is one of the most social places on the continent. The men collect themselves into weekly evening clubs. The ladies . . . are comely and dress well, and scarcely any of them have distorted shapes . . . and, by the helps of a more elevated education, would possess all the accomplishments desirable in the sex."[8] Betsy scandalized New York matrons by riding horseback in breeches, at least as long as she could fit into them. In October 1758, a son was born, Robert, named after both his grandfather and Robert Monckton.

Three years slipped by. Then, just as hope was beginning to fade, Cornwallis's efforts produced an appointment as brigade major to Brigadier General John Stanwix, commander of the Southern Department at Fort Pitt. Still more good fortune, Stanwix was replaced the following May by Gates's friend Robert Monckton, who had won distinction as second in command to James Wolfe at the taking of Quebec. Fort Pitt was on the site of old Fort Duquesne, with its memories of Monongahela and Gates's nearly fatal wound. The French had burned and abandoned it to the British the previous

November. Gates helped Monckton to stage a mammoth Indian peace conference attended by nearly a thousand delegates from most of the western tribes.[9] With these warriors neutralized, a British army under Sir Jeffery Amherst conquered Montreal on September 8, 1760. It was the end of the war in North America.

Not, however, the end of the war in the western hemisphere. In August 1761, Spain signed a treaty of alliance with France. The next step was a British attack on the French and Spanish West Indies, with Havana as the grand goal. Monckton was now the rising star among British generals in America and was awarded the command, along with a dual appointment as governor of New York, where the invasion force was being assembled. Gates went with him as chief aide. The governorship inevitably involved Monckton in New York political feuds. The pro-Royalists, led by the aging, cantankerous Lieutenant Governor Cadwallader Colden, sought to control patronage and dominate the courts. The Whig coalition of New York City lawyers and Hudson River Valley land barons demanded limitation of the governor's prerogative and independence for the judiciary. Conflicting economic interests meshed with the political issues. Colden clashed with William Smith, Jr., and the Livingston clan over upstate land titles. The Livingstons resented Colden's crackdown on illicit trade with the West Indies. Monckton, influenced very likely by Gates, sided with the Whigs. He entertained them with a lavish banquet and they responded with one in return.[10] The Whig sympathies that had been aroused in Gates were being encouraged by direct participation. Mixing the army with politics was a longstanding tradition in England, but the combination of soldier and radical Whig was a rarity. It was an unorthodox political education.

Monckton's army headquartered on Staten Island. He was a commander of spirit and imagination. His daily mess was a gala occasion. Forty officers, mostly junior, were invited, and he would welcome them with the remark that he was once a subaltern himself. Gates learned a lesson in leadership: he could never be the handsome, dashing figure that Monckton was, but he might cultivate his own brand of folksy, salty comradeship, inviting cooperation rather than mandating obedience. It was to be the key to his generalship at Saratoga.

The expedition sailed from Sandy Hook on December 24, with Martinique as its first target. At Barbados it merged with a fleet under Rear Admiral George Bydges Rodney. The armada of 173 ships and 11,000 men reached Cas des Navieres, on Martinique's west coast, on January 16. Within nineteen days Monckton's troops outmaneuvered and overwhelmed the

French defenders in an operation remarkable for coordination of land and sea forces. For Gates it was a priceless laboratory. He became familiar with the management of a motley army of regulars, militia, and Indians. He learned that there were times when a commander in the field must make spot decisions independent of home instructions.

Five days after the French surrender, Monckton gave him his reward. He dispatched him on February 10 to London aboard the *Nightingale* to carry the news to the war secretary, the earl of Egremont. Traditionally, the bearer of victory tidings was rewarded with a promotion. The message recommended Gates "to His Majesty's Favour, as a very deserving Officer, and who has now served upwards to twelve years in America, with much Credit." A six-week voyage landed him in England late on the night of March 21, 1762. Two days later, all London read Monckton's letter in the *Gazette Extraordinary*. Within five weeks Gates was named major in his old Nova Scotia regiment, the Forty-fifth Foot, Major Edward Boscawen commanding, and awarded a thousand pounds to use in purchasing a lieutenant colonelcy as soon as a vacancy should arise.[11] It looked as though he had arrived. Betsy and the baby joined him in London.

Alas, the euphoria was short-lived. The new rank carried with it a cut in pay. Lieutenant colonel's commissions were not to be had. Gates requested another assignment. At first it looked as though this could be arranged: Cornwallis had recently married the sister of the secretary at war, Charles Townshend; Townshend supplied a letter to Sir Jeffery Amherst, the commanding general in North America, asking that Gates be appointed deputy adjutant or quartermaster general. Lord Ligonier, who had succeeded Cumberland as commander in chief, sent a similar recommendation. The position normally carried the rank of lieutenant colonel, and in time Gates might be raised to that level. On the strength of these prospects, he took his family back to New York in August 1762. The voyage was a weary one, and at its end there were more frustrations. At Amherst's headquarters, Gates discovered that the post he expected had been filled. He had even lost his former majority in the Forty-fifth, and although his pay was continued he had no assignment. The only occupation available to him was to serve again as political aide to Governor Monckton. He resumed his associations with the Whig Club, and it was no doubt a satisfaction to be able to bring to his friend William Smith Monckton's offer of appointment as chief justice of the province. Smith declined on the ground that the salary was too low. On June 28, 1763, Monckton left for home in England, and with him went Gates's employment. If Gates remained friendlessly in America, he might be assigned, now that the war was virtually over, to a regiment scheduled for deactivation and be retired at half pay.

He decided that he would do better to return to England and try once more for help from Monckton and Cornwallis. Amherst warned that he might be removed from the payroll and suggested that he cover the trip with a fake medical excuse. Gates replied that he "never was sick when his duty called him." Amherst consented, and in August 1763, after a futile year in America, Gates took his family back to England.

In London, the outlook proved no better. "Parliament opens, everybody is bribed," wrote Horace Walpole. The Gateses took rooms at 90 Gerrard Street, not far from the Turk's Head tavern, where Samuel Johnson dined and presided over literary taste. Gates had a disastrous quarrel with Cornwallis's wife, apparently over a dispute in which he became involved with one of her officer friends. She attacked Gates with a fury that threw him "entirely off my guard" and provoked him to an angry reply. It didn't help when he sent Cornwallis an apology describing her outburst as "unmerited and unexpected." After that he could expect nothing from Townshend, who in any case had been replaced as secretary at war by Welbore Ellis, a pretentious incompetent whose overriding concern was to obtain a peerage for himself. "I am Soliciting," Gates wrote bitterly, "from the Hard Hand of Power."[12]

Betsy's health declined, and they moved to Bath to try the cure of the waters. In 1766 they rented a house near Bristol, at St. Michael's Hill. Cares and responsibilities multiplied. Gates tried unsuccessfully to secure the promise of a commission for his son, Bob. Betsy's father died penniless, and her mother pressed Gates to obtain a widow's pension for her. His own mother clashed with Betsy and accused her of instigating the move to Bristol as a "design of discarding us." It was all too much. He turned, an acquaintance reported, to "guzzling and gaming." He tried the consolation of Methodism. He became demanding and obstinate. Offers of majorities in regiments in America did eventually come, but these no longer satisfied him. He insisted on remaining in England to angle for a colonelcy. Learning of an impending vacancy, he tried secretly to sell his commission in advance in order to raise the purchase money, but the scheme, a shady one, fell through. On March 10, 1769, he sold his commission to a younger brother of Monckton and left the army.[13]

One hope remained. Monckton had requested the command of the East India Company's troops, a private force, and he promised Gates the top position under him. Gates banked everything on that. He clung to Monckton, even trying to help him iron out his relations with a feuding mistress. Jack Hale, home from Canada where he had served brilliantly under Wolfe, tried to restrain him, warning that although he might come back from India a nabob and find Lady Harrington "as ready to set her a--e upon your p---- and to pick your pocket into the bargain as she wou'd have been 20 years ago," he could as likely return empty-handed, "like a Dog as you are to his Nasty Vomit." Gates persisted. For four years Monckton's fortunes dragged through tortuous twists. In Parliament in April 1772, his appointment was held up while a select committee under the M.P. for Preston, John Burgoyne, investigated the affairs of the East India Company and considered a motion of censure of Lord Clive. Although Clive was cleared, Parliament determined to exercise greater supervision over the company's policies, and this included control over the appointment of the commander in chief of the Indian forces. In the end, the post went to General John Clavering, not Monckton.[14] In 1773 Monckton was offered the command of the forces in North America. Had he accepted, and had he requested Gates to be assigned to him, they might have been the British guiding spirits at Lexington and Bunker Hill.

The India disappointment brought final disillusionment for Gates with the British system of caste and corruption. The germ of republicanism planted in the Whig Club in New York sprouted. He still heard from William Smith, who wrote of those evenings when, "with the Aid of Bacchus and in the Pride of Philosophy, we laughed at the shining Anxieties of the Great." Now he found friends in England who talked republicanism. Between 1763 and 1768 he often went into Bristol to hobnob with the city's radicals at Mrs. Perry's coffeehouse. One of them was a transplanted New Yorker and a "hot Wilkite," Henry Cruger, Jr., then a member of the city's common council and later the mayor. In February 1766, after the Stamp Act was passed, Cruger spent three weeks with a Bristol delegation in London, "talking as it were for my own life," to persuade members of Parliament to repeal the act. Another guest at Mrs. Perry's, when he was not sitting in Parliament, was the uninhibited, melodramatic Lieutenant Colonel Isaac Barré. It was said that Garrick had offered him a thousand pounds a year to go on the stage. He had lost an eye in the attack on Quebec in 1759 and still had a bullet lodged in the other cheek that gave a "savage glare" to the one eye. Speaking in the

Commons against the Declaratory bill, February 3, 1766, he exploded, "All colonies have their date of independence. The wisdom or folly of our conduct may make it the sooner or later."[15]

Gates's father died in 1766 and his mother in 1768. Betsy no longer had reason to shun the London area, and they moved back, to nearby Sandridge. There Gates, inspired perhaps by the example of his political friends at Bristol, considered running for a seat in Parliament on the platform of opposition to "the present pernicious system of American Politicks," but without any apparent voting support, and he withdrew. His political activism brought a renewed friendship with Jack Hale, who, though risen to colonel of light dragoons, was a convinced, pro-American Whig. He was then on inactive duty, residing on his Yorkshire estate at Gisborough, and Gates traveled north to visit with him. Hale introduced Gates to a club of Yorkshire radicals, the Demoniacs, who met at Crazy Castle, a six-hundred-year-old fortress owned by John Hall Stevenson, a handsome, hypochondriac litterateur and friend of Laurence Sterne, whose *Tristam Shandy* had appeared in 1760. Rabelais's *Gargantua and Pantagruel* was their libertarian guide. During the day they gathered along the beach, "as even as a mirour of 5 miles," said Sterne, and raced their chaises "with one wheel in the Sea, & the other in the Sand." In the evenings they reveled at the castle, proclaiming war against all sham.

One of the Demoniacs was Charles Lee, who after his service under Burgoyne in Portugal had served as aide to the King of Poland, and then, when he could rise no higher in the British army than brevet lieutenant colonel, had retired at half pay and was now living at Bury St. Edmunds. He had served with Gates in Braddock's expedition to the Monongahela. Nicknamed "the vagabond," he was tall, spare, slovenly, and conspicuous with a huge, beaked nose. Even among British aristocrats he was an eccentric, not least in being an intellectual. He had read the Greeks and the Romans, the essential John Locke, the popular French historian of England, Paul de Rapin-Thoyras, and, his favorite, the "divine and incomparable" Jean-Jacques Rousseau. Gates, listening to Lee pontificate in his rough voice, had reservations about Rousseau. He was, he said, "the greatest man or the greatest humbugger." But Lee's fondness for Rapin must have reminded him of the talk of William Livingston in New York, who thought Rapin "an estimable treasure of knowledge." Rapin viewed British history as beginning with an ideal representative government in Saxon times, which was destroyed by the conquest, recovered in the Glorious Revolution of 1689, and corrupted by the Hanoverians and their ministers. Gates became more and more receptive to this country-versus-court ideology.[16]

The radicals' battle cry of "Wilkes and Liberty!" struck a responsive note at Crazy Castle. Stevenson set the tone. Wilkes was a physically ugly, combative man with an unsightly squint in one eye but with considerable cultivation and charismatic appeal, especially for women. His famous attack on the ministry in the magazine *North Briton* had resulted in his prosecution, exile, expulsion from Parliament (at the king's insistence), and incarceration in King's Bench Prison. Rioting mobs and mammoth petitions proclaimed him a symbol of democracy, and in the end he was elected Lord Mayor of London. Gates may have met him at meetings of the Demoniacs. Where Gates's sympathies lay is indicated in two letters he received from Hale. On May 12, 1766, hearing that Gates had turned Methodist, Hale wrote, "You may indeed with some reason Abandon Politicks as it is next to Impossible to settle things upon [James] Harrington's Plan." Clearly, Hale considered Gates a confirmed republican. On August 30, 1771, Hale wrote in like spirit:

> Knowing His Majesty as you do and loving him as well as you know him, with what astonishment and even Horror will you hear that the following lines were one day posted upon his Palace Gate, supposed to be wrote by some Incendiary who had only supposed himself injured

> > Scourge of thy People violent and base
> > Sent in Gods Vengeance on a slavish race
> > Who Lost to Every Sense of Freedom past
> > Are dead to Wrongs or this had been thy last.

In May 1770 an acquaintance had called Gates a "red hot Republican." A friend, Charles Davers called him "a great Politician." Gates again considered running for Parliament and went so far as to draft a campaign speech.[17]

He would have been an advocate for America, probably more radical than his friend Benjamin Franklin. On March 12, 1768, Franklin invited Gates, whom he had probably met in 1755 in Braddock's camp at Frederick, to a gathering of veterans of America in his lodgings at 36 Craven Street. Present also that evening were Charles Lee and Robert Monckton. It is an open question whether Gates and Lee argued more heatedly against British colonial measures than Franklin. Franklin had at first supported the Stamp Act, and although he had recanted on that, he had spoken only mildly against the Townshend duties of 1767. He had no use for Wilkes radicalism, but he and

Gates had common interests. They shared a passion for chess. Franklin owned two thousand acres in Nova Scotia and was eager to obtain firsthand information to help promote settlement of them.[18] And Gates's thoughts were turning more and more toward America.

By 1772 there was nothing left to hold him in England. A failure in the stock market in 1769 had hurt his lifetime savings. Monckton told him curtly that he had "distresses enough of my own." Why not put England behind him and start again in America? He still had the thousand pounds Parliament had awarded him for his service in Martinique, invested in 4 percent Consolidated Bank annuities. That might suffice to buy a wilderness tract, erect a house, buy a few slaves, and set up as a country squire. It would mean that he would have to swallow a few scruples, as Jack Hale was quick to point out. "He who walks at large by the favour of another might allmost as well be dead." Hale could afford to moralize. He had won the rewards Gates had been denied. After the Quebec victory, Hale had been delegated by Monckton to carry the news to London, and now he had risen to major general and was living comfortably on the Gisborough estate that came with his wife's dowry. Hale knew that Gates was too distraught to stop. "I shall not be at all affronted," he sighed, "if you shou'd wipe your A--e with my advice."[19]

Virginia seemed a likely place. George Washington was the example of the nontitled planter who might rise to eminence there. Gates wrote him for advice. The reply was not enthusiastic, but it was not discouraging. Gates wrote to Colonel Robert Hunter, his old paymaster in Braddock's army and a successful Virginia businessman. Hunter urged Virginia. That settled it. Inquiries unearthed an attractive land purchase in Maryland. Belongings were packed. The Gateses waited a month at Bristol for suitable passage; in August 1772 they sailed. A jaded, embittered man watched the crowded quays of Bristol fade in the distance. "I fear I shall have a task to support his spirits," Betsy told herself.[20]

❧ 6 ❧

"The Soldier Draws His Sword
with Alacrity"

For Burgoyne, 1772 was a year
of self-assessment. Until this point he was a major general without a command and a member of Parliament without distinction. It had been ten years since his campaign in Portugal. Now he seemed more a man of fashion than of adventure. He was approaching his fiftieth birthday. His brother-in-law and patron, Strange, had died on June 1, 1771, at Bath, of apoplexy. Unless some new field of opportunity opened for him, he might sink into obscurity. He needed a new cause, a vehicle to give play to his talents and restore the luster to the image of the hero of Valencia de Alcántara.

Early in 1772, there appeared in the London bookstalls a work entitled *Considerations on Indian Affairs,* by William Bolts, a Dutch employee of the British East India Company who had been expelled from Bengal for disruptive activities. The book claimed to be an exposé of monopoly, extortion, and cruelty during the regimes of Governor Robert Clive and his successor, Harry Verelst. It raised, Horace Walpole reported, a "general clamour." The press took up the cry. At issue was the very survival of the East India Company, which not only traded with India but governed it. While Parliament had contributed naval support for its conquests, the company's nabobs had amassed private fortunes. Now the company teetered on the verge of bankruptcy. The directors were divided among themselves into warring factions, the stock was subject to wild speculation on the market, and the unstable military relations with the native rulers threatened to invite an attempt by France to regain control. While a disastrous famine devastated Bengal and tea rejected by the American boycott accumulated in London warehouses, the directors declared a bountiful year's dividend of 12 1/2 percent.

Belatedly, in the face of the threat of Parliamentary intervention, the company introduced a judicature bill in the Commons on March 30 providing for a mild administrative reform that would bar the governor and council from engaging in personal trade. The bill triggered a storm of recriminations among Commons members who were also company directors. Burgoyne sensed an opportunity. He conferred with the duke of Grafton, his supporter during the election troubles of 1768. On April 13, he rose to move, in the form of an amendment to the judicature bill, that before any legislation was attempted a select committee be created to investigate the complete affairs of the company. A token restructuring was not going to be enough. He proposed a no-holds-barred inquiry into "the present narrow and rotten system of Indian Government." In an obvious bid for the committee chairmanship— "His own abilities and his own modesty," William Hazlitt observed, "took up half his speech"—he warned that "if by some means sovereignty and law are not separated from trade, India and Great Britain will be sunk and overwhelmed never to rise again." And he advocated nothing less than the extension of the liberties of the British Constitution to the downtrodden millions of India. "Good God! what a call! The native of Hindostan, born a slave,—his neck bent from the very cradle to the yoke,—by birth, by education, by climate, by religion, a patient, submissive, willing subject to Eastern despotism, first begins to feel, first shakes his chains, for the first time complains under the pre-eminence of British tyranny!"[1]

Here was a Burgoyne unknown to military men or politicians. His concept of constitutionalism was benevolent. Human rights were the prerogative of every British subject. The British Empire, although paternalistic, must not be repressive. Governmental authority, as defined in that uniquely British mystical amalgam, "the King in Parliament," fanned out to the colonies from London, but its operation must be in the spirit of the Glorious Revolution of 1688.

The heated debate that Burgoyne's motion aroused lasted until 11 o'clock at night and revealed the gulf between the company's defenders and detractors. Yet the motion passed overwhelmingly. The committee named included partisans of both sides, among them Clive himself. Predictably, Burgoyne was elected chairman. At the first meeting, George Johnstone, a former governor of West Florida, company official, and enemy of Clive, struck the keynote. A friend of Burgoyne, he was a coarse, combative man with an impressive store of information and a "half-savage eloquence, restrained by no delicacy of language." He demanded that the committee begin with an investigation of individual misconduct. Clive became the prime target of attack. Records were assembled and witnesses called, including Bolts and

Clive. The most dramatic revelation was Clive's own testimony, detailing the defeat and dethronement in 1757 of the nawab of Bengal, young Siraj-ud-daula (dubbed "Sir Roger Dowler" by English servicemen). Clive employed as his secret agent a double-dealing Sikh merchant from Calcutta, Omichand, who negotiated the defection of Siraj-ud-daula's uncle, Mir Jafar. In order to obtain Omichand's services, Clive deceived him with a bogus promise of 5 percent of the nawab's treasures and a cash payment of three hundred thousand pounds, which he formalized in a bogus contract to which he forged Admiral Charles Watson's name. Subsequently, at the Battle of Plassey, Mir Jafar was one of Siraj-ud-daula's chief generals and stood by while Clive brilliantly routed his nephew's troops. Clive then crowned Mir Jafar the new nawab of Bengal. Siraj-ud-daula was captured and beheaded by Mir Jafar's son. Mir Jafar rewarded all the leaders in the victory, and Clive received a munificent £234,000. Two years later, he was also awarded the *jaghire,* an honorary position paying £30,000 a year for life, in effect a transference of the same sum that the nawab received as a yearly quit-rent from the East India Company. "By God, Mr. Chairman," Clive brazenly told the committee, "at this moment I stand astonished at my own moderation!"[2]

On May 26, Burgoyne presented a progress report to the Commons, printed in 152 pages of the House journal's oversize folios. In June, the company's problems exploded into a financial crisis. The London and continental bourses collapsed, and in September, East India stock plummeted from 219 to 160. The company could not meet its loans or pay its customs taxes, yet it declared its intention to issue the next half-yearly dividend. The shareholders and speculators were dismayed at this irresponsibility. Some critics, including Burgoyne, urged that the company reduce its dividend to 6 percent or less, thereby exempting it from the recently imposed government levy of four hundred thousand pounds, effective whenever the yield was higher, but the directors refused. Government intervention was now mandatory. Lord North, pressured by the Bedford Whigs among his own supporters and resisted by company partisans among the Rockingham Whigs, desired a mild reform less damaging to the reputation of Clive, whom he counted among his wealthy supporters, and less thoroughgoing than the sensational revelations of the Burgoyne committee threatened. He therefore proposed the creation of a new secret committee, composed exclusively of his supporters, to formulate a plan of reform he could control. Burgoyne indignantly asked why a new committee was necessary and whether the intention was to protect the guilty and cater to the stockholders. North adroitly replied that the company's confidential books could not be released for the public investigation assigned to Burgoyne's committee and that both committees would continue in their separate functions. Edmund Burke, whose patron was a company shareholder, afterward charged that the Secret Committee was a cover-up for a scheme secretly concocted, that it was "pregnant before wedlock."[3]

The members of Burgoyne's committee viewed their function as downgraded. Attendance declined to a point where it became difficult to assemble a quorum of seven. Burgoyne kept on doggedly. It took almost a year before two further reports were submitted. At the same time, on May 3, 1773, North introduced his Regulating Bill, a moderate proposal to reorganize the company's leadership and place Bengal's judicial system under governmental control. Burgoyne wanted more than that. "Not to proceed against persons who by the reports appear guilty," he charged, "will be to give encouragement to others hereafter to offend." The perfidy of Omichand had been of the *"blackest* dye," but with heavy sarcasm, Burgoyne declared that the crimes of the British were of the *"whitest* kind." Another member of his committee, Charles W. Cornwall, warned North that "the Government would be irreparably disgraced if nothing was done this Session." North hedged. He gave Burgoyne nominal support but did not marshal his administration behind him. Burgoyne plunged ahead. On May 10 he introduced three resolutions, castigating "crimes which it shocked human nature even to conceive" and making it clear that he intended to follow them up with a specific condemnation of Clive:

1. That military conquests and treaty acquisitions belonged to the state.
2. That it was illegal for civil or military employees to appropriate such acquisitions.
3. That money and property from Bengal had been so appropriated from the princes of India.

The speeches were heated, but the first two resolutions passed without a head count and the third was adopted four days later. On May 19, Burgoyne arose for the personal assault. Clive, he said, had deposed Siraj-ud-daula for his own gain. Huge grants to individuals had been concealed with evidence obtained from witnesses under duress. "What I ask," he demanded, "is a Bill for the satisfaction of sufferers out of the private estates of persons who received sums of money unwarrantably." He moved that Clive had "illegally acquired the sum of £234,000 to the dishonor and detriment of the state."

The debate was a veritable trial of Clive. In that long, galleried, paneled chamber, lit by three round-topped windows at one end and a three-tiered chandelier at the center, with the sweating members ranged around in four rows of benches, the man who had conquered India was to be judged, according to the usages of the British Constitution, by elected representatives each of whom in that function counted himself his equal. Clive, jowly and paunchy now and pain-ridden with gallstones, spoke in his own defense. He had been examined by Burgoyne's committee "more like a sheep-stealer than a member of this House." The attack on him had been inspired by vindictive company dissidents led by the recent deputy chairman, Lawrence Sulivan. Far from his having oppressed the Indians, "it pleased God to make me the instrument of their deliverance." He had deposed Siraj-ud-daula because the nawab had broken his word. He had accepted presents because they were a just reward. "I have one request to make of the House," he concluded with an accusing flourish, "that, when they come to decide upon my honour, they will not forget their own."

Whether or not this was intended as a slur against Burgoyne, Solicitor General Alexander Wedderburn took up the cue, citing the four-year-old "Junius" charges of bribery and cardsharping to suggest that Burgoyne look to his own record before criticizing others. Burgoyne furiously replied, "If that wretch Junius is lurking here in any corner of the House, I now tell him to his face he is an assassin, a liar, and a coward."

Although Clive's guilt was clear, it was also clear that the House recoiled from branding him a wrongdoer. Even Hans Stanley, Burgoyne's previous ally, moved that the condemnation be struck out, leaving only a simple, uncensuring statement that Clive had received £234,000. Burgoyne attempted to reinstate the censure, and the debate lasted from 3:00 in the afternoon to 5:00 in the morning. Clive spoke again. "Take my fortune, but save my honour," he ended, and strode out. Finally, Wedderburn moved that "Robert Lord Clive did at the same time render great and meritorious services to his country." It was carried without a division.[4]

Burgoyne took the exoneration as a personal blow. A year of painstaking labor seemed lost for purely political reasons. North, he believed, had "acted with duplicity." On the surface, North had supported Burgoyne's Select Committee and had voted for all of its proposed resolutions, including the condemnation of Clive. But he had left his followers free to vote as they chose, and they had understood this to be an encouragement to undercut the committee and whitewash Clive. "Nothing short of proposed enmity," Burgoyne was convinced, "could place me further than I found myself from the confidence of this minister." And when Burgoyne voted with the opposition, which was more often now, conviction might be mingled with spite. In

February 1773, the opposition attempted an inquiry into a recent military expedition to suppress an uprising of dispossessed Carib tribes of St. Vincent in the West Indies. The Caribs had been resisting settlers' occupation of their lands (including purchasers of a large tract granted to Robert Monckton, whose armada against Martinique in 1762 had also conquered St. Vincent). The expedition had lost almost as many men from disease as were killed and wounded. Critics charged callous invasion of the Caribs' rights. North disclaimed responsibility for the affair and threatened to resign if it were made an issue against him. Burgoyne apparently opposed exploitation of the Caribs for the same reasons he had championed Indian rights. North succeeded in defeating the motion for an investigation.[5]

The following year found Burgoyne again in the opposition. In February 1774, the Grenville Election Act, designed to curb abuses at the polls, came up for renewal. North, with a national election in the offing, wanted no roadblocks in the way of his obtaining a Commons majority. Burgoyne, concerned to prevent repetition of the violence at Preston, desired legal safeguards. This time he voted with the majority. The act was retained.[6]

But the great issue that overshadowed all else in 1774 was the American crisis, and on that Burgoyne joined with North. On May 10, 1773, the very day that Burgoyne introduced his three East India Company resolutions, Parliament had inconspicuously passed a Tea Act intended to help the company's sale of tea by repealing the tax of 1d. per pound paid in England. Two members of Burgoyne's Select Committee, Cornwall and Johnstone, argued that the Townshend duty of 3d., collected in America, should be removed as well. North replied that the Americans were "little deserving of favour from hence."[7] As much as any man, he had lit the fuse for the American Revolution. Fleshy, complacent, and unenterprising, he disliked confrontation but would not budge from an innate conservatism. Burgoyne, tolerant, humane, and constitutionalist, likewise took as God-given a world of hierarchies and subordinations.

On January 20, 1774, John Hancock's ship, *Hayley,* arrived in England with the news that on the sixteenth of the previous month a band of Bostonians, thinly disguised as Mohawk Indians, had boarded three East India merchant vessels anchored in Boston Harbor and thrown nine thousand pounds' worth of tea overboard. It was America's unequivocal answer. North, faced with a direct challenge, advocated a punitive response, the Coercive Acts, which closed the Port of Boston until the tea was paid for, transferred trials of enforcement officials to Britain, annulled the Massachusetts charter, and legalized the quartering of troops in occupied buildings. The opposition, led by Rockingham and Chatham, demanded repeal of the Tea Act. In the debate, on April 19, Burgoyne rallied to North's side. "I look upon America as our child," he declared, "which we have already spoilt by too much indulgence. . . . It is the right of taxation which they dispute, and not the tax." For a general to speak so pugnaciously aroused an uproar. One member jeered that the author of such bombast "belonged rather to the heavy than the light horse." Burgoyne sat down, adding—what could cause even greater concern—that he "wished America convinced by persuasion rather than by the sword."[8] He was now publicly aligned on the side of coercion.

It was a monumental misjudgment of the mood of the colonists, but it was consistent with all he had ever said about the empire. He was familiar with constitutional arguments. "I am no stranger," he wrote a year later, "to the doctrines of Mr. Locke, and others of the best advocates for the rights of mankind, upon the compacts always implied between the governing and governed, and the right of resistance in the latter when the compact shall be so violated as to leave no other means of redress. I look with reverence almost amounting to idolatry upon those immortal Whigs who adopted and applied such doctrine during part of the reign of Charles the First, and in that of James the Second." But he could not place himself in the position of the colonists so as to enable him to understand their problems as they saw them. When it came to the empire, the august institution he so much revered, he was adamant for the central authority: "The vital principle of the constitution, in which it moves and has its being, is the supremacy of the King in Parliament—a compound, indefinite, indefeasible power, coeval with the origin of the empire, and coextensive over all its parts.[9] He might have added the almost universal confidence of British officers that British soldiers could always defeat colonial militia. That unspoken misjudgment proved fatal at Saratoga.

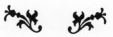

Nothing better illustrated the casual, pleasure-as-usual attitude of the British aristocracy in the midst of the American crisis than a gala social extravaganza staged by Burgoyne on June 9, 1774. His nephew, Edward Smith-Stanley, son of Lord Strange and heir to the Derby earldom, had become engaged to Lady Betty Hamilton, daughter of the duke of Hamilton.

No expense was spared to celebrate the marriage. The event was in the form of a fête champêtre, the first ever in England. The place was the Burgoynes' Surrey residence, the Oaks, site of today's Derby races. Robert Adam was engaged to build a pavilion for dancing and theatricals. David Garrick was entrusted with dramatic arrangements. More than three hundred guests were invited, so many of them members of Parliament that Lord North found himself without a quorum and adjourned for the weekend. Each arriving carriage at the Oaks was greeted with a salvo of French horns. Soon the front lawn was crowded with elaborately costumed shepherds and shepherdesses. At a signal, Burgoyne led them through the house to the back lawn for a masque performance. A throng of local residents, many perched in trees, watched from an adjoining road. Two Cupids presented each guest with a bouquet. From a grove of orange trees, a troupe of singers serenaded Lord Stanley and his queen of the Oaks, accompanied by a band and followed by a dance of sylvans. Then Stanley and his lady led the way inside to an octagonal, colonnaded dance hall decorated with flowers and lined, chairback-high, with white Persian and gold fringe and with seats covered in deep crimson.

The evening's feature was a two-act play, *The Maid of the Oaks,* specially written by Burgoyne and produced by Garrick. The setting was a fête champêtre for the coming marriage of the lead couple. The plot was a mix of concealed identities, dominated by Lady Bab Lardoon, an advocate of women's equality. She determines to humiliate Dupely, an authentic male chauvinist, by baiting him in the guise of a shepherdess. While he attempts to make advances to her, she expounds on the cause of the "superior set." "We have our *Bill of Rights* and *Constitution,* too," she tells him, "we drop in at all hours, play at all parties, pay our own reckonings, and in every circumstance (pettycoats excepted) are true, jolly fellows." Garrick liked the play so well that he expanded it into five acts and produced it five months later at the Drury Lane Theatre, where it had a run of several nights, a success for those days.[10]

Following the performance came minuets and cotillions until 11:30, when six gold-fringed curtains were raised to reveal a large supper room spread with hot dishes and rich desserts. Then came more singing and dancing of minuets composed by the earl of Kelley. Country dances were struck up until past 3:00 in the morning. Outdoors, four pyramids of lights illumined a troupe of Cupids carrying a float of an Ionic portico with four pink, transparent columns and a pediment topped with a quartered shield of the Hamilton and Stanley arms. One estimate put the cost of the fête at twelve thousand pounds.[11]

The Coercive Acts infuriated the colonists. A continental congress met in Philadelphia and adopted a nonimportation, nonexportation, and nonconsumption agreement. The Massachusetts House of Representatives converted itself into an autonomous provincial congress. At Portsmouth, New Hampshire, an insurgent band overpowered the garrison and seized arms and munitions. Pamphlets by Thomas Jefferson, James Wilson, and John Adams proclaimed that the colonies owed no obedience to Parliament and only a nominal one to the king.

North and his cabinet divided on how to react. He would not yield to the colonists, but he wanted an effort of conciliation. The only minister who supported him was his stepbrother, Lord Dartmouth, the colonial secretary, who went as far as to confer with Franklin through two secret agents. The rest of the cabinet members, led by the Bedfords, favored military repression. Most significant, so did the king. They were unhappy with the recently appointed military governor of Massachusetts, Thomas Gage, who they felt should have suppressed the disturbances. He had demanded twenty thousand troops before he would move. When, in September, he recommended that the Coercive Acts be suspended, the king and North agreed that he should be replaced. Their choice was Sir Jeffery Amherst. The king conferred with him and told him that he would be sent "with an olive branch on one hand, while the other should be prepared to obtain submission."[12] But Amherst, whose wife was an American, could not bring himself to accept a mission of repression.

The king took counsel with his personal adviser, Charles Jenkinson, a junior treasury official who was later to become secretary at war. He was a somewhat mysterious court figure, described by Walpole as the king's "sole confidant" and "director or agent of all his Majesty's secret counsels." Burke whispered to Rockingham that "Jenkinson governs everything." Jenkinson had served on the Secret Committee on the East India Company. He was a brother-in-law of Burgoyne's Select Committee colleague, Charles Cornwall. He knew Burgoyne as an audacious general, fiercely loyal to the empire, and had apparently been thinking of him for the American command for some time. In order to sound him out, Jenkinson edged near him in the crush leaving the House of Commons after a day of debate on the American crisis late in January 1775. Burgoyne could not fail to catch the signal of Jenkinson's peculiarly graceless motions toward him. When they came side by side, Jenkinson gave him a meaningful look and observed that he wished Burgoyne were in America. Burgoyne understood immediately. He replied that "every soldier must go where he was ordered," although "*that* service would not be desirable to any man."

Much as the king might desire Burgoyne, however, there was an insurmountable difficulty of seniority. As a major general, Burgoyne was junior to William Howe, who had experience in North America, and to Henry Clinton, who had grown up in New York while his father was the colony's governor. All three generals had been promoted to their present rank on the same day, but Burgoyne had the least service. The king decided to leave Gage temporarily in command and to send all three major generals to Boston, supposedly as Gage's assistants. In fact, Howe was to replace Gage at the first opportunity. Clinton was second in command. Burgoyne, in the end, seemed intended primarily to infuse spirit into the others.

On February 2, Lord Barrington, still secretary at war, called Burgoyne to his home in Cavendish Square. Burgoyne was prepared. Earlier that day, North had introduced in the Commons a proposal that Massachusetts Bay be declared to be in a state of rebellion. He had also hinted, what had already been decided in cabinet meetings, that additional forces would be dispatched and a blockade imposed on New England. Burgoyne knew that his name had been making the rounds of the gossip circuit. Clearly there were plans in the wings. In this private meeting, Barrington began with discursive talk on the Commons debates of the preceding day. He had a lisping, tediously precise manner of speech. The conversation wandered into general chitchat. ("We sat late, it was very tiresome.") Abruptly, with no change of expression, Barrington remarked that "he did not doubt that everything in America would mend" when Burgoyne and the two other generals he was appointing would arrive there. Burgoyne was not caught off guard. He had no intention of entrusting his future to Barrington's hands alone. He asked whether the king had requested him as "particularly necessary." In that case he would forego considerations of family and fortune and obey the call of duty. Barrington poured on compliments ("a language," Burgoyne acidly noted, "in which he is always ready"), assured him that the king had personally selected him, and revealed that the other two nominees, Howe and Clinton, had accepted a few hours earlier. Having opened a channel to the king, Burgoyne accepted, as he had no doubt intended to do from the start.

But he meant to define his own assignment, not to travel as standby baggage. The post he decided upon was military governor of New York. New York, he saw, with its Hudson River–Lake Champlain route from Canada and its Mohawk River avenue to the interior, was the arterial focus of the continent, as the French and Indian War had demonstrated. Little had been done to prepare the colony for its logical role. Governor William Tryon, an absentee in London, had rendered himself ineffective by taking sides with the Livingstons against the DeLanceys in the colony's bitter factional politics. The resident lieutenant governor, Cadwallader Colden, was also a controversial figure, well into his eighties. Burgoyne reasoned that with a military presence of three or four newly dispatched regiments he might negotiate a settlement. Failing that, he would be in a strategic position to cut New England off from the other colonies. It may be that he knew of Shelburne's recommendation of him for the New York governorship eight years earlier and had been thinking of it ever since. Plainly, he already had the Saratoga route on his mind.

It was pointless to attempt to win Barrington over for such a project. Although Burgoyne did not know it, Barrington favored a general withdrawal of troops from America and reliance instead on a naval blockade to bring the colonies to terms. In any case, the governorship of New York was a political appointment, out of Barrington's jurisdiction. Burgoyne determined to swallow past resentments and go directly to Lord North. He negotiated a meeting with North's secretary, William Cowper. North received him cordially. Burgoyne laid himself out to please. He had differed with North, he said, from principle, never out of rancor. He stood foursquare behind North's American policy. North responded flatteringly. Burgoyne explained his scheme for the New York governorship. He did not seek, he emphasized, "to interfere in military command with my colleagues" but rather to secure a political post more challenging than "the bare superintendence of a small brigade." North was noncommittal but promised to discuss the proposal with the king.[13] Burgoyne could really not expect more. He would have to wage a wider campaign if he was to achieve his goal.

He made a point of delivering a warlike speech in the Commons. Protesting that he had not sought his appointment, he proclaimed that "the soldier draws his sword with alacrity." He had enough, he said, of disputes over "real and virtual representation, external and internal taxes, revenue and regulation, till one's head grows dizzy with distinctions." The issue was "whether we have spirit to support our conviction."[14] His militant credentials reaffirmed, he canvassed the ministry for support. He found that only

Dartmouth and Lord Suffolk, secretary of state for the southern department, opposed him. They supported Howe for the New York post. He went to see Howe. A tall, swarthy, large-boned man, genial but closemouthed, Howe admitted only that he "wished to avoid going to Boston if possible." Presumably, this was because he did not wish to fight Bostonians, who had affectionately raised a statue to his eldest brother, George, who had been killed near Ticonderoga in 1758. Actually, he had a low opinion of Gage and disliked the prospect of serving under him. During the next few weeks Burgoyne could learn nothing more and became resentful. He told North that he had not accepted the assignment merely "to see that the soldiers boiled their kettles regularly." At a breakfast on March 30 with Thomas Hutchinson, former governor of Massachusetts, he inveighed against "the want of one vigorous direction, the indecision in all the Councils, the aptness to procrastination," and the absence of formal instructions for the three generals.[15] He attended a cabinet dinner on April 3 at Lord Dartmouth's in St. James's Square and was frustrated to find that they "talked of every subject but America."

Finally, Burgoyne turned to the king. He obtained an interview, ostensibly to discuss an assignment for a relative, but could find no opening to broach his own affairs. Then he wrote a letter, enclosing a paper with his views. The king was impressed. "I am sorry Howe seems to look so much on the command in New York as the post of confidence," he wrote North, "as I think Burgoyne would best manage any negociation." Instructions were drawn up for Gage, authorizing him to make his own choice between Howe and Burgoyne and sending him four regiments from Ireland to be assigned to New York. The three generals were not informed, in order to circumvent a commitment to Howe. Did the king hope that Gage would prefer Burgoyne, a Westminster classmate, to Howe, an Etonian? For the present, he urged that North have a "full conversation" with Burgoyne so as to send him off "in good humor."

North met with Burgoyne and informed him of the decision. Not to be put off, Burgoyne shook his head. "Do me at least the honor," he fumed, "to treat me like a man not totally ignorant of the world." Why couldn't Gage be instructed to name him? North could only answer that the king had "early and unadvisedly" made "some promise" to Howe. Burgoyne went back to the king. This time, pleading concern for Lady Charlotte's precarious health, he requested permission to return home in the winter, when military operations were suspended. He could then renew his efforts to obtain an independent command. The king, sensing that Burgoyne could serve as a confidential conduit "to suggest what falls in conversation to the Commander-in-Chief," approved.[16]

Charlotte had long been suffering from severe asthma, and her condition was indeed alarming. A painting done of her by Ramsay in the early 1770s depicts a frail, sad-eyed woman, much changed from the lively, outgoing girl Burgoyne had eloped with twenty years before. He agonized over "the levities, the inattention, and dissipations" he had imposed upon "the tenderest, the faithfullest, the most amiable companion and friend that ever man was blessed with." Aware that even his intimates might smile at his professions, he hid his feelings from the world, and, lest her anxiety be aggravated, from Charlotte herself, "not, I hope," he afterwards wrote, "to doubt that I felt— but rather to be ignorant *how much* I felt." Impulsively, he dashed off a letter to the king, to be delivered in the event of his death, recommending Charlotte to his "compassion and generosity."[17] He had little else to leave her.

It was an apprehensive Burgoyne who left London on the Saturday afternoon of the Easter weekend. Parliament was in recess. A glorious spring had come early. The city seemed uncaring of the crisis across the ocean. A coach took the three generals to Portsmouth. There they waited five days for their ship to make ready. On April 20, the *Cerberus,* thirty-six guns, Captain James Chadds commanding, hoisted sail from Spithead.[18] The day before, on Lexington Common, a series of volleys from a British force led by Major John Pitcairn had left eight Minutemen dead and ten wounded on the spring grass.

"America Must Be Subdued or Relinquished"

FOR FIVE WEEKS THE THREE MEN who were to direct British fortunes at Saratoga dined together, paced the ship's pitching deck together—the voyage was a stormy one, and Howe and Clinton both lost their favorite horses—and discussed battlefield experiences, Parliamentary politics, and American affairs. Aristocrats all, they had all distinguished themselves for bravery: Howe under Wolfe on the Heights of Abraham at Quebec, and Clinton in the campaigns in Germany under Prince Charles of Brunswick. "A triumvirate of reputation," Burgoyne characterized them, but their careers had stopped short of the summit, and after declaring themselves reluctant to serve in America they had yielded to the lure of advancement under the cloak of duty. Howe had the self-assurance of a court favorite reputed to be illegitimately descended from George I and had performed brilliantly as a light-infantry battalion commander in the taking of Quebec. Clinton, although self-styled a "shy bitch," was the son of a former governor of Newfoundland and of New York and a relative by marriage of the duke of Newcastle, and he had been wounded at Johannesburg in 1762 while serving with distinction under Prince Ferdinand of Brunswick. A small, introspective man, he had a keen mind and excelled as a planner. Burgoyne and Howe charmed him out of his diffidence, and he declared that he "could not have named two people I should sooner wish to serve with in every respect." Burgoyne afterward wrote that "the sentiments of Howe, Clinton and myself have been unanimous from the beginning." Yet Howe, in his silent, uncommunicative way, played his cards close to his chest. He was not really at home with Burgoyne, a colorful possible competitor, or Clinton, a military intellectual. Clinton was a member of the meticulous "German school," detested by Howe's clubby "American school." "We of course differ in opinion," he hinted.[1]

When the *Cerberus* neared Boston it was met by an outbound packet headed for Newport with the astounding news that Boston was under siege. "What!" Burgoyne exclaimed when the skipper described the rebel force, "Ten thousand peasants keep five thousand king's troops shut up! Well, let *us* get in, and we'll soon find elbow-room." Before long, the rebels were calling him "Elbow Room." The *Cerberus* dropped anchor in Boston Harbor on May 25, within range of rebel cannonade. A motley assembly of militia from all over New England semicircled Boston's Back Bay from Roxbury to Chelsea. Gage's troops were cut off from the interior and reduced to subsistence on salt provisions.

The three generals found quarters in homes vacated by departed Whigs. Burgoyne took over the mansion of James Bowdoin, a member of the rebel Committee of Safety, on Beacon Street at the northeast corner of the Common, the present Bowdoin Street. Clinton occupied the John Hancock house, and Howe a house at the corner of Oliver and Milk streets.[2]

Gage learned from the generals that reenforcements were on the way from Britain—the Thirty-fifth, Forty-ninth, Sixty-fourth, Sixty-fifth, and Sixty-seventh regiments. He dispatched a frigate, the *Mercury,* to cruise off New York, where the transports with four of the regiments were heading, and redirect them to Boston. For Burgoyne, this immediately suspended any hope of a separate New York command. Gage's next move, in accordance with Dartmouth's instructions, was to declare martial law and offer pardons to all who would return to the fold, excepting Samuel Adams and John Hancock. Burgoyne drafted the proclamation, a grandiose manifesto. It addressed the Whigs as "infatuated multitudes" deluded by such "well known traitors and incendiaries" as Adams and Hancock, whose offenses were "of too flagitious a nature to admit of any other consideration than that of condign punishment." The rebels were a "preposterous parade of military arrangement." The officials who were "intrusted with the supreme rule" would "prove that they do not bear the sword in vain." When a copy arrived in London, Lord Germain immediately recognized the authorship. The proclamation may have sat well with the hawks in Parliament, and it may have fueled Burgoyne's drive for a higher command, but in Massachusetts it inspired derision. The Provincial Congress drew up a mock counterproclamation offering pardon to repentant Tories, excepting Gage, Admiral Samuel Graves, and three members of the council, who were pronounced unforgivably guilty of "flagitious" offenses and deserving of "condign" punishment.[3]

After this, Lord North must have been nonplussed when he received a letter from Burgoyne, proposing himself as a conciliator. Burgoyne asked that he be dismissed from the army and unofficially commissioned, as a member of Parliament, to enter into discussions with colonial leaders of all persuasions in New York, Philadelphia, and other centers of agitation. He would present himself as a "friend to human nature, and a well-wisher to the united interests of the two countries, to obtain such lights as might enable me to assist the great work of conciliation." He would leave Boston in October and return with his findings to England by Christmas. His report could help North to "come to Parliament with a more positive plan than could be suggested in the present uncertainty of things." Could a British general who viewed the Whigs as gullible provincials, who privately confided that there was "hardly a leading man among the rebels, in council, or in the field, but at a proper time, and by proper management, might have been bought," and who insisted that the colonists must acknowledge the principle of Parliamentary supremacy, hope to fashion a compromise? Sublimely self-confident though he was, did he truly believe in conciliation if he could write, as he did ten days later to his friend Lord Rochford, secretary of state for the southern department, that, had he been appointed governor of New York, he would have used military power "to encourage and to terrify"?[4] Not surprisingly, North displayed no enthusiasm for the experiment.

In the meantime, the generals decided that the army must assume the offensive. New troop arrivals had augmented Gage's forces to approximately six thousand men. The rebels must be given a demonstration of strength and the British must be aroused, Burgoyne declared, from "a sort of stupefication." The targets were to be Dorchester Heights to the southeast and Charlestown Peninsula to the north. These two elevated positions were vital to the protection of Boston, because the rebels, if they occupied them, could use them as bases from which to bombard the town. The first goal was Dorchester Heights. Burgoyne would provide artillery cover from the approach at Boston Neck, while Howe and Clinton would each lead assaults with troops ferried over in transports. The operation was set for June 18. But news of the scheme reached the patriots, apparently from incautious remarks of Burgoyne. To forestall the attack on Dorchester, General Artemas Ward sent Colonel William Prescott with one thousand men to occupy Bunker Hill, the highest elevation on the Charlestown Peninsula. The troops moved on the night of June 16. At the insistence of Connecticut's impulsive and bullish General Israel Putnam, they bypassed Bunker Hill and entrenched on Breed's Hill, fifty feet lower, at the southeast end of the peninsula where their rear was unprotected. Clinton, ever reconnoitering, spotted the American activity and reported it to Gage, who ignored it. At 4:00 in the morning, the British generals were awakened by the sound of shells from the warship *Lively,* which had detected the patriots on Breed's Hill. A hasty council of war was convened at Province House. Clashing views surfaced. Clinton proposed that Howe, with the main army, attack Breed's Hill from the front, while he would land at the isthmus to the rear with a detachment of five hundred, cutting off the rebels' retreat. But Gage would have no part of tactics from "a man bred up in the German school." Howe, contradicting his own experience in amphibious operations and light-infantry deployment, maintained that a frontal assault was sufficient without an attack to the rear. Perhaps this was the first concrete evidence of his resistance to anything Clinton might propose, a resistance that proved fatal at Saratoga. Burgoyne, aware that as the junior officer he could expect only a minor role, maintained a discreet silence. The Howe plan was adopted. Burgoyne was assigned to provide artillery cover for the left from the mainland at Copps Hill. Warships would provide cover for the right, and Clinton would remain with Burgoyne in reserve at Copps Hill.

That afternoon Howe landed in force on the southern shore of the Charlestown Peninsula. He delayed his attack for two hours. Fearing sniper fire from Charlestown, a largely abandoned town of three to four hundred houses, he ordered the floating batteries and Burgoyne on Copps Hill to lob incendiary shells ("red hot balls" and "carcasses") and set the buildings ablaze. Whole streets fell in ruin, church steeples sent up pillars of flame and smoke, and burning ships sank in the harbor. Then Howe, personally leading the right wing of his twenty-two-hundred-man force, charged the entrenched rebels in traditional open-field formation. Repulsed with heavy losses, he regrouped and charged again. The British left, under Brigadier General Robert Pigot, was especially hard hit. Clinton, watching with Burgoyne from Copps Hill, which gave a view of the entire battle, concluded that Pigot would be submerged if aid were not sent to him. Without waiting for orders, and asking Burgoyne to defend him to Howe, he gathered the guards and the ambulatory wounded and dashed to Pigot's side in the nick of time. Howe, determined to persevere, then led a third bloody charge. Prescott's men, now out of powder and mercilessly bayonetted by the British, retreated to Bunker Hill. Clinton wished to pursue the rebels for "a Compleat finishing to a great and dear bought Victory." Howe called him back, "I thought," Clinton noted, "a little forcibly."[5] Howe may have been right. The British had suffered fearful casualties: 42 percent dead and wounded. But he was not treating Clinton tactfully.

Burgoyne believed that the British sacrifices at Bunker Hill were necessary in order to "efface the stain of the 19th of April." He had lost close
friends. Captain Nicholas Addison, descendant of the author of *The Spectator,*
who had arrived from England only the day before and was to have dined
with him the day of the battle, died of a bullet under the heart. Major John
Pitcairn, who had commanded the advance to Lexington, was shot by a black
militiaman and carried back to the boats by his own son, Thomas, a lieutenant in his battalion. Nevertheless, the principle had to be established that
"trained troops are invincible against any number of undisciplined rabble."
There could be no more thought of conciliation. With such rabble-rousers as
Adams in the saddle, America "must be subdued or relinquished. She will
not be reconciled." Burgoyne wanted to follow up the victory at Bunker Hill
with a two-pronged offensive: first, occupy the Dorchester Heights Peninsula, thus averting repetition from there of a Bunker Hill type of attack.
Then, leaving three thousand men to protect the Charlestown and Dorchester heights, release the remaining two thousand, and such frigates as
could be spared, to harass the entire coast, with emphasis upon an expedition
against New York. This would be expanded with an advance up the Hudson,
while a northern army would descend from Canada, the operation he had
proposed before he left England. And, because Clinton had volunteered to
remain with the contingent of troops at Charlestown, the way would be
opened for a field command for himself. But large numbers of foreign mercenaries must be recruited abroad, and supplies must be shipped to arm
Indian attacks in the north and slave insurrections in the south. "You can
have no probable prospect of bringing the war to a speedy conclusion with
any force that Great Britain and Ireland can supply," he wrote Rochford.[6]

At this point a disturbing letter arrived from Burgoyne's old comrade of
Portugal days, Charles Lee, now a major general in the newly created rebel
Continental Army. Released in advance to the press, it artfully attempted to
open old wounds. Invoking for Burgoyne the memory of the ministry's
"wickedness and treachery" in the East Indian investigation and the "black
business of St. Vincents," it conjured him not to heed Gage's "tissue of
misrepresentation, injustice, and tortured inferences from mis-stated facts."
Appealing to Burgoyne's humane convictions, it exhorted him not to engage
in an unjust war against "the last assylum of persecuted liberty."

Burgoyne instantly recognized his jeopardy. He must not allow North to
believe that Lee spoke for him. He would turn Lee's "paltry jargon of invec-
tive" into an opening wedge for a negotiation to lure Lee back to the British
side. Why not, he replied, meet and discuss the issues at the Brown general

store, a British outpost on Boston Neck (on Washington Street, south of Blackstone Square)? If the primary issue was taxation, it was "in the power of the Colonies to put an end to the exercise of taxation immediately, and for ever." Let them tax themselves, and it would "never be the interest of Britain after her late experience to make another trial." This seemed a revival of North's olive branch offer. Lee, willing to talk, submitted Burgoyne's letter to the Massachusetts Provincial Congress. The rebel militants, however, feared that the proposal might prove seductive to faint hearts. Lee declined the invitation. In any case, as North afterward informed Burgoyne, the king disapproved of the negotiation, ostensibly because Burgoyne might be taken hostage. There were political rumblings against Burgoyne's presumption in proposing to speak for the ministry. Had he conferred with Lee he might have been repudiated.[7]

Yet there was little else for him to do than "draw a pen instead of a sword." A message arrived on August 11 from Washington protesting the British refusal to treat captured Patriot officers as prisoners of war and threatening to retaliate "exactly by the rule which you shall observe." Burgoyne drafted Gage's reply in the same overbearing tone he had used in the proclamation two months earlier: "No rank that is not from the King" would be acknowledged from wielders of "usurped authority." Washington, possibly amused by this rodomontade, did not carry out his threat. Burgoyne turned to writing for charity theatrical productions staged in Faneuil Hall. He contributed a rhymed prologue and epilogue to an adaptation of Voltaire's *Zara,* inveighing against American "minds diseased" and ridiculing Puritan prudery. One of Washington's secretaries, on receiving a playbill, lamented that the Continental Army lacked the powder to convert the performance into a real-life tragedy. Burgoyne also wrote an entire play, *The Blockade of Boston,* which lampooned Washington as a bumbling figure with an oversized wig and trailing sword. A Whig dramatist countered with *The Blockheads.*[8]

By mid-July there was still no word from North on his proposed invasion of New York. "I begin to despair," Burgoyne wrote Rochford. "Enterprise is not ours. Inertness, or what is equal to it, attention to small objects, counteracts or procrastinates undertakings, when no visible objection lies to them." Was no move possible before winter set in? On August 13 he submitted a new proposal to Gage. He asked to lead an expedition of two thousand against Rhode Island. This would force the withdrawal of Rhode Island militia from Boston for local defense. The expedition might be expanded or contracted as developments dictated. It could become a diversion or a springboard for the eventual attack on New York. But Gage would not budge without authorization from home. As the frustrated Burgoyne wrote Germain, Gage had not "resolution to act upon the occasion; in events which the King's servants at home could have foreseen, to substitute reason and principle for orders."[9] Gloom descended over the beleaguered British in Boston. Food became scarce and sickness spread. The rebel poet Philip Freneau versified Gage in torment: "Three weeks, ye gods! nay, three long years it seems / Since *roast beef* I have touched, except in dreams."[10]

Then, when the prospects seemed darkest, two startling letters arrived on September 16 from Lord Dartmouth. Gage was to return home, a decision made three days after the arrival in London of the news of Bunker Hill with its casualties. In his absence, his command was to be divided between Howe in Boston and Guy Carleton in Canada, but in the event of a juncture of the two armies, Carleton, as the senior officer, was to take precedence. The invasion of New York was approved. Clinton was to remain with the troops in New England. Burgoyne was to be second in command to Howe in the expedition against New York. At last, the long awaited opportunity! With Howe he could expect action. Howe at Bunker Hill had shown himself an aggressive leader, and he had afterward declared for a decisive strike to nip the rebellion in the bud.

A few days after the Dartmouth letters, another vessel arrived bearing the long awaited permission from North for Burgoyne to return home. Should he go? Charlotte was gravely ill. The transport ship *Pallas* was readying to leave Boston with Gage on October 11. But what if some change of schedule or unforeseen crisis should set the army in motion and deprive him of a share in the glory? Might North even take advantage of his return to sideline him permanently? He decided to wait. He became ill with a malady (unspecified in the records) that required surgery, but still he delayed.[11]

Life in Boston grew more pinched and deprived. Driving snows came early, forcing the troops on Charlestown Heights to strike their tents and withdraw into Boston, where soldier and civilian competed for food and fire. Smallpox broke out, an unlooked-for shield against rebel attack. The soldiers tore down old houses for fuel, including the Old North Meeting House, but Burgoyne saved the Old South as a riding school for his light dragoons, with the pulpit, pews, and seats removed and a bar installed over which officers galloped their horses. Looting became widespread despite punishments of hangings and whippings. A private's wife was sentenced to one hundred lashes on her bare back with a cat-o'-nine-tails and three months' imprisonment. Burgoyne, in his quarters at the Bowdoin house, set back from Beacon Street above a high entrance flight of stone steps, lived a block east of Clinton at the Hancock house. Together, and with growing camaraderie, they supervised the town's west defenses.[12]

In November the waiting ended. The impenetrable Howe, drawn more to the company of Elizabeth Loring, wife of an army provisioner, and more to his subordinates than to his equals, had kept his plans jealously to himself. He could not, however, ignore a query from Dartmouth that arrived on November 9; nor could he conceal his reply from Clinton and Burgoyne. The letter, written November 26, proposed that Boston be evacuated in the spring, to be followed by simultaneous invasions of New York City and Rhode Island. Howe would command at New York, Clinton at Rhode Island. No command or function of any kind was mentioned for Burgoyne. So he was to be shunted aside and his requested project of the Rhode Island expedition handed to Clinton, who didn't want it! Howe, suspicious of competitors, had no intention of giving a second chance to Burgoyne, who had challenged him in London for the New York command.

There was no longer any point in remaining in Boston. There need be no open rupture. He could claim medical leave for himself as well as the urgency of his wife's condition. On December 5, he boarded the ship of the line *Boyne* for the voyage home. Howe made him the bearer of his letter to Dartmouth, and if Burgoyne required any further proof of Howe's coolness it was in the concluding, pallid reference to him: "If His Majesty's service has not more essential service for him and it should be his inclination to return to this country, I hope I may not be deprived of an officer of his experience and ability for the ensuing campaign."[13]

Strong winds sped the ship to England in three weeks, and London's mild weather was a welcome relief. Burgoyne rode at once to Kensington Palace, where Charlotte maintained apartments during his absence. The surprise Christmas gift of her husband's arrival brought momentary color to her faded cheeks, but his worst fears were confirmed. It was plain that she had not long to live. He gave orders for them to move back to their Hertford Street house for their remaining time together.

In the evening he dressed for an audience with the king. At the Queen's House (at the site of the present Buckingham Palace), in its magnificent library where, eight years later, John Adams found "every book that a king ought to have always at hand," the conference was long and private. The king was cordial and questioned Burgoyne closely about events in Boston. Burgoyne made clear his willingness to return to America and his desire for an active command. He was gratified to hear that a major cabinet change had taken place the previous month: Germain had replaced Dartmouth as secretary of state for the colonies. Dartmouth, he could not forget, had passed him over for Howe, while Germain had "upon all occasions" shown himself "communicative and friendly." Germain could have no love for the baleful Barrington in the War Office, for it was Barrington who in 1760 had arranged Germain's court-martial.[14]

Between Dartmouth and Germain there was a profound difference in strategic thinking: Dartmouth believed that the rebellion was an internal, adjudicable dispute, while Germain maintained that it must be treated like a war against a foreign enemy, in which crucial territory must be occupied and resistance ruthlessly crushed. Dartmouth had aimed for a show of strength by occupying New York City and penetrating northward up the Hudson Valley into New England. Auxiliary expeditions were to be launched against North Carolina and Rhode Island. Clinton had already been named to head the southern operation, and it was expected that this would be concluded in time for him to lead the Rhode Island foray as well. These limited ventures, Dartmouth hoped, would bring the Americans to the conference table. He was not aiming for a decisive stroke, such as a seizure of the Lake Champlain–Hudson River line of communication and isolation of New England from the other colonies. The brothers Richard and William Howe were authorized to meet with rebel spokesmen and offer revokation of taxes in return for colonial acceptance of Parliamentary supremacy.

Germain, in stark contrast, advocated the use of "the utmost force of this Kingdom to finish the rebellion in one campaign." Success for him would be a compensation for the shadow that had darkened his entire career. He had begun in the army, and as a son of the duke of Dorset, with a quick intelligence, enormous energy, an imperious, large-boned presence, and language that the *London Chronicle* described as "elegance itself" (but a voice "not very appealing"), he seemed certain to rise to commander in chief. Then, at the Battle of Minden in the Seven Years' War, he was accused by Prince Ferdinand of Brunswick of disobedience of orders. There had been no previous question of his physical courage (he had been wounded at Fontenoy), but he was caught in a political contest between Pitt, whose conduct of the war in Germany hinged on support for Ferdinand, and opponents of the war led by the British crown prince and Lord Bute. Contemptuous of criticism, Germain had demanded a court-martial. He was convicted and dismissed from the service. For fifteen years, haunted by "The Ghost of Minden," he had been barred from cabinet office. "I do not conceive," said Lord Shelburne, "that anything but the checks which stopped his military career, could have prevented his being Prime Minister."[15] The crown prince, when elevated to the throne as George III, had returned him to political life.

Two mornings after Burgoyne's audience at the Queen's House he was asked to return, this time with Germain, Dartmouth, and Gage. They conferred for two hours on North American affairs. The news from the field was almost all bad. In October and November, the Americans had captured the forts at Chambly and St. Johns on the Richelieu River. Montreal had fallen when the French populace had opened the gates to the invaders. Quebec was still in British hands, but one American army under Richard Montgomery was reported advancing toward it along the St. Lawrence and another under Benedict Arnold along the Chaudière River. Carleton might already be a prisoner. When Burgoyne was asked for his opinion, he submitted a lengthy paper, "Reflections upon the War in America." Returning to his favorite scheme, he proposed a reorientation of the campaign from a southern to a northern focus. Mating armies, northward from New York City and southward from Canada, would seal off New England from the other colonies. The emphasis this time would be on the northern invasion. He cautioned against underestimating the Americans' skill in forest fighting, and he urged the addition of twenty-six light infantrymen to each regiment of light dragoons. Supporting the entire operation must be a more effective blockade of the coast, with frigates and sloops assisted by smaller craft adapted for "peeping into every hole and inlet."[16]

Burgoyne's ideas matched Germain's. Germain had little enthusiasm for the southern expedition to North Carolina and still less for the Howes' chimerical mission of conciliation. He decided to dispatch at least ten thousand troops northward to Carleton by the first or second week in March. As Carleton was in danger of death or capture, a second in command must be provided. Clinton, senior among the major generals in North America, was selected. He could be back from the south by the spring, in time to join Carleton. Because large numbers of Hessian troops would have to be hired for the North American armies, both Clinton and Burgoyne were promoted to lieutenant general in order to insure that they would be senior to the ranking Hessian officer, Lieutenant General Wilhelm Knyphausen.[17]

Burgoyne was too prudent to push too hard for a major role for himself. His committed, confident manner was his best advocacy. He was delighted, he wrote Lord Huntingdon, to see American affairs aggressively carried forward "in the able hands of Lord Germain." Perhaps he sensed that the naming of Clinton as second to Carleton was not final. Within four weeks it developed that Clinton was going to be delayed too long in the south to arrive in Canada early enough for an offensive. The ordnance ships for his expedition, scheduled to leave Britain on December 1, had been held up a month at Spithead, first by lack of supplies and then by unfavorable winds. At Cork, further delays kept eight Irish regiments from sailing for another five weeks. By February 1, Germain decided that Burgoyne would have to replace Clinton as Carleton's second in command.[18]

There was a more pointed reason for Germain to prefer Burgoyne to Clinton: he wanted Burgoyne, as a trusted personal agent, to promote the strategy he had adopted. He considered Carleton indecisive and unwilling to employ the all-out tactics necessary for a quick victory. Carleton at that time had only eight hundred British soldiers under him in all Canada and had failed to raise French Canadian militia, yet he had rejected the only other reservoir of manpower—the Indians of the Iroquois confederacy. Guy Johnson, acting superintendent of Indian affairs for the northern district, had assembled seventeen hundred of them at Montreal, but Carleton had kept them idle until they dispersed in disgust. They might have prevented the city's capitulation. Johnson was so outraged that he had come to England to register his protest. London was just now agog with excitement over two Indians he had brought with him. Thayendanegea (known to the English as Joseph Brant) and Oteronghyanento had been given commissions as British officers, but they appeared at public occasions in Indian dress. The government billeted them at the Swan with Two Necks Inn in Southwark and underwrote all their expenses. Fashionable society competed for their attendance, the earl of Warwick commissioned Romney to do a painting of the tall, flamboyant Brant, and Boswell interviewed him for the *London Magazine*. Johnson, an athletic man with finely chiseled features of oriental cast (as painted by Benjamin West), introduced the Indians to Germain, whom they addressed as "Brother Gorah." They told him, he reported to Burgoyne, that "had Gen. Carleton permitted them to act last year, Canada would not have been in the hands of the rebels."[19] Germain was all too willing to believe. And how preferable to Carleton was the enterprising Burgoyne, who long ago had written to urge the use of Indians.

"I would not even suffer a savage to pass the frontier, though often urged to let them loose on the rebel provinces, lest cruelties might have been committed and for fear the innocent might have suffered with the guilty," Carleton had written Dartmouth.[20] Germain and Burgoyne maintained that the colonists had brought their calamities upon themselves. They themselves had first enlisted Indians in the forces besieging Boston. Indians, in any case, would be indispensable as scouts and guides for an army cutting its way through the wilderness. Germain and Burgoyne had no conception of how profoundly the Indians' scalping, torture of prisoners, and above all murder of women and children infuriated the American people. All America at one time or another had been frontier, exposed to the Indians, and the memory of the barbarities of Pontiac's War only thirteen years earlier was still fresh. Nor could Germain and Burgoyne understand the welling up of American outrage at the employment of foreigners in the British armies. To Americans the Hessians were invaders, hired brigands let loose on unprotected households and incapable of appreciating the American struggle for the rights of Englishmen. Without the Indians and the Hessians, the invasion was impossible. With them, all New England would rise with a newborn nationalism to repel the intruder.

The rapport between Burgoyne and Germain was so complete that Burgoyne believed Germain the previous year had wished to see him replace Gage as commander in chief in North America. Everywhere Burgoyne went in London he put himself forward as the advocate of militant policy and of the invincibility of the British army. From his seat in the House of Commons he heatedly defended the regulars at Bunker Hill from charges of cowardice by Barré. "It is the fashion here," reported Lieutenant William Feilding, "to wish that Boston may be Attack'd as Genl. Burgoyne assures every Body, that if they do Attack, the Enemy must be Repulsed." There was even a rumor that Burgoyne had replaced Carleton, this despite the arrival of news that Carleton had turned back the attack of Montgomery and Arnold at Quebec.[21] Late in February, Burgoyne prepared to leave for Cork to supervise the preparations of six infantry regiments that were assembling for embarkation. These were to join with three English and three German regiments leaving from Spithead and Portsmouth.

Suddenly, as if Charlotte's condition were not grave enough, she received the shock that became the finishing touch. Her father and mother died within a week of each other. Barely a week later, a servant mistakenly delivered to her a note with the news that her favorite sister, Mary, was terminally ill. "In my soul," Burgoyne wrote Germain, "I believe that my immediate separation against which, however, she would not say a word, would convey her to the family grave before it is closed." He requested leave to remain with her until the troops left, and then to sail separately from Plymouth to join them in Canada. He had no thought of withdrawing. The duty of suppressing an internal rebellion, he declared, "supersedes every private consideration."

Germain could hardly ask for greater devotion. He had in any case anticipated Burgoyne's need by arranging for him to sail from Spithead aboard the *Blonde,* a frigate assigned to convoy Brunswick troopships. The delay also gave Burgoyne a respite to undergo surgery.[22]

The Brunswick troops arrived at Spithead March 28, and Germain immediately sent Burgoyne his traveling orders, with a reminder that the Indians were to be "managed with attention." Burgoyne was also given a letter to Carleton instructing him to "pass the Lakes as early as possible." No detailed orders were included on the ground that, without knowledge of latest developments, it was "impossible to give any other than general instructions without the hazard of misleading." Earlier, however, on February 17, Germain had written that "Major-General Burgoyne will be so fully instructed in every point in regard to the important services that are to be carried on, on the side of Canada, that it will be unnecessary now for me to say anything on the subject." It appeared that he had chosen to communicate with Burgoyne rather than Carleton, a sign of a personal as well as a policy difference. Gossips noted that Carleton was a friend of the duke of Richmond, who had testified against Germain at his court-martial.[23]

Charlotte moved back to her apartments in Kensington Palace. Burgoyne tried to conceal from her his fears over her health. She had never, he agonized, "given me a moment's pain, except upon a bed of sickness or in an hour of parting." That hour, which they both knew was their last together, came on March 30. He was himself still unwell after surgery. He said his farewell and left to embark at Portsmouth. Three months later in Canada he received word that she had died, and it rendered him "an unconnected cypher. . . . Interest, ambition, the animation of life is over."[24]

But there remained the duty to suppress rebellion, so he had persuaded himself.

8

"To Preserve the Liberty of the Western World"

T HE GATESES ARRIVED AT HAMP-
ton, Virginia, in October 1772 to find that the land they had expected to
purchase was already sold. It took five months of hunting and dickering to
locate another, a 659-acre tract on the upper Potomac River in the Shenan-
doah Valley, in what is now West Virginia. Shepherdstown, six miles east and
with a population of one thousand, was the largest community. Ten miles
south of Shepherdstown was Harewood, home of George Washington's im-
provident brother Samuel.

Gates built a limestone house with a three-dormered gabled roof and a
chimney at each end and called it Traveller's Rest. He bought "Six working
Black Slaves" and wished for even more. He attempted, unsuccessfully, to
borrow money from a brother-in-law of Robert Monckton to buy a couple
and child from Samuel Washington. Gates accepted an appointment as a
justice in the local court of oyer and terminer that tried slaves accused of
capital crimes. Whippings "well laid on" were common punishments. In
November 1776, while he was away in the army, one of his slaves was hanged
for stealing a chest of money from the cellar of Traveller's Rest. Gates was
awarded seventy pounds for the loss of the slave.[1]

He prospered. The land was well watered and richly wooded with wal-
nut, hickory, and black oak. He cleared 140 acres as meadow for cattle, sheep,
and hogs and built barns, stables, and outbuildings. He boarded his son,
Robert, at school in Annapolis. He was appointed a lieutenant colonel of local
militia. "I have every thing requisite & necessary about me both for Comfort
& Convenience," he wrote to Charles Mellish, Monckton's brother-in-law. "I
was such a Fool to stay so long in England, Vainly hoping for what I never
Obtained."[2]

Yet America had her class divisions, too. "I lead a Life very different from you Elegant Virginians," he wrote a friend from the tidewater, "as I seldom see Company, Drink Little, & never Game."[3] His old resentments took new form. He joined with other small gentry to challenge the entrenched James River plantation aristocracy of the east. Colonel Adam Stephen, a comrade of the campaign with Braddock, was a nearby neighbor at The Bower, on the present site of Martinsburg. He had advised Gates about land purchases. Formerly a physician, profane and hard drinking, he was now the commander of George Washington's old regiment and was probably responsible for Gates's appointment as lieutenant colonel. During the war he had been a trusty lieutenant to Washington, but in 1761 he had dared to run against him for election to the House of Burgesses, a presumption his former superior never forgot.

The leader of the dissidents was Richard Henry Lee, an organizer of the Virginia Sons of Liberty and of riots against the Stamp Act (although he had earlier applied, then withdrawn, for appointment as Stamp Distributor). Tall and spare, red haired and sharp featured, he spoke with a melodious voice and the graceful wave of a maimed hand bandaged in black silk. A member of an old Virginia family, educated in England, fluent in the classics, he was a speaker rated second only to Patrick Henry. He was a younger son whose inheritance was insufficient to provide for his own large brood of children. Merit and integrity, he declared, must rank above wealth and rapacity. In 1766 he had spearheaded the exposure of the greatest scandal in Virginia's history, the defalcations of House of Burgesses Speaker John Robinson. His investigations implicated many members of the province's first families and earned for him their hatred as a traitor to his class.

Patrick Henry, famed orator against the Stamp Act, teamed with Lee to win a reduction in the powers of the Speaker. An immensely popular politician from backcountry Hanover, with high forehead, pointed face, and deep-socketed eyes, he was a spellbinding orator. "I can give You no Idea of the Music of his Voice," wrote Silas Deane of Connecticut to his wife, "or the highwrought, yet Natural elegance of his Style, and Manner." Henry and Lee were paired as "the *Demosthenes,* & *Cicero* of America."[4] With two such leaders in the House, the outnumbered radicals carried more than their weight among the conservatives.

The newest addition to the ranks of the radicals was Charles Lee, Gates's brother officer and fellow Demoniac, who had also emigrated to America. His enormous nose, spidery figure, and small hands with slender fingers, two of which had been lost in a duel, marked him out in any company. Aristocratic, yet outspokenly devoted to the republican "spirits of Cato, Brutus,

Hampden, and Sidney," he did not shrink from the prospect of separation from Britain.[5]

Nor did Gates. In two short years he had become an ardent American nationalist. "The News from this Continent [he told Mellish] is that we are going Silently, & I believe Surely, on to Empire. Our prodigious Increase from all Causes, is astonishing; Germany, Great Britain, & Ireland, pour their Subjects in Multitudes upon us, this, added to the natural Increase, (long before many upon your side the Atlantic think of it,) will make No. America a most Opulent and Independent State." When the news arrived of the Boston Tea Party and the Intolerable Acts, he welcomed the confrontation: "The Tea *so kindly sent* by the India Company, has been all thrown into the Sea & the Colonys to the Southward have utterly refused to receive an Ounce of it; four Millions of People, in every thing (but Wealth, & Luxury) equal to yourselves, sepperated from you by an Ocean 3000 Miles wide, are not be be awed by Fear, nor Cajoled by Cuning, however they may be influenced by Favor, and Affection."[6] When Charles Lee wrote that he was prepared to contribute "in whatever Mode my service is required," Gates answered with his own pledge: "I am ready to risque my life to preserve the liberty of the western world."[7]

But just then the call to service came unexpectedly from another and unwelcome quarter. Virginia's Governor Dunmore organized an expedition against the Indians of the Ohio Valley. It was a drive prompted by land speculators to open western Pennsylvania and Kentucky for settlement, and it ignored Indian tribal claims. Adam Stephen's regiment was ordered to join the expedition. Gates recoiled: "As to the Indians, the behaviour of certain of the White people is beyond all comparison abominable towards those unhappy Natives, not content with quiet possession of all the Land on this side of the Ohio, they demand as a preliminary to a peace, all the Land between that River & the Mississippi."[8] The implication was plain: he would serve only in a just war. The expedition, he flatly told Stephen, was illegal. Stephen passed the letter to Dunmore, who brushed it aside and ordered Gates to report. Gates blandly replied that he was confined by a "Violent inceptive Fever." Ironically, the excuse was good enough afterward to win for him a veteran's bonus in the conquered territory—five thousand acres in Fincastle County, on the Ohio River.[9]

He remained at Traveller's Rest for a year, watching political tensions build. With the passage of the Intolerable Acts, a convention of county representatives at Williamsburg in August 1774 adopted bans on all trade with Britain and elected seven delegates to a continental congress in Philadelphia, including Richard Henry Lee, Patrick Henry, and George Washington. All the colonies felt threatened. Gates was elected to a county committee to report tea purchases. "Lord North has disclosed," Adam Stephen exploded, "that he has a Rod in piss for the Colony of Virginia & province of Maryland—Could I see him in America, in Spite of all the armies of Commissioners, Customhouse Officers & Soldiers, I would make the meanest American I know piss upon him."[10] At a second Virginia convention in Richmond, late in March 1775, Patrick Henry shocked the conservatives by calling for armed resistance. He attacked George III, said a witness, as "a Tyrant, a fool, a puppet and a tool to the ministry." His biographer, with a little improvising, rendered the speech immortal: "I know not what course others may take; but as for me, give me liberty or give me death!"[11]

April 29 brought word of the clash at Lexington. Gates was ready. He set out immediately across the Blue Ridge Mountains. On May 2, two days before Washington was to leave for Philadelphia, Gates was at Mount Vernon. A stream of callers had come during the past two weeks, including Charles Lee. Richard Henry Lee and his brother, Thomas, appeared while Gates was there. The weather was prematurely hot; the guests moved to the lawn by day and the parlor by night. They anticipated that Washington would be named to the supreme command of the army that the Continental Congress was sure to raise. He voiced no strong objection. Gates let it be known that he was available for a military post. Washington silently approved: here was one of the few men in North America who had high-level staff experience with large-scale combat engagements. Gates returned to Traveller's Rest to await the outcome.[12]

Washington wore his telltale uniform of blue and buff into Philadelphia. He told his friends that he did not wish the command, but this was seen only as the carapace of his natural reserve, perhaps a defense against touchy New Englanders. For the New Englanders had their own candidate in Artemas Ward, the popular but colorless Worcester militiaman in charge of the troops converging on Boston. Some New Englanders even favored Charles Lee, and one, wealthy and popular John Hancock, strongly favored himself. Southerners united behind Washington, partly out of sectional pride, partly out of fear that a New England hothead might instigate independence and then use New England military might to dominate the other colonies. There was never any real doubt, though, that the final choice would be Washington.

John Adams brought the issue to a head by declaring on the floor of Congress that Washington could "unite the cordial exertions of all the colonies better than any other person in the Union." The opposition quickly dissolved. Washington was not a "harum Scarum ranting Swearing" southerner, Connecticut's Eliphalet Dyer wrote home, but a "Sober, steady, and Calm" gentleman, "if any thing too modest."[13]

Neither was he diffident. As soon as he was sworn in, he insisted on having Charles Lee and Gates to help him organize his army. There was resistance. The two men were only recent arrivals in America, it was said, lacking the loyalties that came with native roots. "Nothing has given me more Torment, than the Scuffle We have had in appointing the General Officers," wrote John Adams. "Dismal Bugbears were raised. There were Prejudices enough among the weak and fears enough among the timid, as well as other obstacles from the Cunning." The two Adamses and Thomas Mifflin of Pennsylvania argued that Lee and Gates had clearly cut their ties with the British establishment. Gates had committed himself to America by the purchase of a large estate. Lee, who was present in Philadelphia, busily offering advice and helping to whip the Pennsylvania militia into shape, hastily wrote Gates to purchase for him a two thousand–pound plantation in Virginia. In the end, as a concession to the New Englanders, Ward was named the senior major general, second in rank to Washington. Lee was named major general next in line. Gates was appointed brigadier and adjutant general.[14]

Washington waited a week in Philadelphia while Congress named two more major generals and eight brigadier generals. On June 22, unofficial reports arrived of a bloody clash at Bunker Hill. He hurried off to Boston.

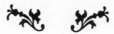

At Traveller's Rest on June 21, Gates received from Washington orders to report immediately to Boston, where the fledgling army urgently needed him to set up procedures. He sent what may have seemed a presumptive reply: "I shall Obey your Commands with all possible Expedition, & hope to be in Philadelphia Thursday next, & wish earnestly to find you there. I must take the Liberty to entreat it of you, not to leave the Congress, until you are provided, not only with all the Powers, but all the Means, their Power can bestow." Did Washington need to be instructed how to negotiate with Congress? There was already in Gates the embryo of the politician-general. "My grateful Thanks are most Respectfully due to the Congress," he wrote, "for the very Handsome manner in which they conferr'd their Commission."[15] The self-congratulation and the presumptuous flattery could grate.

He arrived in Philadelphia to find Washington gone. It was just as well; he really wanted the chance to mingle on his own with the politicians. His friend Richard Henry Lee and his brothers had formed an alliance with John and Samuel Adams of Massachusetts—what afterward came to be called the "Lee-Adams Junto." They were the "violents," pushing for independence ahead of the majority of moderates who continued to "breathe reconcilia-tion." Gates fitted into their concept of a military man in a democracy. He had the credentials of a professional but was not imperious or charismatic, he welcomed the supremacy of civilian over military authority, and he was himself a politician of sorts. Unlike the intimidating Washington, he was homey, gregarious, even vulnerable with his gullible vanity and thin-skinned resentments. As a British Whig in the republican tradition of Trenchard and Gordon, he brought to the American rebels a comforting sense of the trans-atlantic continuity of their cause. He made it plain that he stood with the violents against the pacifiers, prepared to risk all that he had come to the New World to gain. And, in resisting Dunmore's War, he had shown that he was not a land-hungry Virginia expansionist, pandering to lawless frontiersmen and threatening to dominate the other colonies. "Nothing has given more concern and disgust to these northern colonies," Richard Henry Lee re-ported, than that war.[16]

If the stop at Philadelphia was a touchstone to Gates's future, so was his next one at New York. There Philip Schuyler, commander of the northern army, was preparing to depart for an invasion of Canada. With him were his second in command, Richard Montgomery, and a force of two thousand Connecticut militia under David Wooster. Gates found Schuyler quartered at the home of his former Whig Club friend, William Smith, Jr., at 5 Broadway. The last he had seen of Smith, in 1761, had been when Gates, as aide to Governor Monckton, had brought him an offer of a commission as chief justice of the province. Smith had declined, but now he was serving as a member of the legislative council. Then he had seemed an incipient rebel; now he was all but a confirmed Loyalist. Schuyler, a cousin of Smith, was conducting his business at Smith's home and consulting with him on matters of congressional policy. Directly across the way from Smith lived Governor William Tryon, and only a week earlier, when Washington had passed through the city, great pains had been taken to prevent the two men from meeting. Schuyler, nevertheless, called on Tryon and was rebuffed. A wealthy scion of Albany's leading family, Schuyler was a revolutionist only to the extent of wishing to continue control of colonial government by colonial aristocrats. His appointment as major general had been a concession to "Sweeten, Add to, & keep up the spirit" of conservative New Yorkers.[17]

Montgomery, son of a baronet and a capable former captain in the British regular army who had fought in 1759 at Ticonderoga and Crown Point, was an old comrade of Gates. They had served together under Monckton at Martinique and had returned on the same ship with the news of the British victory.[18] Montgomery had since resigned his commission and come to New York to marry a daughter of Judge Robert R. Livingston. Established on his estate, Grassmere, near Rhinebeck, in Dutchess County, he had, through family connections, obtained prominence and an appointment as brigadier general.

Wooster was a contrast to Schuyler and Montgomery. Although a Yale graduate and a son-in-law of a Yale president, he was a failed businessman whose only claims to distinction were insubstantial experience in the French wars and his job as collector of customs in New Haven. He was, however, an adept at winning militia elections and at the age of sixty-three had advanced to the rank of major general in Connecticut. When he was offered a lower rank as brigadier general in the Continental Army, he was so incensed that he declined. He was therefore serving at New York as a Connecticut officer, not officially under Schuyler's command, and he resented taking orders from a haughty New York land baron.[19] All of New England detested New York, partly for its aristocratic leadership and partly for its claim to the New Hampshire Grants that eventually became the state of Vermont.

For the observant Gates, the Schuyler-Wooster dichotomy was a lesson in the distinctive civilian-soldier character of the entire Revolution. The Patriots undertook to win a war against a professional army. Although the Continental Army was created and national enlistments were solicited, traditional state militia units were the indispensable backbone. Undisciplined, short termed, and ridden with local factionalisms, they were nevertheless the reflection of the democratic distrust of standing armies. Elected officers relied more on popularity than on punishment for enforcement of orders, which frequently resulted in ineffective leadership. This approach called for the unique skills of the officer who knew how to cajole and control amateur soldiers. The common militiaman trusted an officer risen from the ranks, or at least one with a common touch, rather than the aloof aristocrat. Many aristocrats thought themselves above serving in the militia. General Montgomery's wife wrote that in New York "no gentleman offered to take commissions in the army. The mechanics alone offered, and General Montgomery accepted them without demur. When the brigade was filled several gentlemen came forward, but he refused them the places, telling them they should have been first, and were too late." One of those gentlemen, Gouverneur Morris, had applied, but when he was offered a commission to serve under a shoemaker he refused, sneering that "a herd of Mechanicks are preferred before the best Families in the Colony."[20]

Considering that Gates had the longest and highest-ranking military experience and that he had served extensively in Canada and upper New York, he might well have thought himself better qualified for the command of the invasion army than Schuyler. But even if he had come north earlier, it would have made no difference. He had no eminent connection, no New York constituency. He owed his commission to the urgent need for his expertise as a staff man and to his chance acquaintance with Washington. Yet Wooster was visible evidence that a new era was dawning. A general who could manage the American civilian soldier might surpass the traditional product of privilege. In war, opportunities would arise through death, disease, and reverses in the field. With the backing of the Adams-Lee junto in Congress, Gates might in time challenge the conservative New Yorkers who championed Schuyler.

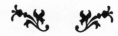

Gates found the army at Cambridge, the lovely college town converted to a military encampment. The common was now a parade ground. Harvard educational functions had been transferred to Concord. Earthworks had been thrown up in Harvard Yard, and Massachusetts, Stoughton, Hollis, and Harvard halls and little Holden Chapel had been taken over as barracks. The president's house was serving as Washington's headquarters until the Brattle mansion (the present Longfellow House) could be readied for his occupancy. Some of the private homes, especially those of departed Tories, had been converted to hospitals. In every usable open space, soldiers had erected makeshift shelters of boards, sailcloth, stone, turf, brick, and brush. Only the Rhode Islanders came equipped with neat regulation tents.

The militiamen came in their daily homespun, many without blankets or weapons. Like all eighteenth-century soldiers, they each cooked their own rations (fortunately plentiful), and they denuded the local woods of timber for their campfires. Their guns were of such varied caliber that they "rolled their own" cartridges. They were earthy, acquisitive, and provincial. They insisted on serving only in companies of their own townsmen and under officers whom they personally knew. They demanded their pay, for, as New England Revolutionary historian Allen French says, "no Yankee ever served for nothing." They expected furloughs to attend to their private affairs, and when their enlistment terms were up they departed punctually for home, no matter what the battlefield emergency. Bored with inaction, they quarreled over seniority, traded uniforms and equipment without compunction, and allowed their quarters to become stinking and unsanitary. Connecticut's Israel Putnam, an old campaigner but "no shake hand body," wanted his men at work, if only to dig and fill the same ditch. Yet these provincials were devout Congregationalists who confidently expected the succor of the god of battles. The worst the watchful and exhorting chaplains who marched with them could complain of was hearing "shocking oaths and imprecations; and the tremendous name of the great God taken on the most trifling occasions."[21]

The technique of mobilizing this raw reservoir of manpower had still to be developed. The Massachusetts militia system had been intended for community protection; now it was called upon to deliver a revolution. Before Washington's arrival a beginning had been made. The first requirement was to purge the regiments of their Loyalist commanders. This was accomplished locally in the towns, where the offending colonels were forced to resign and the old militia was replaced with minutemen units, whose officers were elected. Next, with the prospect of protracted hostilities, the Massachusetts Provincial Congress created a wholly new volunteer army of 13,600, enlisted for the remaining eight months of the year and led by appointed officers who were to recruit their men before they could receive permanent commissions. The other New England colonies were requested to supply 6,400 men. All told, a total of some 16,600 materialized—no mean accomplishment, considering problems of local jealousies, disputes over promotions, family hardships, and administrative confusion. "We have just experienced the inconveniences of disbanding an army within cannon-shot of the enemy, and forming a new one in its stead," reported Rhode Islander Nathanael Greene from camp on June 4. "An instance has never before been known. Had the enemy been fully acquainted with our situation, I cannot pretend to say what might have been the consequence."[22]

Washington's task was to transform this conglomeration into a regular army. Gates's assignment was to provide the substructure of military usage. Washington created three subdivisions: Artemas Ward commanding on the Dorchester Peninsula at the right, Charles Lee on the Charlestown Peninsula at the north, and Israel Putnam at the center. A stream of directives quickly issued from headquarters: returns of manpower must be prompt; latrines must be dug to prevent disease; uniforms must be standardized; and above all, incompetent officers must be cashiered. "I dare say the Men would fight very well (if properly Officered) although they are an exceedingly dirty & nasty people," Washington confided to his brother Lund. By August he wrote Richard Henry Lee, "I have made a pretty good Slam among such kind of officers as the Massachusetts Government abound in since I came to this Camp, having Broke one colo. and two Captains for Cowardly behaviour in the action on Bunker's Hill—Two captains for drawing more provisions and pay than they had men in their Company—and one for being absent from his Post when the enemy appeared there, and burnt a House just by it. Besides these, I have at this time one Colo., one Major, one Captn, & two Subalterns under arrest for tryal."[23]

But to persuade the Massachusetts eight-months army to enlist in sufficient numbers for long-term service proved impossible. Washington had to call for reinforcements from the other colonies. Some few companies of riflemen, previously authorized by the Continental Congress, arrived from Virginia, Pennsylvania, and Maryland. From Virginia's Frederick County came Gates's friend, flamboyant Daniel Morgan, with ninety-six men dressed in long, Indian-style hunting shirts, each woodsman carrying a tomahawk and scalping knife along with his long rifle. As sharpshooters, they picked off British sentries with uncanny accuracy, but they wasted precious ammunition with unnecessary sniping. Their drinking and brawling plunged the camp into turmoil. In one of the Pennsylvania companies of "shirtmen," a riot over the arrest of a sergeant required the combined intervention of Washington, Lee, and Greene and the court-martial of thirty-four men.[24]

Between Washington and Gates a fundamental cleavage was developing over the use of militia. Washington, repelled by the rabble, disdained them. Gates declared before a visiting group of politicians that he "never desired to see better soldiers than the New-England men made." He learned how to work with them: to explain the purpose of his directives rather than to demand mindless obedience; to ask service only when it was needed immediately, so that the men could go home for planting and harvesting; to promote officers who were not only capable but popular; and above all to let it be known that he liked the militia and sought their confidence. Washington, essentially a conservative, still hoped for conciliation with Britain. Gates from the start was so "mad an enthusiast" for independence, reported Charles Lee, that he frightened the moderates "out of their Wits."[25]

Gates's closest friend at camp was Colonel Thomas Mifflin of Pennsylvania, the quartermaster general. Short yet posture perfect, he was sensuously handsome, his eyes "keen coal black." He walked with a quick, graceful step and conversed in a "brisk and easy tone." Although a member of Philadelphia's upper social stratum, he was a crowd-pleasing orator, a favorite with the militia, and an early advocate of independence. "Popularity and the bustle of public life were hobby-horses he could not dispense with," a Philadelphia conservative cuttingly noted. "He must mount them, therefore, though at something more than a risk of being spattered by the dirt which he raised."[26]

In the circle vying for Washington's favor, Mifflin's competitor was Brigadier General Nathanael Greene. Alexander Hamilton said that Washington's "discerning eye" marked him out from the first as "the object of his confidence." Thirty-five years old, with high colored complexion and hair just beginning to turn grey, he was heavily built and walked with a noticeable limp caused by a stiff right knee. A former ironmonger in the family business, he was self-taught but widely read and delighted friends with his impersonation of *Tristam Shandy*'s Doctor Slop. Ambitious and headstrong, he could be anxious and resentful, especially when he suffered from recurrent asthma attacks. "I have not slept six hours in four nights," he once wrote. "The common People," he believed, are "exceeding Avaricious. . . . The Sentiment of honour, the true Characteristicks of a Soldier, has not yet got the better of Interest." He wished to erase New England provincialism: "If the Southern and Northern troops were exchang'd it would . . . cure the itch for going home on Furlough."[27]

Allied with Greene was Colonel Henry Knox, a former bookseller and now chief of the as yet nonexistent artillery. Reading interests and similar opinions had drawn him and Greene together. Knox was only twenty-five years old, a huge man at 280 pounds, with a low forehead and small, brilliant eyes. He had lost the third and fourth fingers of his left hand in a shooting accident, and he wound and unwound a black silk handkerchief around it, never allowing the disfigurement to show.[28]

The bonds developed among the wives paralleled those of the husbands. Martha Washington arrived in Cambridge on December 11, and "Kitty" (Catherine) Greene and Lucy Knox quickly became her intimates. Kitty, a bride of a year, was pregnant; in February she gave birth to a boy christened George Washington Greene. Washington teased her that he would redeem her from her Quaker preacher husband. Lucy, as overweight as her husband, was light on her feet, and Washington delighted to lead her down the line at dancing assemblies. Aloof to the Greene and Knox women, Betsy Gates paraded her aristocratic ancestry and defied propriety in her mannish dress, while Sarah Mifflin, lovely and highbred (as captured by Copley), cared only to fend off her husband's women admirers. "I do not know whether her husband is safe here," observed Abigail Adams. "Bellona and Cupid have a contest about him."[29]

Washington did not at first sense antagonism. He himself became an ardent advocate of independence when he learned of the king's speech of October 26, which announced a policy of military suppression and the employment of mercenaries.[30] Although he did not feel comfortable with the militia, it was at least reassuring to know that Gates and Mifflin could obtain these men's support for him. If he perceived the rivalry between the factions in his staff, he was not disturbed enough to curb it. And for the moment it was undeniable that Gates was a first-rate adjutant general.

In March 1776, the besieging Americans triumphed at Boston. Fort Ticonderoga had been taken by Ethan Allen and Benedict Arnold, and Henry Knox's men had dragged the captured cannon all the way down to Boston. On the night of March 4, two thousand men under John Thomas had occupied Dorchester Heights, and the newly arrived cannon were trained down on Boston. The next morning, the anniversary of the Boston Massacre, the British found themselves trapped in the very predicament against which both Burgoyne and Clinton had warned. Unable to elevate their guns within fire power of the American parapets, they remained, Gates reported to John Adams, "Sullen and Sulkey in Boston, suffering our Works upon the Heights be carried on without any other molestation, than now, and Then, a Feint Cannonade."[31] That evening a drenching rain driven by a cold, cutting wind from the south destroyed the Britons' last hope of displacing the Americans: a seaborne landing on the Dorchester Peninsula. Howe's position in Boston was untenable. On March 17, his entire army embarked on troopships in the harbor. Places were found for one thousand Loyalists who refused or feared to remain behind. Nine days later the fleet sailed. For three days it lingered at Nantasket Road and then stood out to sea, its destination, Halifax, a closely guarded secret.

To the elated Gates the victory made conciliation unthinkable. "I was disappointed," he wrote John Adams in Congress, "in not receiving you[r] High Mightiness's Act of Independency," and he threw in a quote from Alexander Pope decrying fence-sitting. "My dear Friend Gates," Adams replied, "our Misfortunes arise from a Single Source, the Reluctance of the Southern Colonies to Republican Government." "Let those who doat upon Dependency dream on," Gates wrote back, "Constitutional Dependency, is a Creature, that America, so Abounding in Monsters, cannot from Cape

Horne to Newfoundland produce," and this time he summoned a quote from Shakespeare to demolish "those Vermine," the "Crowds of Tories." Adams, delighted, in turn cited John Milton against "Thrones, Dominations[,] Princedoms, Powers."[32]

The two men had struck up a friendship when Adams visited camp in December and January. Adams harbored thwarted yearnings for military eminence. "I, poor Creature," he wrote his wife, "worn out with scribbling, for my Bread and my Liberty, low in Spirits and weak in Health, must leave others to wear the Lawrells which I have sown."[33] But he found in Gates a surrogate. The undramatic brigadier was no more martial looking than the short, balding congressman. The rapport grew, especially when Gates sent Adams a letter which confirmed fully that he was not only a republican but a strategist whose ideas harmonized with New England interests. Neither Philadelphia nor the southern colonies were in danger of British attack, he stated. The targets would be Canada and New York. The measures under-way at New York would suffice there, but preparations in Canada were not going well. Wooster, who had replaced the fallen Montgomery, was "too inert to leave so long in Command." And the Indians must be won to the American side: "By good Management, I think they would have put you in Possession of Niagara before now, that, and D'Troit." If Adams had not already been convinced that he had found the general for New England, he was now. "A letter from you," he wrote, "cures me of all Anxiety and ill Humor, for two or three Days at least; and, besides that, leaves me better informed in many Things and confirmed in my good Resolutions, for my whole Life." A command in the field, not a desk job as adjutant general, was the place for Gates. "I wish you was a Major General," Adams finished, "what say you to it?"[34]

The promotion, of course, was what Gates was bent on all along. "If the Congress think me deserving of the Honour you Mention," he promptly replied, "I shall Gratefully accept." He had been cultivating friendships with other congressmen, too—Benjamin Franklin and Robert Morris of Pennsylvania, Samuel Adams of Massachusetts, Richard Henry Lee and Thomas Jefferson of Virginia, and Thomas Johnson and Samuel Chase of Maryland—and to them all his message was that he was a committed republican, that he sided with the popular party against the aristocrats, and that he had no compunctions about facing former British comrades across the battle lines. When he learned in December that Burgoyne was about to return to England, he wrote Franklin, "If there is an honest Mob left in England, Gage and He, cannot ride the Streets of London in Safety." The way in which

Gates was received by republicans was expressed by Mercy Otis Warren, historian, feminist, and wife of James Warren, president of the Massachusetts Provincial Congress. She found Gates "a brave soldier, a high republican, a sensible companion, an honest man, of unaffected manners, and easy deportment."[35]

With Gates and his aides-de-camp, Washington left Boston to take over the defense of New York from Putnam. Gates's talents could now prove useful to Washington, who had to face the prospect of an extended conflict. The makeshift militia somehow had to be replaced with long-term professionals. Long-range plans must be developed for operations in the Canadian, middle, and southern theaters. These were all fundamentally matters for legislative purview. Washington sent Gates to Philadelphia to speak for him to the Continental Congress, carrying with him a letter of praise for Gates's "zeal and attachment to the cause of America" and a recommendation of him to the "Notice and favors" of Congress. He also sent Thomas Mifflin, a key figure in Pennsylvania politics, to persuade Philadelphia's Committee of Safety to lend the Continental Army two or three thousand stand of arms and very likely to lobby for Pennsylvania's support for independence.[36]

Mifflin arrived in Philadelphia on May 13, at the climax of the dispute over independence. The nucleus of the radical movement was in the militia organizations, styled "Military Associators" because they wished to associate with the Continental Army. Inspired by Thomas Paine's defiant *Common Sense,* they demanded not only independence but democratization of Pennsylvania government. They feared a British attack on Philadelphia and asked for the assignment of several battalions to be commanded by their "favourite fellow-citizen," Thomas Mifflin. The independence advocates in Congress sided with the militia as a means of winning Pennsylvania. John Adams was a leader in this group, and he worked closely with Mifflin, who, with all his popularity, was not a leveling radical and could help ward off extremist factions.[37]

Unfortunately for Washington, his effort to promote a standing army collided with the supporters of militia at this very point. From camp at Cambridge, he had sent Congress on February 9 an attack on the militia system and an urgent request for reform. Profoundly moved by what he considered the unnecessary death of Montgomery at the siege of Quebec, he had "not the most distant doubt" that the policy of short enlistments had forced Montgomery to attack prematurely, before the troops' enlistment terms had expired. In any case, raw and undisciplined troops could not be relied upon in combat. Not patriotism but fear of punishment must be the prime incentive. "A coward, when taught to believe that if he breaks his ranks, and abandons his colours, will be punished with death by his own party, will take his chances against the enemy." Such discipline becomes impossible without long enlistments. "Men engaged for a short, limited time only, have the officers too much in their power; for, to obtain a degree of popularity, in order to induce a second inlistment, a kind of familiarity takes place, which brings on a relaxation of discipline, unlicensed furloughs, and other indulgenses." His own ordeal, the disbanding of one army at Boston and raising another at the same time, was "such as no man, who had experienced it once, will ever undergo again."[38]

Was this a threat to resign? Was he throwing the gauntlet down to Congress? The men at Philadelphia debated and delayed an answer for three months. Elbridge Gerry observed that militia would agree only to short absences from home. Roger Sherman of Connecticut declared that "long enlistment is a state of slavery." And John Adams warned that the union was threatened just as much by the aristocratic character of the south as by the egalitarian militia practices of New England. Let those who wished sign up for the duration, but they would be "the meanest, idlest, most intemperate and worthless." Such were not soldiers of freedom. "We must have tradesmens Sons and farmers Sons," and they must be accepted for short terms. Thomas McKean, of Delaware, agreed that in Pennsylvania even "the most desperate of imported Labourers cannot be obtained in any Numbers on such terms." Robert H. Hanson, of Virginia, stung by Adams's disparagement of the south, sarcastically proposed that all outside forces be withdrawn from Boston and the New England colonies granted three million dollars yearly to fight their battles alone.[39]

On May 16, Congress came to a decision. It smoothed Washington's ruffled feathers with encomiums for his expulsion of the British from Boston. Then it adroitly shelved his long-term enlistment proposal. Two new battalions for the army at Boston would be recruited in Massachusetts and Connecticut. The assemblies of these colonies were advised that "if the men cannot be prevailed on to inlist for two years, that they be inlisted for one." A general popular with militia would replace Ward at Boston; Gates was selected and promoted to major general. Mifflin, promoted to brigadier general, was named second in command. The assignments, however, were technically to be made by Washington, and he was requested to come to Philadelphia to review the entire program for the coming campaigns.[40]

Gates rode into Philadelphia on May 21 to learn that he was no longer a spokesman for Washington but a major general with a command of his own and that his advancement had been linked to a rejection of Washington's proposal for long-term enlistments. He was requested to await Washington's coming and then, with Mifflin, to join in the discussions with a congressional conference committee. The committee included militia partisans John Adams, Richard Henry Lee, William Whipple, and Roger Sherman. It confirmed what Congress had already decided. Gates and Mifflin were of no help to Washington. They were the reminders that a sympathetic officer could make militia effective. Washington had to acquiesce. Twenty thousand militia were to be recruited for service in Canada and New York. Another ten thousand would be formed into a "Flying Camp" for the protection of the middle colonies. These soldiers would not be lured with bounties, as Washington had requested, and they would serve only until December 31. Plans were made for a vigorous Canadian campaign. The British were not to be permitted to move further south than the mouth of the Richelieu (Sorel) River. Up to two thousand Indians were to be enlisted. Here Gates had the opportunity to display his knowledge of Canada and the Canadians; the policy on Indians was adopted at his insistence.[41]

It was the kind of self-promotion in which Gates excelled, and Washington watched it with distaste. Three years later, when enmity between the two men broke out into the open, Washington recalled, "I discovered very early in the war symptoms of coldness and constraint in General Gates behavior to me. These increased as he rose into greater consequence." Washington may at this time have begun to fear that Gates and Mifflin, in combination at Boston, might hatch some self-serving scheme. He argued that the British would not return to Boston and that Mifflin was needed more at New York. Gates was deeply resentful. He had information, he wrote the Massachusetts delegates in Congress, that the British did contemplate an attack on Boston. Could he possibly have known of Howe's proposal to Germain, four months earlier, for an expedition under Clinton against Rhode Island, which might be extended into an advance against Boston? For Washington to say "where the enemy will not come is too mighty for my judgment . . . when the freedom of this continent is at stake we can't have too much wisdom nor too many arms employed to save it." Mifflin could not "be half the Use in Acting as a Simple Brigadier at N. York as he might be with me at Boston."[42]

On the day of this outburst, April 8, a messenger brought news from Canada that ultimately sent Gates there instead of Boston. John Thomas, who had replaced Montgomery at Quebec, had died of smallpox. He had never been vaccinated, although he was by profession a physician, and the disease had been so violent that it had blinded him before he succumbed. Schuyler, officially the supreme commander of the northern army, was too ill to take the field and had remained in Albany. Wooster was next in command, but he had had a falling out with Schuyler so severe as to make it difficult for them to work together. On the scene in Canada during this crisis was a congressional commission sent from Philadelphia with powers to oversee the army and fill vacancies. Its leader, Samuel Chase of Maryland, accused Wooster of incompetence, a convenient charge as he was overage, garrulous, touchy on seniority of rank, and intolerant toward the French Canadians. The other commissioners, infirm Benjamin Franklin and Charles Carroll of Carrollton, a wealthy Catholic who had been named in the hope that he would appeal to Canadian Catholics, agreed. Reinforcements arrived in the meantime under Brigadier General John Sullivan of New Hampshire. The commissioners installed him in Wooster's place until Congress should make a permanent appointment.[43]

Chase, however, had made up his mind: he wanted Horatio Gates. Gates had the administrative experience the job required, and, at least as important, he was not a New Englander but was popular with New Englanders, which would quiet the objections of Wooster's partisans. Soon afterward, the commissioners set off for Philadelphia to present their findings to Congress. Illness had already forced Franklin to leave early. On June 9, Chase and Carroll stopped off at New York and discussed the Canadian command with Washington and Gates. Washington was equivocal. He could not support Sullivan, who, although "active, spirited, and Zealously attach'd to the Cause," had "a little tincture of vanity" and "an over desire of being popular, which now and then leads him into some embarrassments." This reservation might apply equally to Gates. Washington preferred loyal subordinates who looked to him rather than Congress for promotion. How much more gratifying was dependable Nathanael Greene, who told him, "Modesty will forever forbid me to apply to that House [Congress] for any favors. I consider myself immediately under your Excellency's protection and look up to you for justice."[44]

Gates himself was not at first eager for the Canadian assignment. His sights were set on the comfortable post at Boston, especially if Mifflin could be sent with him. The northern army was in such a state of chaos that it might prove a graveyard for the ambitions of any officer sent there. He had a low opinion of Schuyler and feared that he would be difficult to work with. But Chase was difficult to resist. Big, burly, and red faced, he argued with supreme conviction that the opportunity was yet there for a good organizer to salvage American prospects. He listened sympathetically to Gates's proposals for army reforms, including the definition of his authority, and promised to advance them in Congress. Carroll, short and slightly built, balanced Chase's exuberance with quiet assurance. "See with your own eyes," he urged, "and all your suspicions will vanish. I am confident that you will judge very differently of him [Schuyler] on acquaintance, and you will find him a diligent, active and deserving officer."[45] Gates was persuaded.

Chase carried the message to Philadelphia. Richard Henry Lee, the Adamses, Gerry, and Sherman lined up behind him. He was sure he had a majority, and he wrote Gates that he would have "the powers of a Roman Dictator. Many of the Congress have cast their Eyes on You, and I doubt not, you will be appointed to this great & important Command." On June 17, Gates was appointed "to take the command of the forces" in Canada. He was given powers until October 1 to fill up vacancies and appoint or suspend "such other officers as he shall find necessary for the good of the service." This was authority broader than that given to any other theater commander. John Adams, newly named chairman of a congressional board of war, wrote, "We have ordered you to the Post of Honour, and made you Dictator in Canada for Six Months, or at least untill the first of October. We don't choose to trust you Generals, with too much Power, for too long Time."[46]

But Congress had not clarified the division of command between him and Schuyler. Schuyler was still the titular commander of the "northern army" in upper New York, Gates the commander of the army "in Canada." If the army in Canada should be driven back into New York, it might be considered to fall under Schuyler's jurisdiction. Two days before Gates's departure northward, news arrived that made the issue immediate. General John Burgoyne had reached Canada with an army to reinforce Carleton. Sullivan, without adequate reconnaissance, had sent a two-thousand-man force under Brigadier General William Thompson to attack Trois Rivières on the St. Lawrence. The Americans had been routed and Thompson and a considerable number of his officers captured. It was feared that Burgoyne would continue southward along Lake Champlain to the Hudson. Was the American withdrawal from Canada to reduce Gates to an emissary of Schuyler, carrying out orders from headquarters at Albany? That was not the assignment he had bargained for, and it was not the one for which he intended to settle.

9

The Lost Victory

The flotilla of thirty-six sail with which Burgoyne left England zigzagged its way westward for seven weeks through the North Atlantic's buffeting headwinds. Captain Hugh Dalrymple, the convoy commander, took the lead aboard the frigate *Juno,* followed by sixteen transports of Brunswick troops, four of Hesse-Hanau, six of English artillery, two of supplies, and six of the English Twenty-first Regiment. The *Blonde,* with Burgoyne aboard, brought up the rear. Ships that strayed from formation were warned into line with cannon shots from the *Blonde* and fined two guineas for each shot.

Toward noon of April 20, at the Azores, a fleet of forty-six transports from Glasgow and Cork appeared, commanded by Lieutenant Colonel Simon Fraser and carrying 770 men of the Ninth, Twentieth, Twenty-fourth, Thirty-first, Thirty-fourth, Fifty-third, and Sixty-second regiments. The new arrivals kept at a remove to the right. A violent sea on April 16 scattered the fleet entirely for a day. "We fell out of our beds, and the sailors had to tie themselves to the masts," wrote a Brunswick grenadier, Johann Bense. On the night of May 7, the flotilla passed the Grand Banks of Newfoundland in a fog so dense that Lieutenant William Digby, of the Fifty-third Regiment aboard the *Woodcock,* wrote that "the sailors on deck cried out we were most on shore." At last, on May 19, they entered the St. Lawrence River, "reddish instead of the beautiful blue-green of the Atlantic," observed a Hessian officer.[1]

Seven days later at Ile du Bic, the convoy found the frigate *Surprise* waiting with the news that Quebec was saved. An advance squadron from England had brought Carleton the Twenty-ninth Regiment and one hundred marines, with which he had completely routed General Thomas's Americans. Three thousand miles of wind and water had not dulled Burgoyne's instinct to attack: he proposed to dash ahead with a detachment of twelve fast ships and cut the Americans off at Sorel, where the St. Lawrence meets the southbound Richelieu River. Captain Dalrymple refused. At sea he had supreme authority, and he would not divide his convoy. Disgusted, Burgoyne that evening boarded the *Surprise* and sailed on alone. "Not one of the enemy would have escaped," he wrote Germain.[2]

The *Surprise* dropped anchor on May 28 in the Basin of Quebec, which was abloom with the spring's first foliage. To the right were the magnificent roaring Falls of Montmorency. Burgoyne and his aides stopped for a night's rest and the next morning set out in search of Carleton, who was forty miles upstream at the town of Champlain.

Burgoyne found a stonily self-contained man. Carleton's calm, unblinking eyes betrayed no emotion, revealed no concern. Intelligent, competent, twice wounded in action, he scorned to please and sought no advice. An officer who knew him considered him "one of the most distant, reserved men in the world." Yet, more than any British general who served in America, he had given compassionate thought to the problem of governing a far-flung colonial empire composed of diverse peoples and cultures. Local established institutions must be preserved. Colonial loyalty must be won through persuasion rather than compulsion. He was the architect of the Quebec Act, which guaranteed religious freedom for Catholics, reinstated French civil law for Canada, and protected the French Canadians from political domination by a tiny minority of newly arrived English. Whatever his officers and men thought of him, the French provincials regarded him as their friend and advocate. If aroused by any imagined official slight they would cry, "I will tell General Carleton."[3] Although this goodwill did not inspire an outpouring of Canadian volunteers for the British militia and Carleton had suffered a series of disastrous defeats for lack of manpower, it did achieve what in the long run proved almost as valuable: the neutrality of the transplanted Bretons. Immersed in their absorbing concern of wresting a primitive livelihood from the briefly thawed soil, they remained impervious to appeals from the rebelling Anglo-Americans to join in the fight for a self-government of which they had no experience.

Burgoyne was dismayed to discover that Carleton was not straining for a decisive victory. Instead of pursuing the fleeing Americans, he was heading for Trois Rivières, a trading village midway between Quebec and Montreal, to set up a base for attacks on Sorel and Montreal. He assigned Burgoyne to lead the British troops up the north bank of the St. Lawrence. Major General Baron Friedrich Adolphus von Riedesel and his Brunswickers would take the south bank.

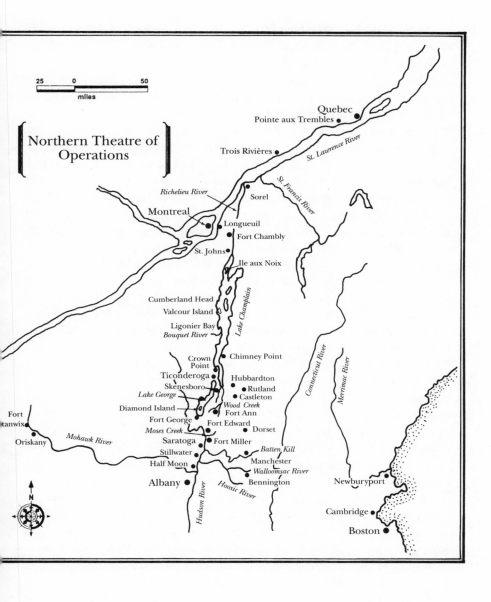

Northern Theatre of Operations

25 0 50
miles

Quebec
Pointe aux Trembles

Trois Rivières

St. Lawrence River

St. Francis River

Richelieu River
Sorel

Montreal
Longueuil
Fort Chambly
St. Johns
Ile aux Noix

Cumberland Head
Valcour Island
Ligonier Bay
Bouquet River

Lake Champlain

Crown Point
Chimney Point
Ticonderoga
Hubbardton
Skenesboro
Rutland
Lake George
Castleton
Diamond Island
Wood Creek
Fort George
Fort Ann
Fort Edward
Moses Creek
Dorset
Fort
Stanwix
Saratoga
Fort Miller
Oriskany
Mohawk River
Stillwater
Batten Kill
Half Moon
Manchester
Walloomsac River
Albany
Bennington
Newburyport
Hudson River
Hoosic River
Connecticut River
Merrimac River
Cambridge
Boston

N

At Trois Rivières they found that an advance force under colonels Simon Fraser and Barry St. Leger had overwhelmed a detachment of General John Sullivan's army the previous day. The captured commander, Brigadier General William Thompson, had a weakness for melodramatics. On seeing Burgoyne, he threw his arms around him and proclaimed their friendship as "subjects of the same King."[4] Carleton released all the prisoners except Thompson on the condition that they promise not to return to fight. He might have pursued the rest of Thompson's men and caught up with them before they reached their getaway boats on Lake Champlain. Then he could have hurried down to Sorel and annihilated the reduced main army, already incapacitated by smallpox, dissention, and desertion. Instead, he opted for a ponderous pincers movement: one column, under Fraser, was to advance northward to Montreal, there to join forces with river-borne troops arriving under Carleton himself; a second column under Burgoyne was to proceed southward to Sorel, with instructions to slow its progress if necessary in order to effect a timed meeting with Fraser, who was to turn southward after the taking of Montreal. Between Fraser and Burgoyne, the Americans retreating from Montreal and those already at Sorel would be trapped.

The calculations miscarried. Unfavorable winds delayed Carleton's ships at Varennes, ten miles below Montreal, and Arnold escaped southward with his army to Fort St. Johns. Burgoyne sailed from Trois Rivières on June 13 with four thousand troops and six cannon and reached Sorel on the fifteenth to find the Americans there also gone. He then transferred to land and crossed the river on a bridge the Americans had failed to destroy. At first he made rapid progress, traveling at night to avoid the torrid sun, but he slowed down as instructed. When he arrived at Fort Chambly on the fifteenth, the Americans were gone again. Twelve miles remained to St. Johns on Lake Champlain, where the Americans could escape aboard their waiting boats. Burgoyne addressed his troops in person and ordered music and drums to urge them forward. The Americans were only five hours away, but now the British found the bridges in their path destroyed. Fretting at the delay, Burgoyne sent ahead the Canadian volunteers and three light-infantry companies under Captain James Henry Craig. They arrived at St. Johns at dusk, just as the last rebel boat, bearing Arnold, pushed off. It was too close to nightfall to follow. The Americans under Sullivan and Arnold, performing prodigies of endurance, had overcome the rapids and carried off two thousand sick, wounded, and dying aboard three captured British schooners. When Burgoyne appeared, a half-hour later, he found the fort a deserted, burning shell.[5]

At Crown Point on Lake Champlain, the Americans were busy assembling a formidable fleet protected from larger British oceangoing ships by the impassable, shallow draft of the narrow Richelieu River. Carleton decided that he would have to destroy this fleet before he could move south by land. He would build a new navy on the lake from scratch. If this took too long to permit a southern invasion before winter set in, the expedition would have to be postponed until the following year.

Burgoyne was unwilling to wait. Ridding Canada of the Americans was for him only the tantalizing beginning. A junction of the northern and southern British armies could still be achieved that very year. Howe had by then left Boston and landed at New York City. Burgoyne wrote Clinton, in whom he had come to confide since their transatlantic voyage, that he cherished "sanguin hopes, the favorite idea upon which I lay my head every night to my pillow, of joining you and my friend Howe before Winter."[6] He had a plan for a "secret and separate expedition": he would lead a force of three battalions westward up the St. Lawrence to Lake Ontario. At Oswego he would turn eastward down the Mohawk Valley toward the Hudson. The threat to Albany would draw the Americans southward away from Ticonderoga, thus speeding Carleton's passage south on Lake Champlain toward a meeting with Howe. A contingent of Indians was essential for the expedition, and two thousand of them under Caughnawaga were then gathering at Montreal for negotiations. Carleton asked his generals to attend, an opportunity for Burgoyne to push his plan. He rode north, and at the meeting on June 24 in the Church of the Jesuits, he conferred with Loyalist Sir John Johnson (Guy's elder brother), who agreed to raise a regiment in the Mohawk Valley. But Carleton, after first approving, reversed himself.[7]

Burgoyne persisted. If not a western expedition, he would strike southward down the east shore of Lake Champlain, bypassing the Americans at Ticonderoga. One column would seize the landing place at the junction with Lake George. A second would destroy the shipyard at Skenesboro, twenty miles to the south, where the rebels were constructing their navy. If successful he might, although he didn't explicitly say so, proceed nonstop to Albany, forcing the Americans to follow and engage on his terms. Carleton would have none of that scheme either. It was easy to find objections. He lacked the supplies for an extended operation: shipments from England had been inadequate, the Canadians had not come forward with contributions and there could be no hope of subsisting on the Americans. Furthermore, the lake's eastern shore was impenetrable: no road had been cleared through the dense forest that grew down to the water's edge.[8]

Returning from Montreal, Burgoyne waited idly at Chambly with his four regiments—the Ninth, Twenty-first, Thirty-first, and Forty-seventh—while the navy was being assembled ten miles to the south at St. Johns. Chambly was an idyllic spot at a fork of the Richelieu River where the rapids emptied into a placid basin. With his penchant for the spectacular, he built a colonnaded headquarters that he christened The Bower, with domed roof and gothic windows. It was a sad substitute for action.[9]

Horatio Gates, accompanied by Philip Schuyler and Benedict Arnold, arrived at Crown Point on the evening of July 5 amid a howling storm. They found the ragged, disease-ridden Americans more a mob than an army, huddled in makeshift brush shelters and tents and exhausted from their harrowing five days' journey up the lake from Ile aux Noix. Fully half of them lay suffering with smallpox. On the crowded Crown Point Peninsula, a flat finger a mile wide extending from the lake's west coast, the diseased men could not be separated from the uninfected. Medical services were virtually nonexistent, and the only available food was rancid salt pork and flour. "I did not look into a tent or hut in which I did not find either a dead or dying man," wrote Gates's adjutant, the artist Colonel John Trumbull. Sometimes there were as many as fifteen deaths in one day.[10]

The confined quarters aggravated tensions between the "Damn'd Yankees" (already a southern epithet) and men from the middle and southern states. New England officers complained of the disproportionate number of southern generals. Southern officers sneered at the freedom between New England officers and men. Colonel Thomas Hartley of Pennsylvania advised Gates that his men had best be kept separate from the New Englanders: "Our Policy and Manners are so exceedingly different that it would require a much greater Time than can now be spent to blend them properly together."[11]

The encampment was virtually defenseless against enemy attack. The old fort, burned in 1773, was in ruins, its four massive redoubts crumbled down, the log walls rotted away, and the casements fallen in. Not one cannon was mounted on the exposed terrain to counter shelling from any British naval force that might occupy the half-mile-wide bay that separated the peninsula from the mainland. "It would take Five times the Number of Our Army for several Summers to put Those Works in Defensible Repair," Gates wrote.[12] A British land offensive could choke off and force the surrender of the entire army.

Within three days of their arrival, Schuyler and Gates met in a council of war with the three brigadier generals: John Sullivan, Benedict Arnold, and Baron de Woedke. They listened to a report from Trumbull, who had been dispatched to reconnoiter the defensive possibilities of the shore across the lake to the east of Fort Ticonderoga. He described it as an excellent location, protected at the north by a large creek and sunken terrain and at its other sides by a fifty to seventy-five foot wall of rock at the water's edge. The lake at that point narrowed to a half mile, allowing passage for only two ships at a time. Between a fortification on the east side and Ticonderoga on the west, the British would be exposed to destructive cross fire from shore batteries. The solution was obvious. The council decided unanimously to move the healthy troops "to the strong ground on the east side of the Lake opposite to Ticonderoga" and the sick with smallpox to a hospital to be erected at Fort George at the southern end of Lake George. At the same time, naval construction would be pushed to assure American superiority on Lake Champlain.[13]

The decision incensed the colonels from New England. Sullivan had already set them an example of rebelliousness by refusing to serve under Gates. Led by John Stark of New Hampshire, all but John Paterson of Connecticut signed a protest charging that Crown Point would become "an assylum for the savages, from which they may much easier make excursions upon the frontier settlements." They would not concede that Crown Point was untenable or that the shore opposite Ticonderoga was defensible. They implied that Schuyler was disobeying the directive of Congress "to dispute every inch of the ground in Canada." Seven colonels from Pennsylvania, New Jersey, and Canada refused to sign, among them Arthur St. Clair and Anthony Wayne. To Schuyler this was another case of New England animosity. He replied, firmly and flatly, that the evacuation of Crown Point was "not only prudent, but indispensably necessary," and, rather than have Washington hear from the malcontents themselves, he sent him a copy of their remonstrance.[14]

The response from New York was astounding. Washington sided with the colonels. He assumed that Gates was responsible for the decision and instinctively reacted against it. This would be an excellent opportunity to separate Gates from his New England constituency. To Schuyler he wrote, with elaborate concern for his sensibilities, that he did "not design any Thing I have said, by Way of Direction, trusting, that whatever is best to advance the Interest of the important Struggle we are engaged in, will be done." To Gates he sent a blistering letter. "I expected 'ere this to have heard from you;

as I have not I will open the correspondence." He considered the decision to leave Crown Point as nothing less than "a relinquishment of the Lakes, and all the advantages to be derived therefrom." He echoed the charge of the colonels that the British would secure a free and uninterrupted passage into the three New England states. "Nothing but a belief that you have actually removed the Army from the point to Ticonderoga, and demolished the Works at the former; and the fear of creating dissensions, and encouraging a Spirit of remonstrating against the conduct of Superior Officers by inferiors have prevented me, by Advice of the Genl. officers here, from directing the Post at Crown Point be held till Congress should decide."[15]

But he had made a damaging slip of the pen. In citing the "Advice of the Genl. officers here" he was setting them up as judges of their equals at Crown Point. Gates promptly replied that Washington's staff "could not see, nor did not know the Circumstances of this Army" when they presumed "to Censure the Conduct of those who are in Nothing inferior to themselves." Washington's letter was as much a censure of Schuyler as himself, and he made sure that Schuyler read it. Schuyler instantly detected in it another affront to his authority as the northern commander. He fired off to Washington a protest over the "outrage" and a demand for an apology: "I cannot, consistent with my honor, remain in the army, unless the council at New York are censured for the assertion, by Congress or your Excellency, or unless, conscious of the impropriety of their conduct towards us, they make a candid and full acknowledgement thereof."

Too late Washington realized that he had gone too far. In attempting to alienate Gates from the New England colonels, he had created a common ground between Gates and Schuyler. He could explain only that there had been no formal council meeting, that he had had only individual consultations (he did not reveal that Nathanael Greene had been the severest critic).[16]

Until this, relations between Gates and Schuyler had been strained. Gates, learning on his way north that there was no longer an American army in Canada, had insisted that he was still its commander, no matter where it might be, and had attempted to install his own appointees in charge of the commissary and quartermaster departments. Schuyler had maintained that he was the army's commander as soon it crossed back over the border, and he had voided Gates's appointments. Rather than "be a suicide and stab his own honor," Schuyler wrote Washington, he would resign. Congress had supported him. And Gates had written John Adams: "I have been Deceived, and Disappointed in being removed from a place where I might have done the publick Service, and Fix'd in a Scituation where it is exceeding Doubtfull, if it will be in my Power to be more than the wretched Spectator of a ruin'd Army." He would have been still more furious had he known that Washington had tried to convince Congress to return him to his former post as adjutant general.[17]

Now Schuyler and Gates drew together. Schuyler saw in Gates a fellow sufferer. How consoling to find the very idol of his tormentors sharing in the same abuse! With Gates on his side he could throw the accusations of the New Englanders back in their teeth. "It is our duty," Schuyler wrote him, "to go Hand in Hand opposing the Enemies of the public" and to "join in defeating the insidious Foes who basely aim at the Destruction of our Characters." His tone toward Congress became increasingly shrill. He challenged its appointments of the heads of the quartermaster and commissary departments and lost. He demanded and did not receive exoneration of all blame for the failure of the Canadian invasion. Finally, he submitted his resignation as commander of the northern army. And while he waited for Congress to accept it he did not look upon Gates as an opponent and did not recoil at the prospect that he might succeed him. "I can readily conceive," he reassured him, "that you have neither sought nor solicited the Command in this Department, but it must devolve of Course on you, as I have sent my Resignation—a Step which Congress drove me to." For the present, he trustingly turned over the field command at Ticonderoga to Gates and devoted himself to negotiations with the Indians at German Flats on the Mohawk River and to the coordination of operations from his headquarters at Albany. Gates, for his part, decided that his best course was to bide his time, leaving it to his friends in Congress to champion him while he remained on good terms with Schuyler. "It is a matter of Moon shine to me, who is Commissary, so the Troops are well Supplied," he asserted to Schuyler, even though Gates's nominees were contending with Schuyler's. The command of the northern army would be "an Honour from the possession of which I cannot receive the smallest Satisfaction, unless you will suffer me to hope that you will continue to give every Aid which Your Experience, Interest, and Authority, so preeminently Supply."[18]

The rapprochement bore quick fruit. While the army was still in Canada, Schuyler had named Jacobus Wynkoop, a self-important New York infantry captain, to command the ships on the lake. Gates judged him totally incompetent to lead the enlarged fleet being constructed at Skenesboro. He replaced him with Benedict Arnold, an appointment enthusiastically endorsed by Washington. Wynkoop, however, signing himself "Commander of Lake Champlain" from aboard his ship, the *Royal Savage,* declared that his commission from Schuyler gave him precedence and fired a shot across the bow of a vessel approaching under Arnold's orders. Gates ordered his arrest and expulsion from the lake, and Schuyler loyally upheld him.[19] The navy rapidly took shape. At Albany, Schuyler hastened procurement of axes and food shipments. Gates sent Brigadier General James Waterbury, Jr., of Connecticut to superintend the construction crews at Skenesboro. At Crown Point, Arnold whipped the arriving ships and men into an effective fighting force.

The mercurial Arnold required careful management. "As I am entirely unacquainted with marine Affairs," Gates told him, "I shall not presume to give any Directions, respecting the Duty and Discipline of the Seamen and Marines, on Board the Fleet." But to restrain Arnold's pugnaciousness Gates also warned, "It is a defensive War we are carrying on; therefore, no wanton Risque or unnecessary Display of the Power of the Fleet is at any time to influence your Conduct." Under the right conditions Arnold was an asset, and Gates was willing to stretch the rules of good behavior in order to keep him. Arnold had become embroiled in court contests with colonels Moses Hazen and John Brown over mutual charges of stealing from Montreal merchants. In the trial of Hazen, he had behaved so disrespectfully toward the judges that they had demanded his arrest. Gates responded by dissolving the court. In the case of Brown, Gates ignored directions from Congress and Schuyler to try his charges against Arnold and referred the dispute to the Board of War, where it would probably be buried. "I was obliged to act dictatorily," he notified Hancock. "The United States must not be deprived of that excellent Officer's Service, at this important Moment."[20]

The best that could be hoped for from the hastily built flotilla was to delay the superior British force. "Our fleet is only our advanced guard," Gates told his men, "that defeated, the defense of the United States and the support of American freedom falls upon this army." His greatest task was to forge Ticonderoga into an impassable bastion. Conditions there were only a shade better than at Crown Point. There were no barracks and no established hospital. The skeletons of James Abercromby's slaughtered men in the disastrous attack on the fort in 1759 were still strewn about; the threadbare arrivals from Crown Point used the skulls for drinking cups and the shin and thigh bones for tent pins. Colonel Anthony Wayne of Pennsylvania swore that Ticonderoga was "the last part of world that God made," and "finished in the dark."[21]

The immediate enemy was smallpox, more dreaded than the British. "Our men dare to face them," declared Governor Jonathan Trumbull of

Connecticut, "but are not willing to go into a hospital." From Crown Point, three thousand suffering invalids were rowed southward to Fort George, where trees were felled and planks cut at nearby sawmills to house them. Hemlock branches served for beds. Under the capable supervision of Gates's friend Dr. Jonathan Potts, understaffed physicians and apothecaries strove to provide treatment despite shortages of jalap, ipecac, bark, and opium. Appeals to the countryside brought in contributions of old sheets, shirts, and aprons. Gates drafted women camp followers as nurses. He issued strict orders to inoculate recruits well before arrival or not at all so as to prevent spread of the disease to the uninoculated troops in camp. He established standards of sanitation for privies, cooking, and housing. By September he reported, a little prematurely, that "the Smallpox is totally eradicated from among us." Dysentery, too, gradually yielded to improved living conditions, although Gates himself suffered from it on and off all during the war.[22]

Recruiting for the pestilence-ridden northern army had been hard going. Even in New Hampshire, where the threat of invasion was imminent, draftees were offering payments as high as fifty dollars for substitutes. Massachusetts and Connecticut had had to double their bounties for Canadian service over those for Boston and New York. Gates's reforms brought reassurance. The Connecticut Council of Safety dispatched a smallpox specialist, Dr. John Ely, to Ticonderoga, and he reported that the disease was arrested. The Connecticut militia promptly turned out, taking the newly built northern road through Bennington to Skenesboro. Troops from New Hampshire and Massachusetts also lined the Connecticut River roads toward a rendezvous at Charlestown, and Gates sent a four-hundred-man work force to clear the way through the flooded terrain for the rest of their way to Skenesboro. At Skenesboro, flatboats carried the wet and weary recruits the final thirty miles to Ticonderoga.[23]

The militia constituted for Gates the margin of difference between victory and defeat, without which, he said, "this Country will infallibly be exposed to the Invasion of the Enemy." Many more enlistments were required than the numbers who might be counted upon to be fit for duty. Although the northern army had grown by September 29 to 11,180 rank and file, 4,434 were still incapacitated. Hardly had smallpox been conquered when a new scourge resembling yellow fever appeared among the troops who were clearing the brush for their encampment at Mount Independence. John Trumbull believed that it came from "exhalations from the earth, which was now, for the first time, exposed to the rays of a midsummer sun, combined with the fog which rose from the pestilent lake." For two months there were no medicines in camp to treat it. "It would make a heart of stone melt to hear the moans and see the distresses of the sick and dying," reported Dr. Samuel Wigglesworth. "I scarce pass a tent but I hear men solemnly declaring that they will never engage another campaign without being assured of a better supply of medicines."

Gates blamed the shortage on the failure at New York to send ten chests of medicines promised for troops sent northward the previous spring. He imagined he saw again the hostile hand of Washington, and he wrote to the secretary of the New York Provincial Congress to intercede. "I cannot be long answerable for the consequences of the shameful neglect of the Army in this department," he warned, and, in words that amounted to going over Washington's head, he demanded that the civilian authorities "comand the same attention to be paid the health of their soldiers here as elsewhere." He sent the northern army's director of hospitals, Dr. Samuel Stringer, to get the medicines. Stringer was a friend of Schuyler and so enmeshed in jurisdictional bickering that the medicines did not arrive until October.[24]

Gates's solicitude for his men, his no-nonsense, evenhanded discipline, and his sure command of army regulations soon won him both respect and popularity. Order and efficiency began to appear. Supplies of warm clothing arrived, new housing sprang up, and rum rations were increased in rainy weather. Civilian profiteering and counterfeiting were curtailed, and so was soldiers' plundering of civilians. The men turned out at drumbeat every morning to their alarm posts, drilled until breakfast at the manual of arms, and toiled during the day at fortifications. Gates could be strict with his New Englanders. He dressed down three Massachusetts brigades at Mount Independence for "supineness and indolence." He court-martialed a New Hampshire lieutenant for "degrading himself by voluntarily doing the duty of an Orderly Sergent, in violation of his rank as an officer." He could also be flexible. Lieutenant Benjamin Whitcomb of the New Hampshire Rangers, when sent as a spy into Canada, ambushed and killed British Brigadier General Patrick Gordon near St. Johns—a deed Carleton branded assassination. Whitcomb was a tough, six foot, pockmarked scout clad in leather vest and breeches and a flapped hat bound with yellow cord. He was a type indispensable for dangerous missions. Gates warned him that on spy missions he was "positively forbid to fire upon, to kill, to wound, to scalp, or in any way, to injure the Life or person of any one engaged in the Service of the Enemy, Except in your own defence" but at the same time recommended him to Congress for the command of two companies.[25]

Gates divided the army into five brigades. Three, chiefly from Massachusetts, Connecticut, and New Hampshire, with some units from New Jersey and New York, were assigned to Mount Independence on the east side of the lake. They built earthern parapets behind which two batteries were mounted in position to shell approaching enemy ships. The bulk of the fourth and fifth brigades was put to work repairing the redoubts that the French had thrown up on the high ground north of old Fort Ticonderoga and on the low ground to the east. Work at Mount Independence progressed slowly, partly because the New Hampshire and Connecticut troops brought no tents and lost time constructing huts. They were the ones that Gates admonished. Fortunately, Mount Independence was virtually invulnerable to attack. Work on the old French lines progressed more rapidly. A rampart six to eight feet thick was erected behind a stockaded ditch ten feet wide and five feet deep. After ten nonstop weeks of labor in the summer heat, Gates decreed a day off for September 22, with compulsory divine services in every brigade. Two weeks later, gun carriages, sponges, rammers, powder, lead, flints, and cartridge paper arrived to complete the readiness of the fort's 120-gun armament. It was a vastly different army than the one that had come limping out of Canada. But if only those medicines had arrived earlier. "One Half of this Army are Sick; one Third of the other Half are feeble, or poorly," Gates wrote Schuyler on October 4.[26]

As summer slid by and the nights grew long and cold, Carleton still, amazingly, kept to his harbor at St. Johns. On September 23, Arnold brought his fleet to Valcour Island, where he anchored in the concealed half-mile-wide channel separating the densely wooded island from the western shore of the lake. Southbound enemy vessels could detect him only after they had passed the island and then would be forced to turn back against the current to attack him. While he waited, a storm lashed the island on September 29, followed by a succession of gales. He wrote Gates on October 7 that if the British did not come by the middle of the month they "would not pretend to Cross the Lake after that Time." On October 11, Gates warned his men that "the long stillness and seeming supineness of the enemy, strongly indicate that they are meditating some stroke of importance."[27] On October 12 there were heard at Ticonderoga sounds of the firing of many cannon to the north. Cannon fire was heard again all the next morning. At ten o'clock a letter arrived from Arnold with an account of the engagement, a disaster. Carleton's formidable fleet, with firepower of fifty-three guns, had sailed southward before a strong northerly wind past Valcour Island, not discovering the Americans until he was two miles beyond them. He had turned back into the channel. In the following hours, Arnold's little fleet of thirty-two guns was furiously battered. Arnold had escaped at night, only to be ripped apart again the next day at Split Rock. He had then beached and burned his ships at Buttonmould Bay and marched ten miles south to Crown Point, where he had left the fort in flames to the British. He had lost eleven ships, including the *Washington,* which Waterbury, its commander, had surrendered. Arnold himself arrived, exhausted and ill, at Ticonderoga on the morning of October 14. He brought with him six vessels, all that remained of his fleet, and Hartley's sixth Pennsylvania regiment that had garrisoned at Crown Point, with its women and children.[28]

The next evening, a group of enemy rowboats neared, displaying a flag of truce. The fort's defenders were amazed to discover that Carleton was releasing on parole Waterbury and the entire 110 crew members of the captured *Washington* on condition that they pledge not to take up arms again. The liberated prisoners were so loud in their praises of Carleton that Gates feared their effect on the garrison's morale. He isolated them and the same night hurried them off to Skenesboro and to their homes for discharge.[29]

The ultimate trial now awaited. Burgoyne's troops occupied Crown Point on October 18 and 19 in rainy, raw weather. The next move would be a direct assault on Ticonderoga. The danger infused new life into the troops, determined, said Colonel Jeduthan Baldwin, to "defend the place to the Last Extr[emity]." Nerves were taut. A spy from Crown Point reported that "Carleton said he would be in possession of Ticonderoga before Sunday & on his way to Albany." Jumpy sentries in the evening mistook an ox for the enemy and fired upon it when it failed to give the countersign. Gates cautioned the men not to "throw away their shot in a random, unsoldierlike manner." The Reverend William Tennent, chaplain of the Connecticut troops, chose as his text Nehemiah 4:14: "Be ye not afraid of them: Remember the Lord which is great and terrible, and fight for your brethren, your sons, and your daughters, your wives and your houses." The British were "engaged in a wicked and unrighteous cause, which the righteous Lord abhoreth. . . . Reward your enemies, and your country's enemies, even as they have rewarded you, and render double to them."[30]

Fortunately, the winds on the lake, coming from the south, delayed the attack; Gates needed every extra moment to prepare. Persistent sickness aggravated critical manpower shortages, and he asked Schuyler to call up additional militia. Schuyler agreed, but he had little faith in their value. "If

General Gates was not so very importunate to have them at Ticonderoga I should certainly dismiss many of them," he wrote Washington.[31] The New England militia, 827 strong, responded quickly. Those from New York, more concerned with the threat to the west than the north, moved slowly, some even deserting rather than marching to Ticonderoga. Gates also coaxed from Schuyler the transfer of Colonel Elias Dayton's Third New Jersey regiment from Fort Stanwix. The brunt of the British attack on the west side of the lake was expected against the old French lines; to resist it, an advance post named Mount Hope was erected a half mile before it. On the east side, in order to obstruct the enemy's approach from Crown Point along the shore, a detachment of one hundred Continentals was dispatched to plug the road with felled trees. To guard against an attack on the rear of the American outposts, a boom of heavy logs chained together was flung across the water between Mount Independence and Ticonderoga. To facilitate troop transfers from one side of the lake to the other, a four-hundred-yard long pontoon bridge, resting on twenty-two piers, was erected on the south side of the boom. Scouting parties constantly patrolled the shores as protection against surprise.[32]

Even so, a potentially fatal flaw remained in the defense, and John Trumbull alone detected it. The future "Painter of the Revolution" gaged the distance from Fort Ticonderoga to Sugar Loaf Mountain, immediately to the west and seven hundred feet high, and decided that enemy cannon mounted on the summit would be within firing range of the Americans below. He chose as the forum to air his view an officers' mess at Gates's table. Young and abrasive, he "rarely erred by excess of meekness." The response was derision: the distance was prohibitive; the steep hill was insurmountable. Trumbull was certain. He staged a demonstration. A common six-pound cannon was wheeled into the fort and a gunner fired a ball that reached the summit. He enlisted the aid of Arnold and Wayne, and with them clambered to the top of the hill. Then he drew up a report, arguing that five hundred men and twenty-five heavy guns stationed at the summit could effectively replace the ten-thousand-man garrison below at one-tenth the cost, and sent copies to Gates, Schuyler, and the Continental Congress. Gates said afterward that he was persuaded, except that he preferred howitzers to guns. Schuyler, however, "thought it wrong to throw away labor in preventing an evil that could never happen." And there was not a howitzer to be had at Ticonderoga.[33]

On October 28 the wind shifted to the north. At eight o'clock in the morning an advance guard boat boomed the signal that the enemy fleet was coming. An hour later, five of the largest British gunboats landed troops and

Indians at Three Mile Point, on the western shore, three miles north of Fort Ticonderoga. Two of the boats started toward the eastern shore but were turned back by fire from the redoubt there and from the row-galley *Trumbull,* which had been anchored near the boom. Gates concluded that the enemy was preparing a major attack on the west side against the French lines and redoubts, and he transferred three regiments from the eastern side across the bridge. "Nothing could exceed the spirit and alertness which was shown by all officers and men," he reported. The defenses that were exposed to the full view of the British appeared formidable. "The whole summit of cleared land, on both sides of the lake, was crowned with redoubts and batteries, all manned, with a splendid show of artillery and flags," Trumbull wrote. If the British had intended an assault they abandoned it. At four in the evening they were seen to embark at Three Mile Point. When five days later Gates sent forces to attack outposts on both sides of the lake, they found that the British had departed from all stations, including their main base at Crown Point. Carleton had decided to retire to Canada.[34]

Gates had vindicated his judgment over Washington's slurs. "I cannot help observing here," he pointedly wrote Hancock, "that the removal of our army from Crown Point to Ticonderoga, was a most fortunate and Salutary Measure; for, had it continued at Crown Point after the Disaster that befell our Fleet, the Enemy might have cut off all our Resources, by stationing their Fleet above the Point. Desperate must then have been the Situation of our Army."[35] He had not won a pitched battle, but better yet he had retained possession of the field without the loss of life. He had demonstrated that he could organize and put spirit into an army.

That success also brought to an end his alliance with Schuyler, who was still commander of the northern army and Gates's superior. Schuyler was a tormented man. He wrote on October 11 that he was suffering from a "violent rheumatick attack in the head and stomach." He imagined enemies behind every disagreement with his policies. Having submitted his resignation, he wished to be begged to stay. Detesting the militia, he resented Gates's popularity with them. Vigilantly he watched for signs of precedence accorded to Gates over himself. He found them. When Congress sent a shipment to the northern army in the name of Gates instead of Schuyler he saw it as an insult. When Congress sent an investigating committee of Richard Stockton and George Clymer to the northern army, he charged that they were bypassing him. "Would you believe," he wrote Robert R. Livingston, "that Mr. Clymer and Mr. Stockton were ordered to repair to Ticonderoga to confer with General Gates? They arrived here on Friday evening, dined and

1. *James Smith-Stanley, Lord Strange, 1771, John Burgoyne's brother-in-law and patron. Print of painting by W. Derby after T. Hudson. National Portrait Gallery, London.*

2. *Charles Paulet, third duke of Bolton, employer of Horatio Gates's parents and patron of Horatio. Print of painting by unknown artist. National Portrait Gallery, London.*

3. John Burgoyne, 1756. After Allan Ramsay. National Portrait Gallery, London.

4. John Hale, friend of Horatio Gates. Print of painting by unknown artist. National Portrait Gallery, London.

5. *Lord George Sackville, 1759, later titled Lord George Germain, advocate and later political enemy of Burgoyne. Mezzotint by James McArdell after Sir Joshua Reynolds. Yale Center for British Art, Paul Mellon Collection.*

6. *Horatio Gates, 1782. Painting by Charles Willson Peale. Independence National Historical Park Collection.*

7. John Burgoyne, 1766. Painting by Sir Joshua Reynolds. Copyright the Frick Collection, New York.

8. *Thomas Gage, 1768, Burgoyne's superior in Boston. Painting by John Singleton Copley. Yale Center for British Art, Paul Mellon Collection.*

9. *Sir William Howe, Burgoyne's superior in the Saratoga campaign. Engraving,*
James Murray, An Impartial History of the Present War in America *(Newcastle-*
upon-Tyne, 1778), vol. 1, facing p. 471. The Beinecke Rare Book and Manuscript
Library, Yale University.

10. *Sir Henry Clinton, c. 1777, whose aid was too little and too late to save Bur-*
goyne. Miniature by John Smart. Courtesy of the Director, National Army Museum,
London.

11. Sir Guy Carleton, Burgoyne's jealous superior in Canada. Copy of a portrait by an unknown artist. National Archives of Canada C 2833.

12. William Phillips, Burgoyne's second in command. Print of painting by Francis Cotes. Frick Art Reference Library.

13. George Washington, 1787, Gates's superior and critic. Painting by James Peale. Independence National Historical Park Collection.

14. Philip Schuyler, 1792, whom Gates replaced in the command of the northern army. Painting by John Trumbull. Courtesy of the New-York Historical Society, New York City.

15. Benedict Arnold [tentatively identified], Gates's daring, unruly subordinate. Print of painting attributed to Cassidy. Frick Art Reference Library.

16. Daniel Morgan, intrepid commander of the Virginia corps of riflemen. Painting by Charles Willson Peale. Independence National Historical Park Collection.

17. *Benjamin Lincoln, Gates's second in command. Painting by Charles Willson Peale. Independence National Historical Park Collection.*

18. Charles James Fox, 1792, Burgoyne's political ally in Parliament. Bust by Joseph Nollekens. Yale Center for British Art, Paul Mellon Collection.

19. Horatio Gates, 1794. Painting by Gilbert Stuart. The Metropolitan Museum of Art, Gift of Lucille S. Pfeffer, 1977 (1977.243).

20. The Surrender of General Burgoyne at Saratoga. *Painting by John Trumbull. Copyright Yale University Art Gallery.*

21. Key to The Surrender of General Burgoyne at Saratoga *by John Trumbull.
Courtesy Yale University Art Gallery.*

KEY TO SURRENDER OF GENERAL BURGOYNE

1. Maj. William Lithgow, 11th Massachusetts Regt.
2. Col. Joseph Cilley, 1st New Hampshire Regt.
3. Brig. Gen. Stark, New Hampshire Militia
4. Capt. Thomas Youngs Seymour, 2nd Continental Dragoons
5. Maj. William Hull, 8th Massachusetts Regt.
6. Col. John Greaton, 3rd Massachusetts Regt.
7. Lieut. Col. Henry Dearborn, 3rd New Hampshire Regt.
8. Col. Alexander Scammell, 3rd New Hampshire Regt.
9. Col. Morgan Lewis, Deputy Quartermaster General, Northern Department
10. Maj. Gen. William Phillips, British, Royal Regt. of Artillery
11. Lieut. Gen. John Burgoyne, British
12. Maj. Gen. Fredrich Adolf von Riedesel, Baron of Eisenbach, German
13. Lieut. Col. James Wilkinson, Deputy Adjutant General, Northern Department
14. Maj. Gen. Horatio Gates

15. Col. William Prescott, Massachusetts Militia
16. Col. Daniel Morgan, 11th Virginia Regt.
17. Col. Rufus Putnam, 5th Massachusetts Regt.
18. Lieut. Col. John Brooks, 8th Massachusetts Regt.
19. Rev. Enos Hitchcock, Chaplain, 10th Massachusetts Regt.
20. Lieut. Col. (brevet) Robert Troup, Aide-de-Camp to Gen. Gates
21. 1st Lieut. Elnathan Haskell, Adjutant, 14th Massachusetts Regt.
22. Maj. John Armstrong, Aide-de-Camp to Gen. Gates
23. Maj. Gen. Philip John Schuyler, New York
24. Brig. Gen. John Glover, Continental Army
25. Brig. Gen. William Whipple, New Hampshire Militia
26. Maj. Matthew Clarkson, Aide-de-Camp
27. Maj. Ebenezer Stevens, Independent Battalion of Artillery, Continental Army

supped with me yesterday, but have not opened their lips on any public business; that is to be transacted with my inferior officer under my very nose." Actually, the congressmen had arrived at Albany too exhausted from their journey to take up business the first day. On subsequent days they held ample discussions with him. Schuyler rode north with them as far as Saratoga, and, when they asked, he sent them a full statement of the army's needs. Unappeased, he laid his grievances before the New York Convention, which sent a sharp warning to Congress that acceptance of his resignation would "endanger the peace and safety of the State."[36]

When Stockton and Clymer arrived at Ticonderoga, two days before the departure of the British from Crown Point, Gates undoubtedly learned from them that before their departure from Philadelphia the warning of the New York Convention had been referred to a committee so loaded with Schuyler's supporters that the rejection of his resignation was a foregone conclusion. He was not, after all, to succeed Schuyler. His reward for stopping Carleton was to continue to take orders from an invalided superior in Albany. He felt that he had to get away. The lake was freezing over at the narrows and he did not have the constitution for a severe winter. He learned that Betsy and Bob had arrived in Philadelphia, and he wanted to see them. Might he not, there, plead his prospects with his political friends? He wrote Schuyler that the next British push would be in the south, across the Delaware, that some northern troops would have to be redeployed to Washington's army, and that he would like to go with them. He appointed Colonel Anthony Wayne, a younger man who had the "health and strength fit to encounter the inclemency of that cold inhospitable region," to command the fort at Ticonderoga.[37]

His boat left for Albany on November 18. The departing view of Ticonderoga was unforgettable. On the lake's west shore the men's cooking fires had ignited huge masses of autumn leaves. The flames leapt up Sugar Loaf Hill from accumulations on boulder after boulder. John Trumbull's artist's eye vividly caught the drama of the scene: "In parts the fire crept along the crevices of the rock; at times an ancient pine tree rose up a majestic pyramid of flame; and all this was reflected in the pellucid surface of the lake, which lay like a beautiful mirror in the stillness of the dark night."[38]

Burgoyne sat powerlessly on the sideline. Every hope and plan he had brought with him from England, every lesson learned at Valencia de Alcántara was frustrated. Carleton clearly had no enthusiasm to follow up the destruction of Arnold's fleet with a land offensive. He had given so little consideration to the army that when he set his navy in motion at St. Johns he had forgotten to leave orders for Burgoyne and had to turn back.

True, Carleton's forces faced severe shortages of food, quartermaster supplies, and barrack equipment. He had not received from England the essential gunboats he had requested. The first snow had already fallen, and supply lines from Canada could not be maintained with the coming of the northern cold and the freezing of the lake. The spirited conduct of the Americans at Valcour Island had shown that their ability must not be underestimated.[39]

Yet if Carleton had been an aggressive commander, willing to take risks, he might have seized an opportunity to end the war that year. Howe had driven Washington out of New York City and opened the way for a march north up the Hudson. Carleton might have captured Ticonderoga by occupying Sugar Loaf Hill and then driven down to Albany in time to join forces with Howe before the lake froze: that winter turned out to be unusually mild, and the lake was navigable through much of December. He was so hesitant that when he sailed on a lakeside reconnaissance of the fort and saw its new redoubts, bristling cannon, and milling militia, he decided that he could not safely leave an exposed garrison at Crown Point through the winter.[40]

For Burgoyne this was the last straw. He would have liked to make an attempt at Ticonderoga. He considered Crown Point indispensable as a staging place for an invasion the next year. With such a lackluster prospect, he could see no point in remaining in Canada and requested leave from Carleton to return home. He could offer inoffensive reasons: his health was poor and he needed treatment; he must attend to Lady Charlotte's estate; and he could serve Carleton best by presenting to Germain his requests for reinforcements and supplies.[41]

Privately, he wrote Clinton that he could be "no otherwise of service" to Carleton "than by silence." He did not openly declare, and he may not fully have admitted to himself, that in London he might maneuver for a separate command. His friend Major General William Phillips, who had accompanied him on the expedition from England, said it for him: "The next year must divide this army, and we go together if it be possible."[42]

It was common knowledge that relations between Carleton and Germain were reaching the breaking point. Germain had sent over with Burgoyne's troops his personal appointee as quartermaster general—Lieutenant Colonel Gabriel Christie, a native of St. Johns who had opposed Carleton's Quebec Act. Carleton had already named his own brother, Major Thomas Carleton, to the job. The disappointed Christie retaliated by filling Germain's mail with accusations against the governor as a slothful, inefficient administrator and bungler who had missed opportunities for victory at Chambly and Ticonderoga.

Germain was sure to listen. "Take care of our cause in England," Phillips enjoined Burgoyne.[43]

~※10※~

Howe versus Burgoyne

To CHARLES LEE, A CASUAL AC-
quaintance, William Howe appeared "naturally good-humored and complacent." Charles Stedman, a subordinate who knew him better, saw, rather
than complacency, an "absurd and destructive confidence" that could not
hide a "monotonous mediocrity." In fact, Howe was a secretive military
politician who devised no plan and made no decision without carefully considering the effect it might have in raising up a potential rival. When crossed,
according to James Wemyss, who later served under him at Brandywine, he
could be "sullen and ungracious"; William Phillips found in him "a damned
vile disposition, great bravery without a ray of conduct."[1]

At Boston he had feared Burgoyne as a rival and had denied him the
command of a Rhode Island expedition. Carleton was a threat because he
outranked Howe in seniority. If the northern and southern armies met up the
Hudson, Carleton could assume the combined command. Howe therefore
wrote Germain in June 1776 proposing that in the event of a junction his
own command would remain separate, "in the same manner as in an allied
army." The result was not at all what he had expected. Germain seized on the
issue as an excuse to install Burgoyne as northern field commander and
restrict Carleton to the function of civilian governor. Because Burgoyne was
junior to Howe, there would be no conflict. Howe received the news on
October 23, 1776. He did not relish the reappearance of the flamboyant
Burgoyne. He did not learn until long afterward that the change of northern
command for 1776 never took place: the ship that carried Germain's instructions failed in three attempts to get through the icebound St. Lawrence and
returned to England.[2] When he heard that Burgoyne had gone back to
England, no doubt to pull strings there, he decided that Burgoyne must be
totally eliminated from Canada. On December 31, Howe wrote to Germain

bluntly requesting that Clinton, "being senior to Burgoyne," be sent in his place to Canada, "the prior command." He wished Burgoyne to take Clinton's post at New York, where he could safely be tethered.[3] This would achieve the added advantage of ridding himself of Clinton, whom he detested.

But Burgoyne proved a jack-in-the-box who could not be restrained.

Burgoyne landed at Portsmouth on December 9, according to one report a very sick man. His business would brook no delay, and he sent ahead, by special delivery, a letter he had brought for Germain from Carleton.[4]

The letter threw Germain into a fury. Ostensibly a commendation of Burgoyne, it was a thinly disguised attack on Germain for supporting Christie:

> I cannot omit on this Occasion, mentioning to your Lordship the great Satisfaction I have received from the Services of General Burgoyne, not only from the Zeal and readiness with which he concurred with me in promoting His Majesty's Service, but from the attention and assiduity which he showed in discountenancing & preventing all faction and party in this Army; Dispositions which, your Lordship must be sensible, when unfortunately they are encouraged by Persons eminent in their Stations, are capable of defeating the most zealous Endeavors, and of rending the best concerted plans of Operation.[5]

If Germain had not previously been determined to remove Carleton, he was now.

Burgoyne was ushered in the following morning. He came, he said, for the purpose of presenting Carleton's proposal for the 1777 campaign that would require reinforcements of four thousand troops. The plan did not accord with his own ideas—it called for an invasion along the Mohawk River and another down the Connecticut, with no mention at all of the Champlain-Hudson route. Carleton later wrote Germain that his only purpose was to provide "a suitable command" for Burgoyne. Burgoyne may have known or suspected this, but he prudently refused to be drawn into open criticism of Carleton lest he be accused of disloyalty. Germain perceived that when Burgoyne saw the king he would defend Carleton, perhaps rescue him.

As soon as Burgoyne left, Germain rushed to the king to head him off. He charged Carleton with all the offenses Christie had reported, and he vehemently urged his recall. His animus was "so manifest," the king wrote Lord

North, "that it would be idle to say more than that it is a fact." He waited to hear what Burgoyne had to report.[6]

Burgoyne came the next morning to a levee at St. James's, and in the afternoon the king had a long talk with him. Burgoyne later said that he "seized every possible occasion" to vindicate Carleton, "careless how ill I paid my court, earnest to meet every attack against his fame."[7] But he also put himself skillfully forward in contrast as the advocate of attack and the planner for a Champlain-Hudson invasion.

Two days later the king communicated his decision to Lord North. He conceded that Carleton was "too cold or not so active as may be wished." It would be "cruel," however, to remove him from his post as governor of Canada. The solution was "to have the part of the Canadian army which must attempt to join General Howe led by a more enterprising commander."[8] The appointment was not officially announced. Howe had yet to be heard from, and the plans for 1777 hinged on the outcome of his campaign at New York.

Burgoyne did not remain idle. He went to the king again and "humbly laid myself at his Majesty's feet for such active employment as he might think me worthy of." He visited Secretary at War Barrington and smoothed over old hostilities. He frankly asked Germain for his support: "I deserve it, inasmuch as a solid respect & sincere personal attachment can constitute such a claim." He managed another hour with the king, riding with him in Hyde Park. He made a show of confidence, and at Brooks's on Christmas day bet Charles Fox fifty guineas that he would be back within a year, victorious.[9]

Germain was not won over. Clinton, he was beginning to think, was after all the better man for Canada. He had not fallen under Carleton's influence, and he had won victories in the field at Long Island and Rhode Island sufficient to offset his failure at Charlestown. When on February 23 Howe's request arrived for Clinton to be named to Canada and Burgoyne to be sent as second in command to New York, Germain made his decision. He informed the king the next day that he intended to propose the appointments to the cabinet. The king, relieved to have salvaged Carleton as governor, acquiesced. Then Germain's vengefulness carried him too far: he would get at Carleton by removing his lieutenant governor, Hector T. Cramahé. The king refused. "I have thrown cold water on that, and Ld. Suffolk and Ld. Gower will oppose it at the next meeting," he wrote North.[10]

That cabinet meeting proved crucial. Suffolk and Gower had as allies Lord Sandwich, first lord of the admiralty, who had long been feuding with Germain, and Viscount Weymouth, secretary of state for the southern department, who was Gower's father-in-law. Joined with North, they constituted a majority of the eight cabinet members, and Germain suffered a major defeat. It was an easy step for his enemies, having opposed him on the dismissal of Cramahé, to oppose him on the appointment of Clinton as well. Burgoyne was the obvious alternative, and he had let it be known that he was already preparing a complete invasion plan. The result was a terse cabinet minute: "Also submitted that General Burgoyne should be again employed in Canada."[11]

Burgoyne quickly moved to improve his footing with Germain. Having achieved his goal without open criticism of Carleton, he no longer felt any obligation to defend him. He sent Germain his campaign plan, "Thoughts for Conducting the War on the side of Canada," and in it he all but declared that he had no confidence in Carleton's commitment to cooperate in supplying provisions of the magnitude required for the expedition, that Carleton's supercaution would find "plausible objections . . . sufficient to crush such exertions as an officer of a sanguine temper, entrusted with the future conduct of the campaign and whose personal interest and fame therefore consequentially depended upon a timely outset, would be led to make."[12]

Germain was not that easily mollified. He saw in Burgoyne's disparagement only the fuel for a new tactic to undercut Carleton. Why not appoint Clinton to the position of commander in chief in Canada? This would further divide Carleton's authority, leaving him only with his demeaning civil function as governor.

Clinton arrived in London on February 28, the day Burgoyne submitted his plan. Germain met with him a few days later and made the offer. He declined. He was not to be deceived with an inactive command, even if it acknowledged his seniority by making him Burgoyne's technical superior. He resented Burgoyne's elevation to the "Road to Glory" and would not be a party to the humiliation of Carleton. He would rather resign his commission. All that Germain could accomplish was to induce him, with the promise of the award of a knighthood of the "red ribbon," the Order of the Bath, to return to his former post in New York as second in command to Howe. Dependent on his officer's salary, Clinton consoled himself with the hope that he might still supersede Burgoyne if the northern army merged with Howe's.[13]

Burgoyne expected that his "Thoughts" paper would be adopted as the basis for his instructions, and he submitted the supporting documents to

Germain's principal undersecretary and military confidante, Christopher d'Oyley. The plan called for an army of not less than eight thousand regulars (including most of the Brunswick troops), artillery that Carleton had already requested, a corps of watermen, two thousand Canadian workmen, and a thousand or more Indians. An additional force would be provided for a diversion by way of lakes Ontario and Oswego to the Mohawk River under Colonel Barry St. Leger, consisting of the Loyalist corps under Sir John Johnson, two hundred British regulars, a body of Indians, and four pieces of light artillery. The invasion would proceed in two stages. The first was an assault on Ticonderoga, preceded by seizure of Crown Point as a supply base. The second stage posed three options: Burgoyne might "effect a junction with General Howe" at Albany; he might proceed alone to Albany in order to divert the Americans from Howe "and thereby enable that general to act with his whole force to the southward"; or he might turn east and march down the Connecticut River for a junction with the force from Rhode Island. He much preferred the last as "the most important purpose to which the Canada army could be employed."[14]

Unlike his previous proposals, it focused exclusively on New England as the political tinderbox of the rebellion. This was the lesson he believed he had learned at Boston. The unnatural uprising had been provoked by New England's "profligate hypocrites." Merely to isolate New England from the southern colonies along the Champlain-Hudson dividing line would not be sufficient. Samuel Adams and his ilk must be suppressed and the penalty for insurrection demonstrated. The undeceived multitude would then return to the benevolent protection of the British constitution.

The decision, however, had already been made across the ocean by Howe, who had no intention of providing Burgoyne with an opportunity to earn laurels as the conquerer from Canada. He switched to a whole new schema for the 1777 campaign, in which the main thrust would be an attack against Philadelphia followed by penetration into Virginia, South Carolina, and Georgia. Unless reinforcements of fifteen thousand foreign levies were provided, he wrote Germain, the force in Rhode Island would be scaled down to two thousand, the garrison at New York City to four thousand, and a limited three thousand vaguely designated to "act defensively on the lower part of the Hudson River to cover Jersey on that side as well as to facilitate in some degree the approach of the army from Canada." His explanation was that the taking of New York had inspired a ground swell of Loyalist support in Pennsylvania and that Washington's army was sure to be stationed there. The king had the final say, but he found that he had little choice, for Germain was in no position to send Howe the reinforcements he requested. "As Sir W. Howe does not think of acting from Rhode Island into Massachusetts," the king decreed, "the Force must from Canada join him in Albany." He refused to authorize the eight thousand men Burgoyne had requested. Only seven thousand could be spared, in order not to "run any risk in Canada."[15]

It was now up to Germain to issue the specific orders to the field commanders, and he was in a difficult position. He had been informed by Howe of his intention to turn south to Philadelphia, but he was politically too weak to order the abandonment of that plan and run the risk of offending Howe. He could only trust that Howe would subjugate Philadelphia in time to turn north and join Burgoyne at Albany. He therefore adopted the device of transmitting his instructions in the form of a letter to Carleton, who was the nominal commander in chief, with copies to Burgoyne and Howe.[16] The result proved calamitous. Burgoyne, who was to "pass Lake Champlain and from thence by the most vigorous exertion of the force under his command to proceed with all expedition to Albany and put himself under the command of Sir William Howe," assumed that Germain would, as he had written Carleton in the letter of instructions, "write to Sir William Howe from hence by the first packet," and that, although Burgoyne and St. Leger were to "act as exigencies may require" until they received orders from Howe, they must "never lose view of their intended junctions with Sir William Howe as their principal objects."[17] Howe afterward insisted that he had never personally and separately been ordered to march to Albany.

If Burgoyne had any misgivings, they were overcome in the exhilaration of command. On March 23 he attended the king's levee and received his good wishes. Four days later he left for Portsmouth and thence to Plymouth, where the *Apollo,* thirty-two guns, commanded by his friend Captain Philemon Pownoll, waited to depart on April 3 for Quebec. At Plymouth, finding the *Albion* man-of-war about to depart for New York, he dispatched a letter to Howe, informing him that he was on his way.[18] With that precaution, it seemed as though everything possible had been done to insure the coordination of the northern and southern armies.

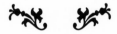

Eight weeks later, on May 18, a letter from Howe dated April 2 reached London. It contained a final revision of his campaign for 1777: "I propose to invade Pennsylvania by sea and from this arrangement we must probably abandon the Jerseys which by the former plan would not have been the case."

He said not a word about a meeting with the northern army, and he set a launching date so far into the year that it would be virtually impossible to turn north in time. In an instant Germain awoke. Burgoyne's entire operation was in jeopardy! He fired off a reply: "His Majesty does not hesitate to approve the alterations which you propose, trusting however that whatever you may meditate it will be executed in time for you to cooperate with the army ordered to proceed from Canada and put itself under your command."[19]

It was too late. By the time the letter arrived, Howe was on his way to Philadelphia by sea.

❦ 11 ❦

Schuyler or Gates?

SCHUYLER RESISTED RELEASING Gates southward, where he might do damage among Schuyler's New England friends in Philadelphia. But orders from Washington left him no choice, and on December 2, 1776, Gates took boat at Albany, at the head of eight regiments severely decimated by disease and all engaged for no longer than the end of the year, and sailed down the Hudson toward the army in New Jersey.[1] It remained to be seen whether his freedom from Schuyler would result in anything better than confinement under Washington. Returning to the adjutant generalship would be a step backward. His accomplishment at Ticonderoga had earned him an assignment to another field command. Would Washington give him his due?

Along the way, a letter was delivered to Gates from Charles Lee that told him he was not alone in daring to challenge the commander in chief. Lee charged that Washington's conduct of the campaign during the past month had demonstrated indecision and vacillation. He had procrastinated in ordering the evacuation of Fort Washington before the approaching British until it was too late, and the entire garrison of three thousand had surrendered. He had abandoned New Jersey to the mercy of the British but then had reconsidered whether to return for raids on the British flanks and rear. This had left Lee uncertain how to react. *"Entre nous,"* he wrote, "a certain great man is most damnably deficient—He has thrown me into a situation where I have my choice of difficulties—if I stay in this Province I risk myself and Army and if I do not stay the Province is lost for ever . . . our Counsels have been weak to the last degree."[2] Lee's letter was written the morning before his capture by a British scouting party, and his captivity was perhaps fortunate: he had gone so far as directly to disobey Washington's orders to join him and might have been court-martialed.

When Gates and his troops, traveling through snow and slush, reached Easton, a letter awaited from Washington with an unmistakable revelation of the treatment he could expect. General Henry Clinton had landed at Newport with six thousand troops and had taken Rhode Island without opposition. Washington was detaching Benedict Arnold from Gates's command in order to join Major General Joseph Spencer, a discredited and overage officer, in organizing the state's militia defense force. Here was an assignment that would have been much to Gates's liking. He would have had a command physically separated from Washington, and he would have been comfortable among his New England friends and involved in an operation that could support the northern army. This bypass might be a first step in elevating Arnold above himself in an assignment to the northern theater. His entire career might be in jeopardy. New strategems must be devised. Previously he had challenged Washington head-on; now he proceeded with subtlety. Washington had left a loophole: he had not specifically stated who would have the supreme authority in Rhode Island. Gates advised Arnold to continue with him to Washington's headquarters for clarification.[3] This would force Washington to decide in favor of Spencer, the senior. Arnold would never consent. Gates could then put himself forward as the senior to whom Arnold could have no objection.

Gates and Arnold, bringing six hundred troops, arrived at Washington's headquarters at Newton on December 20 amid a heavy snow. The conference with Washington produced no satisfaction. He resented Gates's having "induced" Arnold to delay going to Rhode Island. His choice of Arnold and Spencer was unchangeable. Another vacancy, the command of Lee's army while he was in captivity, was given to John Sullivan. If Gates did not shield himself, he might find himself silently shunted to staff duty. It was insufferable. Gates requested sick leave to go to Philadelphia.[4] He did not explain why recuperation was necessary in Philadelphia, but Washington did not press him.

In Philadelphia he discovered that Congress had fled to Baltimore. His friend Robert Morris, however, had remained behind as caretaker, and from him he could not fail to learn the congressional aspect of the appointment to the Rhode Island command. The delegates from Rhode Island, Massachusetts, and New Hampshire, before knowing of Washington's appointment of Spencer and Arnold, had written him recommending Greene or Gates, who were both "greatly belovd in that Part of America."[5] Gates needed nothing more to fortify him in his impulse to turn to the New England delegates for protection against Washington. He was still sick, but he must go on to Baltimore. Betsy was there; his excuse would be that he needed her to nurse him.

He arrived December 28 feeling only slightly better. The streets were dirty and miry, and among the thousand-odd brick houses even the president of Congress, John Hancock, had been able to find lodging only "in a Remote place among the Whores & Thieves," where, he reported, "I had not been Forty eight hours at my house before it was Rob'd." Congress was meeting in a former tavern at the southwest end of Market Street. Gates lost no time in conferring with his friends, especially Sam Adams and Elbridge Gerry. The proposal to send Gates or Greene to Rhode Island had originated with William Ellery, a delegate from that state, who was eager to see a major counteroffensive launched there. Washington had clearly been unenthusiastic. The New Englanders were not happy with his choice of Spencer and Arnold and were talking of a complaint to Congress.[6]

For the present nothing could come of such maneuvering. Washington had just won brilliant victories at Trenton and Princeton, and he was riding high on a fresh crest of popularity. He had emerged as the single symbol of national unification. Congress had delegated to him virtually dictatorial powers for six months in a desperate attempt to arrest failing recruitment and governmental disorganization. Neither did the New England delegates have the votes to oust Schuyler in the north. "General Gates is here. How shall we make him Head of that Army?" Sam Adams wrote his cousin John, but when John arrived in Baltimore on February 1 he had no answer.[7]

So, until the political climate improved, Gates was going to have to go wherever Washington chose to send him. That, strangely and agreeably, proved to be Philadelphia. He was to take over the command of the city, with responsibility for forwarding to the field the incoming reserves of militia. It gave him a much needed rest. He took Betsy with him. His health improved. He enjoyed hobnobbing with Robert Morris and other friends at Mrs. Smith's City Tavern before the fire with a bowl of warm broth.[8]

But it was only an interim assignment, and within three weeks the unwelcome prospect of a return to the adjutant generalship threatened again, this time with the disturbing endorsement of his supposed political friends. Joseph Reed, the incumbent adjutant general, resigned on January 22. A deceptive impression that Gates might accept the post was created in a letter written by his friend Colonel Joseph Trumbull, which had been intercepted by the British and published in the Loyalist *New-York Gazette*. To the congressmen this was an opportunity to solve two problems. They would be relieved of the embarrassment of finding a post for Gates; they would also acquire an agent on Washington's staff who could serve as a watchdog. They had strong reservations over having surrendered so much authority to Washington. John Adams, who had before this spoken of the value of military aides as a check on the commander in chief, on February 19 declared on the floor, "I have been distressed to see some members of this house disposed to idolize an image which their own hands have molted. I speak here of the superstitious veneration that is sometimes paid to Genl Washington. Altho' I honour him for his good qualities, yet in this house I feel myself his Superior. In private life I shall always acknowledge that he is mine. It becomes us to attend early to the restraining our army."[9] The following day the delegates instructed President Hancock to inform Gates of their "earnest desire" that he resume the office of adjutant general with the assurance that he would retain his rank and pay as major general. Should he accept, they would replace him as Schuyler's second in command with Arthur St. Clair, who was promoted, in anticipation, to major general.[10]

The movers of resolutions egregiously misunderstood their man. Gates's ambitions were wedded to the northern theater. He had not refused to serve under Schuyler in order to sink to a staff position. He saw that his protests had been too low-key. He threw aside his habitual language of deference to politicians. "To be expected to Dwindle again into the Adjutant General," he replied to Hancock, "requires some philosophy upon my side, & something more than Words upon Yours." He laid down conditions unlikely to be met: Washington must explicitly make it clear that he wanted him, and Congress must specify that he would retain his former pay of $332 per month and his aides de camp.[11]

Washington was not to be forced into flattery. He would say only that he wished "that the desires of Congress may be gratified; and in that case, that you will repair to this place immediately, as there never was a time when a good Adjutant Genl was more wanted." Gates refused to be satisfied with that. He was surprised, he answered, that Hancock's request had not been preceded by one from Washington. A desk job, after having "commanded last Campaign at the second post upon this Continent," was a comedown. He would "by no means consent" to the assignment unless Washington made it clear that it was not only Congress's but his own "earnest desire." Washington was unrelenting. His aide, Tench Tilghman, drafted a conciliatory statement he rejected: "I do request you to resume the office and request it as a favor, the greatest that can be conferred upon me, as an individual, and the greatest that can be conferred upon the public." The toned-down letter that Washington sent merely told Gates that his return was "the only means of giving form and regularity to our new Army." It agreed, hardly persuasively, that he might find the job "disagreeable" by comparison with his former command. It informed him almost demeaningly that another candidate of much lower rank had been considered for the position, Major Appolos Morris, also "equal to the task," who, however, had turned out to be a suspected Loyalist.[12]

Gates ignored the letter. He would do his business with Congress, which was now close at hand, having returned to Philadelphia. At this crucial point, Schuyler's imprudence opened the way. On the day Congress reconvened, March 12, it took up two abrasive letters from him. The first began with a sharp protest against Congress's removal in January of Dr. Samuel Stringer from the post of director of hospitals for the northern department. Stringer was Schuyler's personal physician. He had been feuding with the national director of hospitals, Dr. John Morgan, and with his own assistant director, Dr. Jonathan Potts, a friend of Gates. "As Dr. Stringer had my recommendation to the office he has sustained," Schuyler wrote, "perhaps it was a compliment to me that I should have been advised of the reasons for his dismissal." Another abrasive complaint demanded congressional intervention in a dispute with commissary-general Colonel Joseph Trumbull: "I confidently expected that Congress would have done me that justice which it was in their power to give and which, I humbly conceive, they ought to have done." The second letter, answering charges that he had misused funds for the northern army, accused the members of Congress's Board of Treasury of "lending willing ears to improbable tales."[13] Schuyler's petulance had carried him too far. The congressmen had here an opportunity to assert legislative supremacy over the military. Gates was within easy call and was the waiting alternative to Schuyler. The next day a committee of five was appointed to confer with Gates "upon the general state of affairs." Four of the members were distinctly in his camp—Sherman, Lovell, Whipple, and the chairman, Daniel Roberdeau, a radical from Pennsylvania. The fifth, Lewis Morris, although a New Yorker, was not committed to the Schuyler faction.[14]

Gates came fully prepared. The northern theater, he declared, was "the Second Post of the Continental Armies." Marshalling expert manpower statistics, he demonstrated that it would require a vastly augmented force of sixteen thousand. This mandated a correspondingly increased staff of general officers, and he specified their rank and distribution: "One Majr. Genl. should be sent to Albany. Two Brigadier Generals to Tyconderoga, one Brigadier General to Number 4 [Mount Independence] and one to Bennington." He would take over the Albany post. For his second in command at

Ticonderoga he requested St. Clair, who had privately asked to serve under him.[15]

To replace Schuyler he had to win over a closely divided Congress, and the key vote was New Hampshire. Of the ten states in attendance, he could safely rely on five in the radical "eastern interest": Connecticut, Massachusetts, Rhode Island, New Jersey, and Pennsylvania. Three states in the conservative "southern interest"—Virginia, Delaware, and North Carolina—could be expected to oppose him. Georgia and New Hampshire were divided. New York, Schuyler's base, lacked sufficient delegates to qualify to vote. Gates threw aside any pretense of political neutrality. He openly bid for the support of New Hampshire by championing the Vermonters in their feud with New York over statehood. The issue centered around the appointment of Lieutenant Colonel Seth Warner to head a Continental Army battalion of "Green Mountain Boys." The New York Committee of Safety objected that it might be interpreted as a recognition of Vermont. Schuyler complained to Congress that Warner had failed to recruit the men he had promised. Warner replied that Schuyler had withheld bounty payments, and he offered to raise the money from the Vermont towns if Congress would permit him to match the higher bounties offered by the other New England states. Gates endorsed his petition: "The Inlisting all the Men possible upon the Grants, has a Double Good Effect, it will Strengthen Our Army, defeat any designs the Enemy may have form'd to inveigle the men of the Grants."[16] This move may have done him more good in New Hampshire than he realized, for there was a movement there by Governor Meschech Ware to obtain the northern command for native son John Sullivan. He won his majority. On March 15, Congress resolved that the language of Schuyler's letter of complaint about the removal of Dr. Stringer was "highly derogatory to the honour of Congress; and that the president be desired to acquaint General Schuyler that it is expected his letters, for the future, be written in a stile more suitable to the dignity of the representative body of these free and independent states, and to his own character as their officer." The language likewise of his charge against Joseph Trumbull was, "to say the least, ill-advised and highly indecent." The rebukes were followed on March 25 with a resolution that Gates be "directed immediately to repair to Ticonderoga, and take command of the army there."[17]

Gates chose to consider that he had replaced Schuyler. The resolution was not that clear. On the one hand, Gates could be viewed as the chief commander of the army that happened to be at Ticonderoga. On the other, because Schuyler was not specifically removed, he might be thought to continue in the supreme command at Albany. Gates wishfully maintained that Congress had "at length Resolved" to approve all the appointments he had recommended to the committee, including his own as the sole major general at Albany. Congress did, indeed, name St. Clair as his second in command and instruct him, as Gates had advised, to remain temporarily in Philadelphia as manpower and material coordinator. Also, Gates's nominee to replace Dr. Stringer, Dr. Jonathan Potts, was appointed director of hospitals for the northern army.[18] But Gates could not erase the maddening ambiguity of that congressional resolution. The truth was that the narrow majority that favored him had not been strong enough unequivocally to remove Schuyler.

On the day Gates left Philadelphia to take up his post, he learned that New York had begun a campaign to recall him. Schuyler and William Duer arrived in town as the state's newly elected delegates to Congress. The annals of April 7 do not record whether he met with them; it made no difference. Their presence signified that the New York Provincial Congress was now under the control of the speculators in New Hampshire lands. The state's former delegates—Francis Lewis, William Floyd, and Lewis Morris—had been recalled. They had not opposed the Vermonters or prevented the appointment of Gates. Schuyler, as one replacement, had been elected over Lewis's objections in a stormy session of the state legislature. Duer, a second replacement, had been a state representative of Charlotte County, which claimed within its borders the contested land in the New Hampshire Grants west of the Green Mountains. The remaining two New York congressmen shortly to arrive in Philadelphia were James Duane and Philip Livingston. Duane, a speculator in enormous New Hampshire tracts, was a brother-in-law of Schuyler's nephew, Walter Livingston, who had been forced to resign as deputy commissary of the northern department by Gates's friend Joseph Trumbull. Philip Livingston was an uncle of Duane's wife. A coterie more united behind Schuyler and hostile to Gates would be difficult to find.[19]

Gates encountered Duane on his way north. Wearing a brown broadcloth coat, striped dimity waistcoat, and leather breeches, Duane was hurrying his horse to Philadelphia. With a sly look, he remarked that the northern department could not be directed from Ticonderoga. Gates detested him as the ringleader of the "New York gang." Either Duane was implying that Gates's assignment to Ticonderoga was a subordinate one, or he was urging him to expose himself at Albany to the charge of usurping Schuyler's place.[20]

Gates had already decided to set up headquarters at Albany until July, when he expected the British assault. Then he would transfer to Ticonderoga. When he arrived at Albany he found a dispirited and disorganized army. "Apathy seems to have pervaded Our whole System," he wrote Hancock, "which, I am apprehensive, nothing but the Cannon of the Enemy will awaken." The immediate problem, he quickly decided, was the vulnerability of old Fort Ticonderoga. It must be evacuated and the defenses concentrated on the east side of the lake at Mount Independence. Again he had to contend with the opposition of the New York legislature. Gouverneur Morris, writing for his colleagues at Kingston, warned that "the Temper of the People will not bear any more Retreats." Gates appealed to Congress, but Congress dodged the responsibility; it gave him freedom to make his own decision.[21] This was more than an isolated denial of support; it was the harbinger of his removal from the northern command. He learned on May 1 from his friend Lovell that Schuyler's allies in Philadelphia were arguing that Schuyler was the "one single man" who could keep New York united for independence. Duane, indeed, had laid down the line they would take: Ticonderoga was too confined a location from which to direct the operations of the entire northern department. Gates had been assigned to Ticonderoga, not Albany, and that established his subordination to Schuyler. Gates poured out his rage on Lovell:

> Unhappy State: that has but one man in it who can fix the wavering minds of its inhabitants to the side of freedom! How could you sit patiently, and, uncontradicted, suffer such impertinence to be crammed down your throats? . . . Nothing is more certain, than that the enemy must first possess that single rock [Ticonderoga] before they can penetrate the country. Where, then, ought the commanding general to be posted? Certainly, at Ticonderoga. If General Schuyler is solely to possess all the power, all the intelligence, and that particular favorite, the military chest, and constantly reside at Albany, I cannot, with any peace of mind, serve at Ticonderoga.[22]

It was a calculated rage. Calculation is the only explanation for a succession of outbursts that in the end won for him his coveted command. The first step was to make it officially clear that he would never again serve under

Schuyler. To this end he wrote Hancock, pretending that he had heard from him the news of his impending replacement that in fact had come from Lovell. If he was to "be degraded," he stormed, he would request "an Honourable Dismission."[23] His purpose was to prevent being ordered to revert to second in command.

The second step was to neutralize any effort to return him to the adjutant generalship. To accomplish this, he seized on a disagreement with Washington so as to magnify it into a dispute that would make clear their incompatibility. Washington had rejected Gates's requisition for tents on the ground that the northern army was stationary and could build huts. Gates heatedly replied, "Refusing This Army, what you have not in your power to bestow is one thing; but saying This Army has not the same Necessities, or does not require the same Comforts, as the Southern Armies, is another; . . . the Service to the Northward, required Tents as much as any Service I ever saw." He then dug deeper and appealed over Washington's head to Hancock. Predictably, Washington was incensed. He answered with a charge that Gates had given him tardy news of reports of a planned enemy offensive against Ticonderoga, which, although later discredited, might have inspired attacks by Howe to the south. Gates fired back that the rumor had been received long before he arrived at Albany, and that the delinquent report had been sent by Wayne, the commandant at Ticonderoga. He countered with a charge of his own, that Washington was contravening the orders of Congress: "Your Excellency says this Army will be Stationary:—if by that, You mean they are to be fixed solely for the defence of a particular post, or posts, I should be glad immediately to receive Your Command thereupon, having already received a Resolve of Congress upon that Subject.—I wish to know if Your Excellency's Orders Correspond with their Resolve." The rupture was complete. "Let an Impartial, moderating Power, decide between Us," he demanded of Lovell, "and do not suffer Southern Prejudices, to Weigh heavier in the Balance than the Northern." He would not even comply with Washington's request for monthly returns, being too occupied with more important duties, and not being "infected with Caeoethes Scribendi."[24]

An hour before this letter reached Lovell, Congress reinstated Schuyler in the northern command. The New Yorkers had conducted a skillful campaign. New Congressmen were entertained with lavish hospitality. Schuyler was exonerated of financial irregularities. His explanations of the offensive letters he had sent to Congress were accepted. A last minute-attempt by Gates's supporters to reassign Schuyler as second in command to Washington was fought back. A move to designate Ticonderoga as a command separate from Albany was defeated. Gates might still have won if Rhode Island had been represented and if two radicals from New Jersey had been present to swing their state. The vote was 5 to 4. Gates was instructed to choose between serving under Schuyler or returning to the adjutant generalship under Washington. Curiously, twelve days after his removal he was informed by the Board of War that a thousand tents were on their way to the northern army.[25]

Gates's friends in Congress urged him to remain patiently at Ticonderoga and trust to them to advance his interests. He refused. They argued that the Schuyler forces had made a serious blunder that would redound to Gates's benefit. They had put Schuyler up for election as governor of New York. If he won, he would have to resign the northern command voluntarily or be forced to do so on a charge of dictatorial concentration of power. If he lost, he would also lose his credibility as the indispensable unifying force in New York. Either way the path would be opened for Gates to return to the command. He would not be persuaded. He liked better the counsels of younger, more impetuous advisers. His aide James Wilkinson angrily told him that Congress had "insulted" him and was "guilty of the fellest Ingratitude." His own son Bob hotly pressed him to resign and "not tarnish the hitherto unspotted honour of your family."[26]

Gates himself was only deceptively impetuous. He was not going to allow himself to be pressured into yielding to the unpalatable alternatives Congress had handed him. Ticonderoga, in view of Congress's evasion of the responsibility for its evacuation, was an impossible assignment. Schuyler's refusal to approve the fortification of Sugar Loaf Hill made the old fort virtually defenseless. Schuyler favored operations in western New York over those in the Champlain Valley. His unpopularity with the New England militia was discouraging the massive turnout Gates considered essential for an expanded northern army. The adjutant generalship, of course, was out of the question.

Schuyler, after his own political junket, could not refuse to grant him leave to carry his refusal to Congress in person. He was in Philadelphia by June 16, and he promptly arranged with Roger Sherman to be admitted to the floor of Congress.[27] Two days later he presented himself at the door of the meeting chamber in the State House. Sherman informed the members that he wished admittance. "For what purpose?" demanded hostile William Paca, of Maryland. "To communicate Intelligence of Importance," Sherman replied. Gates was ushered in. What followed was reported by William Duer. Gates "sat himself in a very Easy Cavalier Posture in an Elbow Chair." He drew from his pocket a set of notes and began to recite a rosy summary of the salutary reforms he had introduced at Ticonderoga. His voice rose. After these services, he railed, he had been dismissed "without any previous Reason Assigned—without any Cause of Offense given—without having lost one single Hour that could be usefully employed in the Service of the United States." He had "quitted an easy and happy Life" to fight for the "Liberties of America." He recited his qualifications and years of experience: "My Rank, my Station, my Services entitled me to more Regard than such unceremonious Treatment." To the charge that his appointment was only to a secondary command at Ticonderoga, he replied that Ticonderoga was "the proper and only Post for the Commander in Chief of the Northern Army." To the criticism that he had headquartered at Albany in violation of his assignment to Ticonderoga, he answered that he had planned to transfer there in mid-June, in time to meet the British attack due in mid-July. He declared that Duane's deep-seated animosity had revealed itself in their meeting on the road two months earlier. Duane rose to protest the personal attack. Paca moved that Gates be ordered to withdraw. Duer seconded the motion and charged Gates with unbecoming conduct. "I plainly saw that he was brought in with an Intention to browbeat the New York Members, whom he considers as his Mortal Enemies," Duer wrote Schuyler, "and I was determin'd to let him see that it was indifferent to me whether I offended him or not." More opponents and defenders of Gates entered the fray. He joined in the shouting. "His Manner was ungracious and Totally devoid of all Dignity," wrote Duer, "his Delivery incoherent and interrupted with frequent Chasms, in which he was poring over his Scattered Notes, and the Tenor of his Discourse a Compound of Vanity, Folly, and Rudeness." Finally he stormed out. He was informed that in future he must submit all communications in writing.[28]

The New Yorkers' elation was undisguised. "I must put up with the General's displeasure," said Duane, "Which I find myself disposed to do with great Resignation and Philosophy." Duer even gloated that he might have goaded Gates to a duel and was perfectly prepared to "act with Spirit, to enable me to discharge with Fidelity the Trust reposed in me."[29]

Twelve days later Congress resolved that it never intended the raising and officering of Seth Warner's regiment of Green Mountain Boys to be the opening wedge for recognition of the New Hampshire Grants as a separate state.[30] The New Yorkers' victory seemed complete.

Except that Schuyler was defeated for the governorship of New York State by George Clinton, the small-farmers' candidate. Was he indispensable?

❧12❧

Ticonderoga

I N QUEBEC ON MAY 6, BURGOYNE handed Carleton Germain's letter of dismissal. He read it with unconcealed outrage. This replacement by "an inferior officer" to whom he was to "act in a subaltern office," he harshly wrote back, was the blow intended from the beginning to follow "every kind of slight, disregard, and censure." Toward Burgoyne he put on a show of good sportsmanship. He would, he assured him, extend full and unstinted cooperation; he would not hold him responsible for Germain's venality. But he held on jealously to his authority as long as the army remained in Canada, and he delayed yielding up a copy of Germain's instructions until the expedition was about to cross over into New York. "My situation," Burgoyne confided to his friend Brigadier General Simon Fraser, "is critical and delicate." Fraser was not so restrained. Carleton, he declared, was "a proud, austere, narrow-minded man, disappointed in all his views of ambition, environed by flatterers, Dependants & Sycophants."[1]

If Carleton's zeal was less than sufficient, what might be expected of his protégé, Baron von Riedesel, whose German troops constituted half the entire invading army? He was camped at Trois Rivières, midway to Montreal from Quebec along the St. Lawrence. Burgoyne left Quebec on May 15 for Montreal, the expedition's operations base, and planned to stop at Trois Rivières. The road, thick with mud from the spring thaw, lay along the north bank of the St. Lawrence. Nine miles outside Quebec, a tavern run by a Dutch proprietress provided sausages and beer. White-painted stone houses lined the shore, and at each mile was a fifteen-foot-high wooden cross at which the *habitants* never failed to stop for their devotions. At Trois Rivières, the St. Francis flowed into the St. Lawrence to form the majestic Lake St. Pierre. The town was a declining trading center of some three hundred wooden houses which had lost out to Montreal in competition for the fur trade. Now it swarmed with two dragoon squadrons and three infantry companies of Brunswickers. The former government house had been converted to a barracks, and the Ursuline convent to a hospital.[2]

The troops were a conglomerate of unemployed workers, peasants, and criminals who had been lured or pressed into service in order to obtain rental money for their petty princes. The contract signed by the duke of Brunswick gave him an additional £7 4s. 4-1/2d. for every soldier killed or wounded. The recruits obeyed their officers without question, although occasionally they succumbed to fits of homesickness. In battle they were fearsomely proficient with the bayonet. Between them and the British there was no love lost. In a recent scuffle at Montreal, an English officer had called a Hessian cannoneer a "Dutch bugger," at which the Hessian cut his cheek with his sabre, declaring that there was "not a single 'bugger'" in the Hessian army, "only brave soldiers as good as they were themselves."[3]

Riedesel received Burgoyne at his quarters in the parish priest's house. A Hessian by birth, he had resigned from his country's army when passed over for promotion and had obtained a lieutenant colonelcy in the Brunswick service, not scrupling to fight against his own brother in the Saxon army, who once, in night action, unknowingly shot his horse out from under him. His real preference was for service under Frederick II of Prussia. Service under the English, whom he considered "drunk with haughtiness," was for him an unavoidable obligation. Carleton, however, had placed under him a separate corps comprising not only the Brunswick troops and a Hessian artillery company but an English battalion and a force of three hundred Indians. "I cannot deny," Riedesel wrote the duke of Brunswick, "that I am exceedingly flattered."

After dinner, Riedesel lit his pipe and listened while Burgoyne discussed the coming campaign. The two men had in common their scorn of the rebels. "There are only a few dozen ambitious people who direct this whole affair and who make the whole land unhappy," he wrote his wife three weeks later. "As for the others, they do not know why they fight."[4] But although he allowed no displeasure to show through his mask of politeness, he did not welcome Burgoyne's displacement of Carleton.

Burgoyne outlined his plans: the British troops, led by himself, would march down the west bank of Lake Champlain. Riedesel and his Germans would take the east bank. The fleet, under Captain Skeffington Lutwidge, would provide cover from the water. Lieutenant Colonel Barry St. Leger (pronounced Sellinger) would lead his Thirty-fourth Regiment, with Loyalist and Indian support, on a sweep through Fort Stanwix to Albany. Burgoyne assured Riedesel that he would at all times welcome the free expression of his opinions and continued on his way to Montreal.

Two weeks later, Carleton passed through Trois Rivières and remained closeted with Riedesel for more than an hour. It was plain that Carleton intended to resign before the year ended. Riedesel's distaste for Burgoyne deepened. "God knows what he will do with the Canadian army which has already been a whip to his ambition," he wrote the duke of Brunswick.[5]

In Montreal, at last, loyal friends awaited. Burgoyne's second in command, his personal choice, was Major General William Phillips, an artilleryman with an outstanding record at Minden and Warburg in the Seven Years' War. Had it not been for his preparations during the winter and spring, the invasion would not have been possible. He was a close friend of Henry Clinton but bore no grudge against Burgoyne for having preempted the Canadian command. Self-indulgent, he ordered his servants about, said an acquaintance, with "the single nod of his black head or the wave of his lily-white hand."[6]

Simon Fraser was camped across the St. Lawrence at Boucherville with his elite advance corps of fifteen hundred, and he lined it up for Burgoyne's inspection along a route of a mile and a half. Major John Dyke Acland's battalion of grenadiers, picked for their height, stood still taller in their high, brass-plated caps. Their red coats had been shortened so as to make patches with the tails, and incidentally were more suitable for summer. Major the earl of Balcarres exhibited his light-infantry battalion of skirmishers drawn from the entire army. Their cumbersome, three-cornered felt hats had been trimmed down to lightweight caps. Major Robert Grant displayed his Twenty-fourth Foot, wearing trimmings of red lined with white. Captain Alexander Fraser (Simon's nephew) put his seven-months-old corps of sharpshooters through the open-formation woodland maneuvers he had taught them.

Phillips also staged a grand review in Montreal on the heights behind the Fauburg de Recollets. Bands played and banners waved as 42 artillery guns were drawn by—24-, 12-, 6-, and 3-pounders, 2 to be assigned to each regiment and 10 to remain as a separate gun park. (There were 96 more pieces waiting on shipboard to be transported down Lake Champlain for use against Ticonderoga.) Phillips introduced the two brigade commanders of the army's right infantry wing. Brigadier General James Hamilton led the Ninth Regiment, wearing red trimmings faced with yellow; the Forty-seventh, also wearing red faced with yellow; and the Fifty-third, wearing red faced with red. Brigadier General Henry W. Powell led the Twentieth, wearing red faced with pale yellow; the Twenty-first, wearing red faced with blue; and the Sixty-second, wearing red faced with yellowish buff. Burgoyne addressed the men, praising them and exhorting them to high adventure, conveying warm comradeship. "The troops are in a state of health almost unprecedented," he wrote home to Adjutant General Edward Harvey.[7]

But there were not enough of them. Recruiters in Britain garnered what unemployed artisans, poverty-stricken Scotch highlanders, and commuted criminals they could find, yet even with enlistment terms shortened to three years instead of the usual life term most Englishmen had no desire for the army's low pay, harsh discipline, alternating boredom and butchery, and despised social status. The shortage had to be made up with nonnationals. In his "Thoughts" paper, Burgoyne had called for an army of 8,000 regulars, 2,000 Canadians, 1,000 Indians, and a corps of watermen. Germain authorized 7,173 regulars, and 7,251 actually joined Burgoyne—4,135 British and 3,116 Germans. Only 150 sullen and unarmed French Canadians were assembled at Montreal, and Burgoyne complained to Carleton that he had expected "six times the number of these Companies." Carleton replied that "if Government laid any great stress upon assistance from the Canadians for carrying on the present war, it surely was not upon information proceeding from me." Not a single work party levied by corvée could be induced to cross the American border. A paltry total of approximately 500 French Canadians eventually served with Burgoyne, and General Phillips reported that "most of them run away, in such a way that the Transport of provision is nearly stopt." The number of Indians, too, fell far below Burgoyne's expectations. A thousand were obtained for St. Leger's expedition, but even after enlisting the support of former French officers La Corne St. Luc and Charles Michel de Langlade, who were popular with the western Ottawas, only 500 Indians in all joined Burgoyne, chiefly Algonquins, Abenakis, and Hurons from lower Canada.[8]

Still more ominous were deficiencies of land transport and supply. Carleton's thinking and preparations during the winter had gone no further than a lakeside attack on Ticonderoga. Commissary general Nathaniel Day, a friend of Burgoyne, had stockpiled sufficient provisions for that operation at St. Johns, the expedition's launching point. Captain Lutwidge had assembled a formidable flotilla. The newly constructed *Royal George,* twenty-four guns, and the *Inflexible,* twenty guns, were the largest vessels. In addition, there were the *Carleton, Lady Maria,* and *Loyal Convert* and the three American ships captured at Valcour Island, the *Washington,* the *Lee,* and the *New Jersey.* Five hundred bateaux would serve as troop transports, twenty-eight craft as gunboats, and the *Thunderer* as a bomb ketch. Lieutenant John Schank, a brilliant naval engineer, had provided a self-navigating, floating bridge to connect Crown Point with the eastern shore of the lake and large booms to destroy the American bridge near Ticonderoga. But beyond Ticonderoga, Carleton had made no provision for transport of equipment between Lake Champlain and Lake George or maintenance of an extended supply line from home base. As early as January 26, Day had called Carleton's attention to this omission, but he had done nothing.[9]

When Burgoyne arrived at Montreal, Day warned him that to subsist a ten-thousand-man army on the march it was imperative to obtain 1,125 carts, each capable of carrying thirty days' provisions of eight hundred pounds. Alarmed, Burgoyne sent Carleton an urgent request for the hiring of seven to eight hundred horses and a corvée of a thousand French Canadians to drive them. When Carleton, though agreeable, could not promise prompt delivery, Burgoyne took matters into his own hands. The best he could do was to contract with Jacob Jordon, a Montreal merchant, for four hundred artillery horses and five hundred two-horse carts. These could each carry only fourteen days' provisions, and they would not be able to transport bateaux, tents, and baggage from Lake George to the Hudson. He would have to pick up horses and wagons on the way.

The task of establishing a supply line from Montreal to the lakes he turned over to Phillips, who weedled from Carleton the loan of the Thirty-first Regiment to man a chain of posts at Sorel, Fort Chambly, Fort St. Johns, Ile aux Noix, and Point au Feu from which the French Canadians of the corvée could be supervised.[10]

It was a far different situation than Burgoyne had allowed himself to expect. As late as May 19 he had written Harvey that he was "exceedingly satisfied with all that has been done" and was planning to put his troops in motion without awaiting the arrival of fleets from England and Ireland. But a month later he was writing Germain that his difficulties were delaying him to a degree "unknown in other services."[11]

He might plausibly have argued that the expedition should be held up until transport could be assured for the last and most crucial leg of the long trek to Albany. He might even have decided that the attempt should be abandoned. He did not. Afterward he steadfastly insisted that he had no choice; his instructions expressly ordered him "to pass Lake Champlain and from thence by the most vigorous exertion of the force under his command to proceed with all expedition to Albany and put himself under the command of Sir William Howe." At least that was what he wished to believe. Not to go forward meant losing the last hope of achieving the glory and eminence for which he yearned, and there was a physical reason, perhaps the uppermost of all: he dreaded northern winters. His return to England the two previous winters had been motivated in considerable measure by desire to escape the subzero cold. If his invasion was to take place at all, it must be early, before another northern winter set in. It was not difficult to convince himself. His image had been built upon audacity. A campaign of risk was in character.

Having already made his mind up, he was hardly likely to be deterred by a discordant letter from Howe that Carleton brought to Montreal. "The force your Excellency may deem expedient to advance beyond your frontiers after taking Ticonderoga will I fear have little assistance from hence to facilitate their approach," Howe wrote Carleton. He could not even promise to "communicate with the officer commanding it as soon as I could wish." Then, in typical evasive style, he hedged that he would "endeavor to have a corps upon the lower part of Hudson's River sufficient to open the communication for shipping through the Highlands, at present obstructed by several forts erected by the rebels for that purpose, which corps may afterwards act in favour of the northern army."[12] Burgoyne brushed the letter aside. It had been written April 5, too early for Howe to have received instructions from Germain or letters that Burgoyne had sent him before embarking from England and after arriving at Quebec. Burgoyne was, of course, totally in the dark concerning Howe's long-gestated and elaborately contrived design to downgrade the northern invasion. He believed that Howe was just as duty bound to meet him at Albany as he was to force his way south and no more free to vary Germain's instructions than he was to veer instead through New England toward Newport for a junction with Clinton's force in Rhode Island. In any case, it was too late to change plans.

The issue of Howe's letter raises a damaging question about Carleton. He had received the letter on May 26 but had held onto it for two weeks before sending a copy to Burgoyne on June 10. Carleton had joined Burgoyne a week earlier in Montreal and could have given it to him then. He recognized the significance of the letter, for when he did transmit it he included the acid comment that Howe was "wishing you a happy and Successful Campaign."[13] If Burgoyne had received it earlier, he might have canceled the expedition before preparations had gone too far. Why, then, did Carleton delay? It would seem that, as he was already withholding Germain's instructions until Burgoyne departed, it was consistent to do the same with Howe's related letter. But in so doing he was allowing his animus toward Germain and his protectiveness of his own supremacy of command as long as the expedition remained in Canada to overrule Burgoyne's need to know. Burgoyne was clearly not going to shake off the disability of a divided command at least until he crossed over the border to New York.

That would happen only when the expedition actually embarked from St. Johns, where the troopships were waiting. Burgoyne arrived there on June 11; Carleton joined him the next day. That afternoon, Phillips hosted a farewell dinner for all the generals. In the midst of the festivities, a messenger from Quebec was admitted with word that a convoy of thirty-nine vessels had arrived. Fifteen were transports, carrying eleven British companies and four hundred chasseurs from Hanau; the rest were supply ships. For Riedesel there was the special news that his wife and three children were aboard. The following morning Carleton reviewed the troops. Atop the mast of the *Thunderbird,* anchored in the Richelieu, the Royal Standard was unfurled, normally displayed only when a member of the royal family was present. A day later Carleton returned to Quebec. Burgoyne boarded his flagship, the *Lady Maria,* and signaled the start of the voyage down the Richelieu into Lake Champlain.

The troops were to rendezvous on the western shore of the lake at Sandy Bluff, now Cumberland Head and the present site of the city of Plattsburgh. Contrary winds kept them there, their first occupation of American soil, for three days. To his officers, Burgoyne breathed confidence. His army of professionals—"they could not have been selected more to his Satisfaction"—would overcome all obstacles against a conglomeration of undisciplined provincials. The officers were to "inculcate in the men's minds a Reliance upon the Bayonet," the trump to the Americans' "whole dependence in Entrenchments and Rifle pieces." Retreat was not to be considered except against far superior numbers.[14]

On the morning of June 20, two cannon of the *Lady Maria* boomed the signal for the resumption of the main army's advance up the shore of the lake to the next stop, twenty miles south at Ligonier Bay. Not a breeze was stirring, and the lake, wrote Sergeant Roger Lamb of the Ninth Foot, looked like "an indefinitely extended mirror." The armada "moved majestically along in perfect order." The Indians led the way in their birch canoes, each of which contained twenty or thirty warriors. Next, in lines four bateaux abreast, came the advance guard of Brunswickers, consisting of a company of chasseurs (*jägers*), forty Rangers from England, a battalion of light infantry, and a battalion of light grenadiers, commanded by Lieutenant Colonel Heinrich Christoph Breymann, an intrepid martinet. Behind them followed Riedesel's own regiment of dragoons, then the *Royal George* and the *Inflexible,* towing Schank's battering booms, and the rest of the brigs and sloops. At a distance of four hundred yards was Powell's First British Brigade. (Hamilton's Second British Brigade had been detained at Sorel to protect the transports and magazines there.) Now came Burgoyne on the *Lady Maria* and Phillips and Riedesel in their pinnaces. Bringing up the rear were the First German Brigade, under Brigadier General Johann Friedrich von Specht, and the Second German Brigade, under Brigadier General W. R. von Gall, which included his own Hesse-Hanau regiment.

When the flotilla arrived at Ligonier Bay at midday, Burgoyne turned over the command to Riedesel and sailed ahead to join Simon Fraser's advance corps five miles to the south, which had made camp at the Bouquet River, thirty miles north of Crown Point.[15]

Before moving against Crown Point, Burgoyne issued a proclamation to the Americans. He came, he announced, on a crusade to restore the "general privileges of Mankind." The rebel leaders had traduced the British Constitution. He would strike down "the completest system of Tyranny that ever God in his displeasure suffer'd for a time to be exercised over a froward and stubborn Generation," and he would reestablish the "blessings of legal Government." He invited the Americans to join in this "glorious task." He would not molest noncombatants if they remained quietly in their homes, made available their cattle, corn, and forage, and did not destroy roads and bridges in the path of the army. If, however, they continued stubborn, he would "stand acquitted in the eyes of God and Men in denouncing and executing the vengeance of the state against wilful outcasts." He would "give stretch to the Indian Forces under my direction" to wreak "devastation, famine, and every concomitant horror" upon the miscreants.[16]

More than anything he had until then written, this threat revealed how profoundly he failed to comprehend the temper of the Americans. He persisted in viewing the rebellion as an aberration. Puritan republicanism he considered a "profanation of religion." The gullible masses had been deluded; they might as easily be intimidated. There is no evidence that he had ever conversed with an American Patriot. In London he had listened to embittered Thomas Hutchinson; in Boston he had met only Tories who had preferred to remain within the British lines. Now, in his invasion army, his closest advisor was Philip Skene, "a famous marplot" and the proprietor of a

56,350-acre estate, Skenesboro (at the present Whitehall), twenty miles south of Ticonderoga on the east side of Lake Champlain. Two other doctrinaire Loyalists in the expedition, John Peters and Ebenezer Jessup, had even persuaded Burgoyne that they could recruit several battalions from among the settlers of the Champlain and Hudson valleys.[17]

Yet Burgoyne was not inhumane. Very different from his proclamation was an address he delivered in person to the Indians the next day. Four hundred Iroquois assembled at the Bouquet River on a refugee's estate. "I positively forbid blood-shed, when you are not opposed by arms," he warned. "Aged men, women, children, and prisoners, must be held sacred from the knife or hatchet . . . on no account or pretence, or subtilty, or prevarication, are they [scalps] to be taken from the wounded." It was a dangerous game to play. He was confident, he wrote Howe, that he could "keep up their terror and avoid their cruelty." But when a copy of his speech was received in England, Edmund Burke heaped ridicule on the contradiction. Suppose, he asked in the House of Commons, there was a riot in the menagerie in the Tower of London. "What would the keeper of His Majesty's lions do? would he not fling open the dens of the wild beasts, and then address them thus? 'My gentle lions, my humane bears, my sentimental wolves, my tender-hearted hyenas, go forth; but I exhort ye, as ye are Christians and members of civilized society, to take care not to hurt any man, woman, or child.'"[18]

Instead of announcing a crusade, Burgoyne's proclamation branded his coming as an invasion of barbarians. The mere mention of Indians was enough to send a horrified chill down the spine of every farmer and every townsman who had known in his own family or community of an atrocity. "We offer our heads to the scalping-knife and our bellies to the bayonet," jeered pamphleteer Francis Hopkinson. Governor William Livingston of New Jersey promised that the Patriots would soon prove that the struggle for liberty was more than a "civil hickup."[19] The populace that Burgoyne aimed most to intimidate was the most aroused. The nervous frontiersmen of the New Hampshire Grants saw themselves as the first victims in the path of the horde from the north.

Simon Fraser's troops landed at Crown Point on June 25 and found it deserted, its little garrison fled. The main army arrived the next morning. A rear hospital was erected. Across the bay, at Chimney Point, a supply depot was established. Hamilton's brigade had now rejoined the expedition, and,

139

except for a force of Ottawas on the way from western Canada, it was complete. It had only to await the arrival of the vessels carrying the heavy artillery and the bulk of the provisions. In the meantime, the bateaux were caulked with oakum by workmen at Chimney Point. The troops paraded under arms and practiced rapid firing motions. Powder, balls, and paper were distributed for each man to make up one hundred cartridges. By June 30 all was ready for the final leg of the journey to Ticonderoga. Food rations were issued for eight days. Twin advance forces were sent ahead to establish footholds three miles from the fort on both sides of the lake—Fraser's on the west and Breymann's on the east. Burgoyne's order of the day was read to the troops:

> The Army embarks tomorrow to approach the Enemy. We are to contend for the King and the Constitution of Great Britain, to vindicate the Law and to relieve the Oppressed. A Cause in which His Majesty's Troops and those of the Princes His Allies, will feel equal Excitement.
>
> The Services required of this particular Expedition are critical and conspicuous. During our progress occasions may occur, in which nor difficulty nor labour nor life are to be regarded. THIS ARMY MUST NOT RETREAT.[20]

At dawn the following morning the men struck their tents and stored them aboard the bateaux. At five o'clock the drumbeat signaled the embarkation. Captain Thomas Hosmer's division of gunboats started at the center of the lake, which was there a mile wide. Riedesel's dragoons formed the advance guard. The British right wing brigades moved in a column of bateaux along the west shore, the German brigades along the east. The sun shone brightly. The drummers and fifers struck up their regimental tunes, and the armada began the eight miles to its destination. The British camped at Four Mile Point (so named for its distance from the fort), the Germans on the opposite side of the lake. The gunboats, the *Royal George,* and the *Inflexible* were within reach of the fort's batteries.[21]

Arthur St. Clair (pronounced Sinclair), as Wayne's replacement, was now in command of the fort. Grandson of a Scottish laird, he had fought as a lieutenant under Wolfe at Quebec and had then married a wealthy Boston heiress and settled on a large estate in the Ligonier Valley of western Pennsylvania. He had served the previous year at Ticonderoga under Gates and subsequently under Washington in Pennsylvania and New Jersey. Congress had dispatched him to Ticonderoga with assurances that any attack on the fort would be no more than a feint designed to forestall northern troops from being sent south to Washington's relief. Burgoyne's army, Washington be-

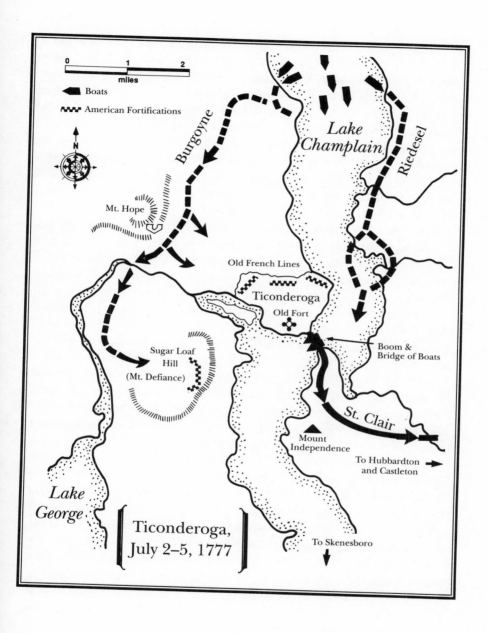

Ticonderoga,
July 2–5, 1777

lieved, would head by sea to join Howe in taking Philadelphia. He was so sure of this that he thought Ticonderoga overmanned. St. Clair was so persuaded that his assignment would be quiet that he took his eleven-year-old son with him, expecting to have time to tutor him. When St. Clair arrived at Albany, he found that Schuyler believed, rather, that Burgoyne would invade in the north but that the British thrust would be either westward toward Fort Stanwix or eastward through New Hampshire; an attack on Ticonderoga would still be a feint. In view of the limited manpower available, Schuyler instructed St. Clair to deemphasize Fort Ticonderoga and concentrate the defense at Mount Independence. Two to three thousand men, he believed, would be sufficient there.

When St. Clair arrived at Ticonderoga, however, he found that a British spy, William Amsbury, captured on the Onion River, had disclosed that Burgoyne was amassing an army of ten thousand, part of which was to penetrate the Mohawk Valley and the remainder to cross Lake Champlain. That put a totally different construction on the situation. Alarmed, St. Clair wrote Schuyler that he was "very ill prepared" for such a siege. He had a total force of only 2,200: 1,576 Continentals, 52 of Whitcomb's rangers, a small crew of artificers, three Hampshire regiments of militia and two of Massachusetts who might at any time decide to return home. With barely seven weeks' supply of meat on hand, he could not request more militia for fear that they might "eat us out before either the arrival of the enemy or the supplies." The powder magazines were leaking fifty pounds a week and there was no paper to make cartridges. He could not see how Mount Independence and Ticonderoga could be defended separately.[22]

Schuyler was already on his way north. He found the situation at Ticonderoga every bit as bad as St. Clair had written. Not only was the old fort on the lake's west side vulnerable, but Mount Independence on the east had been denuded of an essential abbattis (a barrier of felled, interlaced trees), which had been used for firewood during the winter. Construction of the bridge across the lake was going slowly because there were no draught cattle to do the hauling. The boom was unfinished because all the caissons had not been sunk and there was not sufficient rope for the cables. The men were in rags, some of them without shoes. An epidemic of measles was spreading. If St. Clair's entire force were strung in single file along the lines of defense, the men would hardly be within shouting distance of each other.[23]

The crisis called for new thinking, a challenge to which Schuyler was unequal. In the face of British naval superiority, the Americans were never going to prevent their passage up the lake. The best that could be hoped for was to delay their advance while keeping open an escape route to the south. To attempt to hold both Fort Ticonderoga and Mount Independence with limited manpower was futile, as had already been recognized. But it was Mount Independence, not Fort Ticonderoga, that had to be abandoned. Mount Independence could too easily be isolated by enemy forces landed above and below it. Fort Ticonderoga, however, had an escape road that led to Lake George, where the British ships on Lake Champlain could not follow because of the two-hundred-foot falls and rapids of the outlet that connected the two waters. A strong American force could be stationed two miles northeast of the fort at Mount Hope, a ridge that overlooked the escape road's timber bridge that spanned the Lake George outlet. A barbette battery had already been built on its flat summit. Mount Hope not only covered the escape route; it also protected the old fort from British occupation of Sugar Loaf Hill (later renamed Mount Defiance), situated immediately on the other side of the bridge, fourteen hundred yards away. The escape route might not even prove necessary, for a British attack on land might well be repelled by the cross fire between the artillery on Mount Hope and at the old fort. If the British force did become overwhelming, the Americans had only to cross and destroy the bridge and then dash over to Lake George, where their bateaux, kept in waiting, would convey them to shelter at Fort George at the southern tip of the lake.

Schuyler could think only of the censure he would provoke if he lost his whole garrison, as had happend at Fort Washington on the Hudson. He had been burned once over the evacuation of Crown Point. He was not an innovator or a risk taker. No more than he had recognized the vulnerability of Sugar Loaf Hill in 1776 did he now perceive the opportunity that a substantial fortification of Mount Hope offered for a phased withdrawal, even for trapping the enemy with a pincers movement from the old fort. He admitted afterward in testimony that by July 20 he had collected five thousand men at Fort Edward, twelve miles below Lake George, who, if adequately supplied, might have been sent up to Mount Hope. But he would make no move unless authorized by Congress. Rather than accept the responsibility, he convened a war council of St. Clair and the fort's brigadiers—Enoch Poor of New Hampshire, John Paterson of Massachusetts, and the Frenchman Matthias Alexis Roche de Fermoy. Only Poor seems to have sensed the need to fortify Mount Hope, if we may judge from his subsequent testimony that "we ought to have had possession of two hills without the French lines, as also the one on the other side of the Lake, known by the name of Mount Defiance," but there is no evidence that he spoke for it. St. Clair had been warned, in a letter from

Gates, of the vulnerability of Sugar Loaf Hill, but there is no evidence that he took notice of it. The strategic potential of Mount Hope seems completely to have escaped him. He had no hope of withstanding a siege. His obsessive concern was to save his army from capture. He argued that both sides of the lake must be garrisoned in order to force the British to divide their forces. If Ticonderoga proved untenable, its garrison must cross the bridge and, together with the force at Mount Independence, flee into the back country. Schuyler said nothing; St. Clair's insistence prevailed. The council unanimously voted that if, after abandoning Ticonderoga, the troops found Mount Independence undefendable, it would be "prudent to provide for a retreat."[24]

With the responsibility now entirely in his own hands, St. Clair's only real remaining decision was the timing of the evacuation. In this his plan was as much political as military. The logical move would appear to have been an immediate withdrawal, but he wished not to appear spineless and planned instead to put up a last-minute token show of resistance. He therefore delayed, claiming ignorance of the overwhelming size of the British army despite the very reports that had aroused his apprehensions. He hoped to lure the British into a frontal assault on Ticonderoga with only the west shore half of their force. The Americans would be strong enough to repel the first attack wave but not a full-scale investment. They would be justified in crossing over to the east and eventual escape.

Burgoyne was as much in the dark about the size of the American force as St. Clair was of the British. Basing his estimates on information from prisoners and deserters, he anticipated a total of between six and ten thousand, of which between three and four thousand would be positioned on the west side of the lake. He therefore waited for the arrival of heavy artillery and ammunition. On July 2, however, at nine o'clock in the morning, smoke was seen to rise westward from the northern end of Lake George. St. Clair had ordered the destruction of the bridge and the shorefront blockhouse and sawmills and evacuation of Mount Hope. He explained to Schuyler that the blockhouse had been "attacked several times and was surrounded yesterday all day."[25] But Burgoyne's dispatch reported no such engagement. St. Clair's precipitous move invites speculation. Was he, after all, indeed sensitive to the vulnerability of Sugar Loaf Hill and attempting to entice Burgoyne to occupy it and force an immediate American evacuation of Ticonderoga so as to eliminate the hazard of even a token resistance?

Such, in fact, was the result. When a scouting party informed Burgoyne that the Americans were evacuating Mount Hope, he ordered Brigadier Simon Fraser forward with a five-hundred-man detachment of the advance corps and a body of Rangers and Indians to occupy the mount and intercept the retreating Americans. The Indians, dizzy with drink, approached too close to the old French lines and provoked a barrage that killed one British officer and two privates, but by the next day Mount Hope was a beehive of redcoats. Phillips had come up with the rest of Fraser's advance corps, Hamilton's First Brigade, and two artillery brigades. To the left of Hamilton's was Powell's Second Brigade, extending eastward to Three Mile Point, where von Gall's Second German Brigade had been brought over from the east side of the lake to fill the gap left by Fraser's corps. The following day the *Thunderer* arrived from Crown Point and began, amid ineffectual American shelling, to unload its battering train and stores. Burgoyne now had the superior strength for a frontal assault on the old French lines, but he had no intention of justifying the Americans' "supposition that we should only attack them upon the point where they were best prepared to resist." He had heard of Montcalm's remark, back in the days of the French occupation, that, for the defenders, Ticonderoga without the accompanying possession of Sugar Loaf Hill was only "a doorway to disgrace for a gentleman." He was amazed to discover that the Americans had done nothing to fortify the hill, a sure sign "that they have no men of military science."[26] A construction crew was put to work rebuilding the bridge across the Lake George outlet. Lieutenant William Twiss, chief of the corps of engineers, climbed Sugar Loaf Hill and reported to Phillips that, from the crest, Ticonderoga was within fourteen hundred yards' firing range, and Mount Independence, fifteen hundred. From that vantage point, any American activity on either side of the lake could be detected, and, with the advantage of a downhill wind, troop and supply movements in boats and across the bridge could be interdicted. Although the hillside was rocky, the incline at its steepest was little more than 15 percent, and a road could be constructed up it within twenty-four hours. The hilltop could easily be leveled for gun emplacements. Burgoyne promptly ordered up a battery of light twenty pounders, medium twelves, and eight-inch howitzers.

Phillips personally directed the operation with a detail of four hundred men. "Where a goat can go a man can go and where a man can go he can drag a gun," he declared. On the northwest side of the hill, hidden from the Americans' view, the men labored in the intense July heat, felling trees, clearing brush, and smoothing the way around the boulders. Cattle hauled the logs aside while others worked their way upward with the cannon. That night, two medium twelve pounders were installed on the top of Sugar Loaf Hill.[27]

St. Clair testified at his court-martial that only on July 3 did he learn the true extent of the invasion army, from a prisoner and some deserters taken at the French lines. The prisoner was an informed old soldier. An American artillery officer disguised as a down-at-the-heels Loyalist was sent with a bottle of rum to join him in the guard room. By midnight the prisoner had revealed the number, name, and strength of every corps under Burgoyne. Only then, St. Clair testified, did he decide that resistance was impossible. He added, however, that to check these figures he sent a spy behind the British lines who returned two days later with a full verification.[28] How, the question arises, was it suddenly so easy to obtain such information?

The spy returned just when St. Clair had detected the British fortification of Sugar Loaf Hill. Some of the British blamed the Indians for lighting a giveaway fire. No matter. St. Clair had an excuse for what he had already decided. At three o'clock that afternoon, he summoned his brigadiers and Colonel Pierce Long, commander of a New Hampshire regiment of Continentals, to a council of war. They knew what he expected of them. He had made up his mind that even if they all opposed him he would go ahead with evacuation. Briefly, he sketched their situation: there were 2,089 rank and file fit for duty out of a total of 3,300, "many of those mere boys, altogether incapable of sustaining the fatigues of a soldier, naked and ill-armed, not above one bayonet to every tenth man," 900 recently arrived short-term militia, a small artillery corps, and 124 civilian workmen. He neglected to mention 457 troops just arrived from outlying duty. The council had no alternative. The only remaining escape route, by the road east of Mount Independence to Castleton, was still open. Despite orders, Riedesel had not as yet occupied the three-quarter-mile neck of land between Lake Champlain and East Creek behind the mount but according to spies' reports was planning to do so the next day, thus denying the Americans access to the road. When the British on the lake broke through the boom, cutting off water escape, the Americans would be doomed. The council voted unanimously to evacuate that night.[29]

The decision was kept secret from the men until the moment of departure in order to prevent leakage to the enemy. Cannon were fired all through the night to distract the enemy's attention. The new moon set early, leaving protective shadow. At midnight the signal was given. A high wind was blowing. Amid inevitable confusion, Colonel Pierce Long and his regiment of four or five hundred carried the sick and wounded and as much of the armament and provisions as they could manage aboard the 2 galleys, 2 schooners, a sloop, and 220 smaller boats moored on the lake, to be sailed thirty miles south to Skenesboro. Some of the cannon left behind were spiked. The rest of the troops streamed over the bridge, still undiscovered by the British. Despite the disorder, by two o'clock they were all across at Mount Independence. There, however, the commander de Fermoy had made no preparations for his men to join them and was found sound asleep. To make matters worse, despite the prohibition of fires, he burned his head-quarters atop the mount. But luck was with the Americans: the British thought the blaze a trick to lure them into a futile attack. Burgoyne, aboard the *Royal George,* slept through the night. At daybreak, St. Clair started his troops through the woods to Castleton.[30]

✳13✳

Escape

IT WAS NOT UNTIL DAWN ON JULY 5 that Fraser, on the west side of the lake, realized, from accounts brought in by three American deserters, that Ticonderoga's defenders had crossed to the east. He immediately dispatched a detail to occupy the evacuated fort, where sixty cannon were found still unspiked, two 2-inch howitzers, two petards, and one 5 1/2-inch mortar, as well as a considerable quantity of round, grape-, and double-headed shot and boxes of shells. Fraser himself sped ahead to the footbridge with eight or nine hundred grenadiers and light infantry. The Americans had attempted to burn the chain of boats, but the water had quenched the fires. The British laid planks across the boats, allowing passage single file. A battery covered the bridge, and four American gunners who were left behind to man it might have raked the crossing British with devastating fire, but they had discovered a cask of Madeira and were lying dead drunk beside their lighted matches. A curious Indian almost did their work for them when he picked up one of the matches and dropped a spark on the priming of one of the cannon, which went off but fortunately was too elevated to hit its mark. Fraser's men crossed safely.[1]

Burgoyne had incomplete intelligence of what had happened. From the size and number of the vessels departing southward, he may have concluded that the primary American escape route was up the lake to Skenesboro. "I turned my chief attention to the pursuit by water," he wrote Germain. But he also ordered Fraser, with his twenty companies of grenadiers and light infantry, to pursue St. Clair by land, supported by Riedesel's infantry regiment and Breymann's reserve corps. Fraser started out at four o'clock in the morning, leaving the slower Riedesel to follow. They covered twenty-four miles in the stifling heat, each man carrying sixty pounds on his back, with no food, over densely wooded hills, swamps, streams, and ponds. By nightfall they

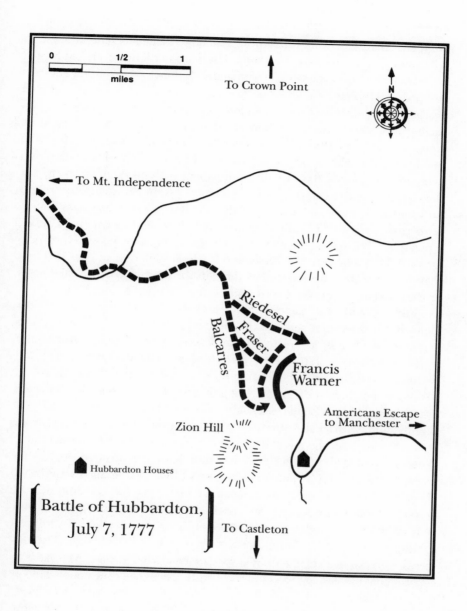

0   1/2   1
miles

To Crown Point

N

To Mt. Independence

Riedesel

Balcarres

Fraser

Francis
Warner

Americans Escape
to Manchester

Zion Hill

Hubbardton Houses

Battle of Hubbardton,
July 7, 1777

To Castleton

stopped, exhausted, near Hubbardton, a small settlement of nine families. St. Clair was six miles away, at Castleton. His rear guard, however, had lagged behind, against his order to its commander, Colonel Seth Warner, and was camped at Hubbardton, three or four miles ahead of Fraser. It included Warner's Green Mountain boys, Colonel Ebenezer Francis's Eleventh Massachusetts Continentals, and Colonel Nathan Hale's Second New Hampshire Continentals. Together with an undetermined number of stragglers from the main body, it totaled approximately 1,000. Fraser estimated them at 2,000 and had himself only 850. Riedesel, impatient with his plodding men, just then came up with a company of jägers detached from Breymann's corps and 80 grenadiers; they camped three miles behind Fraser. Fraser was "much hurt" to discover that Burgoyne had ignored his request for troops, "British, if possible." There were "persons secretly jealous of all my poor endeavors to forward the public service." Fraser and Riedesel conferred and decided that they would both move forward at three in the morning. If the Americans proved too strong, Fraser was to wait for the Germans to join him.[2]

Starting with the dawn's light, Fraser's men sighted Hale's New Hampshires through a notch in the mountains complacently cooking their breakfast beside a little stream, Sucker Brook, without having posted any warning pickets. At 4:40 A.M., Fraser attacked. Hale and his men fled into the woods. One of his captains, James Carr, called after them, "My lads advance, we shall beat them yet," but only a few turned. One who did was a sixteen-year-old fifer, Ebenezer Fletcher. A mere five feet three inches tall and slightly built, with small features and fair complexion, he was still weak from a recent bout with the measles. He took cover and fired his musket once. When he pulled the trigger a second time his piece misfired, and as he brought it up again to his cheek he was hit by a bullet in the small of the back. He crawled for help to his uncle, Daniel Foster, who was standing nearby. Foster and another man carried him back and left him behind a large tree, not far from another wounded man crying loudly in agony. The British were now coming closer and the Americans giving way. Fletcher, though faint and bleeding freely, managed to drag himself on hands and knees eleven yards to concealment under a log in a clump of brush. There he lay in a pool of blood until the battle was over. A British officer, discovering him, exclaimed, "What's such a young rebel as you fighting for?" He had enlisted only a few months earlier, having been a miller's apprentice in New Ipswich, New Hampshire. The bullet had narrowly missed his spine. An obstinate rebel, indeed, he was to escape in a few weeks, although only partially recovered, and eventually serve out the remainder of his three-year enlistment.[3]

Although Hale's men panicked, Warner and Francis had just enough time to rally their troops for a stand. They discharged a volley at the first wave of the charging British; it struck down twenty-one. Major Grant of the Twenty-fourth, who had mounted a tree stump from which to direct his men, was killed instantly. The earl of Balcarres, at the head of his light infantry, was wounded in the left thigh, and five bullets shredded his clothes. The Americans were strung out along an irregular half-mile line, Warner's men on the left near 1,206-foot-high Zion Hill, which guarded the road to Castleton, and Francis's on the right, behind a lower hill. Fraser attempted to turn the American left with an assault on Zion Hill by Major Acland's grenadiers, who were drawn over from the British left. With Fraser in the van, slinging their muskets and hauling themselves up by tree branches and projecting rocks, they reached the top only to find that Francis's men were moving over to the weakened British left. Acland was wounded in the thigh. Some of the Americans fought with no holds barred. According to one British account, a group of sixty of them marched up to two companies of British grenadiers with their arms clubbed, the standard sign of surrender. The British allowed them to advance, but when the Americans were within ten yards they leveled their muskets, fired into their supposed captors, and ran off. The grenadiers gave no quarter to those they caught.[4] Fraser now sent back a desperate plea for help to Riedesel. Riedesel had heard the sounds of the firing and had been pouring imprecations on his troops for their slowness. At last, when the battle had been raging two hours, the jägers and grenadiers arrived. Riedesel, sizing up the situation from an overlooking hill, ordered an immediate charge on the American right by the jägers, led by Captain Carl von Geyso. The grenadiers, under Captain Maximillian Schottelius, were to move around to attack from the rear. With fixed bayonets and a band blaring to give the impression of greater numbers, the jägers advanced, firing while lustily singing their psalms. Fraser's men at first thought they were Francis's Massachusetts covenanters singing Puritan hymns. The contest was furious. Lieutenant Thomas Anburey saw one officer felled by bullets in both eyes, and another, wounded, shot through the heart while being carried off the field. The Americans under Francis fought valiantly, and Burgoyne described him as "one of their best officers." Shot in the right arm, he led his men on. Then a German bullet struck him in the right breast and he dropped dead on his face. "I saw him after he fell," wrote Lieutenant William Digby of the Fifty-third Regiment of Foot, "and his appearance caused me to remark his figure, which was fine & even at that time made me regard him with attention." After that the heart seemed to go out of Francis's men. They saw no relief coming from the main army at Castleton. Three New Hampshire officers, colonels Alexander Scammell and Joseph Cilley and Major Henry Dearborn, had gone forward to Brigadier Poor and pleaded with him to request St. Clair to send his brigade back to Hubbardton, but he had refused. St. Clair, when he heard the firing to his rear, had ordered two nearby militia regiments under colonels Benjamin Bellows and Peter Olcutt to the aid of the beleaguered troops, but they had ignored the command. Only Warner's men fought on. Then Fraser launched a British charge with the bayonet, the weapon Americans feared. This, with the oncoming jägers and their bayonets, was too much. "Scatter and meet me at Manchester," Warner ordered. Many threw down their muskets and ran. A foraging party sent out by Fraser met up with Hale and seventy of his fleeing men, who surrendered without a fight, "a proof," said a British officer, "of what may be done against Beaten Battalions, while their fears are strong upon them." The Battle of Hubbardton was over. In less than three hours the British had suffered 49 dead and 141 wounded, the Americans, 30 killed and 96 wounded. One American colonel, 7 captains, 10 subalterns, and 210 privates were taken prisoner.[5]

A heavy rain descended on the battlefield. The British wounded were placed in hastily built, bark-covered huts that provided scant protection. Logs were piled up in defense against the expected return of Americans from Castleton. A hunting detachment brought back a few wild bullocks, which were roasted without salt and eaten, incongruously, with gingerbread that an officer in occupied Ticonderoga had sent in large quantity as a joke to his brother in the expedition. The prisoners were sent under light guard to Ticonderoga, on threat that if they attempted escape the Indians would be turned loose on them. Riedesel, amid rumors of disagreement with Fraser and mutterings that he was leaving the British exposed to counterattack, departed with his Brunswickers at eleven o'clock the next morning for Skenesboro. Orders for Fraser to follow him arrived a day later. The wounded were made as comfortable as possible and left to await the coming of surgeons and medicines from Ticonderoga, with orders to a subaltern in charge to surrender them if the Americans returned. Captain John Shrimpton of the Sixty-second Grenadiers, who had been wounded in the shoulder by sniper fire after the action, insisted on marching with the brigade rather than remaining behind to fall into the hands of the enemy. Miraculously, he survived the harrowing thirty miles to Skenesboro. At Wood Creek, where trees were felled to provide a single-file bridge, he almost toppled in, but the officer behind him caught him by his clothes.[6]

Meanwhile, Burgoyne had pursued the American flotilla up the lake.

With a few well-aimed cannon shots from the gunboats, the boom on which the Americans had relied so much was cut in two, and in a half hour the British were past Ticonderoga. The unaware Americans sailed unhurriedly ahead, admiring, wrote surgeon James Thacher, the "scene so enchantingly sublime," entertained by the music of drums and fifes and regaling themselves with bottles of choice wine found among the hospital stores. The lake along the last thirteen or so miles to Skenesboro narrows to about a quarter of a mile and is bordered by steep cliffs all the way. No guns had been posted on shore to impede Burgoyne's passage. Sailing before a northerly wind, by three o'clock in the afternoon of July 6 he was at South Bay, the southwestern tip of the lake. Skenesboro, where the Americans had arrived, was three miles away to the southeast at the mouth of Wood Creek, the outlet that led from there twelve miles to Fort Ann. In order to prevent the Americans from escaping into the Vermont woods, he disembarked three regiments on the east shore—Lieutenant Colonel John Hill's "Fighting Ninth," Lieutenant Colonel John Lind's Twentieth, and Major John Squire's Twenty-first— with orders to block the road to Fort Ann. The lightened warships continued up the lake, and at four o'clock in the afternoon Captain John Carter's gunboats came upon the American ships moored below Skenesboro Falls. Within a half hour, in a violent exchange, the schooner *Liberty,* sloop *Enterprise,* and the *Gates* galley were blown up, and the *Trumbull* galley and schooner *Revenge* captured. Long's men set fire to the stockaded fort, mills, and storehouses and fled to Fort Ann, leaving behind some of the wounded, all their cannon and provisions, and most of their baggage. The flames roared in a crescendo up to the top of the hill.[7]

If the three regiments dropped off at South Bay had reached the road to Fort Ann before Burgoyne arrived at Skenesboro, Long's men would have been trapped. A mountain that was steeper and rockier than first appeared obstructed their path, and Long's men were well on their way while the British were still struggling over the slope. The only recourse was to pursue the fugitives. Colonel Hill, who by now had arrived with his Ninth Regiment, was dispatched with half his men. He had only 190 in all, and he did not know that the Americans at Fort Ann had received a reinforcement of four hundred militia from New York under Colonel Henry Van Rensselaer. It took Hill's regiment all day to advance eleven miles through dense woods and across broken bridges. They overtook the boats carrying the invalids, women, and baggage up Wood Creek, but the main body of the Americans had reached Fort Ann. Hill's exhausted men camped that night three-quarters of a mile north of the fort in a rocky gorge through which ran Wood Creek and a bordering path. In the morning, an American appeared who identified himself as a deserter and without urging revealed that there were one thousand dispirited men in the fort in mortal fear of being attacked. Hill immediately sent back to Burgoyne for reinforcements. The pretended deserter turned out to be a spy. He soon disappeared and took back to the fort the knowledge of how few the British were. Within a half hour, Long's men poured out of the fort. They crossed the creek and from a thick wood raked the British left flank. The outnumbered British held firm, but when the Americans recrossed the creek and attempted to surround them, Hill moved his men to the top of a high hill to the rear. Five British officers and thirty-three enlisted men were killed and wounded. Captain William Montgomery, struck in the leg, was taken prisoner, together with the surgeon who was in the act of dressing the wound. Sergeant Roger Lamb, the last to climb the hill, saw, next to him, Lieutenant Richard Westropp shot through the heart, and on the other side, a man spun about with a bullet through the forehead that severed the roof of his skull. Both the Americans and the British were now running out of ammunition.

At this point, a solitary British officer, Captain John Money, arrived at the foot of the hill. He had been leading a party of Indians to the scene, but they had deserted him and he had persevered alone. As if his Indians were still with him, he sounded a high war whoop. The Americans, their ammunition exhausted, turned and fled. Money's ruse, although successful, was in the long run unfortunate. Burgoyne, in the meantime, was personally leading to Hill's assistance the remainder of Powell's First Brigade, the Twentieth Regiment, and some artillery under Phillips. He had been delayed by a violent rainstorm but was due any minute and might have captured Long's entire force. When he did arrive, he found the Americans gone, the fort in flames, and only a sawmill and blockhouse still standing.[8]

Here the headstrong Burgoyne of Valencia de Alcántara would have continued on in search of St. Clair's main force, heedless of fatigue and shortage of rations, hungry for the final kill. The Burgoyne of Ticonderoga, Hubbardton, and Fort Ann halted. He had learned that American soldiers were marksmen to be reckoned with, never continuing twenty-four hours in one place without entrenching and erecting abatis from behind which to level their fire. Unless he had more artillery, he could not proceed ten miles without heavy casualties to his rain-soaked troops. Besides, St. Clair seemed hardly worth the pursuit. "It is my opinion," Burgoyne exulted to Riedesel, "that the army of Ticonderoga is entirely annihilated, as it is in want of all the materials for support and defense."[9] Rather than chase forty miles eastward after St. Clair, who had taken a roundabout route to Fort Edward through Rutland, Dorset, and Manchester in order to avoid entrapment, Burgoyne opted to withdraw to Skenesboro and await the arrival of cannon, carts, and provisions.

He was sure that superior armament and the competence of his superb professionals would guarantee him victory over any rebel force attempting to impede his passage to Albany. "The instruments I have to employ are so good," he wrote Germain, "that my merit will be small." He was so sure that he requested the King's leave to return to England before the snow. "My constitution," he urged, "is not fitted for an American winter."[10]

✲14✲

The American Rubicon

I

N A GREAT STONE HOUSE AT
Skenesboro, Burgoyne meditated his next move. He would have preferred to
turn east into New England and head toward Rhode Island to unite with the
force under Clinton. He claimed afterward in debates in Parliament that he
had written so to Germain on July 11: "Your Lordship will pardon me if I a
little lament that my orders do not give me the latitude I ventured to propose
in my original project for the campaign, to make a real effort instead of a feint
upon New England. As things have turned out, were I at liberty to march in
force immediately to my left, instead of my right, I should have little doubt of
subduing before winter the provinces where the rebellion originated."[1]

The original of this message has not been found, giving rise to the suspicion that Burgoyne fabricated it. However, a letter written the day before by
Phillips, who in all essentials shared Burgoyne's convictions, makes the same
point: "I cannot help repining that our March is *directed* to Hudsons River,
the whole Country of New England Northward and the Connecticut are
open to us—Plans of War made in a Cabinet at several thousand Miles distant
from the scene of action are not *always* good."[2]

Burgoyne's only option was to choose the best route from Lake Champlain to the Hudson River. His men were at Skenesboro and his boats and
supplies at Ticonderoga. How to bring them together? He had written in his
"Thoughts" paper of the previous year that "the most expeditious and the
most commodious route to Albany" was to transfer from Lake Champlain to
Lake George, sail south to Fort George, and transfer again by cart eighteen
miles to Fort Edward, near a crossing of the Hudson. As a water route, this
did indeed seem quickest, but it was not as expeditious as it appeared on the
map. The portage between the lakes was up a 221-foot incline along a three-

mile stretch of road. The road to Fort Edward was hilly and rocky and would require considerable clearing; horses and carts for this operation would be in short supply because of the number to be retained at Ticonderoga for transport across the portage. Despite these drawbacks, Burgoyne chose this as the delivery route for his provisions and most of his artillery—thirty-three pieces. Ten pieces were already at Skenesboro and were to be kept there for Fraser's advance brigade.

At the same time, Burgoyne rejected the idea of doubling back with his men from Skenesboro to Ticonderoga in order to take the passage up Lake George. Such a retrograde movement would be bad for "the capricious workings of the tempers of men." It would also tie up ships for troop transport that otherwise could be used for armament and provisions. He decided to move the army south by land from Skenesboro twenty-three miles to Fort Edward, there to join with the supplies arriving from Lake George. In letters to Germain and Howe, he added that if he had returned to Ticonderoga he would have been held up while investing Fort George, and in the meantime the enemy would have destroyed the road from there to Fort Edward. By advancing on land from Skenesboro to Fort Edward, he would cut the Americans at Fort George off from the Hudson and force their evacuation. Also, the penetration into Vermont would panic the New Englanders into keeping potential rebel army recruits at home for local defense.[3]

There were critics in his army who censored him for not sending the army back to Ticonderoga and up Lake George. Many historians since then have even blamed his ultimate defeat on this supposed mistake. But a consideration of the topography shows the Skenesboro route to have been by no means unfeasible. According to a report to Horatio Gates on May 17, 1777, by his quartermaster general, Colonel Udney Hay, the passage up Wood Creek from Skenesboro to Fort Ann was "tolerably easy." Wood Creek, though narrow, was navigable for the British bateaux. Between Fort Ann and Fort Edward, the chief obstacle was a three-mile morass over which a log causeway had to be repaired. Thirty men could accomplish this in three weeks, while at the same time another fifty men would be smoothing the road with a layer of fresh earth. Some of this work had already been begun by the Americans. The critics have also charged that it was poor planning to haul a train of unreasonably heavy artillery through a wooded route that was sure to be obstructed by rebel axmen. Yet the only artillery that the army carried with it was Fraser's ten light pieces—four 6-pounders, four 3-pounders, and two 5-1/2-inch howitzers. The British deputy quartermaster general, Captain Money, later testified that it took only five or six days to clear the road to Fort Ann and another five or six to complete it to Fort Edward.[4] It could be argued that the Skenesboro route was quicker than the Lake George route.

While the army at Skenesboro waited for the Lake George supply line to be opened, problems of manpower developed. Burgoyne requested from Carleton a reinforcement of troops from Canada to garrison Ticonderoga and was refused on the ground that, according to Germain, Carleton's authority did not extend beyond Canada. This forced Burgoyne to send back north 910 rank and file from the Fifty-third Foot and Prince Frederick's Brunswick Regiment. Carleton had before this introduced another stumbling block by suspending the pay and functions of Burgoyne's brigadiers once they had crossed the Canadian border, this time citing a directive from the secretary at war. Burgoyne chose to keep the order dormant, contending that his was "the army of Canada till it is the army of Sir William Howe."[5]

Relations between the German and British troops became more strained. At the top, Riedesel remained unreconciled to the replacement of Carleton by Burgoyne. From Crown Point on June 28, he had written Duke Ferdinand: "By the appointment of another commander in chief of the army, the theatre of war is so changed that it does not now look like the same one. The new one judges somewhat hastily, and carries out the plan of the ministers. His predecessor went to work more carefully but safely."[6] Burgoyne sent the German troops east to Castleton to keep watch on Seth Warner's force there and to spread alarm among the populace. Unable to procure horses, they had to carry their baggage on their backs over a road in bad repair and, many suffering from dysentery, to sleep in the woods without tents for three or four nights. On July 16 a brawl broke out between some drunken British and Germans in which the British struck a German guard on duty. Riedesel was at this time himself suffering from an ulcerated tooth and a raging fever, and he added his own resentments. He requested permission from Burgoyne to retaliate against pretended Loyalists with an expedition toward the Connecticut River for the purpose of seizing a supply of horses, some to mount his dragoons and some to serve as pack horses in place of the inadequate Canadian carts. Burgoyne was noncommittal.[7]

The Indians Burgoyne had brought with him from lower Canada had proved of no use in pursuing the Americans. "When plunder is in their way, which was the case at Ticonderoga," he declared, "it is impossible to drag them from it. . . . Were they left to themselves enormities too horrid to think of would ensue, guilty and innocent, women and infants would be a common prey."[8] On the morning of July 17, four hundred Ottawas arrived at

Skenesboro, and Burgoyne hoped that, in view of their reputation as more warlike and less rapacious than their southern brethren, they would prove superior substitutes. They were met with a fifteen-gun salute from a frigate at anchor, and two days later a captain's guard, carrying the colors of the expedition's oldest regiment, was sent to conduct them to a conference at headquarters. They came decked out in war paint and feathers, wearing trophies of the hunt, and they looked taller and fiercer than their predecessors. Burgoyne, with the aid of interpreters, welcomed them to the cause on condition that only the dead be scalped. They grunted agreement.

Though the Ottawas were under the overall command of Major John Campbell, superintendent of Indian affairs in Canada, they were more immediately led by two former inveterate enemies of the British. La Corne St. Luc (full name Luc de Chapt de la Corne Saint-Luc) and Charles Michel de Langlade had served with these same Indians under the French and were notorious for their terrorism. Langlade had conducted the ambush of Braddock's army in 1755. St. Luc, father-in-law of Campbell, had led the Indians in the massacre of captives at Fort William Henry in 1757 and now openly declared that "the business must be brutalized."[9]

It took three weeks to accomplish the transport from Lake Champlain to Lake George. Burgoyne sent Phillips to Ticonderoga to supervise this operation. Heavy rains made it necessary to retain a large number of the scarce horses there in order to drag the artillery, boats, and provisions across the uphill portage. From July 14 to 25, a group of rebel prisoners under a brutal British officer, Major Griffith Williams, repaired the road between the lakes and carried guns and stores. On July 27, a force of one hundred men in twenty-six gunboats sailed south and at noon the following day occupied Fort George, evacuated eleven days earlier by the Americans and left in flames.[10] Burgoyne had predicted correctly that the fort would fall without resistance once the Americans realized that they would be cut off by his advance on the east side of the lake to Fort Edward.

Schuyler finally realized that the place of the commander of the northern theater was with his troops in the field. His health was now better than it had been for two years, and he no longer had reason to delegate active command, as he had done to Montgomery in 1775. Neither could he take the time to indulge in private concerns—his beautiful and brilliant eldest daughter, Angelica, had just eloped with an Englishman of whom he disapproved. On

July 7, he set out southward from his home at Saratoga with a small party of militia and was met at Stillwater with the news of the loss of Ticonderoga. Astounded, he wrote St. Clair to meet him promptly at Fort Edward and took charge of the field himself.[11]

He found the old ramparts in such ruin that he could gallop his horse in one side and out the other. The fort had been built for protection against the French, but after the British conquest of Canada there was no further use for it, and its two best buildings had been removed and reerected as private residences. Even in pristine condition it was defenseless against artillery attack. Situated on lowland, it was exposed to point-blank fire from the hills surrounding it. The Americans collected there numbered no more than fifteen hundred, with no provisions, no shelter, no cannon, and only five rounds of ammunition per man. "Every Rain that falls, and we have it in great Abundance almost every Day," Schuyler wrote Washington, "wets the Men to the Skin."[12] He could not remain there, but he waited for the arrival of St. Clair's army and for a contingent of Continental troops under Brigadier General John Nixon that Washington had sent from Peekskill.

In the meantime he sent a Massachusetts militia detachment under Brigadier General John Fellows to break up the roads and bridges between Fort Ann and Fort Edward and to fell trees into the navigable waters of Wood Creek and across any declivities through which Burgoyne's wagons might attempt to pass. He spurred the removal of the cannon from Fort George despite the lack of carriages and was able on July 10 to write Brigadier General Abraham Ten Broeck of the Albany militia that if the enemy would give him three or four more days after St. Clair arrived they would "not see Albany this campaign."[13]

St. Clair arrived July 12 with fifteen hundred men, the remains of his army; Schuyler, with no shelter for them, had to order them to camp at Fort Miller, six miles down the Hudson. Nixon also came that night with 581 men, all the help Schuyler could expect from Washington. For the moment, he had forty-five hundred men. His only hope was for more of the militia he despised. He appealed to the New England legislatures, and when that produced little result he appealed again to Washington. Washington could not send soldiers, but he did send two popular New England officers to attract enlistments: Benedict Arnold, who agreed to retract his threat to resign over being bypassed for promotion, and Major General Benjamin Lincoln of Masachusetts, who was just recovering from illness. On July 23, Schuyler moved his army five miles south to Moses Creek, on the east shore of the Hudson, where hills provided protection and a battery mounted on an island in the river commanded the approach. Arnold had arrived on July 22; Schuyler now divided the army into a left wing under Arnold on one side of the river and a right wing under St. Clair on the other side.

Insubordination and desertion were taking a heavy toll. Increasing Indian raids went largely unrepulsed. Two Massachusetts militia regiments sent as replacements turned around and went home. Schuyler lost nearly half his force. He decided that he must put the Hudson between him and Burgoyne. He moved first to Fort Miller, at the mouth of the Batten Kill, then across the Hudson to Saratoga (now Schuylerville), down to Stillwater, and finally to Van Schaick's Island in the mouth of the Mohawk River, nine miles north of Albany. Brigadier General John Glover, arriving with his tattered brigade early in August, found a "weak & shatter'd" army of three thousand, powerless to make a stand against an enemy advance and in constant dread of "the Cursed War hoop which makes the Woods ring for Miles."[14]

On July 21, American Loyalists brought to the German headquarters the news that the Americans had abandoned Fort George. This was the signal Burgoyne had been waiting for to begin his march from Skenesboro to Fort Edward. First he inspected the route for himself. With a detachment of one hundred men from Fraser's advance corps, he reconnoitered the terrain to Fort Ann and the country beyond. It was a hazardous exposure for a general. On the first day, a rebel deserter came in with word that a party of thirty-four men lay in wait near Fort Ann to kill or capture him. A party of Indians was immediately sent out against them and returned with three scalps and twenty prisoners, among whom was the rebel captain. He disclosed that three thousand of the enemy were encamped eight miles from the fort. On the second day, another rebel party retaliated with an attack that killed one British-allied Indian and wounded fourteen; the rebels in turn had nine dead and eleven wounded. Burgoyne saw how clearing the road had required back-breaking labor. It had been impossible to police the thick forest enough to prevent rebel destruction. Work teams were still cutting through the felled trees and rolling boulders out of the way. Much of the area was swampland, created by the heavy rains and made worse by trenches the rebels had dug to channel the many streams into the roadway. In the two-mile causeway east of Fort Ann, many of the transversely laid logs had sunk beneath the oozing mud and had needed replacement. More than forty broken bridges had had to be rebuilt. There was so much work remaining that he had to postpone the army's march another day. And yet, as Captain Money afterward testified before Parliament, the expedition was not "delayed an hour on that account."[15] The real holdup had been the wait for the supply passage to be cleared through Lake George.

On July 23, Fraser's corps started south from Skenesboro. The army's right wing was to follow two days later, and the left wing, under Riedesel, recalled from Castleton, was to bring up the rear. This phased advance would prevent congestion of the supply bateaux up the narrow reaches of Wood Creek. It took Fraser's men two days, cutting their way through the pines, to cover the twelve miles to Fort Ann. The rebels had burned the barracks at their departure but in their haste had left the square, eleven-foot-high, pallisaded blockhouse standing. The scalping parties of Burgoyne's newly acquired northern Indians had kept the rebels from returning to bury the dead. The stench was suffocating, and Fraser's men could approach one recognizable body, that of Lieutenant Richard Westropp of the Ninth Regiment, only long enough to cover it with leaves.[16]

Burgoyne arrived at Fort Ann on July 26. That evening he received news that, he told Fraser, "fills me with horror." An Indian scouting party brought in two scalps, one of a man, the other with the long black hair of a woman, which an anguished officer of Lieutenant Colonel John Peters's Loyalist battalion immediately recognized as that of his beautiful twenty-three-year-old fiancée, Jane McCrea. She had been visiting near Fort Edward with Mrs. Sarah McNeil, a recently emigrated Scotch cousin of Brigadier Fraser. As nearly as could be learned, the Indians had become involved in a skirmish with Americans from the fort and had run for shelter to the house where they found the two women. A dispute had developed over custody of the girl, and in the fracas one of the warriors had shot her and then scalped, stripped, and mutilated the body. The murder was the more upsetting because the new Indians from the west had at first been treating captives with humanity. But another massacre had occurred the day before on the Batten Kill River, of John Allen and his family and slaves—nine people. Now not even the intended bride of a Loyalist officer was safe. Burgoyne summoned the Indian chiefs to a conference the next day. With Fraser at his side, he demanded that the girl's killer be delivered up for punishment with death. St. Luc, however, stepped forward and argued that this would result in the mass desertion of the Indians, who would only commit worse enormities on their way back to Canada. Fraser also pleaded caution, and Burgoyne yielded. Punishment was left to the chiefs, which meant none at all. Burgoyne had to content himself with ordering that all Indian raids in future be accompanied by a responsible British officer.[17]

From Fort Ann, the southward road to Fort Edward left Wood Creek and turned slightly to the west. The bateaux were no longer of any use. Orders were issued to guard against overloading the two-wheeled carts, cheaply made of green lumber, which were breaking down. The precious horses and oxen were not to be overworked. There seemed no end of huge, felled trees still to be removed in order to make way for the 6-pound cannon, and while the men strained in the sweltering summer heat and daily downpours of rain, they were tormented beyond endurance by the small gnats and oversize mosquitoes of the north country. Indian patrols combed the country for rebel snipers, returning from time to time with fresh scalps. On July 29, Fraser's men emerged from the woods at Fort Edward and found it abandoned and burned. An unsigned letter was found nailed to a tree, warning against crossing the Hudson River: "Thus far shalt thou go and no farther." The soldiers' lively imaginations attributed it to Benedict Arnold, who was thought to have replaced Schuyler. Fraser's men pitched tents on a hill a mile to the south. The rebels were encamped four miles away but apparently did not intend to make a stand. The open vista of the lovely river dotted with myriad small islands was a welcome relief from the gloom and damp of the forest. The way to Albany lay through cleared and settled terrain.[18]

The bare dating of a letter from the Hudson River was the measure of his progress, Burgoyne triumphantly wrote to Germain. The rebels' driving of people and cattle before them as they retreated was "an act of desperation and folly." It could retard him for a time; "it cannot finally impede me." He still expected to fill up Ebenezer Jessup's and Peters's Loyalist battalions, and he still believed he could employ the Indians' ability to terrorize and yet restrain their cruelty. He was disturbed, it was true, that he was "in total ignorance of the situation or intentions" of Howe, although he had dispatched ten messengers to him by different routes. But his confidence was not diminished. He expected soon to cross the Hudson and on his way to Albany to draw off any enemy expedition against St. Leger in the west. If he did not say so, he sounded as though he could manage without Howe's assistance and perhaps even preferred to win all the glory for himself. He was so sure that he again asked leave to return to England in the winter and proposed Phillips as his replacement.[19]

He was not deterred by a near mutiny that broke out among the Ottawas only three days after his arrival at Fort Edward. St. Luc came to him with a message that they were insisting on a council with him. The meeting took place August 4. Without warning, St. Luc announced that the Ottawas asked leave to return home, alleging that they had committed themselves only as long as August 5. It was obvious that they resented the restrictions Burgoyne had imposed. To lose them would deprive him of their expert scouting and protection against rebel raiding parties. He flatly refused them permission to go home, insisted on the prohibitions against scalping, appealed to their loyalty and honor, and promised them more rum. They withdrew to reconsider. That evening a second council was held. The Indians agreed to stay if parties were rotated home in order to gather in the harvest. Burgoyne consented. The chiefs each pledged their support, and one, La Bouf de la Prairie, drew his knife with a flourish and declared that it would not be sheathed until he had revenged the injuries to his father (the king). But the next day they left for home by the score, loaded with their plunder, until hardly any remained of the western tribes who had joined the army at Skenesboro.[20]

Nor was Burgoyne deterred by a letter, written on two strips of paper wrapped around a quill, that at last arrived from Howe on the same day that the councils took place. Sent July 17 from New York, it was the sole answer to three of Burgoyne's letters, the first dated from Plymouth, England. "My intention is for Pensylvania, where I expect to meet Washington, but if he goes to the northward contrary to my expectations, and you can keep him at bay, be assured I shall soon be after him to relieve you. After your arrival at Albany, the movements of the enemy will guide yours; but my wishes are, that the enemy be drove out of this province before any operation takes place in Connecticut. Sir Henry Clinton remains in command here, and will act as occurrences may direct."[21]

Burgoyne could not bring himself to believe that Howe would abandon him. Surely Howe would receive further instructions from Germain and would change his plans and march north after all. The letter could even be interpreted as a directive urging Burgoyne south, for it rejected his proposal for an incursion into Connecticut in favor of an "arrival at Albany." He replied the next day: "I hope . . . to move to Saratogha (where the enemy is at present posted but making disposition to retreat) in a few days, but as I have a carrying-place at Fort Miller and another at Stillwater I do not apprehend it will be possible to be in possession of Albany, even supposing the enemy should not stand a battle, before the 22nd or 23rd. Should the opportunity of any stroke offer, I certainly, where I can convey necessary provision only, shall not wait the carriage of the tents or any other baggage." He glossed over and even misrepresented the troubles he had with the Indians: "During my stay here the Indians have done good service; not a day passes without prisoners brought in, some from miles behind the enemy's camp. I have detachments of seventeen different nations. There is infinite difficulty to manage them. My effort has been to keep up their terror and avoid their cruelty. I think I have in great measure succeeded. They attack very bravely, they scalp the dead only and spare the inhabitants."[22] He had no suspicion of the denouement that had been prepared for him in the councils at Howe's headquarters in New York.

Henry Clinton, arriving in New York early in July to resume his post as second in command, was amazed to find that Howe was planning to depart by sea for Pennsylvania and leave him with only seven thousand troops at Manhattan, mostly provincials and Hessians. He promptly protested that Pennsylvania was a futile objective, that the force left in New York was inadequate for the conquest of the forts in the highlands, which were essential to open the Hudson as a supply line to Burgoyne, and that the ministry in London expected cooperation between the northern and southern armies. Howe replied that the northern army would not advance south far enough to require support, that he hoped Washington would be drawn north so as to leave the field unopposed for the occupation of Pennsylvania, and, as for the orders from home, that Germain had not made his intention clear. During the next three weeks, in meeting after meeting, Clinton persisted. The discussions became heated, and he thought he saw, behind Howe, Lord Cornwallis as the "evil genius" misleading Howe to catastrophe. Howe declared that "he was sorry to find that we had never agreed in any one thing since we started." Clinton complained that Howe "really did not think well of me as an officer." When Howe attempted to reassure him of his confidence, Clinton asked whether, if the northern army did reach Albany and fall under Howe's jurisdiction, he would supersede Burgoyne in the command. This Howe refused. It would be an insult to Burgoyne. Clinton had had his chance; he should have accepted the command when it was offered him in London.[23]

As late as July 18, the day before Howe boarded ship, Clinton still believed that he would "deceive us all, and when the southerly wind blows this afternoon with the flood you will go up the N[orth] River to the Highlands. You can mean nothing else." The next day, an unconfirmed report arrived that Burgoyne had already advanced to Fort Edward on July 10.

Clinton, ever fertile with new ideas, drafted a letter to Howe proposing that he move up the Connecticut River Valley for a junction with Burgoyne east of the Berkshires in Massachusetts. This was the very campaign that Burgoyne had preferred from the start.. But before the letter went out Clinton learned that Howe was attempting to trick the Americans, through a bogus letter to Burgoyne intended for interception, into believing that he was heading for Boston instead of Philadelphia. For Clinton to press his proposal after that would invite ridicule. "Not sent," he endorsed his letter. Howe sailed July 23.[24]

Clinton was now in command in New York, and his concern for Burgoyne gave way to concern for himself. Although Howe had suggested some diversion in favor of Burgoyne, Clinton grew apprehensive that Washington might attack New York, and he feared weakening his defense by detaching an expedition to the north. This supercaution, when the Americans had far greater reason to move against Howe to the south or Burgoyne to the north, seems indecisive in the extreme, perhaps another exercise of the self-doubt that his biographer, William B. Willcox, saw as his dominant characteristic. Equally damaging to Burgoyne was Clinton's procrastination in waiting eighteen days after Howe's departure before writing that he could not help him. Even then he neglected to send several messengers so as to insure delivery, and Burgoyne never received the letter. When a messenger from Burgoyne, dispatched July 31, before he had received Howe's letter, rode into New York with word that Burgoyne intended to continue to Albany, Clinton did not attempt to communicate further. Burgoyne lost the last warning that might have dissuaded him from crossing the Hudson.[25]

Defiance

AS SOON AS BURGOYNE CROSSED the Hudson, his supply line from Montreal would be severed; he must take with him sufficient provisions to last until he reached Albany. The task of buildup was herculean. At Fort George the supplies were transferred from the bateaux to horse-drawn carts for the trip to Fort Edward. At the same time, the bateaux were separately drawn over the same route. At Fort Edward the bateaux were launched on the Hudson and the provisions transferred back to them. The bateaux were then floated six miles down the river to the steep falls above Fort Miller, where the contents were again unloaded onto carts and hauled a quarter of a mile south below the falls. There the provisions were once more reloaded aboard the bateaux for water carriage of another two miles to the nearest crossing point of the Hudson, where a bridge was being built. The carts took a full day to travel the road each way, and many were badly in need of repair. Only a third of the horses contracted for in Canada had arrived, and only fifty yoke of oxen had been collected from the countryside. The cattle were overworked, the rocky road required considerable clearing, and daily thunderstorms made conditions miserable. Often ten or twelve oxen had to be hitched together to haul a single bateau, and after two weeks only ten of the boats had been lowered to the Hudson. A day's labor sometimes brought forward no more than a day's provisions for the army. At best, the trip delivered four days' more.[1]

Burgoyne would not allow these difficulties to delay him. He still had in his pocket Riedesel's proposal of July 22 for an incursion east from Skenesboro toward the Connecticut River in order to obtain mounts for the horseless Brunswick dragoons. He would use the Brunswickers to round up cattle, corn, and carriages and would center their operations to the south, from where the supplies could quickly reach the main army. "I conceived it a favourable occasion to give in to their ideas and solicitations," he explained to Germain, "because in exerting their zeal to fulfil their favourite purpose they necessarily would effect the greater purpose of my own." He could spare the Brunswick dragoons from the main army until they procured their horses. When he next saw Riedesel, at Ford Edward on August 4, he informed him that he wished the expedition to seize a supply depot at Manchester, on the Batten Kill River. To mollify Riedesel, Burgoyne delegated to him the naming of the expedition commander, Lieutenant Colonel Friedrich Baum, and the drafting of instructions. But in fact, as Burgoyne afterward testified in Parliament and published in his *A State of the Expedition from Canada* in 1780, from the beginning he really intended the expedition for Bennington, thirty miles further south. "A man must indeed be void of military and political address," he said, "to put upon paper a critical design, where surprize was in question, and every thing depended upon secrecy." On the morning of August 10, when Baum was already on the road and when Riedesel was away at Fort George, Burgoyne rode into Baum's camp at Fort Miller and informed him that he had just received word from Philip Skene that the largest supply depot was at Bennington, not Manchester, and that Baum should redirect his expedition there. This was a fabricated explanation. "Surely," Burgoyne told Parliament, "there is nothing new or improbable in the idea, that a general should disguise his real intentions at the outset of an expedition, even from the officer whom he appointed to execute them, provided a communication with that officer was certain and not remote."[2]

Baum was assigned a detachment of approximately 750 rank and file consisting of 374 Germans, Peters's corps of 150 Loyalists, 100 Indians, 56 Canadians, and, the sole British contingent, Captain Alexander Fraser's 50 marksmen. The only artillery was two 3-pound cannon. Burgoyne expected no significant resistance: "I undertook the expedition to Bennington upon report, strengthened by the suggestion of *persons of long experience and residence in America; who had been present on the spot when the rebellion broke out;* and whose information had been much respected by the administration in England; *that the friends to the British cause were as five to one,* and that they *wanted only the appearance of a protecting force to shew themselves.*"[3]

The chief person of "long experience and residence" was Skene, who, Burgoyne instructed Baum, was "to assist you with his advice, to help you to distinguish the good subjects from the bad, to procure you the best intelligence of the enemy, and to choose those people who are to bring me the accounts of your progress and success." As Baum could speak no English (his adjutant, Captain Laurentius O'Connell, did), Skene would manage relations with civilians, and, if necessary, impose levies of cattle, grain, and horses on the country and take hostages to insure delivery. Skene was also to spread the impression that Baum's expedition was the vanguard of the main army on its way to Boston and to a junction at Springfield with a corps from Rhode Island. A large, vigorous man, opinionated yet affable, Skene was addressed by Burgoyne as "colonel," although his permanent rank in the army before his retirement was captain. Colonel Baum might not find it easy to overrule Colonel Skene.

Riedesel's original objective of gathering horses for his dragoons seemed almost forgotten. After Bennington, Baum was to continue foraging northeast to Rockingham on the Connecticut River, south to Brattleboro, and thence to cross the Hudson to join the main army. By that time, estimated as two weeks, Burgoyne expected to be in Albany. He could get there without the horses—for that matter without Baum's detachment.[4]

The main army, meanwhile, was not waiting for the supplies from Baum's expedition before moving. The artificers, under an enterprising captain, George Lawes, had demonstrated by August 10 that a bridge of rafts, lashed together with twigs and strips of bark, could be strung across the Hudson in the shallows and narrows below Fort Miller. The bateaux, so slow in arriving from Fort George, were no longer necessary. On August 14, while the bridge was being built, Fraser's advance corps crossed the river in bateaux. The horses and baggage forded a mile below, breasting the water risen from a heavy storm of the night before. The bridge was finished August 16, and orders were issued for the rest of the troops to cross the next day.[5] After that, the main source of supplies would be the Baum expedition.

On the day of Baum's departure, an army of more than a thousand rebel militia arrived at Bennington. The shock in New England of St. Clair's evacuation of Ticonderoga without a fight had given way to resistance. The New Hampshire assembly responded to Vermont's plea for help by reorganizing the state militia and commissioning Brigadier General John Stark to lead a force to Bennington, there to cooperate with Seth Warner's Green Mountain boys posted thirty miles north at Manchester. The assembly's speaker, John Langdon, pledged his personal fortune of three thousand dollars in hard money, another three thousand to be borrowed on the security of his household plate, and seventy hogsheads of Tobago rum. Stark was a popular, intrepid veteran of the French and Indian War. He had resigned from the Continental army when he was superseded by junior officers, and he had demanded and received from the New Hampshire legislature freedom to act independently of Congress and Schuyler. Within six days of recruiting, 1,492 officers and men enlisted, including a contingent that the minister of the Concord church gave leave to depart in the middle of the Sabbath service. "Not a loyalist was found earnest enough to convey me intelligence," Burgoyne afterward recalled bitterly.[6]

The clumsy advance of the Brunswick dragoons was a poorly kept secret. They "marched boldly in the open road" in their knee-high riding boots, big spurs, and thick leather breeches, carrying ten-pound sabers and heavy carbines. Their long, pigtailed wigs and plumed hats bobbed ludicrously through the dense forest. Pretended Loyalists, on the strength only of having taken an oath of allegiance, were allowed to come and go freely, learning the purpose and numbers of the expedition. On August 13, a scouting detachment of thirty Loyalists and fifty Indians surprised a party of thirty or forty local militia at Cambridge, eighteen miles northwest of Bennington, and took five prisoners. Both armies thus learned of each other's presence.

Ironically, Stark was about to depart to join Schuyler at Stillwater. He had at first refused to comply with Schuyler's order, delivered by General Benjamin Lincoln, but then had been cajoled to obey. With the news from Cambridge, he immediately dispatched a force of two hundred men under Lieutenant Colonel William Gregg to take post six miles to the south, at the confluence of the Owl Kill and the Hoosic River, at Sancoick's (also known as Van Schaick's) mill. When Baum arrived there the next morning with his full force, Gregg's men fired a volley from the bushes and, leaving behind the mill's 78 barrels of flour, 1,000 of wheat, and 20 of salt, hastened back to Bennington with word that the British were no small scouting party.[7]

Baum reacted to the news that fifteen to eighteen hundred men were at Bennington with inexplicable aplomb. He expected, apparently with the assurance of Skene, that the militia would flee with the approach of the British. Pausing only an hour, two miles southeastward, to repair a bridge across Little White Creek (a tributary of the Walloomsac) that Gregg's men had burned, Baum continued on to Bennington with the intent to attack Stark early the next day. So he informed Burgoyne, in a letter written in haste "on the head of a barrel," with the confidence that Loyalists were "flocking in hourly."[8] Burgoyne recognized danger and promptly wrote back: "Should you find the enemy too strongly posted at Bennington, and maintaining such a countenance as may make an attack imprudent, I wish you to take a post where you can maintain yourself till you receive an answer from me, and I

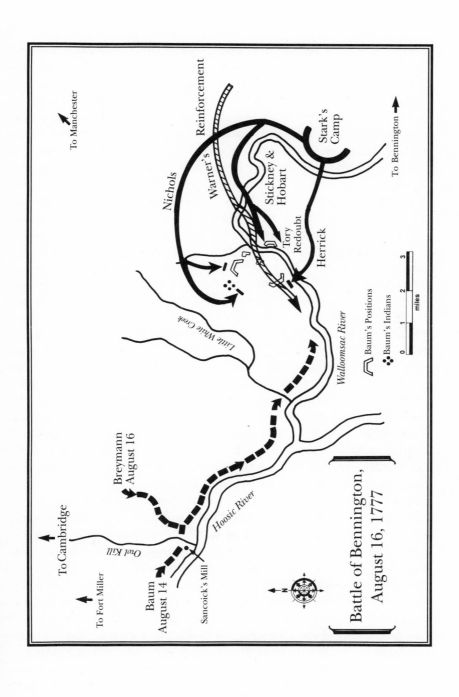

To Manchester

Nichols

Warner's
Reinforcement

Stickney &
Hobart

Stark's
Camp

Tory
Redoubt

Herrick

To Bennington

Little White Creek

Walloomsac River

Breymann
August 16

To Cambridge

Owl Kill

To Fort Miller

Baum
August 14

Sancoick's Mill

Hoosic River

N

⌐ Baum's Positions

∴ Baum's Indians

0   1   2   3
miles

Battle of Bennington,
August 16, 1777

will either support you in force, or withdraw you." Clearly, Baum needed reinforcement. Fraser volunteered his advance corps for the assignment, but Burgoyne still would not risk his crack troops. He dispatched his aide, Sir Francis Clerke, in the night to Riedesel, with an urgent request that he order Lieutenant Colonel Breymann to Baum's relief with a company of jägers and a battalion of chasseurs and grenadiers. Riedesel refused to accept any responsibility for the expedition. Let Burgoyne issue the orders himself, he answered. Clerke brought Burgoyne's instructions to Breymann the next morning.[9]

Stark now advanced with all the troops he had at Bennington, sending orders to Warner at Manchester to join him with his regiment. With this, and with the arrival of Massachusetts militia from Berkshire County and a party of Stockbridge Indians, his brigade now numbered approximately two thousand. Baum's expedition, with the induction of ninety more Tories, had grown to about eight hundred. The presence of the Tories signified the civil strife between New York and Vermont. "We took four or five of our neighbors—two Sniders and two Hornbecks," wrote one of Stark's men after the engagement. "The bigger part of Dutch Hoosick was in the battle against us."[10]

The two forces came within sight of each other on the evening of the fourteenth, when they reached the southeastern and northwestern sides of the Walloomsac River about four miles from Bennington. Stark moved back a mile to a more defensible position. Baum, disregarding Burgoyne's instruction to withdraw if opposed by a superior force, settled down to await Stark's next move. He established his chief post on the right bank, on a high hill commanding the river bridge, and dispersed the remainder of his troops, four detachments, within a half mile radius—a rough breastwork on the enemy side of the bridge, and the other entrenchments west of the river. On the fifteenth it rained all day, and no major move was attempted. If Baum had any second thoughts about retreating, they were dispelled when he received a message at eleven o'clock that night from Breymann saying that he was on his way. Stark took counsel with his colonels and adopted a tactic of double envelopment. Colonel Moses Nichols, with two hundred New Hampshire men, would loop around Baum's left, while Colonel Samuel Herrick, with three hundred Vermont men, would circle to the right. Facing Baum's front would be a force of three hundred, divided between colonels David Hobart and Thomas Stickney. In order for the plan to succeed, Nichols and Herrick would have to attack simultaneously.

Toward nine o'clock the next morning, groups of armed men in their shirtsleeves appeared through the rain at Baum's rear. Taking them for Loyalists, he allowed them to camp unmolested. By midday the rain stopped, and at three o'clock Stark's offensive began. Nichols's and Herrick's encirclements struck at the same time, and the supposed Loyalists at the rear joined the attack with them. Baum was cut off from the detachments he had dispersed around him. At the front, Hobart and Stickney charged the Tories, Canadians, and Indians under Peters. One of Hobart's captains, Jeremiah Post, was an old schoolmate of Peters and a cousin of his wife. Without recognizing him, Peters fired a shot that was to prove fatal. But Post, with the bullet in him, rushed forward with drawn bayonet, crying, "Peters, you d——n Tory, I have got you," and struck him in the left breast. Although Peters survived, his men fled. Stark, at the signal from Nichols and Herrick, moved forward with his main body against Baum's last-ditch position at the top of the hill. Accounts afterward, perhaps a little imaginative, had Stark shouting, "There they are! We'll beat them before night, or Molly Stark will be a widow." His men scaled the steep hillside, under the muzzles of the cannon on the top, and shot down the gunners.

For two hours Baum's one hundred and seventy–odd dragoons and twenty-odd British fought off the attackers. The frenzied firing, Stark said, was "one continued clap of thunder." At last, Baum's ammunition gave out. The dragoons slung their carbines and drew their swords, useful now against the riflemen not equipped with bayonets. The Americans fell back. But in the melee a bullet hit Baum fatally in the abdomen. His men were demoralized, and only twenty-nine dragoons escaped capture.[11]

The battle was only half over. Breymann's men had been slogging ponderously to Baum's assistance through the pouring rain and gripping mire. Each soldier carried forty cartridges. The two 6-pounders had to be drawn one after the other up the many hills and across the brimming ravines, and the ammunitions wagons upset and took much time to be righted. The guide lost his way, and a replacement had to be found. They covered scarcely a half mile an hour. The advance was so slow that it inspired talk that Breymann, who had a long-standing quarrel with Baum, had been heard to remark, "We will let them get warm before we reach them." By nightfall of the fifteenth, they were still seven miles west of Cambridge. The next morning, the artillery horses were so weak that progress was at a snail's pace until, by noon, Skene arrived with fresh horses and carts that, fortunately, had been sent back by Baum. At Cambridge, Breymann halted a half hour to redress his ranks. He arrived at Sancoick's mill at 4:30, six miles from Baum. When he approached the bridge at Little White Creek, he saw a considerable number of armed men occupying a hill on his left. Skene assured him that they were Loyalists. The mistake was the same that Baum had made that morning. The cocksure Skene rode up to the newcomers and called out to them. His answer was a volley, which among its targets found his own horse. Major Ferdinand A. von Barner's battalion then attacked the hill at the front, and the grenadiers and jägers attacked at the right; the two 6-pounders shelled a log house in which the Americans had taken refuge and drove them out.

Stark at first could provide little assistance, for some of his men were tied up guarding prisoners, while the rest had disbanded to gather loot. Warner, however, had ridden up in advance of his regiment and assured Stark that his men were coming from Manchester. They came that evening, 330 strong. At first, owing to a confusion in commands, they deployed to low, exposed, swampy ground to the left of the Germans, instead of to the hill at the right, and had to give way for three-quarters of a mile before the Germans' advance. Breymann attempted to outflank them on their right, and, supported by his two 6-pounders, partly succeeded. But then the freshness of Warner's men told. Supported now by Stark's reassembled men and the two 3-pounders he had captured from Baum, the rebels turned the Germans back. At this point Breymann's last ammunition cart broke apart. He attempted to save his cannon, but most of the men he assigned to the task were wounded. He himself received a flesh wound in the leg. The few horses left were too exhausted to move. Darkness, fortunately, was setting in. He kept his composure, gathered the wounded, destroyed the bridge, and fled west. Stark elected to return to camp. It was the crowning move of a brilliant campaign, for Burgoyne himself was leading the Forty-seventh Regiment to the Germans' relief and turned back when he learned that the action was over. He would have cut Stark to pieces. Two hundred and seven Germans were dead and seven hundred captured; thirty Americans were killed and forty wounded. The Americans took four brass cannon, two hundred fifty broadswords, four ammunition wagons, and several hundred muskets and rifles.[12]

The defeat at the Walloomsac was followed on the eighteenth by still another setback: the collapse of the bridge of rafts on the Hudson below Fort Miller on which the main army was scheduled to cross. The heavy rains had raised the river, and the rush of water had swept apart the weakly bound timbers. The ford where the horses had crossed on the fifteenth was impassable. The planned attack on the Americans at Stillwater had to be abandoned. Using a few bateaux and a large scow for the cannon, Simon Fraser's advance troops at Saratoga struggled back across the current to the east shore on the night of the eighteenth.[13]

Stark had had great good luck. Nichols's and Herrick's encirclements of Baum had worked in perfect unison. Warner's Vermonters' delay had been fortuitous: they arrived fresh and just in time to turn the tide against Breymann. Yet Stark deserves the major credit. He had been the superb leader who personified the New England spirit, inspired the turnout of a whole brigade of amateurs, and understood precisely how to use them against a professional foe.

Burgoyne had suffered a train of misfortunes, without any one of which the result might have been reversed. Baum had ignored Burgoyne's orders to move back if the Americans appeared in force. Breymann had proceeded inexcusably slowly to Baum's rescue, unnecessarily burdening himself with two 6-pound cannon. "Had my instructions been followed, or could Mr. Breyman have marched at the rate of two miles an hour any given twelve out of two and thirty, success would probably have ensued; misfortune would certainly have been avoided," Burgoyne charged.[14]

The Bennington experience revealed the entire campaign in a new and hazardous light. The Indians had proved unreliable: St. Luc had led his warriors back to Canada. The Loyalists in Burgoyne's army numbered no more than four hundred, less than half armed and the rest, he wrote Germain, "trimmers merely actuated by interest." Most ominously of all, those despised rebels stood revealed not as a misled minority but as formidable opponents:

> The great bulk of the country is undoubtedly with the Congress in principle and in zeal, and their measures are executed with secrecy and dispatch not to be equalled. Wherever the King's forces point, militia to the amount of three or four thousand assemble in twenty-four hours: they bring their own subsistence, and the alarm over they return to their farms. The Hampshire grant in particular, a country unpeopled and almost unknown in the last war, now abounds in the most active and most rebellious race of the continent and hangs like a gathering storm on my left.

The main American army, at the mouth of the Mohawk, he now acknowledged was "superior to mine" in numbers and well equipped with artillery. A new urgency crept into his plea for help from Howe: "No operation, my lord, has yet been undertaken in my favour. The Highlands [of the Hudson River] have not even been threatened. . . . I little foresaw that I was to be left to pursue my way through such a tract of country and hosts of foes without any cooperation from New York." To the west, St. Leger, though victorious at Oriskany over Brigadier General Nicholas Herkimer, was stalemated at Fort Stanwix by Colonel Peter Gansevoort. Gone was the confidence of the days before Bennington. "Had I lattitude in my orders," he wrote Germain, "I should think it my duty to wait in this position or perhaps as far back as Fort Edward, where my communication with Lake George would be perfectly secure, till some event happened to assist my movement forward."

But his orders to "force a junction with Sir Wm. Howe" were, he said, "positive." They obligated him to move soon in order to be able, if necessary, to retreat to Ticonderoga before winter set in. He would wait only long enough to collect about twenty-five days' provisions and ammunition and receive German reinforcements on their way from Lake Champlain.[15] In this literal construction of Germain's instructions he denied himself all discretion in the field, even in the face of disaster. He might have relied upon the loophole in those instructions authorizing him and St. Leger to "act as exigencies may require and in such manner as they shall judge most proper for making an impression on the rebels and bringing them to obedience."[16] The truth was that he no longer desired latitude. "Appearances at the time I passed the Hudson's River," he wrote Germain, "would have rendered inaction censurable, had my orders instead of being peremptory been discretionary." He had so firmly made his mind up that he wished no interference. "I did not think myself authorized to call any men into council when the peremptory tenor of my orders and the season of the year admitted no alternative," he declared.[17] That repeated concern over the onset of winter suggests a personal consideration: he might not survive a winter in the north country; better to risk all for victory so as to return home before the snow.

A new bridge, this time of boats instead of rafts, was quickly put together by a detail of Riedesel's light infantry above the rapids (the present Saratoga Falls) by August 19, but a better place was found just below the rapids (two miles above Saratoga, on the west side), and the bridge was dismantled and reassembled at the new location by August 26. At this point, Burgoyne later asserted, "a rapid march to Albany might have been hazarded" if Carleton had been willing to garrison Ticonderoga with troops from Canada, thus releasing the force of 910 there to be brought down to the Hudson and posted at a fortified bridge, which could serve as a retreat route. So it was a shortage not just of provisions but of manpower that was the problem. The question arises whether Burgoyne had a sufficient sense of urgency. Every day of delay was giving the rebel army that lay across the river the time to acquire fresh troops and develop a new spirit. Burgoyne did not recognize this. When he learned on August 28 that St. Leger had been forced to raise the siege of Fort Stanwix by a relief expedition under Benedict Arnold, he concluded that "the first plausible motive in favour of hazardous haste, the facilitating the descent of the Mohawk, was thus at an end." On September 3, the three hundred awaited Germans and two hundred of St. Leger's Indians arrived in camp.[18] He might have used them to fortify an escape bridge and hurried his army across the river.

But he had decided that he had to stockpile a magazine to sustain him for at least twenty-five days after crossing the river. The transport from Lake George to Fort Edward and from Fort Edward to the Hudson was "a d——d hard task," a German officer wrote, "in the hottest part of the year, and one could hardly breathe when sitting still in the tents; dysentery raged among us, but we had to work to maintain life."[19] There were not enough boats because many were in use on the lake for delivery of supplies still in transit from Ticonderoga. For the boats available, there were only twelve boat carriages. Some help did come with the delivery of a batch of horses from Canada, but no more than one hundred and eighty horsecarts could be mustered at any one time. And while the supplies were being hauled, fourteen scows had to be built for the transport of the magazine across the Mohawk once the Hudson was passed.

Twenty-five days after the Bennington defeat, the time Burgoyne had set for himself, his preparations were complete. On September 11, he issued orders to Fraser's advance corps to be ready to cross the river at a moment's notice. It rained all that day and the next, but the thirteenth dawned sunny. At seven in the morning the march began, and by the morrow the entire army of 5,346 effectives was on the west side of the Hudson. The bridge, the last link with Canada, was dismantled. "Britons never retreat," declared Burgoyne.[20]

❧16❧

The Call

"TICONDEROGA! I KNOW WHAT the Public must expect!" exclaimed Rhode Island congressman Henry Marchant. The public wanted Schuyler prosecuted and removed. In vain he protested that he was not present at the evacuation. "It was well known," sneered Samuel Adams, "that he had never been used to keep his own Person near his Army." When Schuyler's defenders countered that New England had not contributed sufficient troops to Ticonderoga, his accusers answered with the supreme charge that the militia refused to serve under him. They would turn out only for Gates, "the darling of the New Englanders," who was close at hand in Philadelphia, waiting for the call in his rooms in Front Street.[1]

On July 26, Jonathan Sergeant of New Jersey moved in Congress that Gates be sent to command the northern department on the ground that Schuyler was repugnant to New England troops and that Gates was their favorite. Benjamin Harrison of Virginia argued that Schuyler was very popular in New York. John Adams recalled dryly that the voters of New York had rejected Schuyler for the governorship. James Wilson of Pennsylvania contended that a man may be unpopular because he is virtuous. Marchant replied that "this congr[ess] depends upon the gen[era]l Opin[ion] of the people. Without attending to this we cannot support this cause." One after another, William Williams of Connecticut, Nathaniel Folsom of New Hampshire, Marchant of Rhode Island, and John Adams of Massachusetts testified that Schuyler was unpopular in their states.[2]

Two days later, the obdurate James Duane returned to the debate with the charge that the attack on Schuyler was the work of a "combination of 4 States." The New Englanders piously denied any design of factionalism, the cardinal political sin of the eighteenth century, and they were supported by their allies from the middle states, Roberdeau of Pennsylvania, and Sergeant. For the moment there was an impasse. All that could be agreed upon was an inquiry into "the conduct of the general officers who were in the northern department at the time of the evacuation," thus including Schuyler among those potentially responsible. Both sides tried to cover their vulnerabilities. The New York delegates warned their home government that if Schuyler continued in command and the New England militia failed to march, New York might be held culpable for any calamity. The New England delegates sent requests home for the tallies of troops sent to Ticonderoga, in order to prove that their states had contributed their share to the defense.[3]

Then, late at night on July 31, Washington arrived in Philadelphia to take over the defense of the city, and the New Yorkers thought they saw an opening. They proposed that he be instructed to name Schuyler's replacement. Lovell went to plead with him for Gates, and Duane against. Seven of the New England delegates, in a joint letter to him, urged that Gates "has on Experience acquired the Confidence, & stands high in the Esteem of the eastern States & Troops." Washington nevertheless preferred Greene, just as he had the year before, and, Greene wrote his wife, "set several persons to sound my inclinations." But a month earlier, Greene had alienated the very New Englanders who championed Gates by threatening to resign if Congress outranked him with a recently arrived French volunteer, Philippe du Coudray, as major general. Washington had to recognize that the demand for Gates could not be resisted, and he grimly wrote the disappointed New Yorker's Council of Safety that, "while the people continue to view what has happened, through the Medium of Suspicion and fear, there is no saying, to what length an enterprising man may push his good fortune." He asked Congress that he be excused from naming Schuyler's successor, as the northern department had always been treated as a separate command. Congress promptly elected Gates, eleven to one, New York unyieldingly objecting that he had supported Vermont statehood.[4]

At the insistence of Duane, Gates was instructed to specify the number of militia he would require; thus New England would have to meet his quotas and he would have to demonstrate his drawing power. He was empowered for four months to suspend and replace officers for misconduct; further, to help him ease the soldiers' fear of Indians, Congress ordered Washington to send him a corps of five hundred riflemen. To loosen Schuyler's grip over the northern army's supply services, James Bleeker was named Deputy Commissary General of Issues. Gates's authority was made so far-reaching that Washington obtained from Congress assurance that it "never intended . . . to supersede or circumscribe" his power as "commander in chief of all the continental land forces within the United States."[5]

Gates immediately wrote the states for 7,750 men: 3,500 from Massachusetts, 750 from New Hampshire, 750 from Connecticut, 1,500 from New York, 500 from New Jersey, and 750 from Pennsylvania. On August 7, he departed to join the army.[6]

Given three more weeks, Schuyler might have been saved. On August 21, Congress received the news of Stark's victory at Bennington, and on September 1, word arrived that the siege of Fort Stanwix had been raised, a triumph resulting from Schuyler's dispatch of a relieving force under Benedict Arnold over the protest of New England officers who had feared to leave their section unprotected.

Yet nothing could have made Schuyler acceptable to New England troops, and New York's canny governor, George Clinton, who at first had been his supporter, was realistic enough to admit it. "Our friend Phil has good qualities," he wrote Duane, "but he has contrived to make himself disagreeable and suspected by the Yankees—prejudices not easily got over. His cursed attachment to the comforts of Albany and doing the fighting business by proxy for two campaigns has destroyed him."[7]

Gates arrived at the northern army's headquarters on the afternoon of August 19, after having stopped at Peekskill to confer with Israel Putnam. He may have delayed assuming responsibility for the command until the militia he had requested should appear. The main army was encamped on Van Schaick's Island, and Enoch Poor's brigade was at Loudon's Ferry, five miles up the Mohawk on the south bank. As of a return on August 17, the entire force totaled 5,888. Schuyler scornfully told Congress that one third of them were "boys, negroes, and men too aged for the field." The men did not forget the slight, and when he attempted to address them he was met with the discharge of a rifle and the whistle of the bullet near his head.[8]

He had been so put out by his removal that for three days he could not be spoken with. Although ordered to report to Washington, he lingered on at the scene, with the excuse that some of his generals had asked him to help manage the militia from his own county of Albany. Certain that he knew what was best for the northern army, he attempted to press upon Gates his plan of operations against Burgoyne—a march back to Stillwater and a recall of Lincoln's two thousand men from Vermont to the east shore of the Hudson in order to threaten the British flank. Gates had already decided to move back toward Burgoyne. The army was located on the Mohawk where it fanned into sprouts that met the Hudson. The surrounding flatland was an unsuitable site for a stand against British formal battlefield maneuver, and Gates deferred to Schuyler's knowledge of the topography in the choice of Stillwater. But he differed sharply about Lincoln's force, which he ordered further north into Vermont to harass Burgoyne's rear and cut off his line of escape to Ticonderoga and Canada. Schuyler, uncomprehending as usual of mass moods, could not recognize that attacks which Lincoln could launch against the forts on Lake Champlain and Lake George could reassure New England and unsettle the British. Gates wanted no more of Schuyler's advice and omitted him from his councils of war.[9]

Gates moved quickly to promote a new spirit in the army. Using the authority Congress had given him, on his second day in camp he issued a general order advising that "the good officer will always find a patron in the General, the bad one must expect disgrace." Among the rank and file, his concern was to instill *confidence in themselves.* This meant first obtaining for them better food, clothing, and equipment, and he sent out a stream of requisitions to the states and to army depots at Peekskill and Philadelphia. Deliveries began to arrive, and commitments came for more. Discipline had to be reestablished, and he introduced daily drills, greater cleanliness in camp and in the hospital, and strict inspections. The improvement was immediately apparent. Colonel Thomas Nixon and the three lieutenant colonels of his Sixth Massachusetts Regiment wrote Gates that "Gladness appear'd in every Countenance, Joy circulated thro the Camp." Major Henry Dearborn of the Third New Hampshire Regiment predicted "a New face upon our affairs," and Glover declared that he now had "not the least doubt of beating or Compelling Mr Burgoyne to return back at least, to Ticonderoga, if not to Canada."[10]

Gates was eager to advance toward Burgoyne not only to establish a more favorable battle location but to dispel the defeatism engendered by encampment at the Mohawk, where the only advantage was refuge from the Indians. He had to wait for his numbers to increase. On August 21, the first of the reinforcements he had requested from New York appeared, Colonel Morris Graham's Ulster County Regiment, assigned to Glover's brigade. On August 31, two vital additions arrived: Arnold's brigade of about 1,200 men from Fort Stanwix, and Colonel Daniel Morgan's corps of 578 riflemen, which Washington, obedient to the order of Congress, had reluctantly sent north. Arnold's victory over St. Leger freed Gates from the danger of attack from the Upper Mohawk. Morgan's Indian fighters relieved Gates's men from the terror of ambush, although for the moment there were so many shirtmen on the sick list that they mustered only 374 effective rank and file. Gates had served with Morgan in the Braddock campaign. Within two weeks he added to his old comrade's command an elite battalion of five newly formed light infantry companies of three hundred men under Major Henry Dearborn. On September 1, two hundred Connecticut Light Horsemen under Major Elijah Hyde came into camp, followed on the sixth by the beginnings of two Connecticut militia infantry regiments under colonels Thaddeus Cook and Jonathan Latimer. These joined Poor's brigade.[11]

Gates seized an opportunity to spur enlistments when a British army physician, Dr. Vincent Wood, appeared under a flag of truce with a message from Burgoyne requesting transmission of baggage and servants for officer prisoners. Burgoyne complained that Tory soldiers who had attempted to surrender at Bennington had been given no quarter. Gates answered with a letter designed for publication "in every Gazette." It was Burgoyne, he proclaimed, "the Soldier and the Scholar," who was the barbarian, the perpetrator of the murder of Jane McCrea:

> Miss McCrea, a Young Lady lovely to the sight, of virtuous Character, and amiable Disposition, engaged to be married to an Officer in your Army, was with other Women and Children, taken out of a House near Fort Edward, carried into the Woods, and there scalped, and mangled in a most shocking Manner. Two Parents and their six Children, were all treated with the same Inhumanity while quietly residing in their once happy and peaceful Dwelling. The Miserable Fate of Miss McCrea was particularly aggravated by her being dressed to receive her promised Husband, but met her Murderer employed by you. Upwards of one hundred Men, Women & Children have perished by the Hands of the ruffians, to whom it is asserted you have paid the Price of Blood.[12]

Pleased with his composition, he called in Lincoln (then briefly in camp for consultation) and Deputy Adjutant General James Wilkinson for their opinions. They hesitated, but when pressed questioned the personal attack on Burgoyne. "By God!" Gates huffed, "I don't believe either of you can mend it," and sent it off.[13]

By September 7, Gates was ready to move. Wilkinson's return of that date listed 7,548 Continentals, including commissioned and noncommissioned officers, present and fit for duty. When to these were added Morgan's

374 riflemen, 248 artillerymen, 200 cavalrymen, 71 engineers, and 1,836 militia, the total came to over 10,000, and Gates wrote Hancock that "The Militia are coming daily."[14] In general orders, he exhorted, "If the Righteous Cause of Freedom, and the Happiness of Posterity be Motives to stimulate the Army to conquer their mercenary and merciless Foes, the Time is now come, when they are called upon by their Country, by their General, by every Reason, human and divine to vanquish their Enemies."[15]

On September 8, at nine in the morning on a bright, sunny day, the main army forded the sprouts of the Mohawk to the village of Half Moon (the present Waterford), where it was joined by Glover's and Nixon's brigades; marched four miles north, where Arnold's division and Morgan's riflemen were added; and after another four miles encamped for the night. The next day, at eleven in the morning, the army reached Stillwater. "The march was made in good order, and the character of the corps seemed renovated," wrote Wilkinson, "courage and confidence having taken place of timidity and distrust." During the army's previous stop at Stillwater, the Polish volunteer engineer, Colonel Thaddeus Kosciuszko, had begun a line of entrenchments, and he now resumed work on them with a fatigue of one thousand men. Colonel Jeduthan Baldwin and his engineers slung a 925-foot bridge of rafts across the Hudson for communication with Lieutenant Benjamin Tupper's Eleventh Massachusetts Continental Regiment, stationed on a hill on the east side of the river, and by nightfall a large drove of cattle and sheep was brought over.[16]

While at Stillwater, the long-gestating antagonism between Gates and Arnold broke into the open. Back in June, Arnold had disregarded Gates's urging to refuse Washington's offer of second in command in Rhode Island. Then, when Washington sent Arnold and Lincoln to join the northern army, Arnold concluded that his best prospects lay with Schuyler. Although Gates had the previous year supported Arnold against charges of misuse of funds and supplies in the Canadian campaign, loyalty was not one of Arnold's supreme virtues. There was in him even a streak of sadism that might delight in arousing apprehension. A fellow clerk who had served with him as apprentice in the Brothers Lathrop apothecary shop in Norwich recalled that he enjoyed dismembering birds and crushing their eggs. When Arnold returned victorious from Stanwix, he took into his military family two of

Schuyler's devoted aides, Lieutenant Colonel Richard Varick and Major Henry Brockholst Livingston. Varick bore a grudge against Gates for having failed sufficiently to punish an officer who had attempted to run him through with a sword when Varick was unarmed during a quarrel at Ticonderoga the previous November. "I wish to God," he wrote Schuyler, "we had a Commander who could see a little Distance before him without Spectacles." Livingston had just returned from Philadelphia, where Schuyler had sent him as the favored carrier of the news of Stark's victory at Bennington, with the expectation of promotion, but Congress had voted against appointing him a lieutenant colonel, New England voting almost solidly in the negative. Gates especially detested Livingston and let Arnold know it in no uncertain terms.[17]

The dispute on September 10 concerned the extent of Arnold's jurisdiction as left-wing division commander. Gates had the day before placed the New York militia under Arnold's command, but then general orders issued by Wilkinson had assigned Colonel Abraham Wemple's Second Albany Regiment, Colonel William B. Whiting's Seventeenth Albany Regiment, and Colonel Morris Graham's Dutchess and Ulster Regiment to Glover's brigade, which came under Gates's own right-wing division. Arnold charged that this put him in "the ridiculous light of presuming to give orders I had no right to do, and having them publicly contradicted." Gates took responsibility for what he said was a mistake and said it would be corrected in future orders, but it never was. It looked as though he was punishing Arnold for keeping Livingston.[18]

On the following day, a captured ensign in Peters's Loyalist battalion gave information that Burgoyne was about to cross the Hudson with his main army and then to press quickly south to attack the Americans. With the British approaching, Stillwater was not a favorable field for a major engagement, as the wide river bank was too extensive at the center to permit occupying it and the heights on the left at the same time. Several of the local townsfolk pointed out that three miles further north there was a narrow defile between the river and a spur of hills, known as Bemis Heights. Through this defile led the only road to Albany on the west side of the Hudson—the one Burgoyne would have to take. Wilkinson had noticed this place earlier, during the army's retreat to the Mohawk, and he, too, thought it superior. Gates sent Kosciuszko and Colonel Udney Hay to check and, when they brought back a favorable report, verified it with a trip of his own. On September 12, he gave the order to move again.[19]

The army took up its position, in the rain, atop a two-hundred-foot elevation at the southern end of the hills, at a farm owned by John Neilson. Below, on the river road, was a tavern kept by Jotham Bemis, a farmer after whom the heights had been named and who was then in the fleet prison at Kingston on suspicion of Toryism. Here Kosciuszko began his fortifications with a line of trenches and earth and log breastworks across the road, and a strong battery at the river edge; Baldwin reassembled his bridge of boats. A mile further north, where Mill Creek descended from the hills to the Hudson, another breastwork was constructed south of the stream, between the road and the river. From the Bemis tavern, rising northwest to the heights, breastworks, with batteries at the southern extremity and the center, were erected along the bluffs for three-quarters of a mile to a commanding knoll, where stood the John Neilson farmhouse, now converted to a closed redoubt for artillery. From there the fortification line turned south for half a mile. The entire layout provided a position from which to sweep the flats along the road on which Burgoyne might approach. There was an exposed point, however, at Fort Neilson (as the farmhouse was christened), where some of the trees had been cut down, and the rough clearing could permit an open engagement.

A mile and a half to the north of the encampment, across Mill Creek, was Freeman's farm, an oblong, east-west clearing of some twelve acres owned by a Loyalist Quaker, Isaac Leggett. Arnold tried to pry from one of Leggett's daughters an admission that her father had sold provisions to the British. "If thee knows better than I, why did thee ask me?" Mary tartly replied. Gates interceded, saying, "Don't be too hard on the young woman."[20]

Burgoyne's position was not precisely known, for Morgan's riflemen, on whom Gates relied as scouts, were as yet unfamiliar with the territory. Because Wilkinson had often traveled between Fort Edward and Albany, he headed a patrol of 150 infantry and 20 riflemen to Saratoga to observe British movements across the river. Starting at night, he reached his destination in the morning of the thirteenth, just in time to see a British column descending from the Batten Kill to the Hudson. Some of the Twentieth Regiment were already on the west near Schuyler's house, and Wilkinson's men seized three of them. The prisoners divulged that Burgoyne was taking his whole army across the river.[21]

The activity at Bemis Heights became feverish. Kosciuszko's work crews sweated at fortifications. Gates sent orders to Lincoln in Vermont "to defeat that Part of the Enemy's Force, yet upon the east Side of the River." To the legislatures of the surrounding states he fired off renewed appeals: "I have Rec'd Certain Intelligence that Genl Burgoyne Designs to Resque all upon one Rash Stroke, it is therefore the Indispensible Duty of all concerned to Exert themselves in Reinforcing this Army without one moment's Delay."[22] And he called upon his men to "live victorious or die free."[23]

❧ 17 ❧

Saratoga

ONCE THEY WERE ACROSS THE Hudson, the eager British and Germans saw themselves on the doorstep of Albany. Burgoyne, Riedesel said, "burned with impatience to advance on the enemy."[1]

On September 15, the army set out from Saratoga south on the river road with colors flying and music pealing—an incongruous spectacle in the wilderness, reminding one observer of a "grand parade in the midst of peace." Burgoyne and his staff stood in review as Fraser's advance corps led the way. To the right, under Hamilton, marched the Ninth, Twentieth, Twenty-first, and Sixty-second English regiments. At the center, making the best of the road that the Americans had left in ruin, rolled the park of artillery under Phillips. Along the meadow to the left of the road came Riedesel and the Germans. Behind the artillery followed eighty-five baggage wagons and, lastly, Breymann's Rear Guard. The provisions were being floated down the Hudson under the protection of the Forty-seventh Regiment.

The prearranged order of march soon had to be abandoned because of the near unusable road, and the whole of the infantry combined into one column, filing along the shore. The inhabitants fled, and the advancing British burned or tore down the homes in their path. Even a Loyalist described it as "a most shocking picture of havoc and wild desolation." After three miles, the army halted for the night at Dovecote (the present Coveville), at the Cummings Kill, where a bridge had been severed by the Americans. Here the Forty-seventh Regiment, with the provisions, joined the army.

In the middle of the night, the tent in which Major John Acland and his wife, Harriet (Christian Henrietta Caroline), were sleeping suddenly caught fire—their Newfoundland dog had overturned a table with a lighted candle. Acland plunged into the flames after Lady Harriet, who was in the advanced

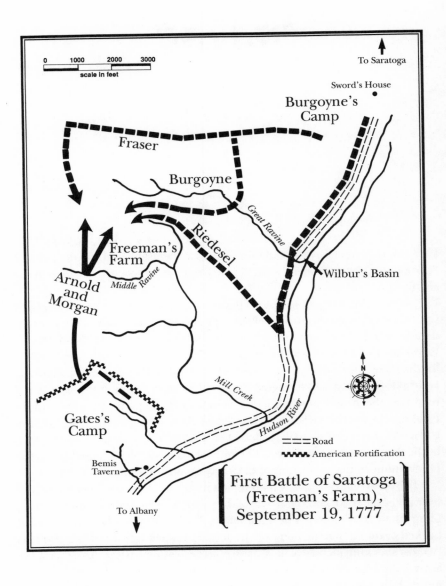

First Battle of Saratoga
(Freeman's Farm),
September 19, 1777

stages of pregnancy, without realizing that she had crept out under the back of the tent. He was pulled out by his orderly, after having been badly burned in the face and body.[2]

The army all the while was without eyes, for only sixty Indians remained after the departure of St. Luc, and they were terrified of Morgan's riflemen. Burgoyne, therefore, himself led a reconnaissance force of 2,000 the following morning, accompanied by two one-hundred-man work crews to repair bridges. The terrain was so difficult that only three miles were covered by nightfall, and when no Americans were encountered, the detachment returned to Dovecote. The next day the whole army struggled along the three miles, stopping in the evening at a dwelling known as Sword's House, on the south side of a spring brook. The enemy was now another three miles away.[3]

On September 18, the army moved a half mile further down the river road to what is now Wilbur's Basin. Here Burgoyne received from deserters information that Gates's force numbered between ten and twelve thousand men. For a payment of £5 13s 4d, the deserters supplied "an exact account of the rebel army, cannon & dispositions."[4] The Americans had established themselves on the heights in extensive fortifications. The right wing, under the immediate command of Gates and consisting of Glover's, Paterson's, and Nixon's brigades, occupied the hills closest to the road and the breastworks leading down to the river. At the center were Brigadier General Ebenezer Learned's brigade and two regiments of militia, and on the heights to the left, under Arnold, were Poor's brigade, Morgan's riflemen, and another portion of militia.[5] If Burgoyne were to take his whole army along the river road, as some historians have faulted him for not doing, he could be caught in a bottleneck, outnumbered and exposed to the entire American force sweeping down upon him from the hills above. His decision was to ascend to the heights in order to attack the Americans at the western end of their fortifications, where they were vulnerable to fire from a commanding hill, and from there speed south along a road that led straight to Albany.

Burgoyne's plan was to advance in three columns, for to move through the woods as one compact body, with the full train of artillery, would have been crippling. Riedesel, accompanied by Phillips, was to lead his three Brunswick infantry regiments, von Gall's Hesse-Hanau infantry regiment, Phillips's Forty-seventh Regiment and artillery battalion, and the auxiliary work crews, a total of 2,978 men, and the Hesse-Hanau artillery—six 6-pounders and two 3-pounders—along the river road. The largest force, 3,003 men under Fraser—consisting of his own Twenty-fourth Regiment, Acland's grenadier battalion, Balcarres's light-infantry battalion, a company of rangers, Breymann's German advance corps, and the Loyalists, Canadians, and Indians—was to ascend a rough road climbing west from Sword's House three miles toward the far side of Freeman's Farm. Artillery support was provided with four 6-pounders and four 3-pounders. Between these two wings would come the center force, accompanied by Burgoyne: Hamilton and the Ninth, Twenty-first, Sixty-second, and Twentieth British regiments, a total of 1,721 British regulars. They were assigned six fieldpieces—six- and three-pounders. The center column was to ascend the road taken by Fraser's right wing for a mile and a half until it reached the vicinity of the North Fork of Mill Creek, where it was to turn south and cross a deep channel known as the Great Ravine. There it was to halt and fire a gun as a signal for Fraser at the west and Riedesel at the east to come abreast and then march in unison upon the American line of fortifications.[6]

In the American camp, there was some confusion, as new troops appeared and others departed. About seven hundred of Stark's Vermont and New Hampshire brigade, temporarily commanded during his illness by Colonel Samuel Ashley, had arrived a week before, but its term of service was about to expire. Despite the appeals of Stark when he arrived and an offer by Gates of ten dollars per man if they would stay until Burgoyne's defeat, these veterans of Bennington marched off punctually at midnight of their severance date, September 18, on the eve of battle.[7] Tensions mounted. In Colonel Henry Beekman Livingston's Fourth New York Regiment of the Continental Line, a fight broke out in which Samuel Hemmenway, plunged a knife into the neck of Dudley Broadstreet, partly cutting the jugular vein.[8] In Arnold's division, Henry Brockholst Livingston became involved in a dispute with another aide, Major Leonard Chester, a militiaman from Wethersfield, Connecticut. Chester had issued a disciplinary order over his own signature, styling himself "Leonardus Chester." Livingston, a violent man and on edge because "General Schuyler's recommendations in my favour have been repeatedly neglected," called him an "impertinint Pedant." The disagreement erupted into a hard-fought duel in which neither man was injured and neither conceded.[9]

The general officers met in council at nine o'clock on the morning of September 17. Some of them still thought Burgoyne might make his main thrust along the river road; others expected him to ascend the hills and skirt the Americans' left wing. Two hours later, Colonel Philip Van Cortlandt, commander of the Second New York Regiment, returned from a reconnaissance trip with news that the British had advanced to Sword's House. Arnold had been pleading to attack the enemy with his division alone, and Gates decided to give him his chance. With his left-wing division of approximately three thousand and Morgan's riflemen, he was to march around northeastward through the woods and down to the river road and "attack the enemy in their march." But he was not to engage unless he could draw the British out from their fortifications. Then the American right-wing division, under Gates, could attack from the south, and the British would be caught in a trap, prevented by the hills from escape to the west.

The army was ordered to turn out with tents struck and baggage loaded at four o'clock the next morning. Rations were issued of bread and half a gill of rum per man. Arnold started at sunrise and arrived northwest of Burgoyne's camp, across the river from the present village of Easton. Some thirty enemy soldiers and women, heedless of danger, were digging for potatoes, their first since landing in America ("Pork at noon, pork at night, pork cold, pork hot," a Brunswick officer lamented), and the Americans killed or wounded four and captured eight. But Burgoyne recoiled from an engagement in which he could not bring his artillery to bear. He could discern through his spyglass seven American regiments but forbade all unnecessary firing. Arnold lingered all afternoon in the area, harassing a work party of four hundred rebuilding a bridge but attempting no major action. At four o'clock he departed back to the American camp.[10]

On the morning of September 19, a thick fog enveloped Bemis Heights. By nine o'clock it lifted, and the British advance began. Fraser, with the Indians, Canadians, and Loyalists at the front and flanks, took the west road up into the hills and crossed the Great Ravine at its head on the far side. There he turned south to a position on a ridge at the western end of Freeman's Farm. Burgoyne and the center column, after a short climb into the hills, crossed the creek at the bottom of the ravine over a small bridge that the Americans had neglected to destroy. At this point he took a westward wagon track for half a mile and halted. It was twelve o'clock, and he waited an hour for the other columns to catch up. Riedesel and Phillips moved south in two columns along the river road, preceded by the few dragoons who had obtained mounts and a hundred light infantry, and followed by the heavy artillery and baggage. Hampered by bridges that required repair, the division arrived a quarter of a mile below Wilbur's Basin by one o'clock. Then the signal guns of the three columns were fired for the general advance.[11]

Gates received news of the British activity from a scouting party under Lieutenant Colonel Andrew Colburn, of the Third New Hampshire Regiment, which he had posted across the Hudson. As the enemy appeared to be ascending the heights toward the American left, he sent out Morgan's riflemen to find and harass them. Arnold once again urged that the army march out in force to engage the British in the woods before they could come near enough to the American lines to use their artillery. Gates, however, was more concerned with the threat of an attack from Riedesel's division on the river road. As a reserve against this threat, he kept under his own direct orders Learned's brigade of four regiments, which formally belonged in Arnold's division, as well as Morgan's and Dearborn's riflemen. Arnold was left only with Poor's brigade of seven regiments.[12] Gates, in his subsequent battle report to Congress, referred to his left wing as only a brigade, without naming its commander. Poor might have resisted taking orders for the internal operation of his brigade from a superfluous superior, yet he seems to have been willing enough to accept Arnold, in effect, as commander of his own brigade.

Morgan's corps moved out in two irregular lines. By about half past twelve they reached an empty log cabin on the south side of Freeman's Farm. Some of the men, under Major Jacob Morris, occupied the house, and the rest positioned themselves along nearby rail fences. Suddenly a band of some one hundred Canadian and Indian pickets, under Major Gordon Forbes of the Ninth Regiment, emerged from the woods. The riflemen immediately opened fire. Within a half hour, every British officer but one was killed or wounded, including Forbes, who persisted despite his wound. Captain David Monin of the Canadians fell as his eleven-year-old son, fought at his side. The Americans did not realize they had encountered a unit of the center of the British line, and they incautiously abandoned their cover and rushed after the fleeing pickets. On hearing the firing, Simon Fraser, off to the British right, led two light infantry companies of the Twenty-fourth Regiment with one cannon to Forbes's rescue. This gave Forbes time to bring the main body of his regiment forward and counterattack the now outnumbered and confused Americans. The alarmed Morgan hastily came up from his customary position at the rear. Wilkinson, who was with him, reported him crying out, in tears, "I am ruined, by God!" and frantically rallying his men with a "turkey call," his signal whistle, to reassemble at a hill eighty feet to his rear.

Forbes's reinforcements, however, were also panicking under the riflemen's deadly marksmanship and were firing so wildly, without orders, that they were hitting many of their own men. Major Robert Kingston, Burgoyne's adjutant general, arrived on the scene and persuaded Forbes to silence the small arms with the warning discharge of a cannonball. Thirteen of Morgan's men had been captured. The Indians were stripping one of them, Captain Van Swearingen, of his money and papers, when a British soldier stepped in and brought him to Fraser. Fraser threatened to hang his prisoner if he did not immediately divulge the American defenses. "You may, if you please," Swearingen answered, and Fraser, impressed, ordered that he not be ill-treated.[13]

Gates at that time was inspecting the battery at the left wing occupied by Poor, and when he learned of Morgan's encounter he ordered out to the north, from Poor's brigade, Colonel Joseph Cilley's First New Hampshire Regiment, and, soon after, Colonel Alexander Scammell's Third New Hampshire Regiment to flank the enemy on their left. Scammell met the British head on, while Cilley found himself flanking them. Morgan's men captured a fieldpiece, and Morgan himself had his horse killed under him. Gates as yet thought the action a limited probe on his left, and he turned over the direction of the engagement to Arnold, who, with Poor's acquiescence, sent out Lieutenant Colonel Winborn Adams's Second New Hampshire Regiment.[14]

But Arnold could not himself keep out of the fray. Captain Ebenezer Wakefield, of Dearborn's light infantry, describes him as "riding in front of the lines, his eyes flashing, pointing with his sword to the advancing foe, with a voice that rung clear as a trumpet and electrified the line." As the action heated up, Arnold sent out Van Cortlandt's Second New York Regiment toward the left to counter Fraser's column; if Van Cortlandt was hard pressed, he was to call for Colonel Henry Beekman Livingston's Fourth New York Regiment. "This order," said Van Cortlandt, "was given me first by General Poor on my parade; and as I was marching also by General Arnold." Van Cortlandt ran into Fraser's advance troops and sent his adjutant back for Livingston's support, but, Van Cortlandt angrily reported, he "disobeyed and fell off to the right, leaving me to contend first with the Hessians' advance of riflemen which I defeated, and who run off; but their place was instantly supplied by the British light infantry, whom we fought upwards of an hour, at which time the Hessians had rallied and gained my left."[15]

The fighting now concentrated at the center, at Freeman's Farm, where Burgoyne's center column arrived at two o'clock. Anticipating an attack in force in the hills on his right, he held most of Fraser's right wing in reserve.

Gates, expecting an attack at the river on his right, at first sent no reinforcements to Poor's brigade. Arnold refused to accept this denial. He rode up to the van of Learned's regiment and demanded three hundred volunteers to assist Poor. Major William Hull, of the Eighth Massachusetts Regiment, offered to command the unit if he could be released from guard duty assigned to him by an order from Wilkinson. Arnold replied that he would excuse him on his own authority. Four companies were quickly filled, and they were deployed by Poor to protect his hard-pressed right.[16]

The brunt of the resistance to Poor's offensive was borne by Lieutenant Colonel John Lynd's Twentieth Regiment on the left, Lieutenant Colonel John Anstruther's Sixty-second in the center, and Hamilton's Twenty-first on the right. Supporting them were four 6-pound cannon commanded by Captain Thomas Jones. The Americans had brought up no artillery but sent off a continuous barrage of small arms fire. By half past three, wrote Glover, there was "One Continual blaze." "Such an explosion of fire I never had any idea of before," Digby marveled, "and the heavy artillery joining in concert like great peals of thunder, assisted by the echoes of the woods, almost deafened us with the noise." The struggle raged in waves back and forth, neither side able to sustain its advance once it had come out into the open field. Arnold, Poor reported, "rushed into the thickest of the fight with his usual recklessness, and at times acted like a madman." Scammell "fought like a hero, leading his regiment where the fire was the hottest, and did not leave his post until he was wounded and taken off the field." His friend Winborn Adams, from their hometown of Durham, had already fallen at his side. The Americans poured forth fresh reinforcements; the British replied with bayonet charges. American sharpshooters climbed trees and singled out officers and gunners. Lieutenant Anburey saw Lieutenant John Don, of the Twenty-first, with a bullet through the heart, spring up as high as a man and fall dead. The Sixty-second took the hottest fire, and among the wounded were both the first and second in command, Anstruther and Major Henry Harnage. Artillery Lieutenant James Hadden, posted to its left with two cannon, lost nineteen of his twenty-two men and himself had his cap shot away while he was spiking a cannon. His superior, Captain Jones, arrived with replacements but was soon mortally wounded, and Hadden had to carry him in his arms back to a hut already crowded with the dying. "I think it is not in the power of men to keep a better fire, both of round and grape-shot, than was successively maintained for several hours that day," Kingston afterward testified. And Burgoyne, through it all, "shunned no danger," reported Sergeant

Lamb; "his presence and conduct animated the troops, (for they greatly loved the general;) he delivered his orders with precision and coolness."

Phillips, meanwhile, had come up from Riedesel's wing at the river to learn what was happening. He promptly sent back to Riedesel for four guns and, personally leading a charge of the Twentieth Regiment to the east and "recklessly exposing himself," repossessed Hadden's guns and permitted the Sixty-second to reform. An aide-de-camp of Phillips, Captain Charles Green, conspicuous on a saddle elaborately laced and embroidered, was shot down from his horse as he was delivering a message to Burgoyne by a rifleman who mistook him for the commander.

By half past four, the British situation had become so desperate that Burgoyne decided to call for Riedesel to attack the Americans' right flank. Leaving Specht behind to guard the bateaux and supply train with his own regiment, the British Forty-seventh Regiment, three companies of the Regiment Rhetz, and the heavy cannon, Riedesel took with him the Regiment Riedesel, two companies of the Regiment Rhetz, and two 6-pounders under Captain Georg Pausch. Ascending west a mile and a half to the scene of the action, he found the three British regiments thinned down to one-half their strength and surrounded by heaps of dead and wounded; the cannon silenced, the ammunition having been exhausted; and the Royal Artillerymen all killed or wounded. Pausch set up his guns on a hill within pistol shot of the Americans, where Phillips was attempting to rally the Twenty-first and Ninth regiments, and fired off a dozen point-blank shots. The Regiment Riedesel now arrived and with shouts and beating drums fired three salvos into the retreating American ranks, following them up with a British-German bayonet charge.[17]

Gates, at his headquarters a half mile south of Fort Neilson, now learned from newly captured prisoners that his forward division faced Riedesel's troops as well as those of the British center. He therefore at last sent ahead all of Learned's brigade of Colonel John Bailey's Second Massachusetts, Colonel Michael Jackson's Eighth Massachusetts (commanded in his absence by Lieutenant Colonel John Brooks), Colonel James Wesson's Ninth Massachusetts, and Colonel James Livingston's New York regiments, as well as Colonel Thomas Marshall's Tenth Massachusetts Regiment from Paterson's brigade. They served to fend off attacks from Fraser's grenadiers and Breymann's light troops.

Arnold had by then returned from the front and was impatiently sitting on his horse next to Gates when Colonel Morgan Lewis, deputy quartermaster general, rode in from the field to report that the outcome of the struggle was still indecisive. This was too much for Arnold. "By God I will soon put an end to it," he exclaimed, clapped his spurs to his horse, and galloped off into the fray. But Lewis, knowing Gates's aversion for Arnold, immediately reversed his report. "You had better order him back," he said, "the action is going well, he may by some rash act do mischief." Gates dispatched Wilkinson after Arnold with an order to return.

With nightfall, the Americans fell back, and it was fortunate that the British did not pursue, for less than forty rounds of ammunition per man remained in the magazine. The British were left in possession of the battlefield, but after the first flush of elation Burgoyne had to admit that "no fruits, honour excepted, were attained by the preceding victory, the enemy working with redoubled ardour to strengthen their left; their right was unattackable already."[18]

The Americans had lost 63 (including two New Hampshire lieutenant colonels, Andrew Colburn and Winborn Adams) and had 212 wounded and 38 missing. The last unit to withdraw, Brooks's regiment, could not bring off its wounded, who lay exposed on the ground in the cold, some to be plundered and scalped by the British army's Indians. One militiaman, shot through the head, wandered about the field all night, until in the morning he chanced on one of the American guards. The fallen who had been rescued faced the agonies of the hospital tent. Glover, who watched, found it heartrending "to see the Amputating of Limbs, (of which there were Six perform'd) to hear the Cries of the Wounded, and groans of the dying, wallowing in their Gore." One of them was a mortally wounded British officer, Ensign Phillips, not more than sixteen years old, who had been hit in the leg and then treacherously shot through the body by a follower of his own army. Wilkinson found him on a visit to the hospital and spoke of him to Gates. "Just heaven!" Gates exclaimed, startled by the name, "he may be the nephew of my wife," which turned out not to be the case.[19]

The British had 160 dead, 364 wounded, and 42 missing. The Sixty-second English Regiment, the hardest hit, lost 53 and had 109 wounded. The dead were buried in mass graves, the officers separate from the men; scattered heads, legs, and arms were left above ground. Three subalterns of the Twentieth Regiment, all aged seventeen or less, lay together. Nineteen-year-old Ensign Henry Young of the Sixty-second, struck in the leg, had at first refused to have it amputated; when gangrene set in and he consented it was too late to prevent death. Also of the Sixty-second, Lieutenant Stephen Harvey, sixteen years old, while being carried away with a leg wound, was shot again, fatally. Asked whether he had any affairs to settle, he replied that he was a minor and there was no need. "Tell my uncle I died like a soldier," was his only request. Lieutenant Anburey, commanding a party to bring in the wounded, found them "perishing with cold and weltering in their blood" while they waited for tents to be erected to shelter them. "Some of them," he wrote, "begged they might lie and die, others again were insensible, some upon the least movement were put in the most horrid tortures."[20]

The Battle of Freeman's Farm was a test of will and spirit between the rank and file of the two armies, not a chessboard match of wits between generals. "Both Armies seemd determin'd to Conquer or die," said Glover, and the British at last had to recognize that they faced a formidable foe: "The courage and obstinacy with which the Americans fought [Anburey wrote] were the astonishment of everyone, and we now became fully convinced that they are not that contemptible enemy we had hitherto imagined them, incapable of standing a regular engagement, and that they would only fight behind strong and powerful works."[21]

The key to that performance had been Morgan's superlative battalion of riflemen, useful not merely for scouting and sniping but for spearheading a major engagement. Gates decided that he would formally attach it to his headquarters command, to be deployed personally by him, and announced this move in a general order on September 22. Morgan's battalion, on loan from Washington's army, had until now not been incorporated into any brigade but had been under Arnold's direction. Arnold immediately reacted to the transfer as the final slight in his festering feud with Gates. He burst furiously into Gates's room, and in an instant the two flew at each other with raised voices and strong language. Arnold charged not only that his command was being reduced but that Gates, in his battle report to Congress, had not given him credit as division commander in the action. Gates hotly answered that he was not aware that Arnold was a major general (a reference to Arnold's attempted resignation) and therefore did not rate a division. Gates had ordered Lincoln to Bemis Heights as division commander, and he should have no further use for Arnold, who could have a pass to go to Philadelphia whenever he wished and apply for reassignment. Arnold returned to his quarters and dashed off a blistering request for the pass.

Gates promptly wrote out the permission, but then it appeared that Arnold had no intention of leaving, counting on his popularity in the army to intimidate Gates with his threat of departure. Poor and his colonels did in fact send Arnold a petition to reconsider, but Learned's officers said nothing for fear of antagonizing Gates. Arnold grew increasingly distraught, watching to see whether Lincoln, who arrived September 23, would in fact take over his division. Once he saw Lincoln giving some directions there and immediately asked him whether this was at Gates's orders. Lincoln assured him that it was not, but Arnold excitedly declared that it would be "certain death" for any officer to interfere in his division, which he would not yield now that an action was impending. Gates was willing to consider a reconciliation if Arnold would demonstrate his loyalty with an act of good faith—the discharge of his aide, Henry Brockholst Livingston. Wilkinson carried the message to Chester, Livingston's former dueling opponent, who relayed it to Arnold. Arnold, according to Livingston, "could scarcely contain himself" and sent Chester back with the answer that he "would not sacrifice a Friend to please the 'Face of Clay.'"

News of the dispute had by now spread through the camp. Poor, who had emerged as perhaps the single general officer on good terms with both Gates and Arnold, now drew up a petition of the generals (with the notable exception of Lincoln) in effect imploring Arnold to make a concession. Arnold would not listen. Gates was too good a politician to antagonize Arnold's supporters; he devised an oblique plan to decrease Arnold's authority without formally removing him. On September 25, in general orders, he assigned Lincoln to the command of the army's right wing, consisting of Nixon's, Glover's, and Paterson's brigades. The seven regiments of New York militia that Arnold had claimed as his own were assigned to Glover. Arnold was left with only Poor's and Learned's brigades. The same orders announced that "the large reinforcements arriv'd and continually arriving makes it necessary that a new arrangement of the Army shou'd soon take place." Nothing was said of Arnold, who had to wait to learn what his command would be. Three days later, another general order, referring again to "an immediate Necessity that a new arrangement of the Army shou'd immediately take Place," called for returns of the effective strength of each brigade as preliminary information. But no new arrangement was ever published. Arnold was left in limbo, uncertain whether he would even have a command. In another wild letter, disclaiming a "Wish to Command the Army, or to out shine you," he accused Gates of "a Spirit of Jealousy," faulting him for not having resumed the offensive the day after the battle and warning him that the militia would go home if he did not take action.[22]

Was it any wonder that Gates wrote home to Betsy, "The Fatigue of Body & Mind, which I continually undergo, is too much for my Age & Constitution. A General of an American Army must be everything, & that is being more than one Man can Sustain. This Campaign must End my Military Labours."[23]

~❧18❧~

Repulse

BURGOYNE STILL BELIEVED, OR
still wished to believe, that his instructions required him to push on to
Albany. But there was no sign of cooperation from Howe, and the disturbing
thought that had before this only faintly intruded itself upon him now returned more insistently—that the campaign was from the beginning
intended merely as a diversion to protect Howe's army to the south, and that
the northern army was seen from Whitehall as expendable. Yet, despite the
carnage of September 19, he had come close to victory. "Had the action
happened nearer the river, so that the left column could have been brought
into action early," he wrote, "not a man would have escaped," and he even
convinced himself that the Americans had suffered a much greater loss than
his own.[1]

He did not yet know what the Americans learned on September 21. That
morning, the British were awakened by the firing of thirteen cannon and
plainly audible shouts of "Hurrah! Hurrah!" from the enemy camp. The
Americans had received news from the north that their force there under
Colonel John Brown had captured Fort George and, although unsuccessful in
attacks on Ticonderoga and Diamond Island in Lake Champlain, had seized
two hundred bateaux, captured three hundred of General Powell's defending
garrisons, and freed one hundred American prisoners. Another American
force had occupied Skenesboro.[2] This meant that even if Burgoyne should
attempt to cross back to the east side of the Hudson his supply lines by land
and water were in serious trouble.

On the night of September 21, a messenger brought a letter from Clinton
in New York, written ten days earlier in code. Burgoyne had lost the decod-
ing mask, a sheet with an hourglass-shaped cutout, but he made another from
memory and read: "You know my good will, & are not ignorant of my pover-

ty. If you think 2000 men can assist you effectually I will make a push at [Fort] Montgomery [in the highlands of the lower Hudson] in about ten days but ever jealous of my flanks; if they make a move in force on either of them, I must return to save this important post. I expect reenforcements every day. Let me know what you would wish."[3]

This offer was accompanied by another communication, delivered orally by the messenger, promising to write again in eight days.[4] That could mean that Clinton would start up the Hudson even without a reply. Burgoyne at once decided to suspend forward movement and wait for Clinton, and he wrote back: "An attack, or the Menace of an Attack upon Montgomery, must be of great Use, as it will draw away part of this Force, and I will follow them close. Do it, my dear Friend, directly."[5]

While he waited, he dug in. The day after the battle, he and his generals rode over the entire front and laid out a two-mile line of defense. The extreme right flank—Breymann's corps and some Loyalists—was pulled back just south of the Great Ravine and protected with a large log palisade named the Breymann Redoubt. From there, southward in the interval to the North Fork of Mill Creek, were two fortified log cabins held by a contingent of Canadians. On the far side of the North Fork was positioned Fraser's corps of light infantry and grenadiers. Immediately east of that, at Freeman's Farm, was Balcarres's light-infantry battalion, protected by a high abatis named the Balcarres Redoubt. East of Freeman's Farm, the North Fork turned south, and east of that Burgoyne established his headquarters and strung the center of the British line—the Ninth, Twenty-first, Sixty-second, and Twentieth regiments—the remainder of the distance further eastward to the river bluff. Artillery were stationed in the spaces between the army's wings. The center was protected along its front by a deep, muddy ditch and a swath cleared of trees. At the riverside north of the Great Ravine were the British Forty-seventh, the Hesse-Hanau and Brunswick regiments, a corps of Loyalists, the hospital, the park of heavy artillery, and the camp of the few remaining Indians. There, on a row of three hills, a great redoubt of fortifications was erected. In the river were moored the provision bateaux, and on the far side was built a floating bridge for access to a source of forage.[6]

Burgoyne expected Clinton "hourly," but no word came. As the nights grew colder and provisions ran dangerously low, he at last had to recognize that he must set a time limit for assistance. On September 27, he dispatched Captain Thomas Scott of the Twenty-fourth Regiment with a verbal message to Clinton, warning that he could not survive if he continued to Albany "unless assured that the communication between that place and New York

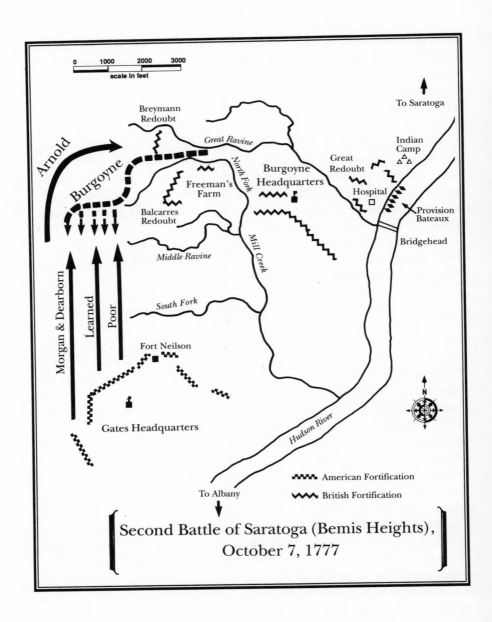

Second Battle of Saratoga (Bemis Heights),
October 7, 1777

was kept open." If Clinton promised help, he could remain at Bemis Heights until October 16. If not, he would have to retreat by the twelfth in order to reach Canada before the ice set in. He requested that Clinton, acting for Howe, send him "an Answer conveying the plainest and most positive Meaning how he should act for the good of His Majesty; whether he should proceed to Albany or to make good his retreat to Canada."[7]

On the day after Scott's departure, the reason for the shouts and cannon shots from the American lines seven days before was revealed to the British. The Americans released a Brunswick prisoner captured at Bennington, Cornet August L. Grafe, who brought the news that the Americans had taken Fort George and Skenesboro. Burgoyne hastily dispatched a second agent to Clinton, Captain Alexander Campbell of the Sixty-second Regiment, with the message that his provisions could last only until October 20, and with the flat declaration that he "would not have given up his communications with Ticonderoga had he not expected a cooperating army at Albany."[8]

Burgoyne's first letter, of September 21, reached Clinton on the twenty-ninth. He was still in New York, having decided to wait for reinforcements from England before acting on his offer of the twelfth to start in ten days. This although seventeen days earlier, on learning of the defeat at Bennington, he had considered leading a detachment northward without delay. The reinforcements came on the twenty-ninth, and he now had no excuse to procrastinate. Leaving four thousand men to guard New York City, he set out with three thousand on October 4 and reached Verplanck's Point, on the river's east shore, opposite forts Montgomery and Clinton.

At this point, Campbell, making better time than Scott, was the first of Burgoyne's later messengers to find Clinton. Clinton was disturbed that Burgoyne should treat his offer of assistance as a proposal for a full-scale juncture with the northern army. He had no intention of acting for Howe, and he sent Campbell back with the chilling reply: "Sir H. Clinton cannot presume to give any Orders to General Burgoyne. General Burgoyne could not suppose that Sir H. Clinton had an idea of penetrating to Albany with the small force he mentioned in his last Letter. What he offered in that Letter he has now undertaken; cannot by any means promise himself Success, but hopes it will be at any rate serviceable to General Burgoyne."[9]

Neither this message nor two duplicates Clinton sent reached Burgoyne.

Campbell, and Scott after him, could not make their way through hostile territory and returned. Another messenger, First Lieutenant Daniel Taylor of the Ninth Regiment, was captured. He swallowed the silver ball in which the message was contained, but the Americans brought it out of him with a strong dose of tartar emetic, "calculated to operate either way," and then hanged him.[10]

Clinton's expedition against the two forts in the highlands was a success. In rapid, combined land and water maneuvers, he defeated American forces under brigadier generals George and James Clinton (the New York governor and his brother) and Major General Israel Putnam. On October 8, Henry Clinton wrote Burgoyne, *"Nous y voila,* and nothing now between us and Gates. I sincerely hope this little success may facilitate your operations." Two days later, emboldened to go further, he sent Scott back to Burgoyne with a verbal message "that if in consequence of my success he should have decided in going for Albany, the Commodore [Sir James Wallace, commander of the squadron in Clinton's expedition] and I would do our utmost to force a communication with him and supply him with provisions."[11] Burgoyne did not receive either message. On October 13, Clinton went so far as to send a force of two thousand under Major General Sir John Vaughan upriver to assist and, if necessary, join Burgoyne.

It was too late. His initial delay removed whatever chance Burgoyne might have had for rescue. Clinton knew when he wrote the letter that Burgoyne was in trouble. He had learned of the defeat at Bennington and the consequent loss of a supply of provisions. Burgoyne had written that he expected to be in Albany by August 23, and he was now, well into September, forty miles away, as Clinton had also learned. The trouble was that Clinton was not committed to helping Burgoyne. He lost valuable time by sending an expedition into eastern New Jersey that accomplished nothing of consequence, aside from acquiring some livestock. He persuaded himself that Burgoyne could survive unassisted until the next spring. His concern in offering to attack Fort Montgomery was really to clear the way for Howe to come back in the spring from Pennsylvania and join Burgoyne at Albany after all.[12]

By October 4, Gates's army at Bemis Heights numbered 11,469 effectives, of which 6,444 were Continentals and 5,025 militia. Burgoyne's army totaled 6,617 effectives, of which 3,068 were British, 2,733 Germans, and 816 Loyalists, Canadians, and Indians. Gates was well aware of his advantage, and he correctly estimated that Burgoyne had no more than three weeks' provisions. Time was on his side, and Burgoyne's inaction suited him very well. He used it to strengthen his western defences, absorb new troop arrivals (including a party of Oneida and Tuscarora Indians), and keep the British on edge with nighttime skirmishes.

In general orders, he told his troops that the enemy "must endeavor by one rash Stroke to regain all they have lost. That failing, their ruin is Inevitable." The jubilant troops became so raucous that the guards complained they could not send an alarm that would be audible in case of an enemy approach, and an order had to be issued to keep the men silent in their tents as soon as the watch was set at eight in the evening. The atmosphere of expectant victory spread to the Patriot civilians of the vicinity. Some twenty frolickers, led by a mock captain in improvised blue and buff uniform, bluffed a British guard patrol of thirty into surrendering to them.[13]

The strain told on the British. "I do not believe either officer or soldier ever slept during that interval without his cloaths," wrote Burgoyne, "or that any general officer, or commander of a regiment, passed a single night without being upon his legs occasionally at different hours, and constantly an hour before day-light." The American patrols were so bold that they circled the right wing of the British and even carried off some English soldiers digging potatoes five hundred yards behind headquarters. Desertions increased, and the Americans sent agents into camp to lure the British from their hard service with promises of lenient treatment. With 800 men in the hospital, Burgoyne was forced to use 120 provincials as replacements in the ranks of the regulars. As foraging parties proved inadequate, he had to reduce the daily food ration by one third to a pound of bread and a pound of meat. To keep the men's spirits up, he announced that "there is reason to be assured, that other powerful Armies are actually in cooperation with these Troops," and distributed twelve barrels of precious rum.[14]

By the evening of October 4, with depletion of provisions, reports of Gates's buildup of manpower, and the virtual severance of the escape route on the east side of the Hudson, Burgoyne decided that he could wait no longer for Clinton; he must advance alone. But he needed to persuade Riedesel. Although he had conferred daily with Phillips and Fraser, Riedesel had not been included in their inner circle. He therefore called a formal conference and presented to them all a proposal that would risk everything on one audacious thrust: eight hundred men would remain at the shore of the Hudson to guard the provisions and keep open the escape route across the bridges; with the rest of the army, he would circle the American left flank, where there was a commanding elevation, and attack it from the rear. Here was the daring Burgoyne of the attack on Valencia de Alcántara, twenty-four years earlier. Not surprisingly, Riedesel objected. It would take three or four days, he said, for the attack force to march through the woods to reach the American left, and during that time the Americans could overwhelm the eight hundred at the shore, capture the provisions, and destroy the bridges. To answer Riedesel, the conferees agreed to inspect the river fortifications before making any decision.

The next morning they rode down to the river and found that the cannon were placed where they could not reach the valleys between the hills, thus opening the way for the enemy to descend to the river road, where the supply trains were inadequately protected. The generals met again in the evening. Riedesel declared that the fortifications were so vulnerable that, in order to strike before the Americans were alerted, the attack force must reach the rear of the enemy left in one day. Considering that, in the battle of September 19, he himself had led reinforcements from the river, up the hills, in a matter of hours, his objection lacked conviction. Nevertheless, he proposed that the entire army recross the Hudson to its old position at the Batten Kill and there await Clinton's arrival. In the meantime, communication could be reopened with Lake George for a restoration of the supply line from Canada and for an avenue of retreat if that became necessary. Riedesel wrote two versions of the meeting afterward: he maintained in one that Fraser and Phillips agreed with him, and in the other that Fraser agreed but that Phillips refused to commit himself. Burgoyne's adjutant general, Kingston, however, afterward stated that he "lived intimately" with Phillips and Fraser and never heard them advocate retreat after the action of September 19.

Burgoyne at first would not hear of a retreat. "I saw . . . that nothing but a successful action would enable me to advance or retreat," he later wrote. Finally, he made his decision, and here again we have two versions of it in Riedesel's memoirs. One version states that, on October 7, Burgoyne would lead a "great reconnoitering expedition against the enemy's left wing, to ascertain definitely his position, and whether it would be advisable to attack him." If so, he would advance the next day with his whole army. If not, he would on the eleventh recross the river to the Batten Kill. The second, more credible, version states that, if an attack were feasible, "he would on that very day, the 7th, immediately attack the enemy."[15] He could not have intended a mere reconnaissance with a large force, which, as it turned out, included artillery of two 12-pounders, six 6-pounders, and two 6-inch howitzers. He could have intended only to initiate an action that would be supported as required with additional troops from the British base at the rear.

On October 7, the heavy rain that had fallen the previous day ceased, and the morning dawned bright and pleasant. Burgoyne briefed a council of all the generals in Fraser's tent. Phillips, Riedesel, and Fraser were to accompany him. Hamilton and Specht were to remain at the British camp on the heights, while Gall would defend the force down at the river. The "reconnaissance" force totaled 1,723, excluding the 180 Indians (of whom a party from Canada had arrived a week earlier), and was drawn from every British and German regiment but the Forty-seventh. Twenty-five men came from every company of British light infantry and grenadiers. So disguised was Burgoyne's intention of a major attack, rather than a reconnaissance, that Phillips's top artillerist, Major Griffith Williams, complained of the risk of losing the heavy 12-pounders in the woods.

At about noon, the march began. The force moved in three columns, veering southwest of the Breymann Redoubt and then proceeding along a wagon road that skirted the northern bank of the North Fork of Mill Creek, south of the Great Ravine. After an hour and a distance of half a mile, with halts for the Indians and Loyalists to feel ahead and for work crews to repair bridges, the force came to a small grain field with a deserted house at one end. The surrounding woods were so dense that attempts to see through them with spyglasses from atop the house roof were fruitless. The march then continued until another stop three-quarters of a mile from the left wing of the American camp. Here Burgoyne sent the company of rangers, Indians, and Loyalists ahead to circle the enemy rear and create a diversion. His intent was still so disguised that Lieutenant Lord Francis Napier, of the Thirty-first Foot, recorded in his diary that the main body was to serve as a diversion to enable the smaller party to conduct observation.

The line of the main body extended over a stretch of a thousand yards. On the right, under Fraser and Balcarres, were the British Light Infantry and Twenty-fourth Regiment, with two 6-pounders. At the center were Riedesel with the detachments of the German line and Breymann's grenadiers, supported by two British 12-pounders at the left-center and two 6-pounders under Pausch on an elevation at the left flank. On a low hill at Pausch's left, under Phillips, were Acland and the British grenadiers, with two 6-pounders and two howitzers. Meanwhile, work crews were ordered up from the rear to cut the grain standing in the field immediately behind the advance force.[16]

Gates was alerted of the advance by a British deserter who had come over that morning. He was not surprised, for he knew Burgoyne, he said, as "an old gamester" who would "risque all upon one throw." Since the engagement of September 19, the arrival of fresh militia had swelled the American army to an effective strength of 13,065, for a total count of 17,228. Almost half of the effectives, 6,444, were Continentals.[17] To block a British retreat across the Hudson, Gates had dispatched General Fellows with a force of 1,500 to cross to the heights opposite Saratoga to observe the enemy movements and if necessary to prevent them from fording.

While Gates sat waiting with his officers at noon mess, dining on ox's heart, an animated discussion took place. Arnold, still on speaking terms with Gates, argued for attack: "The assailant had the advantage; for he can always take his own time, and choose the point of attack; and, if repulsed, he has only to retreat behind his own lines, and form again." Gates preferred to wait for Burgoyne's offensive: "If undisciplined militia were repulsed in the open field, and the enemy pressed upon them in their retreat, it would be difficult to form them again, even behind their own breastworks; for, if they were under a panic, they would keep on retreating, even after they had passed their own lines."

Before this exchange could proceed further, sounds of firing were heard from the direction of an advance picket. Arnold eagerly asked, "Shall I go out, and see what is the matter?" Gates did not reply. Arnold pressed. "I am afraid to trust you, Arnold," he finally answered. Arnold persisted: "Pray, let me go: I will be careful; and, if our advance does not need support, I will promise not to commit you."[18] Gates relented, but he sent Lincoln out with him.

They returned in a half hour with a report that there had been firing at the Hudson, but they believed this to be a feint; a force of fifteen hundred was approaching toward a height on the left, which must be defended at all costs. At this, Gates ordered out Morgan and Dearborn with their riflemen and light infantry. "That is nothing; you must send a strong force," Arnold blurted. This was for Gates the last straw. "General Arnold," he said, "I have nothing for you to do; you have no business here." Here Lincoln stepped in. "You must send a strong force to support Morgan and Dearborn, at least three regiments." Again Gates relented and ordered out three more regiments, two from Learned's brigade and one from Nixon's.[19]

By about three o'clock, it became obvious that the enemy's main move was indeed against the American left. Gates then ordered Poor out with Cilley's First, Reid's Second, and Scammell's Third New Hampshire regiments, all Continentals, to attack the enemy left and Learned's brigade to hold the center.[20]

Poor advanced to a hill facing Acland's grenadiers and halted while he drew up his men for the attack. Acland's jittery grenadiers rained grapeshot and musket balls over their heads. Poor's men then charged, "madly and blindly in the face of a furious fire," reported Captain Pausch. Acland was shot through both legs and was carried to the protection of a fence by Captain John Shrimpton of the Sixty-second. A British flanking party approached through the woods, attempting to surprise Poor's men, but Cilley's regiment intercepted it and, rushing and volleying in the face of a bayonet charge, drove the British back in disarray. A 10-pound fieldpiece exchanged hands five times until it finally fell to the Americans, and Cilley jumped astride it and waved in triumph. It was turned on the British with ammunition left in the boxes. The British were forced further back, as the ground was strewn with grenadiers in the agonies of death. Wilkinson, arriving on the scene, found a teenage American soldier taking aim at a wounded British officer. "Protect me Sir, against this boy," the officer entreated. It was Acland, and Wilkinson and his servant lifted him to a horse, to be taken to headquarters.[21]

Meanwhile, Arnold rode excitedly about camp, mortified at being kept out of the action. At last he could endure it no longer. "Give me a dipperful of that rum," he demanded of the attendant at an open hogshead, and downed it all. Then, on a brown mare lent him by Chester, he galloped to the front. Gates thought him drunk and sent an aide, John Armstrong, to recall him. Arnold kept out of reach and, coming upon a lieutenant in Poor's brigade, stopped him:

"Whose regiment is this?"

"Col. Latimore's, sir."

"Ah, my old Norwich and New London friends. God bless you; I am glad to see you. Now come on, boys; if the day is long enough, we'll have them all in hell before night."

He rode to the head of Learned's brigade as it attacked the British center. The plodding Learned put up no objection to the takeover by Arnold. According to Lieutenant Colonel John Brooks of the Eighth Massachusetts Regiment, Learned was "a weak man." The enemy the brigade faced was commanded by Lieutenant Colonel Ernst Ludwig von Speth, with three hundred men from the regiments Specht, Rhetz, and Riedesel. The retreat of

Acland's grenadiers exposed the Germans' left flank, but Speth formed some of his men on that side in a protective curve and stubbornly resisted. Arnold rode furiously into the fray, behaving, said Sergeant Samuel Woodruff, "more like a madman than a cool and discreet officer." Wildly flourishing his sword, he struck and wounded an American officer on the head and continued away before his victim, Captain Frederick M. Ball, could remonstrate. At this point, Balcarres and his light infantry, on Speth's right, were ordered over to the far right in order to stem the onslaught of the American riflemen. Speth was thus exposed to be raked on both sides, and the Germans fled to the trees in the rear, "each man for himself," Pausch said. Pausch escaped but lost his two 6-pounders. Williams and his 10-pounder, however, were both captured. Among the American wounded was Brigadier General John Paterson, whose brigade, from Lincoln's right wing, had been ordered to reinforce the center.[22]

When Balcarres's men arrived at their new position on the British right, they were struck so hard by Dearborn and Morgan with their light infantry that they were reduced to confusion. Burgoyne galloped about in an attempt to rally them. His horse was hit, and his hat and waistcoat were pierced by bullets. At this point, Fraser, with his Twenty-fourth Regiment, which so far had seen little of the action, arrived to establish a second line of defense to the rear. Recklessly exposing himself, he refused to concede that the battle was already lost. Morgan, concerned that this "devilish brave fellow" might lead a rally, called over one of his best shots, a noted Indian fighter named Timothy Murphy, and instructed him to climb a tree and "single out him on the white horse." Within minutes, the horse received bullets through its crupper and its mane. Another bullet struck Fraser in the body, and he was carried off the field. Burgoyne had already ordered a withdrawal and sent his adjutant, Clerke, forward with the message, but before Clerke could get through he was brought down with a bullet through the ribs and abdomen.[23]

Arnold by now had seized the field leadership of all the engaged American forces and determined to pursue the fleeing enemy to their fortifications. He dispatched Brooks with his regiment toward the Breymann Redoubt, but in order to consolidate the attack he issued orders to Poor and Morgan to pause and reform. This, it immediately became clear, was giving the British time to reach the protection of their battery, and no sooner had Arnold sent the order than he realized his mistake. He raced over himself to counteract it, galloping heedlessly through the fire of his own and the enemy's lines. Then, collecting about twenty riflemen, he circled around to the enemy's rear and joined Brooks's regiment as it advanced on the Breymann Redoubt. His appearance there was the signal for a redoubled general American assault along the front. The remainder of Learned's and Poor's brigades broke through the retreating British lines and joined him. Behind Learned and Poor came Brigadier General Abraham Ten Broeck's brigade of 1,845 Albany County militia, which Gates had ordered up for support. This reinforcement, totaling more than Burgoyne's entire "reconnaissance" force, was the crux of Gates's strategy of engulfing the enemy with the sheer weight of manpower.

No fire was received from the two hundred Germans encamped behind a two-hundred-yard-long rail breastwork fronting the Breymann Redoubt until the Americans came within forty-five yards. Then a tremendous fusillade erupted from the works. One cannonball blew the head off an American infantryman, sending fragments of bone flying in the face of a fifer, Nicholas Stoner, who fell unconscious, with his splattered head on a thigh of the decapitated body. The Americans still advanced, and Arnold rode through a sally port and called upon the defenders to lay down their arms. He was met by a second volley, and a bullet struck his horse. As it buckled to the ground, a German lying wounded shot its rider in the left leg, while the horse pinned him on the other. An American, Private John Redman, ran forward to bayonet the German, but Arnold gasped, "He's a fine fellow—don't hurt him!" Dearborn was close by, and when the horse was lifted he bent over Arnold and asked softly whether the wound was bad. It was the same leg, he answered, that had been hit two years before in the storming of Quebec; he wished it were his heart. A surgeon, seeing that it was a compound fracture, feared amputation might be necessary, but Arnold would not consider "such damned nonsense." "Rush on, my brave boys," he called to the troops and threatened to have himself lifted upon a horse and accompany them. Here Armstrong caught up with his man and with the aid of Sergeant Woodruff carried him back to camp.

Led by Brooks, the Americans mounted the parapet and found the Germans fled and Breymann lying dead. Maddened at the timidity of his men, he had sabred four of them, and then one of them had shot him. With Arnold incapacitated, Learned resumed the direction of his brigade. The sun had set, and, fearing a return of the British, he was on the point of ordering a withdrawal. Just then an aide of Gates rode up with orders to remain where he was.[24]

When Burgoyne learned of the loss of the Breymann Redoubt, he reacted angrily at the opening given to the Americans to fall upon his right flank and rear. With "harsh and cutting words," he ordered a counterattack to retake the entrenchment. Speth, stung by the slurs on his countrymen, collected four officers and fifty men to attempt the impossible mission. Marching blindly at night through the woods, he met a Loyalist soldier who offered himself as a guide and then led them straight into the Americans' hands. Speth and his officers were taken, but his men escaped.

That night, Burgoyne had no choice but to withdraw from his exposed position. Leaving his campfires burning and six cannon behind him, all the horses for which had been killed, he took his whole force back down to the Hudson above the Great Redoubt. There, on an open plain more suited to the European style of engagement than the woods, he desperately hoped still to salvage a victory.[25]

The British main body was now opposite Lincoln's right division, and Gates sent him out during the night, accompanied by Glover, to feel out the enemy's next move. They returned a little before daybreak with the report that the British were preparing to retreat, and Gates ordered Lincoln to attempt the enemy lines. Lincoln at once sent three brigades, each formed in a column, and he was supported by Morgan's riflemen and Dearborn's light infantry, who circled behind the British right. Burgoyne had to move back to a height at the rear. Some of his men began to desert. There was no alternative for him but to retreat further that night in order to avoid being surrounded.

Lincoln had also advised Gates that a body of militia be sent to Fort Edward to prevent the British from crossing the Hudson there, and Gates had agreed. Lincoln appears, however, to have misunderstood. Weary with no sleep, and unthinking that his place was with his division, he assumed that Gates expected him to lead the expedition himself. In the afternoon of the eighth, with little or no rest, he started along a cart path through a thick wood, riding ahead of his force and attended only by Lieutenant Ebenezer Mattoon. At a turn in the road, he suddenly came upon a body of men he took for Americans. Two of them wore scarlet, but he thought nothing of this, for a few of his own soldiers had been wearing captured British uniforms. Others of the group ahead of him wore blue, like the Americans (but also the Brunswick color), and the remainder were in homespun, like the militia. When he had come within a few yards of them, he realized that they were British and checked his horse. Two of the men instantly fired, and Lincoln, normally slow of speech, exclaimed, "The rascals have struck me." A ball had struck his right leg, below the calf. Although he was broad and overweight, he somehow clung to his horse and escaped back around the angle of the road. He had to be hospitalized for the remainder of the campaign, and when the bone healed the leg had shrunk two inches shorter than the other, requiring him to wear an elevated shoe.[26]

That evening, before the British retreat began, Simon Fraser, Burgoyne's "gallant friend," was buried. "Don't conceal anything from me! Must I die?" he had asked when he was brought in the day before. The surgeon reluctantly explained that he had eaten a heavy breakfast that morning which had expanded his intestines, and the bullet had gone through them instead of between them. A bed was hastily set up for him in a log cabin that had been built for Baroness Riedesel, and after a night of anguish he died at eight the next morning. In accordance with his wish, he was buried on a hill of the Great Redoubt, facing the majestic Hudson Valley. Chaplain Edward Brudenell intoned the prayers, never altering his voice while clouds of dust covered him from cannonballs falling around him.

Burgoyne could not yet know that in the American camp he was losing another friend, Clerke, "endeared to me," he said, "by every quality that can create esteem." With words much the same as Fraser's, Clerke asked his surgeon, "Doctor why do you pause? do you think I am afraid to die?" and heard alike that his wound was fatal. Gates gave him his own bed, but after a visit that turned into a dispute over the merits of the revolution, stomped out, declaring that he had never met with "so impudent a son of a bitch."[27]

After dark on October 8, Burgoyne had the pontoon bridge across the Hudson broken up and the boats rowed upriver. The baggage was loaded. Tents were left standing and campfires burning. The hospital, with three hundred sick and wounded, could not be moved, and Dr. John Macnamara Hayes volunteered to remain with them. He was given a note from Burgoyne to Gates asking humane treatment. At nine o'clock, the shaken army started north to Saratoga.[28]

Total British losses in the Battle of Bemis Heights, as the October 7 engagement has been called, were 184 killed, 264 wounded, and 183 taken prisoner. The Americans had about 30 dead and 100 wounded.[29]

❧19❧

Surrender

A HEAVY RAIN SET IN ON OC-tober 9, and Gates allowed Burgoyne to depart unhindered from Bemis Heights. He had no intention of engaging the British in the downpour, when the Americans could not use their rifles and the British could wield their bayonets. He had an army growing daily with new arrivals of militia that had to be equipped, fed, and brigaded into the order of march. He knew that the countryside was with him. "He felt assured there were other and less expensive means of reducing his foe than by blood and carnage," said Major Hull.[1] Burgoyne could be hemmed in on all sides; he would not escape.

Stark had collected a new brigade of New Hampshire militia with which he had recaptured Ford Edward. Fellows, who with thirteen hundred Massachusetts militia had been ordered to the east bank at the Saratoga ford, crossed over to the west side on October 9 and occupied the high ground to the north of Fish Creek. He was replaced at his former position by General Jacob Bayley with nine hundred New Hampshire militia and Colonel John Moseley with a regiment of Massachusetts militia, supported by a company of Continental artillery under Captain Alexander Furnival.[2] These forces could obstruct any enemy attempt to cross the Hudson, and they could interdict foraging expeditions.

Gates learned on October 9, however, that Fort Montgomery had fallen to Clinton; this meant that if the Americans waited too long Burgoyne might be rescued. Nevertheless, another day was lost in drawing and cooking provisions and distributing ammunition and equipment.

While this was being done, the Americans were startled by the arrival of the wounded Acland's pregnant wife, who had insisted on joining her husband in order to nurse him. Dearborn's advance guard found her in the middle of the night, exposed to the incessant rain, approaching in an open bateau under a flag of truce, accompanied by Chaplain Brudenell and attended by a maid and her husband's wounded valet. Brudenell carried an unsealed note from Burgoyne to Gates, stating that he had not been able to refuse Lady Harriet's "request to commit her to your protection." Dearborn put her up for the night in the house he occupied, and in the morning Wilkinson and an army doctor arrived with a horse to conduct her to the American headquarters. Gates found her, he wrote his wife, "the most amiable, delicate piece of Quality you ever beheld." He wrote Burgoyne that he was giving her safe passage despite British "vindictive Malice" in the burning of Patriot farmhouses.[3]

The British army slowly crept north. The road was a sea of mud, Burgoyne insisted on dragging his artillery with him, and progress could be no faster than that of the supply bateaux, which were being rowed upstream against the current. In the middle of the first night of his march, he stopped at Dovecote, where most of the bateaux caught up and rations for eight days were issued. Dovecote was on a gentle spur of higher land where a last stand might successfully be made. So hopeful was he for a major strike that he rejected an opportunity reported to him by Lieutenant Colonel Nicholas Sutherland, who in a reconnaissance had discovered that Fellows's militia force, as yet camped a few miles to the north, was unguarded and could easily be overwhelmed by a single regiment.

But the American main army did not come, and late in the afternoon of the ninth, Burgoyne started north again. The teams of horses and oxen that drew the baggage wagons soon became mired in the mud and had to be abandoned with the baggage. In good weather the march would have taken a half hour, but now it took until evening to reach Saratoga. Hamilton's brigade camped at the shore of Fish Creek. As the bridge had been destroyed, the rest of the army waded, waist-deep, to the other side. The men made no attempt to cut wood and build fires but lay down to sleep in their dripping clothes on the wet ground. The sick and wounded were bedded in the nearby barracks, and Burgoyne set up headquarters in the Schuyler mansion. According to a journal kept by the Brunswick officers, the house "rang with singing, laughter, and the gingling[?] of glasses," but in fact the officers were called out to an accidental fire that consumed the barracks while the wounded were carried to safety.[4] The next morning, Hamilton's brigade crossed the creek and joined the rest of the army.

Burgoyne did not yet know that Stark had taken Fort Edward, and he now proposed to move north to the ford there, cross the Hudson, and reach Ticonderoga by way of Lake George. He did not really wish this step; his

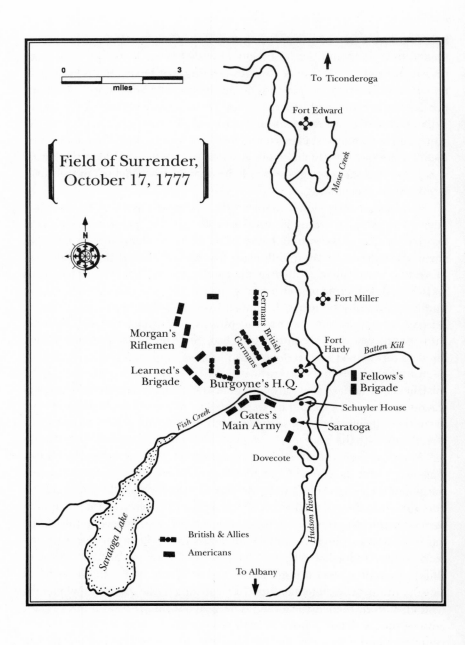

Field of Surrender,
October 17, 1777

To Ticonderoga

Fort Edward

Moses Creek

Germans

British

Germans

Fort Miller

Morgan's
Riflemen

Fort
Hardy

Batten Kill

Learned's
Brigade

Fellows's
Brigade

Burgoyne's H.Q.

Schuyler House

Fish Creek

Gates's
Main Army

Saratoga

Dovecote

Hudson River

Saratoga Lake

British & Allies

Americans

To Albany

0   3
miles

N

instinct was to turn and fight. But Riedesel and his Germans were so insistent upon retreat that he must satisfy them. He therefore sent Lieutenant William Twiss with a party of workmen to repair the bridges and roads to Fort Edward, and Sutherland to protect them with the Forty-seventh Regiment, the company of marksmen, and Captain Samuel Mackay's Canadians.[5]

Violent wind and rain lasted through most of the night of October 9. The morning of the tenth was very cold but clear, and at Bemis Heights Gates issued orders to start after the enemy. Nixon's and Learned's brigades began at nine o'clock, Glover's at eleven, and Poor's at one. They found the road strewn with tents, dead horses, and broken carts and wagons, one with fifteen barrels of gunpowder. At about four o'clock, they arrived at Saratoga where the British were encamped on the heights beyond Fish Creek. Schuyler's house was on fire: it was being burned to clear the view for the shelling of the Americans. Fellows had crossed to the east side of the Hudson in order to avoid being cut to pieces by Burgoyne's main army and was exchanging cannon shots with the British artillery. At the mouth of Fish Creek, a British fatigue party was unloading supplies from the bateaux. Major Ebenezer Stevens ran a couple of light cannon down to the plain near the river and dispersed the group, but he drew the fire of the heavy cannon on the heights and was forced to withdraw after a tumbrel was blown up.[6]

Scouts now informed Gates of the Twiss-Sutherland work force, and he mistakenly concluded that Burgoyne's main army was again on the move, leaving only a rear guard behind. His former caution disappeared. On the morning of the eleventh, he called together his general officers and ordered them to attack in half an hour. The advance began through a thick fog, with the Americans ignorant that they were facing the full strength of the enemy. Burgoyne had anticipated the American move, and he had recalled Sutherland, leaving Mackay's Canadians to guard the work force opposite Fort Edward (they promptly ran off). Morgan's marksmen were the first of the Americans to cross Fish Creek, on a log raft, about three-quarters of a mile southwest of the smoldering Schuyler mansion. They ran into an enemy picket, which immediately opened fire and struck three of them. At this point Wilkinson rode up and promptly returned with news of the predicament to Gates, who ordered Paterson's and Learned's brigades to Morgan's relief.

In the meantime, Nixon's and Glover's brigades approached Fish Creek, with Nixon, as senior to Glover, leading the way. An advance guard of forty volunteers under Captain Nathan Goodale crossed first and surprised and took prisoner a British contingent of thirty-five, and then cut away and set afloat the boats they were guarding. Fellows's militia, across the Hudson, hauled the boats ashore. When Nixon's forward regiment, Colonel John Greaton's Third Massachusetts Continentals, reached the creek, the fog lifted, and the park of British artillery, which was revealed five hundred yards away, opened fire. Colonel Rufus Putnam's Fifth Massachusetts Continentals then came up and covered Greaton's men while they crossed the creek and took shelter under the far bank. Putnam, accompanied by Stevens with two fieldpieces, crossed the creek further east at its mouth and found cover on the opposite shore at the ruins of old Fort Hardy.

As Glover was preparing to follow, a British soldier crossed the stream toward the Americans. He declared himself a deserter and revealed that the whole British army had remained at Saratoga. Glover immediately sent word to Gates and to Nixon, and soon a German deserter confirmed the first report. Nixon, after losing several men, recrossed in the nick of time.

Wilkinson, having witnessed the escape and not having had time to report to Gates, now dashed over to Learned, who was about to lead his brigade across the creek. "Although I have no orders for your retreat," said Wilkinson, "I pledge my life for the General's approbation." Brooks, commanding the Eighth Massachusetts Continentals, and Lieutenant Colonel Benjamin Tupper of the Second Massachusetts Continentals, supported Wilkinson, and Learned agreed.[7]

The American withdrawal eliminated Burgoyne's last chance of a victorious engagement. It was, he afterward said, "one of the most adverse strokes of fortune in the whole campaign." A ring of five American brigades—Poor's, Paterson's, Learned's, Nixon's, and Glover's—flanked to the north by Morgan's riflemen, pinned Burgoyne's army against the Hudson, with Fellows's three thousand militia preventing escape to the other side. Further south lay the remainder of Gates's swelling army. "Attack we could not, and attack they would not," wrote Phillips.[8]

The remnants of the British army lay exposed to continual cannonade and sniper fire from raiding parties, so much so that while Burgoyne and several officers were at dinner a cannonball flew across the table. The wounded had no tents or beds, and the stench from the corpses of the starved oxen and cattle pervaded the camp. One of the few places of shelter was in a house near the Hudson, which was given over to Madame Riedesel. It was exposed to the fire from Fellows's batteries across the water, and she counted eleven cannonballs that pierced the walls. One ball blew off a leg of a wounded soldier lying on a table as he was about to have the other one amputated. Refuge for some of the wounded and the women and children was found in the cellars, while terrified cheaters, claiming wounds, crowded at the door, and the tall, sturdily built Madame Riedesel kept them out only by standing in their way with outspread arms.[9]

In the evening, Burgoyne summoned Phillips and Riedesel to a council of war to consider whether to retreat or to attempt one more thrust. Riedesel proposed leaving the artillery and baggage behind, crossing the Hudson on rafts (the bateaux were all gone) at a ford four miles above Fort Edward, and then marching to Fort George. This passage until now had been made only by Indians or small parties, but it was the only remaining place not known to be obstructed by the Americans. Burgoyne, however, had just received reports that Clinton had taken Fort Montgomery, and he and Phillips still hoped to evade the entire American army by searching for an opening around the enemy's left, between Morgan's corps and the Hudson, and then speeding to meet Clinton at Albany. A decision was postponed.

That night the Americans closed the gap at the northwest end of their besieging perimeter. Stark, leaving a force of two hundred at Fort Edward, arrived at the mouth of the Batten Kill with twenty-five hundred men and crossed the Hudson on rafts. On a knoll at the west shore (since known as Stark's Knob) he immediately set up a heavy battery. The investment of the British army was complete. There was now no way for Burgoyne to resist Riedesel's proposal for retreat. At three in the afternoon the next day he called a second council, to which Hamilton and Gall were added. The supply of provisions, he told them, would be exhausted in twenty days. Although Burgoyne, Phillips, and Hamilton still wished to try circling the enemy's left, the decision was to adopt Riedesel's plan and move either that night or at daybreak. Rations for six days were ordered distributed and patrols were sent to scout out the route of march.[10]

Later that day the patrols returned from the north with a report that the enemy was so entrenched at Fort Edward and in such complete occupation of the country from there to Fort George that a march in that direction would meet with immediate attack. It was too late for retreat. Burgoyne now had reluctantly to consider the growing sentiment in his army for capitulation. In concert with Riedesel, he drew up a draft of the terms to be proposed to Gates, chiefly free passage of the army to Great Britain on a pledge not to serve again in North America. Riedesel urged a demand that the troops return instead to Canada; one wonders whether he was not challenging Burgoyne, in his state of poor health, to a death march in the northern cold. Burgoyne merely answered that the Americans would never for a moment consider it. On October 13, he called a third council to which all field officers of the rank of captain and above who commanded corps were invited, "a full representation of the army." He declared that he was ready "to undertake at their head any enterprise of difficulty or hazard that should appear to them within the compass of their strength or spirit"—he afterward said in Parliament that he meant "to prefer death to dishonour." Then a resolution for a capitulation "upon honorable terms" was put to a vote and passed unanimously. Riedesel presented the proposed terms, and the assembly authorized the following message: "Lt. General Burgoyne is desirous of sending a field officer with a message to M. Genl. Gates upon a matter of high moment to both armies. The Lt. Genl. requests to be informed at what hour Gen. Gates will receive him tomorrow morning."[11]

Burgoyne's message produced a prompt reply from Gates, setting the time for receiving Burgoyne's representative at ten o'clock the following morning. At precisely the hour, a drumbeat from the British advance guard announced the appearance of Kingston, who stepped across the sleepers that had replaced the destroyed bridge over Fish Creek. Wilkinson was waiting for him and demanded that he agree to be blindfolded. Kingston objected to the "indignity" but finally allowed himself to be bound with his own handkerchief and led off by Wilkinson for a walk of a mile to the American headquarters.

At the headquarters tent, the blindfold was removed and Kingston and Gates met with the familiarity of old acquaintances:

"General Gates, your servant."

"Ah! Kingston, how do you do?"

Kingston thereupon announced that he had been empowered by Burgoyne to make certain proposals, which he had committed to paper in order to avoid misunderstandings, and read:

> I am directed to represent to you from General Burgoyne, that after having fought you twice, he has waited some days in his present position determined to try a third conflict against any force you could bring to attack him.
>
> He is apprised of the superiority of your numbers, and the disposition of your troops to impede his supplies and render his retreat a scene of carnage on both sides. In this situation he is impelled by humanity, and thinks himself justified by established principles and precedents of state and of war, to spare the lives of brave men upon honourable terms; should

Major-general Gates be inclined to treat upon that idea, General Burgoyne would propose a cessation of arms, during the time necessary to communicate the preliminary terms, by which in any extremity he and army mean to abide.

As soon as he finished, to the astonishment of both Kingston and Wilkinson, Gates drew from his side pocket a paper and handed it to Kingston. "There, Sir, are the terms on which General Burgoyne must surrender." They amounted to a demand for unconditional surrender. The entire army must ground their arms in their encampment and immediately be considered prisoners of war; officers could keep their side arms, but all other munitions, carriages, and horses must immediately be delivered. The army would then be marched toward Bennington, to be detained somewhere in New England. Gates did agree to an armistice until sunset, when Burgoyne must return an answer. The chagrined Kingston, blindfold replaced, was led back to Fish Creek on Wilkinson' arm, protesting along the way the slight to the army whose six valorous regiments had fought at the Battle of Minden.

When Wilkinson returned to headquarters, he asked Gates whether he did not mean to recede from his extreme demand. "I shall be content to get the arms out of their hands," Gates replied.[12]

Burgoyne received Gates's terms with indignation. At another council meeting he submitted his own proposals: the troops to "march out of their camp with the honours of war"; "free passage to be granted to this army to Great Britain upon condition of not serving again in North America during the present contest"; officers to retain their equipment, baggage, and horses; civilians accompanying the British army to be treated as British subjects; and "Canadians and persons belonging to the establishment in Canada, to be permitted to return there." Each army would appoint two officers to complete the negotiations.[13]

The same day that Gates received this message he also learned that an enemy fleet of twenty sail was moving up the Hudson from Newburgh, carrying Vaughan's troops for an attack on Esopus (the present Kingston), and he had no knowledge of how great that force was. He decided that a quick capitulation from Burgoyne was essential. To the surprise of the British, at ten o'clock in the morning of the fifteenth, Kingston returned with Gates's signature to all of Burgoyne's propositions, stipulating only that the surrender take place at two o'clock that afternoon and that the British army be ready to move toward Boston the next morning.[14]

This sudden acquiescence aroused Burgoyne's suspicions, and, to support a delay, he called another council meeting. He then sent word back to Gates that, while they were in general agreement, a longer time was necessary to settle the details. For that purpose, as he had already proposed, he would name two officers to meet with two from Gates to conclude a treaty "as soon as possible."

Gates was again willing. He appointed Wilkinson and Brigadier General William Whipple, and Burgoyne sent Kingston and Captain James H. Craig, of the Forty-seventh Regiment. A tent was pitched between the advance guards of the two armies near Schuyler's sawmill, and the conferees went earnestly to work. By eight o'clock in the evening they signed and exchanged articles of capitulation and returned to their respective headquarters. At eleven o'clock, a note from Craig arrived for Wilkinson, conveying Burgoyne's approval with the single exception that instead of a "capitulation" the treaty must be termed a "convention." With that alteration, the agreement with Burgoyne's signature would be delivered the following morning. Wilkinson wrote back, "Major-general Gates will admit the alteration required."[15]

Late that night, another factor entered the negotiations. A spy arrived with a report that Clinton had captured Esopus eight days previously and was by now probably already at Albany. Burgoyne at once convened another council and asked for approval, admittedly on the basis of a "report of a man, whom nobody knew," to retract his promise to sign the convention. Only eight officers, including Phillips, Hamilton, and Balcarres, backed Burgoyne against a majority of fourteen. The council decided to play for time. The following morning, the sixteenth, Burgoyne sent Gates a letter stating that he had received a report that Gates, in violation of the armistice, had detached a considerable portion of his army, thereby calling into question its superiority of numbers over the British. Burgoyne requested that two of his officers be admitted to check whether this was true before any treaty could be signed.[16]

Gates was so incensed at the presumption of such a demand that, rather than dignify the response with his signature, he sent Wilkinson to deliver a verbal message that the request was inadmissible, that although several hundred New York militia whose term was up had marched off to Albany the previous evening, no detachment had been authorized, and he gave Burgoyne one hour for an answer. Confronted with "a youth in a plain blue frock, without other military insignia than a cockade and sword," Burgoyne answered, "I do not recede from my purpose; the truce must end," and they set the time, by both their watches, at one hour. But then, as Wilkinson was leaving, Burgoyne called him back and asked for two hours to consult his officers. They again set their watches.[17]

The British council meeting revealed that the eight who previously had favored breaking the treaty now joined the fourteen who opposed it. Still resistant, Burgoyne conferred privately with Riedesel, Phillips, and Hamilton. Riedesel, who had been drinking heavily and considered himself "the most unfortunate man on earth," was blunt: Burgoyne might be faulted in England for the conduct of the campaign, for not having retreated earlier, and for having initiated the negotiations, but he could not now go back on his agreement to capitulate. Hamilton concurred, while Phillips declined an opinion, except to say that he could see no way out of the predicament. Then, the last resort, Burgoyne asked what the sentiment of the men was. The surviving minutes, with names deleted, give the disheartening answer: the men in general wished for the convention. Two corps commanders declared that if the convention were not approved there would be considerable desertion; the Sixty-second Regiment was "not equal to their former exertions"; the other British corps would resist if attacked but had not the "alacrity of spirit necessary for undertaking desperate enterprizes." Riedesel, in his memoirs, declares that the army's left wing, his own, would "defend the present position of the army to the last man," but Burgoyne afterward wrote that the Germans were "dispirited and ready to club their arms at the first fire." The attitude of the German rank and file, a Loyalist lieutenant maintained, was "nix the money, nix the rum, nix fighten."

At last Burgoyne conceded. He would sign, he said, not on the point of honor, but because Gates had promised to permit the British, after the surrender, to verify his numerical superiority, and because Clinton was too far away to bring relief before the remaining three days' provisions expired.[18]

In the meantime, the two hours had lapsed, and Gates lost patience. He dispatched Colonel Greaton on horseback to Burgoyne with a demand for immediate compliance within ten minutes, without which he would launch an attack. Greaton returned in time with the signed "convention."[19]

In the prologue of this narrative, I have described the preliminary meeting of Burgoyne and Gates on the morning of October 17. They then turned to their own troops to prepare for the formal surrender later that morning.

Burgoyne called his staff together for the last time. He began to review the course of the whole campaign, but his voice caught and he could not go on.

Riedesel collected all his troops and told them, "It was no lack of courage on your part by which this awful fate has come upon you. You will always be justified in the eyes of the world." He ordered the German regimental flags taken down and gave them to his wife, who had them sewn into a pillow on which he thenceforth slept.[20]

In the American camp, a chaplain chose from the Old Testament for his sermon of thanksgiving Joel 2:20: "But I will remove far off from you the northern army, and will drive him into a land barren and desolate, with his face toward the east sea, and his hinder part toward the utmost sea, and his stink shall come up, and his ill savour shall come up, because he hath done great things."[21] Gates gave orders that the army was to offer no insult and stay out of sight on the far side of Fish Creek while the British marched out of their camp.

At ten o'clock, the defeated army, in strict formation and with drums beating, began its march down to Fort Hardy. The drums that beat the grenadiers' march, wrote Lieutenant Digby, seemed "almost ashamed to be heard." At the plain adjacent to the fort, in the presence only of Wilkinson and Morgan Lewis, the artillerymen parked their cannon and the rest of the army deposited their muskets and emptied their cartridge boxes. Some of the men angrily knocked off the butts of their weapons and stamped upon their drums.[22]

Then two American officers and a mounted company bearing the new flag of stars and stripes led the British across Fish Creek into the American camp, where the army was drawn up in two long lines. "There was not a man among them who showed the slightest sign of mockery, malicious delight, hate, or other insult," observed a German officer. The rank and file were in civilian clothes, but they stood erect, musket or rifle in the right hand and cartridge box or powder horn slung across the shoulder, left hand on the hip and right foot slightly advanced. They were "so slender, so handsome, so sinewy, that it was a pleasure to look at them." Here and there, too, in that citizen army, were militiamen over fifty, wearing wigs from which their own hair hung down in clumps at the sides and in ponytails at the rear.[23] The bank struck up "Yankee Doodle," a tune originally British and not offensive to the prisoners.

About a hundred feet southeast of the burnt Schuyler mansion, a marquee had been erected, with the sides rolled up for all to see Gates seated with his officers. At noon, Burgoyne and a retinue of his officers rode up. He dismounted and Gates stepped forward. Burgoyne removed his plumed hat and bowed low:

"General, the caprice of war has made me your prisoner."

"You will always find me ready to testify that it was not brought about through any fault of your excellency."

Gates invited him into the marquee, and in a few minutes they came out again. Burgoyne stepped back, drew his sword, and presented it to Gates, who received it in his left hand while extending his right to take Burgoyne's. After a few words he returned the sword. The other British officers in the same manner delivered up their swords and had them returned. Gates hosted Burgoyne to a dinner in his tent on a table of planks laid across barrels. The talk was jovial among the old acquaintances. Toasts were drunk to Washington and to King George. "Your funds of men are inexhaustible," Burgoyne conceded. "Like the Hydra's head, when cut off, seven more spring up in its stead."[24]

Of a grand total of 9,078 men who had marched down from Canada, 5,895 surrendered: 3,018 British, 2,412 Germans, and 465 auxiliaries. 1,728 regulars had been killed or taken prisoner in all the engagements, and 1,297 had been left behind to garrison Ticonderoga and Diamond Island in Lake George.[25] That left 158 unaccounted for, who must be assumed to have deserted.

The credit for the American victory belonged to Gates. Critics have charged that he won with an army organized by Schuyler, against an enemy slowed down by Schuyler's scorched-earth tactics. In fact, Gates had taken over a demoralized army, humiliated by the loss of Ticonderoga without a fight and estranged from Schuyler. Overnight he had inspired a turnout of reinforcements from New England. Uniquely among all American generals, he had mastered the technique of merging Continentals with militia, and although the Continentals had borne the brunt of the fighting, Colonel Thaddeus Cook's Connecticut militia had suffered the heaviest casualties. The mere overwhelming numbers of the militia served as an intimidating menace to the enemy. True, he had been fortunate in having Morgan's riflemen assigned to him by Congress, and in having so daring a wing commander as Arnold, no matter how difficult he was to manage. But the planning had all been his, and when Burgoyne halfheartedly proposed a capitulation, Gates seized on terms less than unconditional, although exposing himself to censure, letting the politicians wrestle with the details while insuring the most sweeping triumph the Americans were to win before the war's end four years later at Yorktown.

On the British side, the defeat had been brought about, above all, by the absence of a single directing intelligence. Lord North, indecisive and subservient to George III, had left the planning and execution of the American war to George Germain, who, lacking a strong political base in the Commons, sought to shore up his position with a quick victory. Into this unstable atmosphere stepped three generals in flagging midcareer—Howe, Clinton, and Burgoyne, each of whom produced a plan for an invasion of New York from Canada. Burgoyne's was the one that won Germain's endorsement, because, in advocating the employment of Indians, it reversed the policy of the Canadian commander, Carleton, whom Germain detested and wished to remove. Once appointed, Burgoyne could not conceive that he would be expected to drive to Albany without the prospect of a junction there with Howe's army moving up from New York City. Howe, however, regarded Burgoyne as a competitor for the glory of winning the war and opted to sail south to invest Philadelphia, while Germain was politically too weak to order him north, as Howe was a favorite of the king. Burgoyne had warning of his peril in two letters from Howe, one before he set out from Canada, and the second before he crossed the Hudson and severed his supply line. Bent on earning laurels, he refused to believe that Germain would permit him to be abandoned at Albany. The expedition's deceptively easy conquest of Ticonderoga confirmed Burgoyne's belief that the Americans were no match for his British professionals. He persisted, until too late, in the conviction that the rebels were temporarily blinded by unscrupulous agitators. His threat of unleashing the Indians only stiffened the American resistance. Even the American victory at Bennington was discounted because it was achieved over the Germans, not his cherished British regulars. At the first battle on Bemis Heights, in the face of punishing casualties, he convinced himself that he had won and would shortly receive the cooperation from Clinton that would take him safely to Albany. In the end his dwindling provisions forced him to face reality. Retreat to Canada was cut off by rebel militia, and his own precarious state of health would have made a march into the cold northern forests a virtual death sentence. He preferred a desperate last stand, but his men were too exhausted or unwilling to attempt it. There was no choice but to capitulate. Critics have accused him of burdening himself with an excessive train of artillery and personal baggage, shortchanging his expedition with insufficient horses and carriages, and electing to cut his way through the woods between Skenesboro and the Hudson instead of taking the water route through Lake George. There are plausible answers to all of these charges, examined earlier in this book, but in any case the army would have been left to starve even if it had reached Albany.

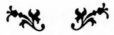

Gates, without consulting Congress, offered Burgoyne passage to England aboard a vessel he would obtain from the Massachusetts legislature. On his own initiative, he wrote a letter to the earl of Thanet, an American sympathizer and his wife's relative, attempting to persuade him to move in Parliament for American independence. Burgoyne could carry the letter, and accompanying him would be Glover, who could speak for the Americans' military prowess. Burgoyne rejected this fanciful scheme, preferring to wait for permission from Howe and from Congress. This, in consideration of his ill health, ultimately was granted and enabled him to embark April 15 of the following year.[26] Congress, despite the convention commitment, refused to allow the army to return to England as long as the war continued. Phillips took charge of the prisoners, and they were marched down to Virginia, there to remain until the peace was concluded.

❧ 20 ❧

The Victor and the Vanquished

T O GATES, THE VICTORY AT Saratoga was only a first step. He thirsted to follow it up with an invasion of Canada, the "bold stroke," he said, that would bring "peace and freedom to America."[1] But Washington refused to beggar the operations to the south for such an enterprise, and the result was that the long-simmering antagonism between the two men erupted into an open breach.

The confrontation began when Gates, instead of communicating the news of his triumph directly to Washington, sent Wilkinson to carry it to Congress, to be relayed secondhand to the commander in chief. On his way, Wilkinson, in a tavern conversation, let fall a quotation from a letter written to Gates by Brigadier General Thomas Conway, an Irish-born French career officer who had volunteered in the American army: "Heaven has been determined to save your Country; or a weak General and bad Counsellors would have ruined it." Conway before this had been making free with invidious comments about Washington. No man, he had been heard to remark, appeared to greater advantage at his table, but as to his talents for command (with a French shrug), "they were miserable indeed." Politicians, too, had been critical of Washington's failure to stop Howe, at Brandywine and Germantown, from occupying Philadelphia. The "American Fabius," some called him, after the Roman general who avoided encounters, and Mifflin boldly declared that he was "fit only to be the head clerk of a London countinghouse." When Wilkinson's quotation from Conway's letter was reported to Washington, it was all that was needed to convince him that a "malignant faction" was plotting to replace him with Gates as commander in chief.[2]

No proof was ever brought forward of any such plot—the "Conway cabal," it has been called. The charge, however, proved an effective smoke screen from behind which to defeat Gates's very real contest with Washington over what in time became his obsession with an invasion of Canada. That contest was underway before the exposure of the Conway letter. More than a month before Burgoyne's surrender, Gates had begun to make his plans. Reports from Canadian spies convinced him that the populace was pro-American and that the British forts at St. Johns and Chambly were poorly garrisoned and open to attack. On September 14, he ordered Colonel Timothy Bedel, a Vermont separatist, to recruit a force of Abenaki and St. Francis Indians, and on November 15 he sent him orders to raise a five-hundred-man regiment and start out on February 1, 1778, from Co'os (now Newbury), New Hampshire, for a strike against St. Johns. In the spring would follow a full-scale assault on Montreal and Quebec. Against an estimated total of twenty-six hundred British troops under Carleton, Gates estimated that he could assemble an American force of two thousand: one thousand regulars to be detached from the army at Albany, Bedel's three hundred New Hampshiremen, Colonel Moses Hazen's two-hundred-man regiment of Canadians ("Congress's Own"), and five hundred prospective volunteers.[3]

In the midst of these preparations, he learned that Congress, without consulting him, had already authorized an expedition against St. Johns under Stark, a political enemy of Bedel and the Vermont separatists with whom Gates had allied himself. Gates realized that if his plans were not to be undercut he would have to channel them through Congress. There his friend Mifflin came to his aid by nominating him president of a newly created five-man board of war empowered to supervise military planning. Washington's supporters, led by Nathanael Greene, charged that this would give Gates an opportunity to dominate and undercut the commander in chief. The "Mifflinites," however, overcame the "Greenites," and Gates secured congressional approval to supersede the Stark expedition with his own. As revised, it was to be a twenty-five-hundred-man force led by the young Marquis de Lafayette, with Conway and Stark as second and third in command. Lafayette had written Gates of his "wish to cultivate your friendschip," and Gates saw in him an inducement for French-Canadian support. Lafayette's orders were to start from Albany, seize St. Johns, invest Montreal, and wait there for reinforcements. He was not told that Gates might then himself resume the field command to drive victoriously to Quebec.[4]

Washington considered the plan a "child of folly" but handed Lafayette his commission without comment. Lafayette, although flattered with the prospect of a conquest, had suspicions, and he demanded the removal of

Conway, who was replaced with Major General Johann de Kalb. At Albany, he found the army undermanned and poorly equipped. Schuyler advised abandoning the project, and Arnold, who labeled Gates "the greatest poltroon in the world," had ordered that no supplies be sent without his authorization. "I have been shamefully deceived," Lafayette wrote Washington, and to Congress he threatened, "I'l publish the whole history, I'l publish my instructions *with notes* through the world, and I'l loose rather the honour of twenty gatess and twenty boards of war, than to let my own reputation be hurted in the least thing."[5] He chose to ignore the preparations that had been made for the expedition by Hazen, Gates's confidential agent, who had 365 men in his regiment, he asserted, "so warm for the expedition that they would consent to go almost naked into Canada," and prospects of 400 more equipped troops from Vermont. Hazen had sent Bedel five thousand dollars at Co'os to enable him to bring his regiment to Albany. He had set up a network of wayside depots along the invasion route with supplies of forage, 174 "fat cattle," snowshoes, felling axes, and leggings, and he had been authorized by the governments of Massachusetts, Vermont, and New York to impress as many carriages and sleighs as he should require.[6]

Congress understood Lafayette's message. The invasion was canceled, and Gates, on April 15, was relieved of his position on the Board of War and assigned to command the army at Fishkill on the Hudson. Undaunted, Gates began planning all over again for an invasion, even to the extent of disregarding a congressional directive to send an expedition against the Seneca and Cayuga Indians in central New York State. On October 13, 1778, however, an unlooked-for factor entered the scene. Lafayette had become infected by the Canadian fever and regretted his impulsive abandonment of the expedition. France had come into the war; why not a joint invasion? He arrived in Philadelphia with a proposal that Congress delegate him to return to France and enlist support for a two-armied, 12,600-man American land invasion through Niagara and Montreal, supported by a French naval squadron sailing up the St. Lawrence.[7]

Washington was not blinded by his affection for Lafayette, and he was appalled. Beside the magnitude of this project, Gates's schemes paled to insignificance. He sent one closely reasoned letter to Congress and a second, privately, to its president, Henry Laurens, asking that they be kept secret from Lafayette. To Congress he set forth the shortage of troops and supplies in the extreme rigors of a northern winter, the folly of dependence on militia, the strength of British fortifications at Quebec, the superiority of British over French naval power, and the danger of weakening American defenses against the British forces still at New York and Rhode Island. On the other hand, a limited, unilateral American offensive could be undertaken against Detroit and Niagara for the purpose of seizing the Great Lakes and subjugating the Indians of the American northwest. He had already begun preparations. The operation from Co'os, unthinkable in the face of British naval power on the St. Lawrence, should be conducted merely as a feint to divert attention from the west.

The letter to Laurens was the most potent. Was it good policy, Washington asked, to tempt the resurgence of Gallic ambitions in Canada by introducing a massive French presence there? He fancied, when he had conferred with Lafayette and his aides, that he had "read in the countenances of some people on this occasion, more than the disinterested zeal of allies." He followed these letters up with a personal interview, and that clinched it. On January 1, 1779, Congress formally shelved the whole project.[8]

Gates was furious, and he made his fatal mistake. He wrote John Jay, the newly elected president of Congress and a staunch friend of Washington, charging that "individuals and not the public" would profit from the Niagara route, and complaining that Washington had not communicated with him for two months. Jay promptly informed Washington, who boiled over. "Malevolence" and "little underhand intrigues," he hotly replied, had long characterized Gates's behavior. Now, "hoping that I had embarked in a scheme, which our situation would not justify, he eagerly seizes the opportunity of exposing my supposed errors to Congress." As for the accusation of neglect, he saw no reason for "multiplying letters without an object" to a correspondent whose replies exhibited "an air of design, a want of candour in many instances, and even of politeness." Congress coldly ignored Gates's letter. "Your Friends," Jay wrote Washington, "thought it merited nothing but Silence and Neglect."[9]

Gates never recovered from that blow. Despairing of northern laurels, he accepted reassignment to the southern command. There, on August 16, 1780, he suffered an ignominious defeat at the Battle of Camden in South Carolina. He was replaced by Greene and never saw action again. Some historians accuse him of complicity, at the army's last encampment on the Hudson, in the "Newburgh conspiracy," an aborted scheme among discontented officers in 1783 to force the thirteen states at bayonet point to grant Congress the taxing power to issue arrears in soldier pay. But by then he was preoccupied with the recent death of his son and the mortal illness of his wife. Three years after her death, he married Mary Vallance, a wealthy, English-born widow, sold his Virginia plantation, and bought Rose Hill Farm, a sumptuous estate three miles north of New York City. To no one's surprise, he ended a confirmed, anti-Washington, Jeffersonian Republican.[10]

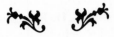

Ultimately, Burgoyne came to concede that American independence was inevitable. He declared himself a "convert."[11]

When he arrived in London, he found that his defeat had become a political issue, and within a year he joined the opposition, led by his friend Charles James Fox. To exonerate himself, he desired an audience with the king, a court-martial, and a Parliamentary inquiry. Germain, determined to escape blame, would allow none of these. He authorized only a preliminary military board of enquiry, which recommended that Burgoyne be ordered to return to his troops in America. Burgoyne replied that, because Parliament had never ratified the Saratoga Convention, he was not legally a prisoner, and in any case Congress had not summoned him. He never received a conclusive hearing. The nearest thing was a review by the House of Commons in May 1779, sitting as the committee of the whole, which did not submit a report. It gave him an opportunity, however, to call his staff to testify and present his case. He argued that his orders were peremptory to force his way to Albany, that the option he had proposed of advancing instead into New England had been deleted from his instructions, and that his expedition had produced a valuable diversion to strengthen Howe's campaign to the south. He accused Germain of mismanaging the entire North American operation. Rather than agree to return to America, he resigned all his appointments save his rank as lieutenant general. It meant the loss of an income of three thousand pounds a year.[12]

Gradually, he recognized that his best defense was that the war was hopeless in the face of the Americans' "most dauntless bravery, and the most obstinate and firm resolution." And when Lord Cornwallis was defeated at the Battle of Yorktown in 1781 and the demand of the opposition for an end to the conflict was mounting in Parliament, he felt free to proclaim that "the American war was but part of a general design levelled against the constitution of this country, and the general rights of mankind."[13]

In like spirit, he voted for a successful motion by Fox for self-government for the Irish Parliament. With the return of Rockingham to power in 1782, he received an appointment as commander in chief of the fifteen-thousand-man army in Ireland. Historian Maurice R. O'Connell writes that 1782 was "the great year of conciliation between the three religious denominations—Anglicans, Catholics, and Presbyterians," but Catholics and Presbyterians still could not serve in Parliament, and although Catholics were allowed freedom of worship, they still could not vote. Civil-military relationships during Burgoyne's tenure were peaceful. He lost his position in 1784 when he advocated reform of Warren Hastings's corrupt administration of the East India Company. He was supporting Fox again, and he was pursuing his long-standing concern for fairness in India, but he was opposing the king, and it was the end of his army career.[14]

He returned to play writing, and at the age of sixty he took as a mistress, by whom he fathered four children, a young actress in his productions, Susan Caulfield, whose husband was still alive. His greatest success in the theater was his play *The Heiress,* a hit comedy that critics acclaimed as a faithful rendering of the upper-class world by one who knew it firsthand.[15]

Until his death in 1792, he retained his seat in the House of Commons, where, in continued loyalty to Fox but in opposition to his other friend, Burke, he aligned himself with sympathizers of the French Revolution.[16] The defeated commander at Saratoga ended on the side of the two great revolutions of his age.

Epilogue:
The Turn of the Scale

WORD OF SARATOGA REACHED
Paris on December 4, 1777. Before that the prospect for the Americans had
been dismal. The fall of Ticonderoga without a fight, and Washington's
failure at the Battle of Brandywine to prevent the British occupation of
Philadelphia, had convinced the French that it was next to impossible for raw
militia to resist a regular and veteran army with success. They expected,
reported Silas Deane, one of the American negotiators in Paris, that "America must accommodate or submit."[1] Nor did it help that Deane and his fellow
representatives, Benjamin Franklin and Arthur Lee, had seriously antag-
onized the French government by illegally using French ports to outfit American warships and sell captured British merchant vessels.[2]

The news of Saratoga, reported Franklin's grandson, William Temple
Franklin, from Paris, "immediately turned the scale." The overjoyed French
acted "as if it had been a victory gained by their own arms." At the same time,
they had to fear that the British might offer concessions sufficient to lure the
rebels back to the fold. Franklin played on that fear; the British also contributed to it by dispatching an agent, Paul Wentworth, to confer with him in
Paris and by sending a commission, headed by the earl of Carlisle, to negotiate with the Continental Congress in America. Louis XVI and his foreign
secretary, the Comte de Vergennes, were willing enough to enter the war if it
could be won. They had been mobilizing their navy for an attack on the
British West Indies, and they were about ready. The day after learning of
Saratoga, Conrad-Alexandre Gérard, an undersecretary to Vergennes, proposed to the American representatives that negotiations be resumed for
conclusion of a treaty of alliance, and two weeks later he informed them that
the king had decided to recognize American independence. The treaty was
signed February 6, 1778.[3]

Saratoga and the French alliance forced the British to back off in America. The war was now global, and Germain's policy of concentrating on reconquest was abandoned. Under the direction in London of Lord Amherst, the army's new commander in chief, and the earl of Sandwich, first lord of the admiralty, a new strategy was adopted. The main thrust would be naval pressure against the rebels' seaports and coastal attacks by the army, mainly in the southern states. Naval stations would be maintained at Halifax in the St. Lawrence, New York in the Hudson, and Hampton Roads or Norfolk in the Chesapeake. Reinforcements were to be sent to Canada, but Clinton, who replaced Howe as commander in chief in America, was left with only three or four thousand men and authorized to withdraw from Philadelphia.[4]

Above all, at Saratoga the Americans proved to themselves that they could take on the pick of Britain's professional army and win. With the elimination of the threat of invasion from Canada, they no longer had to maintain a sizable army in the north. They could focus their efforts upon the enemy in the south, ultimately making possible Washington's decisive capture at Yorktown of a second major British army.

On Bemis Heights in 1777, after the bloodletting of September 19, Henry Dearborn had written in his diary, "We had Something more at Stake than fighting for six Pence Pr Day."[5]

Notes

Prologue. Appointment at Saratoga

1. John Burgoyne to Elizabeth and Harriet Stanley, Oct. 20, 1777, Edward Barrington de Fonblanque, *Political and Military Episodes in the Latter Half of the Eighteenth Century, Derived from the Life and Correspondence of the Right Hon. John Burgoyne* (London, 1876), 316–17; James Wilkinson, *Memoirs of My Own Times* (Philadelphia, 1816), 1:321; Friedrich A. von Riedesel, *Memoirs, Letters, and Journals of Major General Riedesel*, ed. William L. Stone (Albany, N.Y., 1868), 1:189n–90n.

2. Ray W. Pettengill, trans., *Letters from America, 1776–1779, Being Letters of Brunswick, Hessian, and Waldeck Officers with the British Armies During the Revolution* (Boston, Mass., 1924), 113; marginal note attributed to George Clinton in John Burgoyne's orderly book, in William L. Stone, ed., *The Campaign of Lieut. Gen. John Burgoyne and the Expedition of Lieut. Col. Barry St. Leger* (Albany, N.Y., 1877), 118n. I have preferred this version of the Gates-Burgoyne conversation to that in Wilkinson, *Memoirs,* 1:321.

1. Privilege

1. Sir Leslie Stephen and Sir Sidney Lee, eds., *Dictionary of National Biography* (London, 1885–1901), 2:259; Fonblanque, *Episodes,* 4–8; Gerald Howson, *Burgoyne of Saratoga: A Biography* (New York, 1979), 6; Joseph L. Chester, ed., *The Marriage, Baptismal, and Burial Registers of the Collegiate Church or Abbey of St. Peter, Westminster* (London, 1876), 450n.

2. John Sargeaunt, *Annals of Westminster School* (London, 1898), 32, 123, 166–72, 270, 272; Francis Markham, *Recollections of a Town Boy at Westminster, 1849–1855* (London, 1903), 11–12; Basil Williams, *Carteret and Newcastle: A Contrast in Contemporaries* (Cambridge, 1943), 8–10.

3. "The Army List of 1740," *Journal of the Society for Army Historical Research,* Special No. 3 (May 1931); Millard Cox, *Derby: The Life & Times of the 12th Earl of Derby, Edward Smith Stanley (1752–1834)* (London, 1974), 13–17; Winifred Proctor, "The Preston Election of 1768," *Transactions of the Historic Society of Lancashire and Cheshire* 3 (1959): 94; Peter Whittle, *The History of the Borough of Preston, in the County of Lancaster* (Preston, Eng., 1837), 2:123–24; William Dobson, *History of the Parliamentary Representation of Preston* (Preston, Eng., 1868), 45–46; description of Lord Strange by an unnamed friend, Henry Cavendish, *Sir Henry Cavendish's Debates of the House of Commons,* ed. J. Wright (London, 1841–43), 2:410n.

4. James Lunt, *John Burgoyne of Saratoga* (London, 1976), 9–11; Michael Glover, *General Burgoyne in Canada and America: Scapegoat for a System* (London, 1976), 45, 227; Howson, *Burgoyne,* 13–15; "Army List of 1740"; British Public Record Office, WO 25/21, fol. 164.

5. Fonblanque, *Episodes,* 8–9, 122, 134; George J. Armitage, ed., "The Register of Baptisms and Marriages at St. George's Chapel, Mayfair," *Harleian Society Registers* 15 (1889): 188.

6. John Fleming, *Robert Adam and His Circle in Edinburgh & Rome* (London, 1962), 118, 132, 158, 171.

7. Burgoyne to William Pitt (the Younger) [c. 1789], Fonblanque, *Episodes,* 452; Richard Middleton, *The Bells of Victory: The Pitt-Newcastle Ministry and the Conduct of the Seven Years' War, 1757–1762* (New York, 1985), 68–84; William Kent Hackmann, "English Military Expeditions to the Coast of France, 1757–1761" (Ph.D. diss., University of Michigan, 1969), 91–149; F. J. Hudleston, *Gentleman Johnny Burgoyne* (Indianapolis, Ind., 1927), 8, 351; Lawrence H. Gipson, *The British Empire before the American Revolution* (New York, 1936–70), 7:132–34.

8. Barrington to Burgoyne, Oct. 27, 1759, in Shute Barrington, *The Political Life of William Wildman, Viscount Barrington* (London, 1814), 55.

9. Alastair Smart, "The Genuine Portrait of General Burgoyne by Allan Ramsay," *Apollo* 94 (Sept. 1971): 198.

10. Fonblanque, *Episodes,* 14–26; Richard J. Hargrove, Jr., *General John Burgoyne* (Newark, Del., 1983), 29–34; Henry Graham, *History of the Sixteenth, the Queen's, Light Dragoons (Lancers)* (n.p., 1912), 2–4; F. J. Hebbert, "The Belle-Ile Expedition of 1761," *Journal of the Society for Army Historical Research* 64 (summer 1986): 88–93.

11. *Gentleman's Magazine* 34 (1764): 497; drawing of "Brigadeiro Burgoyne," Academia Militar, Lisbon, reproduced in Howson, *Burgoyne,* 2; Thomas Carlyle, *Frederick the Great* (London, 1898), 7:238; John Burgoyne, *The Dramatic and Poetical Works of the Late Lieut. Gen. J. Burgoyne; to which is prefixed, Memoirs of the Author,* (London, 1808), 1:7; Fonblanque, *Episodes,* 26–32; Gipson, *British Empire,* 8:180–84, 155–60; Hargrove, *Burgoyne,* 36–40; A. D. Francis, "The Campaign in Portugal, 1762," *Journal of the Society for Army Historical Research* 59 (Spring 1981): 30–40; Count La Lippe to [Earl of Egremont], Aug. 30, 1762, British Public Record Office, SP 89.57, p. 144; copy of Burgoyne's account in Earl of Loudon to [Earl of Egremont], Oct. 1, 1762, ibid., pp. 19–44.

12. John Burgoyne, *A State of the Expedition from Canada* (London, 1780), "Prefatory Speech."

2. *The Skipjack*

1. Charles E. Pearce, *Polly Peacham: The Story of Lavinia Fenton and the Beggar's Opera* (London, 1913), 46–60, 83–103, 203–32, 280–87; William Henry Irving, *John Gay, Favorite of the Wits* (Durham, N.C., 1940), 244n; Arthur Young to Thomas Tickell, Mar., n.d., 1728, R. E. Tickell, *Thomas Tickell and the Eighteenth Century Poets (1685–1740)* (London, 1931), 144; John Gay to Jonathan Swift, July 6, 1728, John Gay, *The Letters of John Gay,* ed. C. F. Burgess (Oxford, 1966), 76.

2. Lady Mary Montague to Lady Bute, Dec. 8 [1754], in Lady Mary Montague, *The Complete Letters of Lady Mary Montague,* ed. Robert Halsband (Oxford, 1965), 3:75; Horace Walpole to William Cole, June 21, 1782, in Horace Walpole, *Letters of Horace Walpole,* ed. Paget Toynbee (Oxford, 1904), 12:269; Pearce, *Polly Peacham,* 307; W[illiam] W. Watts, *The Seats of the Nobility and Gentry* (London, 1779–86), plate 1.

3. T. P., *London Chronicle,* Aug. 3, 1779; parish registers, St. Alfege Church, Greenwich, England, per J. V. Stacey (verger) to me, Nov. 1, 1972; William A. Shaw, ed., *Calendar of Treasury Books and Papers, 1729–1730* (London, 1897), 107, 197; G. D. H. Cole and Raymond Postgate, *The British People, 1746–1946* (New York, 1947), 48–49; Daniel Defoe, *A Journal of the Plague Year,* in *The Works of Daniel Defoe,* ed. G. H. Maynadier (New York, 1904), 9:123; British Public Record Office, T.11/19, 22.

4. J. Jean Hecht, *Domestic Servant Class in Eighteenth Century England* (London, 1956), 141–92; Letitia Pilkington, *Memoirs of Mrs. Letitia Pilkington, 1712–1750,* ed. J. Isaacs (London, 1928), 214; [Daniel Defoe], *The Great Law of Subordination* (London, 1724), 175; engraving of Westcombe house in Pearce, *Polly Peacham,* 208; rate book of 1769, London Borough of Greenwich, per H. Davis (borough librarian) to me, Mar. 5, 1973; John Rocque, *A New and Accurate Survey of the Cities of London and Westminster* (London, 1748), plate 2; *Cary's New Plan of London and its Vicinity* (London, 1837).

5. "North Country Diaries (Second Series)," *Proceedings of the Surtees Society* 124 (1915): 132n; Mark J. Simmonds, comp., *Merchant Taylor Fellows of St. John's College Oxford* (London, 1930), 59; Horace Walpole, *Journal of the Reign of King George the Third from the Year 1771 to 1783,* ed. D. Doran (London, 1859), 2:200; entry of Mar. 19, 1701, John Evelyn, *The Diary of John Evelyn,* ed. E. S. de Beer (London, 1959), 1067; Ann Allport to Horatio Gates, Apr. 11, 1798, James Gregory, ed. of microfilmed MSS., *The Horatio Gates Papers, 1726–1828* (Glen Rock, N.J., 1978) (hereafter cited as Gates Papers); Pearce, *Polly Peachum,* 231, attributing doggerel to Sir Hanbury Williams; British Public Record Office, T.11/19; *Calendar of Treasury Books and Papers, 1729–1730,* 107.

6. Walpole, *Journal,* 2:200; Isaac Greenwood, "Major General Horatio Gates," *New England Historical and Genealogical Register* 70 (July 1867): 252–56; general return of Horatio Gates's company, Aug. 26, 1756, Gates Papers; Paul David Nelson, *General Horatio Gates: A Biography* (Baton Rouge, La., 1976), 6n.

7. Thomas Gates to Horatio Gates, May 4 and July 7, 1785, June 30, 1787, Oct. 22, 1789, June 17, 1791, Aug. 16, 1792, June 1, 1793, Ann Allport to Horatio Gates, Apr. 11, 1798, all in Gates Papers.

8. Margaret Whinney, *Christopher Wren* (New York, 1971), 183–91; John Summerson, *Architecture in Britain, 1530–1830* (London, 1953), plates 72, 104–05, 45, 107(A).

9. J. W. Kirby, *History of the Roan School (The Greycoat School) and Its Founder* (London, 1929), 53, 56, 62; Beryl Platts, *A History of Greenwich* (Newton Abbot, Eng., 1973), 12–14; Benjamin Rush, *The Autobiography of Benjamin Rush,* ed. George W. Corner (Princeton, N.J., 1948), 154.

10. British Public Record Office T.11/22, f. 163; William A. Shaw, ed., *Calendar of Treasury Reports and Papers, 1739–1741* (London, 1901), 493.

11. *Common Sense* (1738), quoted in Hecht, *Domestic Servant Class,* 193; British Public Record Office, WO 4/39, 45, and WO 64/9, 11, cited in John R. Elting, *The Battles of Saratoga* (Monmouth Beach, N.J., 1977), 17, 76; British Public Record Office, WO 25/21, f. 164. See also Lord Barrington to Judge Advocate General, Feb. 8, 1766, in Anthony Bruce, *The Purchase System in the British Army, 1660–1871* (London, 1980), 173–74.

12. Henry Fielding, *The History of Tom Jones, A Foundling,* Modern Library (New York, 1950), 309; Tobias Smollett, *The Expedition of Humphrey Clinker,* Modern Library (New York, 1929), 227.

3. Luster

1. Count La Lippe, "Orders of the Day," *Gentleman's Magazine* 32 (1762): 498.

2. Sir Lewis Namier and John Brooke, eds., *The History of Parliament: The House of Commons, 1754–1790* (London, 1964), 1:395–96, 2:142, 3:645; Stanley to Newcastle, Oct. 21, 1760, British Library Ad. MSS. 32913, f. 257–58.

3. John Almon, ed., *The Parliamentary Register: History of the Proceedings and Debates of the House of Commons, 1774–1780* (London, 1775–80), 1:252; William Cobbett, ed., *The Parliamentary History of England from the Earliest Period to the Year 1803* (London, 1806–20), 17:295.

4. Namier and Brooke, *House of Commons* 2:142; Charlotte Burgoyne to Viscount Palmerston, Nov., n.d., 1763, in Brian Connell, ed., *Portrait of a Golden Age: Intimate Papers of the Second Viscount Palmerston* (Boston, 1958), 43; George Grenville to Burgoyne, Jan. 28, 1764, and Burgoyne to Grenville, Feb. 16, 1764, in George Grenville, *Additional Grenville Papers, 1763–1765,* ed. John R. G. Tomlinson (Manchester, Eng., 1962), 79–80, 86.

5. Edmund S. and Helen Morgan, *The Stamp Act Crisis: Prologue to Revolution* (Chapel Hill, N.C., 1953), 327–70; Namier and Brooke, *House of Commons* 2:142, 3:455; J. Debrett, ed., *The History, Debates, and Proceedings of both Houses of Parliament of Great Britain, from the year 1743 to the year 1774* (London, 1792), 4:346, 350; R. C. Simmons and P. D. G. Thomas, eds., *Proceedings and Debates of the British Parliaments Respecting North America, 1754–1783* (Millwood, N.Y., 1983), 2:150, 289, 290; Ross J. S. Hoffman, *The Marquis: A Study of Lord Rockinghamm 1730–1782* (New York, 1973), 111–13; Paul Langford, *The First Rockingham Administration, 1765–1766* (London, 1973), 163–64.

6. John Burgoyne, private memorandum, n.d., Fonblanque, *Episodes,* 124; *Gentleman's Magazine* 34 (1764): 146; Charlotte Burgoyne to Viscount Palmers-

ton, May 31, 1764–May 12, 1765, in Connell, *Portrait of a Golden Age,* 52–53, 61–62.

7. Pitt to Burgoyne, July 1, 1766, Burgoyne to Chatham, Aug. 21, 1766, Burgoyne, "Observations and Reflections upon the Present Military State of Prussia, Austria, and France," 1766, Chatham to Burgoyne, Dec. 14, 1766, all in William Pitt, *Correspondence of William Pitt,* ed. William S. Taylor and John H. Pringle (London, 1838), 2:429–32, 3:41–42, and Fonblanque, *Episodes,* 56–83; Basil Williams, *The Life of William Pitt, Earl of Chatham* (London, 1913), 2:234–43; Shelburne to Chatham, Feb. 16, 1767, Chatham Papers, British Public Record Office, cited in Charles R. Ritcheson, *British Politics and the American Revolution* (Norman, Okla., 1954), 89.

8. Namier and Brooke, *House of Commons,* 1:396, 319; Proctor, "Preston Election of 1768," 95–103; "Substance of Col. John Burgoyne's Speech before the King's Bench, Relative to his Election for Preston, in Lancashire, in the year 1769," May 29, 1769, in Lancashire Record Office, DDPr, 131/7, cited in Hargrove, *Burgoyne,* 50–54; Dobson, *Preston,* 7; *Journals of the House of Commons* (London, 1803), 32:27–28, 79–80; Glover, *Burgoyne,* 62–65.

9. Sir Lewis Namier, *The Structure of Politics at the Accession of George III* (London, 1929), 105; Proctor, "Preston Election of 1768," 98; Whittle, *Preston,* 170; Cox, *Derby,* 1–2; Howson, *Burgoyne,* 21, 27, 63.

10. Burgoyne spoke 66 times from 1768 to 1774, "Check List of the M.P.s who spoke in the House of Commons from 1768 to 1774, together with the number of speeches made by each," *Bulletin of the Institute of Historical Research* 35 (Nov. 1962): 223; Howson, *Burgoyne,* 61; Charles R. Leslie and Tom Taylor, *Life of Sir Joshua Reynolds* (London, 1865), 2:99; Hargrove, *Burgoyne,* 44; Henry S. Eeles and Earl Spencer, *Brooks's, 1764–1964* (London, 1964), 22; Anthony Hewitson, *History (from A.D. 705 to 1883) of Preston, in the County of Lancaster* (Preston, Eng., 1883), 355.

11. Cavendish, *Debates,* 2:191; Burgoyne, private memorandum, Fonblanque, *Episodes,* 124; Hudleston, *Burgoyne,* 31n; Cobbett, *Parl. Hist.,* 16:1, 367–68; J. Holland Rose, A. P. Newton, and E. A. Benians, eds., *Cambridge History of the British Empire* (Cambridge, 1929), 1:685–705.

12. To Lord North, Feb. 14, 1771, in George III, *The Correspondence of King George the Third with Lord North From 1768 to 1783,* ed. W. Dodham Donne (London, 1867), 2:57.

13. John Brooke, *King George III* (New York, 1972), 273–77; King George III to Lord North, Mar. 12, 1772, George III, *Corr. of King George the Third with Lord North* 2:96.

14. Alan Valentine, *Lord North* (Norman, Okla., 1967), 1:244–46; Cobbett, *Parl. Hist.,* 17:295; Burgoyne's will, 1783, in Fonblanque, *Episodes,* 463.

4. Merit

1. John Armstrong, Jr., to Jared Sparks, Dec. 4, 1831, Jared Sparks Papers, Houghton Library, Harvard University; Samuel J. Meyrick to John Trumbull, June

1, 1836, in John Trumbull, *Autobiography, Reminiscences, and Letters, 1756–1841* (New York, 1841), 302; Hoffman Nickerson, *The Turning Point of the Revolution* (Boston, 1928; reissued, 1967), 1:10–15.

2. Rose et al., *Cambridge History of the British Empire,* 1:375, 527; Thomas H. Raddall, *Halifax: Warden of the North* (New York, 1965), 20.

3. Horace Walpole to Horace Mann, Nov. 29, 1745, Horace Walpole, *Letters of Horace Walpole,* ed. Paget Toynbee (Oxford, 1903–05), 2:158; Raddall, *Halifax,* 20–37; James S. Macdonald, "Hon. Edward Cornwallis, Founder of Halifax," *Collections of the Nova Scotia Historical Society* 12 (1905): 7–87; Namier and Brooke, *House of Commons,* 2:256–57, 3:149; for a color print of a painting of Cornwallis, see H. Oakes-Jones, "An Unidentified Portrait," *Journal of the Society of Army Historical Research* 6 (Jan.–Mar. 1927): 11; Edward Cornwallis to Robert Gates, Mar. 18, 1750, Gates Papers.

4. John Hale to Horatio Gates, Nov. 30, 1791, Gates Papers.

5. Miniature painting of Mrs. Horatio Gates, artist unknown, New-York Historical Society; Charles Lee to Robert Morris, June 16, 1781, *The Lee Papers, Collections of the New-York Historical Society* (1871–75) 3:458; memorial of Anne Phillips, n.d., Gates Papers; William A. Calneck, *History of the County of Annapolis* (Toronto, 1897), 50.

6. James Boswell, *Boswell's London Journal, 1762–1763,* ed. Frederick A. Pottle (New York, 1950), 46, 215.

7. Dorothy Marshall, *Dr. Johnson's London* (New York, 1968), 123–38.

8. Thomas Robinson to Robert Dinwiddie, July 5, 1754, Jeffrey Amherst Papers microfilm, vol. 71, reel 1119(2); Reed Browning, *The Duke of Newcastle* (New Haven, 1975), 207–13; Thad W. Riker, *Henry Fox* (Oxford, 1911), 194–200; Evan Charteris, *William Augustus, Duke of Cumberland and the Seven Years War* (London, 1913), 2:111–13; Lee McCardell, *Ill-Starred General: Braddock of the Coldstream Guards* (Pittsburgh, 1958), 122–23; Horace Walpole, *Memoirs of the Reign of King George II* (London, 1822), 1:400–01; Namier and Brooke, *House of Commons,* 2:257.

9. Edward Cornwallis to Robert Gates, Mar. 18, 1749, and Thomas Clarke to [?], June 7, 1755, Gates Papers.

5. *"The Hard Hand of Power"*

1. Jonathan Breynton, Certification, Aug. 2, 1757, Gates Papers; Basil Williams, *The Life of William Pitt, Earl of Chatham* (London, 1913), 1:261; Williams, *Cartaret and Newcastle,* 198; McCardell, *Ill-Starred General,* 133.

2. *The Independent Reflector,* Jan. 18, 1753, in Bayrd Still, *Urban America: A History with Documents* (Boston, 1974), 38.

3. Leslie F. S. Upton, *The Loyal Whig: William Smith of New York & Quebec* (Toronto, 1969), 50; Milton M. Klein, *The Politics of Diversity: Essays in the History of Colonial New York* (Port Washington, N.Y., 1974), 56–105; Bernard Bailyn, *The Origins of American Politics* (New York, 1968), 41–117.

4. Entry of Apr. 18, 1755, "Extracts from the Journal of the Proceedings of the

Detachment of Seamen," Archer Butler Hulbert, *Braddock's Road and Three Relative Papers* (Cleveland, 1903), 86; Thomas Clarke to [Thomas Calcraft?], June 7, 1755, Gates Papers; Edward Braddock to Robert Napier, Mar. 17, 1755, Stanley Pargellis, ed., *Military Affairs in North America, 1748–1765* (New York, 1936), 79.

5. Douglas S. Freeman, *George Washington: A Biography* (New York, 1948–57), 2:31; George Washington to John Augustine Washington, May 31, 1754, George Washington, *Writings of George Washington,* ed. John C. Fitzpatrick (Washington, D.C., 1931–44), 1:70; Bernhard Knollenberg, *George Washington: The Virginia Period, 1732–1775* (Durham, N.C., 1964), 26–28; Paul L. Ford, *The True George Washington* (Philadelphia, 1896), 38–39; George Washington Parke Custis, *Recollections and Private Memoirs of Washington* (New York, 1860), 155, 164n; François-Jean, Chevalier de Chastellux, *Travels in North America,* in Gilbert Chinard, *George Washington as the French Knew Him* (Princeton, N.J., 1940), 52.

6. John F. Watson, *Annals of Philadelphia and Pennsylvania* (Philadelphia, 1898), 2:140, quoted in Rupert Hughes, *George Washington, The Human Being and the Hero (1732–1762)* (New York, 1926), 209.

7. George Washington, *The Papers of George Washington, Colonial Series,* ed. W. W. Abbot (Charlottesville, Va., 1983–), 1:294–333; Horatio Gates to Francis Penfold, 1779, Hezekiah Niles, ed., *Principles and Acts of the Revolution in America* (Baltimore, 1822), 496; Horatio Gates to Robert Monckton, Sept. 5, 1755, quoted in Paul E. Kopperman, *Braddock at the Monongahela* (Pittsburgh, 1977), 195.

8. Macdonald, "Hon. Edward Cornwallis, Founder of Halifax," 11–16; William Smith, Jr., *History of the Late Province of New York* (New York, 1830), vol. 1, appendix.

9. Nicholas B. Wainwright, *George Croghan, Wilderness Diplomat* (Chapel Hill, N.C., 1959), 72–73.

10. Klein, *Politics of Diversity,* 155–63.

11. Smith, *New York* 2:361; Gipson, *British Empire* 8:189–95; Monckton to Egremont, Feb. 9, 1762, in *London Gazette Extraordinary,* Mar. 22, 1762, reprinted in *Pennsylvania Gazette,* June 10, 1762; John Armstrong to Jared Sparks, Dec. 4, 1831, Sparks MSS.

12. Nelson, *Gates,* 23–32; John Shy, *Toward Lexington: The Role of the British Army in the Coming of the American Revolution* (Princeton, N.J., 1965), 182; Gates to Edward Cornwallis, Oct. 29, 1763, Gates Papers.

13. Augustin Oldham to Horatio Gates, July 4, 1765, Ann Phillips to Horatio Gates, Oct. 28, 1763, and Robert and Dorothy Gates to Horatio Gates, Jan. 23, 1766, all in Gates Papers; [Mrs.] Sewell to [Elizabeth] Gates, Nov. 28, no year, Letters to and from Gates, n.d., Gates Papers.

14. Robert Monckton to Gates, n.d., and John Hale to Gates, Nov. 26, no year, Gates Papers; Lucy S. Sutherland, *The East India Company in Eighteenth-Century Politics* (Oxford, 1952), 231–67.

15. William Smith, Jr., to Gates, Nov. 22, 1763, and Henry Cruger to Gates, July 6, 1770, Gates Papers; [?] to Gates, n.d., no. 87, reel 11, Gates Papers.

16. Lee Raymond Lombard, "John Hall Stevenson: The Eugenius of Lawrence Sterne" (M.A. thesis, Columbia University, 1934), 7–19; Lawrence Sterne, "The Journal to Eliza," entry of June 28, 1767, Sterne, *The Complete Works and Life of*

Lawrence Sterne, ed. Wilbur L. Cross (New York, 1904), 4:119; Charles Davers to Gates, Jan. 7 and Apr. 12, no years, reel 11, Gates Papers microfilm; *Rushbrook Parish Registers, 1567–1850* (Woodbridge, Eng., 1903), 386–87; [?] to Gates, Feb. 5, 1770, Gates Papers; John Richard Alden, *General Charles Lee, Traitor or Patriot?* (Baton Rouge, La., 1951), 3–5; William Livingston to Noah Welles, Aug. 18, 1759, quoted in Milton M. Klein, ed., *The Independent Reflector* (Cambridge, Mass., 1953), 284; Bailyn, *Idealogical Origins,* 82n–83n.

17. Hale's letters, Thomas Hayes to Gates, May 16, 1770, and Gates's draft of speech, c. 1769, in Gates Papers; Charles Davers to Gates, May 18, no year, Gates Papers.

18. Benjamin Franklin to William Franklin, Mar. 13, 1768, and William Franklin to Benjamin Franklin, Oct. 23, 1767, Benjamin Franklin, *The Papers of Benjamin Franklin,* ed. Leonard W. Labaree and William B. Willcox (New Haven, 1959–), 15:78, 121; Maurice Richards, *Where They Lived in London* (New York, 1972), 26; David Freeman Hawke, *Franklin: What Manner of Man?* (New York, 1976), 271.

19. Monckton to Gates, July 16, 1771, Gates Papers; Andrew Drummond to Gates, May 30, 1765, ibid.; Monckton to George Townshend, September 16, 1759, in C. V. F. Townshend, *The Military Life of Field-Marshal George First Marquess Townshend, 1724–1807* (London, 1901), 248; Hale to Gates, Nov. 26, no year, Gates Papers.

20. Washington to Gates, July 3, 1772; William Allen to Gates, Dec. 17, 1772; Elizabeth Gates to Elizabeth [Lady] Galway, Aug. 1, 1772; [?] to Mr. West, May 11, 1772, all in Gates Papers.

6. *"The Soldier Draws His Sword with Alacrity"*

1. Sutherland, *East India Company,* 220–32; William Hazlitt, *The Eloquence of the British Senate,* quoted in Valentine, *Lord North,* 1:277n; Cobbett, *Parl. Hist.* 17:454–63.

2. Sir John Malcolm, *The Life of Robert, Lord Clive* (London, 1836), 2:296–98; Sir George W. Forrest, *The Life of Lord Clive* (London, 1918), 393–94; John Watney, *Clive of India* (Farnborough, Hants., 1974), 92; Namier and Brooke, *House of Commons* 2:685; *Jour. House of Commons* 33:792–944.

3. A. Mervyn Davies, *Clive of Passy: A Biography* (London, 1939), 480; John Burgoyne, memorandum on East India Company, n.d., Fonblanque, *Episodes,* 95; Malcolm, *Life of Robert, Lord Clive,* 2: 309–10.

4. Malcolm, *Clive,* 2:319–59; "Debates in Parliament," *Gentleman's Magazine* 43 (1773): 579; Namier and Brooke, *House of Commons* 2:143; Sutherland, *East India Company,* 255–58; *Jour. House of Commons,* 34:330–31; Cobbett, *Parl. Hist.* 17:881–82.

5. Burgoyne, private memorandum, Fonblanque, *Episodes,* 123; Valentine, *Lord North,* 1:296.

6. Valentine, *Lord North,* 315; Cobbett, *Parl. Hist.* 17:1074; Charles Shephard, *An Historical Account of The Island of Saint Vincent* (London, 1831), 30.

7. North's speech quoted in Benjamin Labaree, *The Boston Tea Party* (New York, 1964), 72–73.

8. M.P.'s remark quoted in George A. Billias, "John Burgoyne: Ambitious General," in Billias, ed., *George Washington's Opponents* (New York, 1969), 187; Cobbett, *Parl. Hist.* 17:271.

9. To Charles Lee, July 8, 1775, Fonblanque, *Episodes,* 168.

10. Burgoyne, *Dramatic and Poetical Works* 1:65; Hudleston, *Burgoyne,* 324–25; *The Life of Mrs. Abington* (London, 1888), 59.

11. "Account of the Fete Champetre at the Oaks," *Gentleman's Magazine* 44 (1774): 263–64.

12. King George III to Lord Dartmouth, Jan. 31, 1775, quoted in Bernard Donoughue, *British Politics and the American Revolution: The Path to War, 1773–75* (New York, 1964), 229.

13. Namier and Brooke, *House of Commons* 2:676; Burgoyne's private memorandum, Fonblanque, *Episodes,* 120–32; Sylvester Douglas, *The Diaries of Sylvester Douglas,* ed. Francis Bickley (London, 1928), 1:328; Ira D. Gruber, "George III Chooses a Commander in Chief," in Ronald Hoffman and Peter J. Albert, eds., *Arms and Independence: The Military Character of the Revolution* (Charlottesville, Va., 1984), 166–90.

14. Almon., *Parl. Register* 1:252.

15. Thomas Hutchinson, *The Diary and Letters of His Excellency Thomas Hutchinson,* ed. Peter O. Hutchinson (London, 1883), 1:420.

16. King George III to Lord North, Apr. 11, 14, 1775, George III, *Corr. of King George the Third with Lord North* 1:244; Lord Dartmouth to Thomas Gage, Apr. 15, 1775, Thomas Gage, *The Correspondence of General Thomas Gage,* ed. Clarence E. Carter (New Haven, 1933), 2:190–95.

17. Smart, "The Genuine Portrait of General Burgoyne," 94; Lady Mary Coke, *The Letters and Journals of Lady Mary Coke* (Edinburgh, 1892), 2:344, 3:260; Burgoyne, private memorandum, and Burgoyne to King George III, Apr. 18, 1775, Fonblanque, *Episodes,* 122–23, 134.

18. Hutchinson, *Diary,* 1:430.

7. *"America Must Be Subdued or Relinquished"*

1. John Burgoyne, private memorandum, n.d., and to Lord Rochford, [June 25], 1775, in Fonblanque, *Episodes,* 129, 144; Edward M'Gauran, *Memoirs* (London, 1786), 2:189; Charles Stedman, *History of the Origin, Progress, and Termination of the American War* (London, 1794), 1:398; Clinton to [?], June 13, [1775], Clinton Papers, William L. Clements Library, quoted in Henry Clinton, *The American Rebellion: Sir Henry Clinton's Narrative of His Campaigns, 1775–1782,* ed. William B. Willcox (New Haven, 1954), xvii, 18.

2. Richard Frothingham, *History of the Siege of Boston, and of the Battles of Lexington, Concord, and Bunker Hill* (Boston, Mass., 1849), 114n; Justin Winsor, ed., *Memorial History of Boston, including Suffolk County, Massachusetts, 1630–1880*

(Boston, Mass., 1881), 3:iv, 155; Samuel A. Drake, *Old Landmarks and Historic Personages of Boston* (Boston, Mass., 1873), 361–62.

3. Gage to Barrington, June 6, 1775, Gage, *Correspondence* 2:682; Fonblanque, *Episodes,* 136; James Robertson to [?], June 13, 1775, Historical Manuscripts Commission, *Report on the Manuscripts of the Earl of Dartmouth* (London, 1887–96), 2:315; Germain to John Irwin, July 26, 1775, Historical Manuscripts Commission, *Report on the Manuscripts of Mrs. Stopford-Sackville* (London, 1904–10), 1:136; Gage's Proclamation, June 12, 1775, and Journals of Massachusetts Provincial Congress in Peter Force, ed., *American Archives* (Washington, D.C., 1837–53), 4th ser., 2:968–70, 1418 (hereafter cited as *AA*).

4. Burgoyne to North, June 14, 1775, and to Lord Rochford, [June 25], 1775, in Fonblanque, *Episodes,* 138–39, 150, 151.

5. Burgoyne to Rochford, [June 25], 1775, ibid., 143–45; Burgoyne to [Lord Stanley, June 25, 1775], British Library Add. MSS. 5847, f. 378; Allen French, *The First Year of the American Revolution* (Boston, Mass., 1934), 209n; Henry Clinton, loose note, Clinton Papers, quoted in William B. Willcox, *Portrait of a General: Sir Henry Clinton in the War of Independence* (New York, 1964), 48; Henry Clinton, memorandum, Apr. 13, 1785, Clinton, *American Rebellion,* 19n.

6. Burgoyne to Lord Germain, Aug. 20, 1775, Germain Papers, William L. Clements Library; Burgoyne to Rochford, [June 25], 1775, Fonblanque, *Episodes,* 153.

7. Lee to Burgoyne, June 7, 1775, *AA,* 4th ser., 2:925–28; Burgoyne to Lee, ibid., 1610–12; Burgoyne to Lord Dartmouth, July 26, 1775, *Dartmouth MSS.* 2:337; Burgoyne to North, [July 26], 1775, Fonblanque, *Episodes,* 174–79; Journals of Massachusetts Provincial Congress, *AA,* 4th ser., 2:1503–04; North to Burgoyne, July 31, 1775, Historical Manuscripts Commission, *Report on the Manuscripts of the Marquess of Abergavenny* (London, 1887), appendix, part 6.

8. Burgoyne to [Edward] Thurlow, [?], 1775, Fonblanque, *Episodes,* 201; Washington to Gage, Aug. 11, 1775, Washington, *Writings* 3:417; Gage to Washington, Aug. 13, 1775, Gage Papers, American Series, William L. Clements Library, 131; Freeman, *Washington* 3:526–28; Burgoyne, *Dramatic and Poetical Works* 2:238; Stephen Moylan to Joseph Reed, Dec. 5, 1775, William B. Reed, *Life and Correspondence of Joseph Reed* (Philadelphia, 1847), 1:134.

9. Burgoyne to Rochford, [July 26, 1775], Fonblanque, *Episodes,* 180; Burgoyne to Gage, Aug. 13, 1775, Gage Papers, American Series, 131; Burgoyne to Germain, Aug. 20, 1775, Germain Papers.

10. Philip Freneau, "A Voyage to Boston," quoted in Alden, *General Gage,* 276.

11. Dartmouth to Gage, two letters, Aug. 2, 1775, Gage, *Correspondence* 2:202–06; Burgoyne to North, Oct. 10, 1775, Murdock MSS., Houghton Library, Harvard; William Feilding to Lord Denbigh, Dec. 3, 1775, Marion Balderston and David Syrett, eds., *The Lost War: Letters from British Officers during the American Revolution* (New York, 1975), 56.

12. Frothingham, *Siege of Boston,* 280–82, 328; Drake, *Old Landmarks,* 361–62.

13. Dartmouth to Howe, Sept. 5, 1775, Kenneth G. Davies, ed., *Documents of*

the *American Revolution, 1770–1783* (Dublin, 1972–80), 11:99–100 (hereafter cited as *DAR*); Howe to Dartmouth, Nov. 26, 1775, ibid., 191–94.

14. Burgoyne to Henry Clinton, Jan. 5, 1776, Clinton Papers; John Adams's description in John Brooke, *King George III* (New York, 1972), 306; Burgoyne, private memorandum, n.d., Fonblanque, *Episodes,* 126; Piers Mackesy, *The War for America, 1775–1783* (Cambridge, Mass., 1965), 53.

15. "Characters: Lord George Germain," *London Chronicle,* Aug. 27, 1776; George H. Guttridge, "Lord George Germain in Office, 1775–1782," *American Historical Review* 38 (Oct. 1927): 26; Gerald S. Brown, *The American Secretary: The Colonial Policy of Lord George Germain, 1775–1778* (Ann Arbor, Mich., 1963), 1–43; Lord Edmund G. P. Fitzmaurice, *Life of William, Earl of Shelburne* (London, 1875), 1:250, quoted in Mackesy, *War for America,* 52.

16. Frothingham, *Siege of Boston,* 280n; Burgoyne to Germain, Jan. 4, 1776, *Stopford-Sackville MSS.* 1:383–84; Fonblanque, *Episodes,* 208.

17. Germain to William Howe, Jan. 5, 1776, *DAR* 12:33–35; appointment of lieutenant generals, Jan. 1, 1776, ibid. 10:170.

18. Germain to William Howe, Feb. 1, 1776, ibid., 12:55; Mackesy, *War for America,* 63.

19. Barbara Graymont, *The Iroquois in the American Revolution* (Syracuse, N.Y., 1972), 51, 67; Dale Van Every, *A Company of Heroes: The American Frontier, 1775–1783* (New York, 1962), 86–87; [Germain] to Burgoyne, Aug. 23, 1776, *Stopford-Sackville MSS.* 2:40.

20. Oct. 25, 1775, *DAR* 11:166.

21. Burgoyne private memorandum, n.d., Fonblanque, *Episodes,* 126; William Feilding to Lord Denbigh, Mar. 2, 1776, Balderston and Syrett, *Lost War,* 68; James Burrow to Francis Legge, Mar. 9, 1776, *Dartmouth MSS.* 2:599.

22. Burgoyne to Germain, Mar. 3, 1776, *Stopford-Sackville MSS.* 2:23; Germain to Burgoyne, Mar. 1, 1776, Fonblanque, *Episodes,* 212; Howson, *Burgoyne,* 100.

23. Entry of Mar. 28, 1776, Hutchinson, *Diary* 2:31; Germain to Burgoyne, Mar. 28, 1776, and to Carleton, Mar. 28, 1776, *DAR* 10:252; Germain to Carleton, Feb. 17, 1776, ibid. 12:57; Horace Walpole, *The Last Journals of Horace Walpole during the Reign of George III, from 1771 to 1783,* ed. A. Francis Steuwart (London, 1910), 1:522.

24. Burgoyne to Germain, *Stopford-Sackville MSS.* 2:23; Burgoyne to Henry Clinton, July 7, 1776, and Nov. 7, 1776, Clinton Papers.

8. "To Preserve the Liberty of the Western World"

1. Nelson, *Gates,* 35; Millard K. Bushong, *Jefferson County* (Boyce, Va., 1972), 26, 33, 56, 308; Jonathan Ariss to Gates, Aug. 21, 1773, Gates Papers; Gates to Charles Mellish, Apr. 11, 1774, Mellish Papers, University of Nottingham; Gates's commission as justice of oyer and terminer, Apr. 14, 1773, Gates Papers; Berkely County Court proceedings, Nov. 20, 1776, Willis F. Evans, *History of Berkely County, West*

Virginia (Wheeling, W. Va., 1928), 70; F. Vernon Aler, *Aler's History of Martinsburg and Berkely County, West Virginia* (Hagerstown, Md., 1888), 202–05.

2. Gates to Mellish, Apr. 11, 1773, Mellish Papers; Gates's commission as lieutenant colonel, Berkely County militia, Apr. 6, 1773, Gates Papers.

3. Gates to John Winstone, Mar. 15, 1774, Chicago Historical Society, in Gates Papers.

4. William T. Doherty, *Berkely County, U.S.A.* (Parsons, W. Va., 1972), 41; Freeman, *Washington*, 3:55–56; Stephen to Gates, Nov. 24, 1772, Gates Papers; Oliver P. Chitwood, *Richard Henry Lee, Statesman of the Revolution* (Morgantown, W. Va., 1967), 23–27, 46, 62; painting of Patrick Henry by Thomas Sully, Robert D. Meade, *Patrick Henry, Patriot in the Making* (Philadelphia, 1957), 240; Silas Deane to Elizabeth Deane, [Sept. 10, 1774], Paul H. Smith, ed., *Letters of Delegates to Congress, 1774–1789* (Washington, D.C., 1976–), 1:62 (hereafter cited as *LDC*).

5. Alden, *Charles Lee*, 18–72; John Shy, *A People Numerous and Armed: Reflections on the Military Struggle for American Independence* (New York, 1976), 135–62.

6. Gates to Mellish, Apr. 11, 1773, Mellish Papers.

7. Lee to Gates, May 6, 1774, Gates Papers; Gates to Lee, July 1, 1774, *Lee Papers* 1:126.

8. Gates to Lee, July 1, 1774, Lee Papers 1:126.

9. Adam Stephen to [Gates], Aug. 24, 1774; Gates to Stephen, Aug. 26, 1774; and Gates to William Byrd [of Westover], Oct. 6, 1774, all in Gates Papers.

10. Merrill Jensen, *The Founding of a Nation: A History of the American Revolution, 1763–1776* (New York, 1968), 477; Stephen to Richard Henry Lee, American Philosophical Society.

11. The two versions of Henry's speech are in Jensen, *Founding of a Nation*, 544.

12. Freeman, *Washington* 3:416–17.

13. Eliphalet Dyer to Joseph Trumbull, June 17, 1775, *LDC* 1:500.

14. John Adams to Elbridge Gerry, June 18, 1775, and to James Warren, June 20, 1775, ibid., 503, 518; Charles Lee to Gates, May 13, [1775], *Lee Papers* 1:179; Worthington C. Ford, ed., *Journals of the Continental Congress* (Washington, D.C., 1904–37), 2:97 (hereafter cited as *JCC*).

15. Gates to Washington, June 22, 1775, Washington, *Papers of George Washington, Revolutionary War Series* 1:23.

16. Richard Henry Lee to Francis Lightfoot Lee, May 21, 1775, *LDC* 1:366.

17. Eliphalet Dyer to Joseph Trumbull, June 20, 1775, ibid., 521; Don R. Gerlach, *Philip Schuyler and the American Revolution in New York, 1733–1777* (Lincoln, Neb., 1964), 284.

18. Benson J. Lossing, *The Life and Times of Philip Schuyler* (New York, 1860–73), 1:193.

19. Stanley M. Pargellis, "Wooster, David," Allen E. Johnson and Dumas Malone, eds., *Dictionary of American Biography* (New York, 1928–36), 20:524–25.

20. Mrs. Janet Livingston Montgomery, in [Louise L. Hunt, ed.], *Biographical Notes Concerning General Richard Montgomery* (Poughkeepsie, N.Y., 1876), 7; Gouverneur Morris to Lewis Morris, Feb. 26, 1775, Thomas A. Emmet Collection, New York Public Library, quoted in Max M. Mintz, *Gouverneur Morris and the American Revolution* (Norman, Okla., 1970), 57.

21. French, *First Year of the Revolution,* 61; Silas Deane to Elizabeth Deane, July 20, 1775, *LDC* 1:639; James Coggswell to Levi Hart, June 15, 1775, *Bulletin of the Boston Public Library* (Nov. 1900), 390, quoted in French, *First Year of the Revolution,* 177n.

22. French, *First Year of the Revolution,* 39–80; Freeman, *Washington* 3:492–93; Nathanael Greene to Samuel Ward, June 4, 1775, William Johnson, *Sketches of the Life and Correspondence of Nathanael Greene* (Charleston, S.C., 1822), 1:37.

23. Washington to Lund Washington, Aug. 20, 1775, Washington, *Papers of George Washington, Revolutionary War Series* 1:335–36; Washington to Richard Henry Lee, Aug. 29, 1775, ibid., 373.

24. Charles Martyn, *The Life of Artemas Ward, the First Commander-in-chief of the American Revolution* (New York, 1921), 179.

25. "Journal of Rev. Dr. Jeremy Belknap," *Proceedings of the Massachusetts Historical Society* 4 (1858–1860): 82; Charles Lee to Benjamin Rush, Oct. 20, [1775,] *Lee Papers* 1:214.

26. "Lang Syne," in *Poulson's American Advertizer,* Dec. 6, 1828, quoted in Kenneth R. Rossman, *Thomas Mifflin and the Politics of the American Revolution* (Chapel Hill, N.C., 1952), 199; Alexander Graydon, *Memoirs of His Own Time, with Reminiscences of the Men and Events of the Revolution,* ed. John S. Littell (Philadelphia, 1846), 374.

27. Theodore Thayer, *Nathanael Greene, Strategist of the American Revolution* (New York, 1960), 24–26, 65; Greene to Samuel Ward, Sr., Dec. 18 and 31, 1775, Nathanael Greene, *Papers of General Nathanael Greene,* ed. Richard K. Showman (Chapel Hill, N.C., 1980), 1:164, 172.

28. Noah Brooks, *Henry Knox* (New York, 1900), 13, 261, 265.

29. Freeman, *Washington* 3:580; Arthur Gilman, ed., *The Cambridge of 1776: . . . with which is incorporated The Diary of Dorothy Dudley* (Boston, 1876), 49, 68; George W. Greene, *Life of Nathanael Greene, Major-General in the Army of the Revolution* (New York, 1867), 1:142; Thayer, *Greene,* 73–74; Abigail Adams to John Adams, July 31, 1775, John Adams and Abigail Adams, *Familiar Letters of John Adams and His Wife,* ed. Charles Francis Adams (New York, 1876), 93.

30. Freeman, *Washington* 3:244.

31. Mar. 8, 1776, John Adams, *Papers of John Adams,* ed. Robert J. Taylor (Cambridge, Mass. 1977–), 4:47.

32. Gates to Adams, Mar. 8, 1776; Adams to Gates, Mar. 23, 1776; Gates to Adams, Apr. 23, 1776; Adams to Gates, April 27, 1776, all in ibid., 49, 59, 141–42, 148.

33. June 23, 1775, *LDC* 1:537.

34. Gates to Adams, Apr. 23, 1776, and Adams to Gates, Apr. 27, 1776, ibid., 141.

35. Gates to Adams, May 4, 1776, ibid., 165; Gates to Franklin, Dec. 5, 1775, Franklin, *Papers,* 22:284; Mercy Otis Warren to John Adams, Oct. [n.d], 1777, Adams, *Papers,* 3:269.

36. Washington to John Hancock, May 19 and 5, 1776, Washington, *Writings* 5:58, 18–19.

37. Curtis P. Nettels, *George Washington and American Independence* (Boston,

Mass., 1951), 269–72; Eric Foner, *Tom Paine and Revolutionary America* (New York, 1976), 63–66, 115, 134; Anne M. Ousterhout, *A State Divided: Opposition in Pennsylvania to the American Revolution* (New York, 1987), 114–16; "Memorial of the Committee of Privates of the Military Association belonging to the City and Liberties of Philadelphia," *Pennsylvania Gazette,* June 5, 1776; Richard Alan Ryerson, *The Revolution Is Now Begun: The Radical Committees of Philadelphia, 1765–1776* (Philadelphia, 1978), 219–28.

38. Washington, *Writings* 4:315–18.

39. James Duane's Notes of Debates, [Feb. 22, 1776,] *LDC* 3:295–96; John Adams, *Diary and Autobiography of John Adams,* ed. L. H. Butterfield (Cambridge, Mass., 1961), 3:388.

40. *JCC* 4:355–60.

41. Ibid., 383–85, 394–96, 399–401, 412–16.

42. Washington to John Jay, Apr. 14, 1779, ibid. 14:385; Gates to John Hancock, John Adams, Elbridge Gerry, and [Robert Treat] Paine, June 8, 1776, Gates Papers.

43. Samuel Chase and Charles Carroll of Carrollton to John Hancock, May 27, 1776, *LDC* 4:81–84; Charles P. Whittemore, *A General of the Revolution: John Sullivan of New Hampshire* (New York, 1961), 26–27.

44. Chase to Philip Schuyler, May 31, 1776, *LDC* 4:106; Charles Carroll, *Journal of Charles Carroll of Carrollton,* ed. Brantz Mayer (Baltimore, 1876), 104; Washington to John Hancock, June 17, 1776, Washington, *Writings* 5:152; Greene to Washington, May 21, 1776, Greene, *Papers* 1:216.

45. Edward S. Corwin, "Chase, Samuel," *Dictionary of Amer. Biog.* 4:37; Chase to Gates, June 13, 1776, *LDC* 4:201–02; John Sanderson, *Biography of the Signers of the Declaration of Independence* (Philadelphia, 1820–27), 7:260; Charles Carroll of Carrollton to Gates, June 14, 1776, Kate Mason Rowland, *The Life of Charles Carroll of Carrollton, 1737–1832* (New York, 1898), 1:176.

46. Chase to Gates, June 13, 1776, *LDC* 4:201; *JCC* 5:448; Adams to Gates, June 18, 1776, ibid. 4:261.

9. The Lost Victory

1. Riedesel, *Memoirs* 1:39–41, 276–77; Johann Bense, "A Brunswick Grenadier With Burgoyne: The Journal of Johann Bense, 1776–1783," trans. Helga B. Doblib, *New York History* 66 (Oct. 1985) 6:426; William Digby, *The British Invasion from the North: The Campaigns of Generals Carleton and Burgoyne From Canada, 1776–1777, with the Journal of William Digby, of the 53rd or Shropshire Regiment of Foot,* ed. James Phinney Baxter (Albany, N.Y., 1887), 88; August Wilhelm Du Roi, *Journal of Du Roi the Elder,* ed. Charlotte S. Epping (New York, 1911), 20–35.

2. Lord Sandwich to the king, June 24, 1776, *Correspondence of King George III from 1760 to December 1783,* ed. Sir John W. Fortescue (London, 1927–28), 3:387; Burgoyne to Germain, June 1, 1776, *Stopford-Sackville MSS.* 2:33.

3. Paul H. Smith, "Sir Guy Carleton," in George A. Billias, ed., *George Washington's Opponents* (New York, 1969), 104–08; Hudleston, *Burgoyne,* 107; Thomas Anburey, *Travels Through the Interior Parts of America* (London, 1789), 1:72.

4. *London Chronicle,* Aug. 9, 1776, quoted in Howson, *Burgoyne,* 111.

5. Carleton to Germain, June 20, 1776, *DAR* 12:152; Perry E. Leroy, "Sir Guy Carleton as a Military Leader during the American Invasion and Repulse in Canada, 1775–76" (Ph.D. diss., Ohio State University, 1960), 176–81; R. Arthur Bowler, "Sir Guy Carleton and the Campaign of 1776 in Canada," *Canadian Historical Review* 55 (June 1974): 132–33; George F. G. Stanley, ed., *For Want of a Horse* (Sackville, New Brunswick, 1961), 72–73.

6. July 7, 1776, Clinton Papers.

7. Burgoyne to Clinton, Nov. 7, 1776, ibid.; William Phillips to Simon Fraser, Sept. 7, 1776, in C. T. Atkinson, ed., "Some Evidence for Burgoyne's Expedition," *Journal of the Society for Army Historical Research* 26 (Winter 1948): 135; Gabriel Christie to Simon Fraser, Sept. 12, 1776, ibid.; Charles H. Jones, *History of the Campaign for the Conquest of Canada in 1776* (Philadelphia, 1882), 156; "Journal of the Brunswick Corps in America under General von Riedesel," Howard H. Peckham, ed., *Sources of American Independence from the Collections of the William L. Clements Library* (Chicago, 1978), 1:234.

8. Burgoyne to Clinton, Nov. 7, 1776, Clinton Papers; George Germain, "Precis of Operations & Plans," British Public Record Office, CO 5/253, f. 26.

9. Sir Francis Kerr Clerke to Lord Polwarth, July 13, 1776, in Howson, *Burgoyne,* 115.

10. Schuyler to Washington, July 12, 1776, Papers of George Washington (Library of Congress microfilm, 1964) (hereafter Washington Papers); "Journal of Bayze Wells of Farmington, May, 1775–February, 1777, at the Northward and in Canada," *Collections of the Connecticut Historical Society* 7 (1899): 267; Charles Cushing to his brother, July 8, 1776, *AA,* 5th ser., 1:132; John Trumbull to Jonathan Trumbull, July 12, 1776, in Trumbull, *Autobiography,* 302; Uriah Cross, "Narrative of Uriah Cross in the Revolutionary War," ed. Vernon A. Ives, *New York History* 63 (July 1982): 292.

11. July 10, 1776, Gates Papers.

12. To George Washington, July 29, 1776, ibid.

13. Minutes of a Council of War, July 7, 1776, ibid.

14. Remonstrance of field officers to Schuyler, July 8, 1776, *AA,* 5th ser., 1:233–34. The colonels who did not sign can be identified from the officers' address to John Sullivan, July 8, 1776, ibid., 127.

15. Washington to Schuyler, July 17, 1776, and to Gates, July 19, 1776, Washington, *Writings* 5:289–90, 302–03.

16. Gates to Washington, July 29, 1776, Gates Papers; Schuyler to Washington, July 24, 1776, ibid.; Washington to Schuyler, August 13, 1776, Washington Papers.

17. Memo of conversation between Schuyler and Gates, June 30, 1776, enclosed in Schuyler to Washington, July 1, 1776, Washington Papers; Washington to John Hancock, July 4, 1776, ibid.; Don R. Gerlach, *Proud Patriot: Philip Schuyler and the War of Independence, 1775–1783* (Syracuse, N.Y., 1987), 162–65; Gates to John Adams, July 17, 1776, Gates Papers.

18. Schuyler to Gates, Aug. 3, 1776; Gates to Schuyler, Sept. 11 and 12, 1776, all in Gates Papers.

19. Gates to Arnold, Aug. 18, 1776, *AA,* 5th ser., 1:1051; Schuyler to Hancock, Aug. 29, 1776, ibid., 1217.

20. Orders and Instructions for Brigadier General Arnold, Aug. 7, 1776, ibid., 1217.

21. Gates, After-Orders, Sept. 6, 1776, ibid., 474; Anthony Wayne to ?, n.d., quoted in Edward P. Hamilton, *Fort Ticonderoga: Key to a Continent* (Boston, Mass., 1964), 142.

22. Jonathan Trumbull to Schuyler, July 9, 1776, *AA,* 5th ser., 1:145; Gates to Hancock, Sept. 2, 1776, Gates Papers; Benjamin Rush to Thomas Jefferson, March 12, 1803, Rush, *Letters of Benjamin Rush,* ed. L. H. Butterfield (Princeton, N.J., 1951), 2:858.

23. Jones, *Conquest of Canada,* 129–30.

24. General Return of the Northern Department, Sept. 29, 1776, *AA,* 5th ser., 2:618; Wigglesworth to New Hampshire Committee of Safety, Sept. 27, 1776, ibid., 574; Gates to Jonathan Trumbull, Oct. 22, 1776, ibid., 1192; Trumbull, *Autobiography,* 29; Gates to Egbert [Robert] Benson, Aug. 22, 1776, Gates Papers; Lewis Beebe, *Journal of Dr. Lewis Beebe,* ed. Frederic R. Kirkland (New York, 1971), 357; Morris H. Saffron, *Surgeon to Washington: Dr. John Cochran, 1730–1807* (New York, 1977), 28–32; James E. Gibson, *Dr. Bodo Otto and the Medical Background of the American Revolution* (Springfield, Ill., 1937), 104–14; Gerlach, *Proud Patriot,* 190–91; Philip Schuyler to Gouverneur Morris, Feb. 18, 1778, Gouverneur Morris Collection, Columbia University.

25. Hamilton, *Fort Ticonderoga,* 144; *AA,* 5th ser., 1:800; James M. Hadden, *Hadden's Journal and Orderly Books: A Journal Kept in Canada and Upon Burgoyne's Campaign in 1776 and 1777,* ed. Horatio Rogers (Albany, N.Y., 1884), 237; Instructions for Lieut. Whitcomb, Aug. 19, 1776, copy enclosed in Gates to Washington, Aug. 28, 1776, Gates Papers; Gates to John Hancock, Sept. 30, 1776, ibid.

26. *AA,* 5th ser., 1:390; Jones, *Conquest of Canada,* 111–12, 137–40; Gates to Schuyler, Oct. 4, 1776, Gates Papers.

27. Gates to Schuyler, Sept. 30, Oct. 4 and 11, 1776; and Arnold to Gates, Sept. 28, 1776 and Oct. 7, 1776, Gates Papers; Gates, General Orders, Oct. 11, 1776, *AA,* 5th ser., 2:1085.

28. Beebe, *Journal,* 354; Jeduthan Baldwin, *The Revolutionary Journal of Col. Jeduthan Baldwin,* ed. Thomas H. Baldwin (Bangor, Me., 1906), 80–81; Arnold to Gates, Oct. 12, 1776, Gates Papers; Arnold to Schuyler, Oct. 15, 1776, *AA,* 5th ser. 2:1079–80.

29. Beebe, *Journal,* 354.

30. Ibid., 355; Baldwin, *Journal,* 82; Gates, General Orders, Oct. 27, 1776, *AA,* 5th ser., 3:532; Oration of Gilbert Tennent, Oct. 20, 1776, ibid., 2:1144–45.

31. Oct. 29, 1776, Washington Papers.

32. Jones, *Conquest of Canada,* 174–79.

33. Trumbull, *Autobiography,* 30–34, 306–07; Gates to Arthur St. Clair, [June 12, 1777?], Gates Papers.

34. Gates to Schuyler, Oct. 31 and Nov. 5, 1776, Gates Papers; Trumbull, *Autobiography,* 36; Carleton to George Germain, Oct. 22, 1776, *DAR* 10:392.

35. Nov. 5, 1776, Papers of the Continental Congress (National Archives microfilm, 1961).

36. Schuyler to Gates, Oct. 11, 1776, Gates Papers; Schuyler to John Hancock

and to George Washington, Sept. 25, 1776, Washington Papers; Schuyler to Livingston, n.d., Bayard Tuckerman, *Life of General Philip Schuyler* (New York, 1905), 151; Stockton to Benjamin Rush, Oct. 13, 1776, *LDC* 5:342; Stockton and Clymer to John Hancock, Oct. 26, 1776, ibid., 392–93; Schuyler to Stockton and Clymer, Nov. 8, 1776, Benson J. Lossing, *The Life and Times of Philip Schuyler* (New York, 1873), 2:146–48; *AA,* 5th ser., 3:709.

37. Jonathan Rossie, *The Politics of Command* (Syracuse, N.Y., 1975), 128; Gates to Schuyler, Nov. 15, 1776, and Gates to Hancock, Nov. 27, 1776, Gates Papers.

38. Joseph Bloomfield, *Citizen Soldier: The Revolutionary War Journal of Joseph Bloomfield,* ed. Mark E. Lender and James Kirby Martin (Newark, N.J., 1982), 116; Trumbull, *Autobiography,* 37.

39. R. Arthur Bowler, *Logistics of the Failure of the British Army in America, 1775–1783* (Princeton, N.J., 1975), 218–24.

40. Trumbull, *Autobiography,* 36; Leroy, "Sir Guy Carleton," 476–78.

41. Burgoyne to Henry Clinton, Nov. 7, 1776, Clinton Papers.

42. Ibid.; William Phillips to Burgoyne, Oct. 23, 1776, Fonblanque, *Episodes,* 220.

43. Fonblanque, *Episodes,* 220; "Purport of a conversation between Lieut. General Burgoyne and Lieut. Col. Christie," British Public Record Office, CO 42/35, pp. 219–21.

10. Howe versus Burgoyne

1. Lee to Benjamin Rush, June 4, 1778, *Lee Papers* 2:398; Stedman, *American War,* 1:398; Willcox, *Clinton,* 98.

2. Howe to Germain, June 7, 1776, and Germain to Carleton, Aug. 22, 1776, *DAR* 12:146, 187–88; Germain to Carleton, Mar. 26, 1777, ibid. 14:53.

3. *Stopford-Sackville MSS.* 2:54.

4. Dispatch from London, Dec. 11, 1776, in *Pennsylvania Gazette,* Apr. 2, 1777; Burgoyne to Germain, Dec. 9, 1776, British Public Record Office, CO 42/35, pp. 449–51; *London Chronicle,* Dec. 11, 1776.

5. Carleton to Germain, Oct. 22, 1776, British Public Record Office, CO 43/13, f. 138; *London Chronicle,* Dec. 9, 1776.

6. "Memorandum & Observations relative to the Service in Canada submitted to Lord George Germain by J. Burgoyne," [December, n.d., 1776,] (copy) Shelburne Papers, vol. 66, William L. Clements Library; Carleton to Germain, Oct. 16, 1777, *DAR* 14:217; H[ans] Stanley to [Francis, tenth earl of Huntingdon], Dec. 18, 1776, George III, *Corr.,* 3:163; Germain to George III, Dec. 10, 1776, and George III to North, Dec. 13, 1776, ibid., 405–07.

7. *London Chronicle,* Dec. 12, 1776; Burgoyne, *Expedition,* 2, 94.

8. Dec. 13, 1776, George III, *Corr.* 3:407.

9. Burgoyne to [George Germain], Jan. 1, 1777, British Public Record Office, CO 42/36, part 1, p. 1; *London Chronicle,* Jan. 9, 1777, and May 28, 1778.

10. Germain to George III, Feb. 14, 1777, and George III to North, Feb. 24, 1777, George III, *Corr.* 3:421.

11. Valentine, *Lord North* 1:391, 455; Cabinet Minute, Feb. 25, 1777, *Dartmouth MSS.* 2:433. Although Lord North was ill, he attended the House of Commons on Feb. 25. John Robinson to George III, Feb. 26, 1777, George III, *Corr.* 3:421–22; *London Chronicle,* Feb. 27, 1777.

12. Feb. 28, 1777, *DAR* 14:43.

13. Henry Clinton, "Journal from Recollections and Papers," filed at the end of Jan. 1790, Clinton Papers, cited in Willcox, *Clinton,* 135, 161–62.

14. Burgoyne to Germain, Jan. 1, 1777, British Public Record Office, CO 42/36, part 1, pp. 1–22; "Removal of Lord Germain," n.d., Historical Manuscripts Commission, *Manuscripts of Miss M. Eyre Matcham; Captain H. V. Knox . . .* (London, 1909), 273; "Thoughts for Conducting the War from the Side of Canada by Lieut.-General John Burgoyne," Feb. 28, 1777, *DAR* 14:44.

15. Howe to Germain, Nov. 30, 1776, and Dec. 20, 1776, 264–65, 268; "Remarks on the Conduct of the War—from Canada," Mar. 5, 1777, and "Remarks on the Requisitions & observations," Mar. 5, 1777, George III, *Corr.* 3:443–44; George III, "Remarks on the conduct of the War from Canada," n.d., Add. MSS. 18738, f. 196, British Library.

16. Howson, *Burgoyne,* 151–52. Ira D. Gruber, however, believes that "Germain was in no mood to evaluate critically the conflicting plans. He was eager to avoid asking Parliament for an increase in the army in America and anxious to believe that Sir William Howe, his own nominee, would win the war if persuaded to act more ruthlessly." Gruber, *The Howe Brothers and the American Revolution* (Chapel Hill, N.C., 1972), 180.

17. Germain to Carleton, Mar. 26, 1777, *DAR* 14:53–56.

18. Burgoyne to Philemon Pownoll, Mar. 6, 1777, Clinton Papers; *London Chronicle,* Apr. 9, 1777; Burgoyne, *Expedition,* 6.

19. Howe to Germain, Apr. 2, 1777, and Germain to Howe, May 18, 1777, *DAR* 14:64–66, 84.

11. Schuyler or Gates?

1. Gates to John Hancock, Nov. 27, 1776, and Robert H. Harrison to Gates, Nov. 26, 1776, Gates Papers; Nelson, *Gates,* 73; Wilkinson, *Memoirs* 1:98.

2. Lee to Gates, Dec. 13, 1776, *Lee Papers* 2:348.

3. Washington to Gates, Dec. 14, 1776, and Washington to Arnold, Dec. 14, 1776, *AA,* 5th ser., 3:1216–17, 1258.

4. Freeman, *Washington* 4:297, 309; Washington to Gates, Dec. 23, 1776, Washington Papers; Samuel White Patterson, *Horatio Gates: Defender of American Liberties* (New York, 1941), 109.

5. Dec. 12, 1776, *LDC* 5:603.

6. John Hancock to Philip Schuyler, Dec. 30, 1776, ibid., 702; John Adams to Abigail Adams, Feb. 6, 1777, ibid. 6:224; Samuel Adams to James Warren, Jan. 1, 1777, ibid. 6:3; William Ellery to Nicholas Cooke, Dec. 25, 1776, ibid. 5:654;

Elbridge Gerry to James Warren [?], Dec. 23, 1776, ibid., 641; Hancock to Robert Treat Paine, Jan. 13, 1777, ibid. 6:91.

7. Jan. 9, 1777, ibid., 65.

8. Washington to Gates, Feb. 5, 1777, Gates Papers; Robert Morris and George Clymer to Gates, Feb. 24, 1777, *LDC* 6:335.

9. Joseph Trumbull to William Williams, Nov. 18, 1776, *AA,* 5th ser., 3:1498; Benjamin Rush's Notes of Debates, Feb. 19, 1777, *LDC* 6:323–24.

10. *JCC* 7:136; James Wilson to Arthur St. Clair, [Feb. 20, 1777,] *LDC* 6:333.

11. Feb. 28, 1777, Papers of the Continental Congress.

12. Washington to Gates, Mar. 3 and 10, 1777, Washington, *Writings* 7:232, 267, and n; Gates to Washington, Mar. 7, 1777, Gates Papers.

13. *JCC* 7:170; Saffron, *Surgeon to Washington,* 28–31; Schuyler to John Hancock, Feb. 24, 1777, Papers of the Continental Congress.

14. *JCC* 7:175; H. James Henderson, *Party Politics in the Continental Congress* (New York, 1974), 106–07.

15. "Some papers drawn up in the conference with Genl. Gates to be laid on the Table for the Information of any of the Members of Congress," no. 154, vol. 2, ff. 382, 374, Papers of the Continental Congress; St. Clair to Gates, Feb. 18, 1777, Gates Papers.

16. For congressional attendance records, see *LDC* 6:xv–xxii. For identification of radicals and conservatives, see Henderson, *Party Politics,* 106–07; *Journals of the Provincial Congress, Provincial Convention, etc., of the State of New York, 1775–1777* (Albany, 1842), 2:378, cited in *LDC* 6:173; Schuyler to John Hancock, January 4, 1777, Papers of the Continental Congress; petition of Seth Warner, February 26, 1777, ibid.; "Some papers drawn up in the conference with Genl. Gates," no. 154, vol. 2, ff. 373–74, ibid.

17. *JCC* 7:180–81, 202.

18. Gates to Anthony Wayne, Mar. 18, 1777, Gates Papers; Saffron, *Surgeon to Washington,* 29, 31.

19. William Whipple to Josiah Bartlett, Apr. 17, 1777, and Francis Lewis to John McKesson, Jan. 31, 1777, *LDC* 6:550, 171; *Journals of the Provincial Congress of New York, 1775–1777,* 1:855; William Smith, *Historical Memoirs,* ed. William H. W. Sabine (New York, 1956), 2:137–38; Matt Bushnell Jones, *Vermont in the Making, 1750–1777* (Cambridge, Mass., 1939), 276; Edward P. Alexander, *A Revolutionary Conservative: James Duane of New York* (New York, 1938), 40, 70–74.

20. Alexander, *Revolutionary Conservative,* 124; Horatio Gates's Notes for a Speech to Congress, [June 18, 1777], *LDC* 7:307.

21. Gates to Hancock, Apr. 22, 1777, and Morris to Gates, May 7, 1777, Gates Papers; *JCC* 7:307.

22. Lovell to Gates, May 1, 1777, *LDC* 7:4–5; Gates to Lovell, May 12, 1777, Gates Papers.

23. Gates to Hancock, May 11, 1777, Papers of the Continental Congress.

24. Gates to Washington, May 13 and 24, 1777; Washington to Gates, May 19, 1777; Gates to Hancock, May 14, 1777; and Gates to Lovell, May 25, 1777, all in Gates Papers.

25. Lovell to Gates, May 22, 1777, *LDC* 7:105–06; James Duane to Robert R.

Livingston, John Jay, Gouverneur Morris, and Robert Yates, Apr. 19, 1777, and Philip Livingston, James Duane, and William Duer to the New York Convention, Apr. 21, 1777, ibid. 6:617, 630; William Duer to Robert R. Livingston, May 28, 1777, ibid. 7:140–41; Board of War to Gates, June 4, 1777, ibid., 168; *JCC* 7:326, 336, 364, and 8:375.

26. Samuel Adams to Gates, May 24, 1777, and James Lovell to Gates, June 8, [1777], *LDC* 7:115, 177–78; Wilkinson to Gates, June 7, 1777, and Robert Gates to Gates, June 6, 1777, Gates Papers.

27. Schuyler to Gates, June 9, 1777, Gates Papers; Francis Lightfoot Lee to Richard Henry Lee, June 17, 1777, *LDC* 7:203.

28. Duer to Philip Schuyler, June 19, 1777, and Horatio Gates's Notes for a Speech to Congress, [June 18, 1777], *LDC* 228–29, 213–15.

29. Duane to Schuyler, June 19, 1777, and Duer to Schuyler, June 19, 1777, ibid., 225, 230.

30. *JCC* 8:509–11.

12. Ticonderoga

1. Carleton to Germain, June 26 and May 22, 1777, *DAR* 14:122, 93; Burgoyne to Germain, May 15, 1777, Atkinson, "Some Evidence for Burgoyne's Expedition," 139; Fraser to [John Robinson], July 13, 1777, Benjamin F. Stevens, ed., *Facsimiles of Manuscripts in European Archives Relating to America, 1773–1783* (London, 1889–95), 16: no. 1571.

2. Burgoyne to Germain, May 19, 1777, *DAR* 14:86; Anburey, *Travels* 1:99–110.

3. Anburey, *Travels* 1:161–62; Georg Pausch, *Journal of Captain Pausch,* ed. William L. Stone (Albany, 1886), 110–12. On the English soldier's scorn for foreigners, see Christopher Duffy, *The Military Experience in the Age of Reason* (London, 1987), 31–32.

4. Riedesel, *Memoirs* 1:2–9, 242; Riedesel to Baroness von Riedesel's mother, May 24, 1776, and to Baroness von Riedesel, June 28, 1776, Frederika von Riedesel, *Baroness von Riedesel and the American Revolution: Journal and Correspondence of a Tour of Duty, 1776–1783,* trans. Marvin L. Brown, Jr. (Chapel Hill, N.C., 1965), 171, 178.

5. "Jour. of the Brunswick Corps," 257; Riedesel, *Memoirs* 1:237, 252.

6. Burgoyne to Germain, July 11, 1777, *DAR* 14:136; Richard Cox to Henry Clinton, June 20, 1760, Clinton Papers, quoted in Willcox, *Clinton,* 24; Hadden, *Journal,* 359.

7. Digby, *Journal,* 18–19; Anburey, *Travels* 1:197, 205; Hadden *Journal,* lxxi–lxxii; Pausch, *Journal,* 121–22; Hargrove, *Burgoyne,* 118–21; Burgoyne to Harvey, May 19, 1777, Burgoyne, *Expedition,* xxxi.

8. Burgoyne, *Expedition,* xxvii–xxviii; Charles W. Snell, "A Report of the Strength of the British Army under Lieutenant General John Burgoyne," (Saratoga National Historical Park, 1951), 8, 32–35; Burgoyne to Carleton, May 26, 1777, British Public Record Office, CO 42/36, p. 401; Carleton to Burgoyne, May 29,

1777, *DAR* 14:100; Phillips to Carleton, June 17, 1777, British Public Record Office CO 42/36, p. 497; Burgoyne to Germain, May 14, 1777, *DAR* 14:78–79.

9. Hadden, *Journal,* 53; Bowler, *Logistics,* 226.

10. Bowler, *Logistics,* 227n; Burgoyne to Carleton, June 6, 1777, and Carleton to Burgoyne, June 7, 1777, and Phillips to Carleton, June 17, 1777, and Carleton to Phillips, June 18, 1777, British Public Record Office, CO 42/36, ff. 437–42, 445, 501.

11. Burgoyne to Harvey, May 19, 1777, in Burgoyne, *Expedition,* xxxi; Burgoyne to Germain, June 22, 1777, *DAR* 14:119.

12. Germain to Carleton, Mar. 26, 1777, and Howe to Carleton, April 5, 1777, *DAR,* 55, 66.

13. For the date of arrival of Howe's letter, see Howe to Germain, April 2, 1777, and Carleton to Germain, May 27, 1777, ibid., 97; Carleton to Burgoyne, June 10, 1777, British Public Record Office, CO 42/36, f. 449.

14. "Jour. of the Brunswick Corps," 266–67; Hadden, *Journal,* 52–55; John Burgoyne, *Orderly Book of John Burgoyne,* ed. Edmund B. O'Callaghan (Albany, 1860), 2–3.

15. Roger Lamb, *Memoir of His Own Life* (Dublin, 1811), 172; Burgoyne, *Orderly Book,* 1; "Jour. of the Brunswick Corps," 268–70.

16. Proclamation, June 20, 1777, Hadden, *Journal,* 59–62.

17. Ibid., 67n–74n; Doris Begor Morton, *Philip Skene of Skenesborough* (New York, 1959), 26; Burgoyne to Germain, June 22 and July 11, 1777, *DAR* 14:120, 140.

18. Burgoyne's speech to the Indians, June 21, 1777, British Public Record Office, CO 42/36, pp. 571–74; Burgoyne to Howe, Aug. 6, 1777, *DAR* 14:156; Burke's speech, reported in Horace Walpole to William Mason, Feb. 12, 1778, Walpole, *Horace Walpole's Correspondence,* ed. W. S. Lewis (New Haven, 1937–83), 28:355–56.

19. [Francis Hopkinson], "To John Burgoyne," *Pennsylvania Packet,* Aug. 26, 1777, Hopkinson, *Comical Spirit of Seventy-Six: the Humor of Francis Hopkinson,* ed. Paul M. Zall (San Marino, Calif., 1976), 94; William Livingston, in *Pennsylvania Packet,* Aug. 26, 1777, in Livingston, *The Papers of William Livingston,* ed. Carl E. Prince and Dennis P. Ryan (Trenton, N.J., 1980), 2:42.

20. Hadden, *Journal,* 65; Burgoyne, *Orderly Book,* 12–17.

21. Burgoyne, *Orderly Book,* 17–19; Hadden, *Journal,* 306–07; Lamb, *Memoir,* 168; Digby, *Journal,* 201.

22. Arthur St. Clair, *The St. Clair Papers,* ed. William Henry Smith (Cincinnati, 1882), 1:6, 54–59; Schuyler to St. Clair, June 5, 1777, "Proceedings of a General Court Martial . . . For the Trial of Major General Schuyler," *Collections of the New-York Historical Society* (1879): 98; St. Clair to Schuyler, St. Clair, *Papers* 1:396–400.

23. Schuyler to Continental Congress, June 25, 1777, Papers of the Continental Congress; Schuyler to Washington, June 25, 1777, Washington Papers; appendix, St. Clair, *Papers* 1:54n.

24. Wilkinson, *Memoirs* 1:174, 178; "Proceedings of a General Court Martial, Held at White Plains, in the State of New-York, By Order of his Excellency General Washington, Commander in Chief of the Army of The United States of America, For

the Trial of Major General St. Clair, August 25, 1778," *Collections of the New-York Historical Society* 13 (1879): 105–06, 79, 24–27, 157.

25. "Court Martial of St. Clair," 70; "Jour. of the Brunswick Corps," 275.

26. Burgoyne to Germain, July 11, 1777, *DAR* 14:134–36; Burgoyne to Earl Hervey, July 11, 1777, Fonblanque, *Episodes,* 247. Sugar Loaf Hill was more important as an observation post than as an artillery mount because, at its distance of 1,400 to 1,500 yards from the fort, a shot from a 12-pounder would be spent and inaccurate; John A. Williams, "Mount Independence in Time of War, 1776–1783," *Vermont History* 35 (Apr. 1967): 100–01.

27. Hoffman Nickerson, *The Turning Point of the Revolution* (Boston, 1928, reprint ed., Port Washington, N.Y., 1967), 1:143–44; Anburey, *Travels* 1:319–21; Hadden, *Journal,* 83–84.

28. Wilkinson, *Memoirs* 1:183–84; "Court Martial of St. Clair," 151.

29. "Court Martial of St. Clair," 157; St. Clair to James Bowdoin, July 9, 1777, St. Clair, *Papers* 1:425; Stanley, *For Want of a Horse,* 106–09; Hadden, *Journal,* 84.

30. "Court Martial of St. Clair," 111–13.

13. Escape

1. Francis Napier, "Lord Francis Napier's Journal of the Burgoyne Campaign," ed. S. Sidney Bradford, *Maryland Historical Magazine* 57 (Dec. 1962): 299–300; Anburey, *Travels* 1:323–25; Digby, *Journal,* 208–09; Simon Fraser to [John Robinson], July 13, 1777, Stevens, *Facsimiles,* 16: no. 1571.

2. Stevens, *Facsimiles,* 16: no. 1571; Riedesel, *Memoirs* 1:114–16; Burgoyne to Germain, July 11, 1777, *DAR* 14: 136–38.

3. Ebenezer Fletcher, *The Narrative of Ebenezer Fletcher,* ed. Charles I. Bushnell (New York, 1866), 5–43.

4. Lord Lindsay, *Lives of the Lindsays* (London, 1858), 2:343; Anburey, *Travels* 1:326–39.

5. Anburey, *Travels* 1: 339; Burgoyne to Germain, July 11, 1777, *DAR* 14: 137; Digby, *Journal,* 212; "Court Martial of St. Clair," 113; Wilkinson, *Memoirs* 1:186–87; Arthur St. Clair to James Bowdoin, July 28, 1777, St. Clair, *Papers* 1:436; Francis B. Heitman, *Historical Register of the Officers of the Continental Army during the War of the Revolution,* ed. Robert H. Kelly (Baltimore, 1973), 418; Hadden, *Journal,* 88; Napier, "Journal," 300-03; Howard H. Peckham, *The Toll of Independence: Engagements and Battle Casualties of the American Revolution* (Chicago, 1974), 37; William L. Stone, *History of Beverly* (Boston, 1843), 76.

6. Anburey, *Travels* 1:339–43.

7. James Thacher, *Military Journal of the American Revolution* (Boston, 1827), 83–84.

8. Stanley, *For Want of a Horse,* 109–10; Roger Lamb, *An Original and Authentic Journal of Occurrences during the Late American War* (Dublin, 1809), 141–43; Burgoyne, *Orderly Book,* 52; Benson J. Lossing, *The Pictorial Field-Book of the Revolution* (New York, 1850), 1:141; Burgoyne, *Expedition,* 61.

9. Burgoyne to Riedesel, July 7, 1777, Riedesel, *Memoirs* 1:268.
10. Burgoyne to Germain, July 11, 1777, *DAR* 14:142.

14. The American Rubicon

1. Burgoyne, *Expedition,* appendix, xxi. The manuscript version of this letter in the British Public Record Office does not contain this passage. *DAR* 14:140–42. See also the discussion in Howson, *Burgoyne,* 257–71, 327–30.
2. Phillips to duke of Newcastle, July 10, 1777, Newcastle Papers, University of Nottingham.
3. Burgoyne, *Expedition,* 113; Burgoyne to Germain, July 11 and 30, 1777, *DAR* 14:139, 153; Burgoyne to Howe, Aug. 6, 1777, ibid., 156.
4. [Ernst Johann Friedrich Schüler von Senden,] "Denkwürdigkeiten aus den hinterlassenen Papieren E. Schüler's von Senden," *Zeitschrift für Kunst, Wissenschaft und Geschichte des Krieges* 47 (1839): 170, 186–87; Digby, *Journal,* 227–28; Hadden, *Journal,* 94–95, 90, 154; Hay to Gates, May 17, 1777, Gates Papers; William H. Hill, *Old Fort Edward Before 1800* (Fort Edward, N.Y., 1929), 322; Burgoyne, *Expedition,* 39.
5. Burgoyne, *Expedition,* 109; Burgoyne to Germain, July 11, 1777, *DAR* 14:141.
6. Riedesel, *Memoirs* 1:238.
7. Ibid., 121–22, 246; Burgoyne, *Orderly Book,* 45.
8. To Germain, July 11, 1777, *DAR* 14:140.
9. Burgoyne, *Orderly Book,* 45; Digby, *Journal,* 228–29; Hadden, *Journal,* 519–28; William Tryon to William Knox, Apr. 21, 1777, *DAR* 14:71.
10. Hadden, *Journal,* 96, 100–07.
11. Schuyler to St. Clair, July 8, 1777, "Documents in Relation to the Part Taken by Vermont in Resisting the Invasion of Burgoyne In 1777," *Collections of the Vermont Historical Society* 1 (1870): 176–77; Schuyler to Washington, July 9, 1777, Washington Papers; Lossing, *Schuyler* 2:206, 209, 214.
12. Schuyler to Washington, July 14, 1777, Washington Papers.
13. Lossing, *Schuyler* 2:229.
14. Ibid., 248–49, 255–57; Gerlach, *Proud Patriot,* 264–300; Glover to James Warren, Aug. 6, 1777, John Glover, "General John Glover's Letterbook," ed. Russell W. Knight, *Collections of the Essex Institute* 112 (Jan. 1976): 26.
15. Max von Eelking, *The German Allied Troops in the War of Independence, 1776–1783,* trans. J. G. Rosengarten (Albany, 1893), 129; Burgoyne, *Expedition,* 39; Burgoyne to Riedesel, July 23, 1777, Riedesel, *Memoirs* 1:270–71.
16. Riedesel, *Memoirs* 1:270–71; Digby, *Journal,* 233–34.
17. Atkinson, "Some Evidence for Burgoyne's Expedition," 142; Charles Neilson, *An Original, Compiled and Corrected Account of Burgoyne's Campaign* (Albany, N.Y., 1844), 68–78; Burgoyne, *Expedition,* 49; Stanley, *For Want of a Horse,* 122–23.
18. Digby, *Journal,* 239–41.

19. Burgoyne to Germain, July 30, 1777, *DAR* 14:153–55.

20. Stanley, *For Want of a Horse,* 127; Burgoyne, *Expedition,* 100.

21. Howe to Burgoyne, July 17, 1777, Burgoyne, *Expedition,* appendix, xxvi–xxvii; Napier, "Journal," 308.

22. *DAR* 14:156–57.

23. Clinton-Howe conversations, July 6, 8, 13 [1777], Clinton Papers, cited in Willcox, *Clinton,* 153–61.

24. Ibid., 163–64.

25. Ibid., 164–66; Clinton, *American Rebellion,* 60–65; Clinton to Howe, July 21, 1777 (draft), Clinton Papers; confession of Daniel Taylor, Oct. 9, 1777, George Clinton, *Public Papers of George Clinton,* ed. Hugh Hastings (New York, 1900), 2:399.

15. Defiance

1. Burgoyne, *Expedition,* 108–09.

2. Ibid., 107; Burgoyne to Germain, Aug. 20, 1777, *DAR* 14:165; Riedesel, *Memoirs* 1:128, 252–54; Riedesel to Germain, Aug. 28, 1777 (trans.), House of Lords Record Office, 6.16/22.

3. Burgoyne, *Expedition,* 103.

4. "Instructions for Lieutenant Colonel Baume, on a secret expedition to the Connecticut River" and "Instructions to Colonel Skeene, upon the expedition to Bennington," ibid., appendix, xxxiv–xxxviii, xxxix–xl; Hadden, *Journal,* 294n, 516.

5. Burgoyne, *Orderly Book,* 71–76; Digby, *Journal,* 249.

6. Burgoyne, *Expedition,* 106; Herbert D. Foster and Thomas W. Streeter, "Stark's Independent Command at Bennington," *Proceedings of the New York Historical Association* 5 (1905): 24–33.

7. Vermont Council of Safety to Colonels of State Militia, Aug. 13, 1777, Baum to Burgoyne, Aug. 13 and 14, 1777, and Stark to the New Hampshire Council, Aug. 18, 1777, all in "Docs. in Relation to the Invasion of Burgoyne," 197, 199–200, 204; John Carroll Cavanagh, "The Military Career of General Benjamin Lincoln in the War of the American Revolution, 1775–1781" (Ph.D. diss., Duke University, 1969), 117–18.

8. Baum to Burgoyne, Aug. 14, 1777, "Docs. in Relation to the Invasion of Burgoyne," 200–01.

9. Burgoyne to Baum, Aug. 14, 1777, ibid., 201; Hadden, *Journal,* 118–19; Riedesel to Duke Charles William Ferdinand of Brunswick, Sept. 3, 1780, and Breymann to [Riedesel], Aug. 20, 1777, Riedesel, *Memoirs* 1:263, 256; "Relation of the Expedition to Bennington," enclosed in Riedesel to Germain, Aug. 28, 1777, House of Lords Record Office, 6.16/22c.

10. Joseph Rudd to his father, Aug. 20, 1777, Henry D. Hall, "The Battle of Bennington," *Proceedings of the Vermont Historical Society* (Oct. 1896): 63.

11. Ibid., 129–31; Burgoyne to Germain, Aug. 20, 1777, *DAR* 14:163–64; Theodore Dwight to William L. Stone, Sept. 27, 1866, Stone, *Campaign of Burgoyne,* 287–88; Stanley, *For Want of a Horse,* 132n; Stark to the New Hampshire

Council, Aug. 18, 1777, "Docs. in Relation to the Invasion of Burgoyne," 204–05; Eelking, *The German Allied Troops in the War of Independence,* 132.

12. "Docs. in Relation to the Invasion of Burgoyne," 204–05; Breymann to [Riedesel], Aug. 20, 1777, ibid. 223–25; Philip Skene to the Earl of Dartmouth, Aug. 30, 1777, Stevens, *Facsimiles* 18: no. 1665; Hadden, *Journal,* 136.

13. Hadden, *Journal,* 138; Digby, *Journal,* 252–53.

14. Burgoyne to Germain, Aug. 20, 1777, *DAR* 14:165.

15. On Burgoyne's mistaken expectations of a large Loyalist turnout, see Philip Ranlet, *The New York Loyalists* (Knoxville, Tenn., 1986), 96–105. Burgoyne to Germain, Aug. 20, 1777, *DAR* 14:166.

16. Germain to Carleton, Mar. 26, 1777, *DAR* 14:56.

17. Burgoyne to Germain, Oct. 20, 1777 (two letters), ibid., 236, 239.

18. Riedesel, *Memoirs* 1:137n; Burgoyne, *Expedition,* 115, 114, 78; Hadden, *Journal,* 140.

19. German officer's letter, Nov. 15, 1777, Pettengill, *Letters from America,* 97.

20. Burgoyne, *Expedition,* 108–10; Burgoyne, *Orderly Book,* 98; Digby, *Journal,* 267; Frederika von Riedesel, *Baroness von Riedesel,* 47.

16. The Call

1. Marchant to Cooke, Aug. 5, 1777, *LDC* 7:427; Samuel Adams to James Warren, July 31, 1777, ibid., 396; Charles Thomson's Notes of Debates, July 26, 1777, ibid., 382–83; "General Gates, the darling of the New Englanders," in a German officer to [?], Nov. 15, 1777, Pettengill, *Letters from America,* 98; Jacob Hiltzheimer, *Extracts from the Diary of Jacob Hiltzheimer, of Philadelphia, 1765–1798,* ed. Jacob C. Parsons (Philadelphia, 1893), 34. See also Benjamin Rush to John Adams, Aug. 8, 1777, Adams, *Papers,* 5:267–68.

2. Charles Thomson's Notes of Debates, July 26, 1777, *LDC* 7:382–83.

3. Charles Thomson's Notes of Debates, [July 28, 1777], ibid., 388–89; Duer to Schuyler, July 29, 1777, ibid., 389–90; New York Delegates to the New York Council of Safety, July 29, 1777, ibid., 393–94; Samuel Adams to James Warren, July 31, 1777, ibid., 397; Thomas Burke to Richard Caswell, July 30, 1777, ibid., 396; *JCC* 8:585.

4. *JCC* 8:596, 603–04; John Adams to Abigail Adams, Aug. 1, 1777, *LDC* 7:400; Lovell to William Whipple, July 29, Aug. 1, 4, 11, 1777, ibid., 390, 402, 412, 458; New England Delegates to Washington, Aug. 2, 1777, ibid., 405; William Williams to Jonathan Trumbull, Sr., Aug. 6, 1777, ibid., 434; Nathanael Greene to Jacob Greene, July 13, 1777, and to Catherine Greene, July 17, 1777, Greene, *Papers* 2:119, 121–23; Washington to New York Council of Safety, Aug. 4, 1777, Washington, *Writings* 9:12; Rossie, *Politics of Command,* 159–66; *JCC* 8:603–04.

5. *JCC* 8:614, 617, 642, 649, 668.

6. Gates to Jonathan Trumbull, Aug. 6, 1777, Gates Papers; Samuel Adams to John Langdon, Aug. 7, 1777, *LDC* 7:435.

7. George Clinton to Duane, Aug. 27, 1777, in John Armstrong to Jared Sparks, Dec. 4, 1831, Jared Sparks Papers.

8. Ibid.; Gates to Washington, Aug. 22, 1777, and to Arthur St. Clair, Sept. 6, 1777, and to John Hancock, Aug. 20, 1777, all in Gates Papers; Jedediah Huntington to Andrew Huntington, Aug. 12, 1777, *Collections of the Connecticut Historical Society* 20 (1923): 363; Schuyler to John Hancock, Aug. 4, 1777, Papers of the Continental Congress; James Wilkinson, "General Return of the Troops at and in the Vicinity of this Post under the Command of the Honble. Major General Schuyler," Aug. 17, 1777, enclosed in Schuyler to Washington, Aug. 17, 1777, Washington Papers; Christopher Tappen to George Clinton, Aug. 8, 1777, Clinton, *Papers* 2:194–95.

9. John McKesson to George Clinton, Aug. 10, 1777, Clinton, *Papers* 2:206; Schuyler to Gouverneur Morris, Sept. 7, 1777, Gouverneur Morris Collection; Schuyler to John Jay, Aug. [Sept.?] 18, 1777, Jay, *John Jay: The Making of a Revolutionary,* ed. Richard B. Morris (New York, 1975), 1:435–36; Cavanagh, "Lincoln," 119; Gates to St. Clair, Sept. 6, 1777, and to Lincoln, Aug. 19, 1777, both in Gates Papers.

10. Gates's General Order, Aug. 20, 1777, in Wilkinson, *Memoirs* 1:225; Gates to St. Clair, Sept. 5, 1777, and address of Nixon's officers to Gates, Aug. 23, 1777, Gates Papers (Thomas Nixon should not be confused with John Nixon, in whose brigade he served); Heitman, *Officers of the Continental Army,* 38, 415; Henry Dearborn, *Revolutionary War Journals of Henry Dearborn, 1775–1783,* ed. Lloyd A. Brown and Howard H. Peckham (Chicago, 1939), 102; Glover to Jonathan Glover and Azor Orne, Sept. 5, 1977, Glover, "Letterbook," 40.

11. Morris Graham to Gorge Clinton, Aug. 31, 1777, Clinton, *Papers* 2:265–66; John Glover to Jonathan Glover and Azor Orne, Aug. 31 and Sept. 5, 1777, Glover, "Letterbook," 38, 40; Dearborn, *Journals,* 103, 104; Enos Hitchcock, "Diary of Enos Hitchcock, D.D., A Chaplain in the Revolutionary Army," ed. William B. Weeden, *Publications of the Rhode Island Historical Society,* n. s., 7 (July 1899): 130; Charles W. Snell, "A Report on the Organization and Numbers of Gates' Army, September 17, 1777, and October 17, 1777, including an Appendix with Regimental Data and Notes" (Saratoga National Historical Park, 1951), 6–10, 13.

12. Burgoyne to Gates, Aug. 20, 1777, and Gates to Burgoyne, Sept. 2, 1777, Gates Papers.

13. Gates to [Jonathan] Trumbull, Aug. 24, 1777, ibid.; Wilkinson, *Memoirs* 1:231–32.

14. James Wilkinson, "A General Return of the Continental Troops under the Command of the Honb: Major General Gates," Sept. 7, 1777, Gates Papers; Snell, "Report on the Organization and Numbers of Gates' Army," 4–12; Gates to Hancock, Sept. 3, 1777, Gates Papers.

15. [Gates,] General Orders, Sept. 6, 1777, Gates Papers.

16. Hitchcock, "Diary," 133; Wilkinson, *Memoirs* 1:232; Orderly Book of Lt. Col. Joseph Storer's York County, Massachusetts Regiment, Sept. 10, 1777, New-York Historical Society; Henry B. Livingston to Philip Schuyler, Sept. 11, 1777, Philip Schuyler Papers, New York Public Library; Gates to Hancock, Sept. 15, 1777, Gates Papers; Snell, "Organization and Numbers of Gates' Army," 61; Benjamin Warren, "Diary of Captain Benjamin Warren on the Battlefield of Saratoga," ed.

David E. Alexander, *Journal of American History* 3 (1909): 210; Neilson, *Burgoyne's Campaign,* 114; Richard Varick to Philip Schuyler, Sept. 12, 1777, Schuyler Papers.

17. Richard Varick to Philip Schuyler, Sept. 12, 1777, Schuyler Papers; James Duane to Philip Schuyler, Aug. 23, 1777, *LDC* 7:536. Arnold's fellow clerk was Ezekiel Huntley. L. H. Sigourney, *Letters of Life* (New York, 1868), 13–14; Richard Varick to Philip Schuyler, Nov. 18 and 20, 1776, in Rossie, *Politics of Command,* 215–18; Richard Varick to Philip Schuyler, Sept. 16, 1777, Schuyler Papers; *JCC* 8:665; Henry Brockholst Livingston to Philip Schuyler, Sept. 11, 1777, Schuyler Papers; Henry Brockholst Livingston to William Livingston, Sept. 14, 1777, in Edwin Brockholst Livingston, *The Livingstons of Livingston Manor* (New York, 1910), 250.

18. Richard Varick to Philip Schuyler, Sept. 12, 1777, Schuyler Papers; Arnold to Gates, Sept. 22, 1777, Gates Papers; Snell, "Report on the Organization and Numbers of Gates' Army," 13.

19. Richard Varick to Philip Schuyler, Sept. 12, 1777, Schuyler Papers; Robert Troup to John Jay, Sept. 14, 1777, Jay, *Correspondence and Public Papers of John Jay,* ed. Henry P. Johnston (New York, 1890), 1:165; John Armstrong to Jared Sparks, Dec. 4, 1831, Sparks Papers; Wilkinson, *Memoirs* 1:232; Neilson, *Burgoyne's Campaign,* 114.

20. Neilson, *Burgoyne's Campaign,* 115–17; Christopher Ward, *The War of the Revolution,* ed. John R. Alden (New York, 1952), 2:502–03; William L. Stone, ed., *Visits to the Saratoga Battle-Grounds* (Albany, 1895), 67n–68n, 321; John Ashton and Jotham Bemus to George Clinton, Sept. 17, 1777, Clinton, *Papers* 2:329.

21. Wilkinson, *Memoirs* 1:232–34; Gates to Lincoln, Sept. 13, 1777, Gates Papers; Henry B[rockholst] Livingston to Philip Schuyler, Sept. 13, 1777, Schuyler Papers.

22. Gates to Lincoln, Sept. 15, 1777, and Gates to several committees of Albany, Bennington, and Berkshire, Sept. 17, 1777, Gates Papers; Gates to Vermont Council of Safety, Sept. 17, 1777, "Docs. in Relation to the Invasion of Burgoyne," 232.

23. General orders, Sept. 13, 1777, Reuben Aldridge Guild, *Chaplain Smith and the Baptists* (Philadelphia, 1885), 207.

17. Saratoga

1. Burgoyne, *Expedition,* 46, 47, 51, 57; Riedesel, *Memoirs* 1:140.

2. Riedesel, *Memoirs* 1:140–41; Digby, *Journal,* 267–69; Henry Brockholst Livingston to Philip Schuyler, Sept. 16, 1777, Schuyler Papers; anonymous Loyalist letter, quoted in Howson, *Burgoyne,* 238; Stone, *Campaign of Burgoyne,* 41; Stanley, *For Want of a Horse,* 145.

3. Pettengill, *Letters from America,* 99; Stone, *Saratoga Battle-Grounds,* 200n; Hadden, *Journal,* 152.

4. Neilson, *Burgoyne's Campaign,* 133–34; [Senden,] "Denkwürdigkeiten," 178; entry of Sept. 17, 1777, "Brig. Fraser's Accounts of Contingencies," British Public Record Office, T.1/572, bundle 3, cited in Howson, *Burgoyne,* 323.

5. Richard Varick to Philip Schuyler, Sept. 16 and 17, 1777, Schuyler Papers; Wilkinson, *Memoirs* 1:235–36; Neilson, *Burgoyne's Campaign,* 134; Ward, *War of the Revolution,* 2:505–06; Nickerson, *Turning Point of the Revolution,* 2:301.

6. Nickerson, *Turning Point of the Revolution,* 304–05; Hadden, *Journal,* 152–60; Burgoyne to Germain, Oct. 20, 1777, *DAR* 14:229–30; Riedesel, *Memoirs* 1:143–45; Snell, "Strength of the British Army," 96–97.

7. Hitchcock, "Diary," 133; "Lieutenant Thomas Blake's Journal," in Frederic Kidder, *History of the First New Hampshire Regiment* (Albany, N.Y., 1868), 33; Wilkinson, *Memoirs* 1:248–49; Snell, "Organization and Numbers of Gates' Army," 88; Henry Brockholst Livingston to Philip Schuyler, Sept. 16, 1777, Schuyler Papers; John Stark to the Commanding Officer of the Militia destined for the Northern Army, on the Way from the State of New Hampshire, Sept. 17, 1777, "Docs. in Relation to the Invasion of Burgoyne," 235.

8. Entry of Sept. 17, 1777, Hitchcock, "Diary," 147.

9. Morgan Lewis to Philip Schuyler, Sept. 17, 1777, Richard Varick to Philip Schuyler, Sept. 17, 1777, and Henry Brockholst Livingston to Philip Schuyler, Sept. 26, 1777, Schuyler Papers; Henry R. Stiles, *The History of Ancient Wethersfield, Connecticut* (New York, 1904), 2:216; Wilkinson, *Memoirs* 1:274; Chester's order, Sept. 15, 1777, "Orderly Book of Colonel Thaddeus Cook," 13.

10. Richard Varick to Philip Schuyler, Sept. 17, 18, 25, 1777, and to Henry Brockholst Livingston, Sept. 17, 1777, all in Schuyler Papers; Ebenezer Wild, "The Journal of Ebenezer Wild (1776–1781)," *Proceedings of the Massachusetts Historical Society,* 2nd ser., 6 (1890–91): 94; letter of a German officer to [?], Nov. 15, 1777, Pettengill, *Letters from America,* 99; Thomas Anburey, *With Burgoyne from Quebec,* ed. Sydney Jackman (Toronto, 1963), 171–72; Stanley, *For Want of a Horse,* 145; Riedesel, *Memoirs* 1:143–44.

11. Riedesel, *Memoirs,* 1:145–46; Wild, "Journal," 94; Hadden, *Journal,* 161–62; Stanley, *For Want of a Horse,* 146–47.

12. Wilkinson, *Memoirs* 1:238–40; Gates to John Hancock, Sept. 22, 1777, and Arnold to Gates, Sept. 22, 1777, both in Gates Papers; Burgoyne, *Expedition,* 44.

13. Burgoyne, *Expedition,* 61; Napier, "Journal," 316; Digby, *Journal,* 272–73; Pettengill, *Letters from America,* 102; Dearborn, *Journals,* 105–106; Don Higginbotham, *Daniel Morgan, Revolutionary Rifleman* (Chapel Hill, 1961), 65–67; Hadden, *Journal,* 162–63; Anburey, *With Burgoyne from Quebec,* 172–73.

14. Richard Varick to Philip Schuyler, Sept. 19, 1777, Schuyler Papers.

15. Diary of Captain [Ebenezer] Wakefield, Stone, *Saratoga Battle-Grounds,* 152; Philip Van Cortlandt, "Autobiography of Philip Van Cortlandt, Brigadier-General in the Continental Army," *Magazine of American History* 2 (May 1878): 286.

16. Burgoyne to Germain, Oct. 20, 1777, *DAR* 14:229–31; Wilkinson, *Memoirs* 1:240; Maria H. Campbell, *Revolutionary Services and Civil Life of General William Hull* (New York, 1848), 92–96.

17. Glover to Jonathan Glover and Azor Orne, Sept. 21, 1777, Glover, "Letterbook," 43; Digby, *Journal,* 273–74; "Letter from General Enoch Poor," n.d., in Frank Moore, *The Diary of the Revolution* (New York, 1860), 1:497–98; Charles Coffin, *The Lives and Services of Major General John Thomas, Colonel Thomas Knowlton, Colonel Alexander Scammell, Major General Henry Dearborn* (New York, 1845),

86, 269; William O. Clough, "Colonel Alexander Scammell," *Granite Monthly* 14 (June 1892): 269; Anburey, *With Burgoyne from Quebec,* 174–75; Hadden, *Journal,* 162–66; Burgoyne, *Expedition,* 79, 122n; Lamb, *Journal,* 101; Riedesel, *Memoirs* 1:145–51; Pausch, *Journal,* 135–140; Burgoyne to Germain, Oct. 20, 1777, *DAR* 14:231.

18. Pausch, *Journal,* 141; Gates to John Hancock, Sept. 22, 1777, Gates Papers; Neilson, *Burgoyne's Campaign,* 143; Elting, *Battles of Saratoga,* 54; Wilkinson, *Memoirs* 1:245–46; Burgoyne to Germain, Oct. 20, 1777, *DAR* 14:231.

19. Campbell, *William Hull,* 97; Warren, "Diary," 212; Glover, "Letterbook," 43. The return of the dead, wounded, and missing Americans is in Kidder, *First New Hampshire Regiment,* 35, but see also a return of 51 killed, 182 wounded, and 40 missing in Rufus Lincoln, *The Papers of Captain Rufus Lincoln of Wareham, Mass.,* ed. James Minor Lincoln (Cambridge, Mass., 1904), 27; Wilkinson, *Memoirs* 1:246.

20. Snell, "Strength of the British Army," 90 (a judicious balancing of varied returns); Pettengill, *Letters from America,* 101–02; Anburey, *With Burgoyne from Quebec,* 176–77; Frederika von Riedesel, *Baroness von Riedesel,* 48–49.

21. Glover, "Letterbook," 43; Anburey, *With Burgoyne from Quebec,* 175. But see Arnold's reprimand to company officers for pushing on in front of their men instead of bringing up the rear and for not punishing laggards with "Instant Death." Division Orders, Sept. 20, 1777 (copy), in "Orderly Book of Colonel Thaddeus Cook," 18.

22. Wilkinson, *Memoirs* 1:253–61; Henry Brockholst Livingston to Schuyler, Sept. 23, 24, and 26, 1777, and Varick to Schuyler, Sept. 22, 24, and 25, 1777, all in Schuyler Papers. Gates General Order, Sept. 22, 1777; Arnold to Gates, Sept. 22, 23, and 27 and Oct. 1, 1777; Gates to Arnold, Sept. 23 (two letters) and 28, 1777; and Gates to Hancock, Sept. 23, 1777, all in Gates Papers. Gates General Orders, Sept. 25 and 28, 1777, "Orderly Book of Colonel Thaddeus Cook," 27, 31.

23. Gates to Elizabeth Gates, Sept. 22, 1777, Gates Papers.

18. Repulse

1. Burgoyne to Henry Watson Powell, Sept. 21, 1777, Emmett Collection, New York Public Library; Burgoyne, *Expedition,* 58.

2. Pausch, *Journal,* 148; Warren, "Diary," 213.

3. Stanley, *For Want of a Horse,* 149; Clinton to Burgoyne, Sept. 11, 1777, Clinton Papers.

4. Riedesel, *Memoirs* 1:160, referring to Howe and Clinton, speaks of "the former's promise to send word in the course of eight days." As Howe's last letter had been written July 17, when he was about to sail south, there was no reason for him to write in eight days. The promise, therefore, could meaningfully have come only from Clinton; Riedesel, writing afterward, appears to have made a slip of the pen. The translation by the editor of the memoirs, William L. Stone, is faithful to the original: Max von Eelking, *Leben und Wirken des Herzoglich Braunschweig'schen General-Lieutenants Friedrich Adolph Riedesel, Freihern zu Eisenbach* (Leipzig, 1856), 2:162.

5. Burgoyne to Clinton, Sept. 21, 1777, Clinton Papers.

6. Riedesel, *Memoirs* 1:151–54; Pausch, *Journal,* 145–49; Elting, *Battles of Saratoga,* 55–56.

7. Burgoyne, *Expedition,* 53; Burgoyne to Clinton, Sept. 27, 1777, *DAR* 14:190–91; journal of Thomas Scott, May 16, 1778, Fonblanque, *Episodes,* 287–90.

8. Riedesel, *Memoirs* 1:156–57; Burgoyne to Clinton, Sept. 28, 1777, *DAR* 14:191–92.

9. Clinton to Burgoyne, Oct. 5, 1777, *DAR* 14:192; Henry Clinton, memorandum, October, "after taking the forts," 1777, Clinton Papers; Henry Clinton to William Howe, Sept. 4, 1777 (draft), ibid.; Willcox, *Clinton,* 179–81.

10. Willcox, *Clinton,* 184; Clinton, *Papers* 2:398–99, 413, 443–44.

11. Clinton, *American Rebellion,* 72–78; Clinton to William Howe, Oct. 9, 1777, and William Hotham to Richard Howe, Oct. 9, 1777, *DAR* 14:197–202; Clinton to Burgoyne, Oct. 8, 1777, Clinton Papers; Willcox, *Clinton,* 180–84.

12. Willcox, *Clinton,* 177.

13. Snell, "Organization and Numbers of Gates' Army," 20; Snell, "Strength of the British Army," 98, 99; Gates to President of Congress, Oct. 5, 177, Gates Papers; general orders of Sept. 26, and Oct. 2, 1777, "Orderly Book of Colonel Thaddeus Cook" 28, 38; Neilson, *Burgoyne's Campaign,* 157–60; Burgoyne, *Expedition,* 124.

14. Burgoyne, *Expedition,* 124; Burgoyne, *Orderly Book,* 125; Riedesel, *Memoirs* 1:158–60.

15. Riedesel, *Memoirs* 1:160–62; Riedesel's Memoire no. 2, end of Oct., 1777, Riedesel Letters, 1776–1783, Hessian no. 46, in Bancroft Papers no. 63, New York Public Library; Burgoyne, *Expedition,* 80, 81; Burgoyne to Clinton, Oct. 25, 1777, Clinton, *American Rebellion,* 74n.

16. Dearborn, *Journals,* 108; Wild, "Journal," 97; Pausch, *Journal,* 159–60; Snell, "Strength of the British Army," 99–100; Napier, "Journal," 321; [Richard Pope,] Journal of the British Army, p. 109, probably compiled by a member of the Forty-seventh Regiment of Foot, Huntington Library, photostat copy in New York Public Library; Stone, *Campaign of Burgoyne,* 56–57.

17. Gates to George Clinton, Oct. 4, 1777, Gates papers; Snell, "Organization and Numbers of Gates' Army," 20; Digby, *Journal,* 286–87.

18. W. H. Sumner, "Colonel [John] Brooks and Captain Bancroft," *Proceedings of the Massachusetts Historical Society* 4 (Feb. 1858): 273, 275.

19. Ebenezer Mattoon [an artillery lieutenant in the battle] to Philip Schuyler, Oct. 7, 1835, Stone, *Campaign of Burgoyne,* 371–72.

20. Benjamin Lincoln to John Laurens, Feb. 5, 1781, Jared Sparks, ed., *Correspondence of the American Revolution* (Boston, 1853), 2:535; Benjamin Lincoln to [?], Mar. 19, 1799, Francis Bowen, *Benjamin Lincoln* (Boston, 1847), 260–61; Dearborn, *Journals,* 108; Campbell, *William Hull,* 101; Hitchcock, "Diary," 153; Blake, "Journal," 36; Pausch, *Journal,* 166–67. According to the account written long afterward by James Wilkinson, who became a sworn enemy of Gates, he advised Gates to attack, whereupon Gates replied, "Well, then, order on Morgan to begin the game" at the enemy right. Morgan then advised that a simultaneous attack be made at the front. Gates appears to have been a cipher. Wilkinson, *Memoirs* 1:267–68.

21. Wilkinson, *Memoirs* 1:270–71; Neilson, *Burgoyne's Campaign,* 167–68.

22. On Arnold's drinking, see statement of Dr. Edmund Chadwick, surgeon in

Scammell's regiment, in Elliott C. Cogswell, *History of Nottingham, Deerfield, and Northwood* (Manchester, N.H., 1878), 345–46. Sumner, "Brooks and Bancroft," 274; Samuel Woodruff to William L. Stone, Oct. 31, 1827, Stone, *Campaign of Burgoyne,* 325; Wilkinson, *Memoirs* 1:273; Riedesel, *Memoirs* 1:163, 205–06; a German officer to [?], November 15, 1777, Pettengill, *Letters from America,* 105; Pausch, *Journal,* 167; Frank A. Gardner, "Colonel John Paterson's Regiment," *Massachusetts Magazine* 8 (1915): 35.

23. Dearborn, *Journals,* 108–09; Lamb, *Journal,* 163–64; Anburey, *With Burgoyne from Quebec,* 184; Burgoyne to Clinton, Oct. 20, 1777, Clinton Papers; "A Recollection of the American Revolutionary War. By a British Officer," *Virginia Historical Register* 6 (July 1853): 210; Stone, *Saratoga Battle-Grounds,* 246n; Burgoyne, *Expedition,* 82, 125.

24. Sumner, "Brooks and Bancroft," 273–74; Henry Dearborn, "A Narrative of the Saratoga Campaign," *Bulletin of the Fort Ticonderoga Museum* 1 (Jan. 1929): 8–9; Van Cortlandt, "Autobiography," 287; Nicholas Stoner to Jeptha R. Simms, n.d., 1848, Stone, *Campaign of Burgoyne,* 66–67; Ellen Hardin Walworth, *Battles of Saratoga, 1777* (Albany, N.Y., 1891), 99n, citing manuscript of an unnamed Brunswick major.

25. Burgoyne to Germain, Oct. 20, 1777, *DAR* 14:233; Riedesel, *Memoirs* 1:207.

26. Benjamin Lincoln to John Laurens, Feb. 5, 1781, and to William Heath, Mar. 19, 1799, Benjamin Lincoln Papers, Massachusetts Historical Society; Gates to John Hancock, Oct. 12, 1777, Gates Papers; Dearborn, *Journals,* 109; Stanley, *For Want of a Horse,* 163; Burgoyne to Germain, Oct. 20, 1777, *DAR* 14:233; E[benezer]. Mattoon to Josiah Quincy, Feb. 3, 1837, *Collections of the Massachusetts Historical Society,* 3rd ser., 6 (1837): 284; William Sullivan, *The Public Men of the Revolution* (Philadelphia, 1847), 128; Cavanagh, "Benjamin Lincoln," 125, 128.

27. Frederika von Riedesel, *Baroness von Riedesel,* 51–53; Burgoyne, *Expedition,* 125–26; Wilkinson, *Memoirs* 1:269n–70n.

28. Wilkinson, *Memoirs* 1:282.

29. Snell, "Strength of the British Army," 90; Thacher, *Journal,* 102.

19. Surrender

1. Wilkinson, *Memoirs* 1:283; Campbell, *William Hull,* 106–07; see also Jonathan Trumbull, Jr., to Jonathan Trumbull, October 14, 1777, "The Trumbull Papers," *Collections of the Massachusetts Historical Society,* 7th ser., 2 (1902): 164.

2. Caleb Stark, *Memoir and Official Correspondence of Gen. John Stark* (Concord, N.H., 1860), 74; John Fellows to Horatio Gates, Oct. 8, 1777, and to Benjamin Lincoln, Oct. 9, 1777, Gates Papers; Jacob Bayley to Benjamin Lincoln, Oct. 8, 1777, ibid.; Ebenezer Mattoon to Philip Schuyler, Oct. 7, 1835, Stone, *Campaign of Burgoyne,* 89, 376; Burgoyne, *Expedition,* 83, 84.

3. James Wilkinson to George Cinton, Oct. 9, 1777, Wilkinson, *Memoirs* 1:274; Dearborn, "A Narrative of the Saratoga Campaign," 10–11; Burgoyne to Gates, Oct. 9, 1777, and Gates to Burgoyne, Oct. 12, 1777, Gates Papers.

4. Anburey, *With Burgoyne from Quebec,* 190–91; Burgoyne, *Expedition,* 129; Riedesel, *Memoirs* 1:170; Burgoyne, *Orderly Book,* 129; Stone, *Campaign of Burgoyne,* 87 and n; Lamb, *Journal,* 181; Wilkinson, *Memoirs* 1:281.

5. Burgoyne to Germain, Oct. 20, 1777, *DAR* 14:233; Burgoyne, *Expedition,* 55, 82; Riedesel, *Memoirs* 1:171.

6. Hitchcock, "Diary," 155; Wild, "Journal," 98; Wilkinson, *Memoirs* 1:281, 284–85.

7. Wilkinson, *Memoirs* 1:285–89; conversation between William Gordon and Glover, Mar. 18, 1785, cited in William Gordon, *The History of the Rise, Progress, and Establishment, of the Independence of the United States of America* (London, 1788), 2:567–69; Rufus Putnam, *Memoirs of Rufus Putnam,* ed. Rowena Buel (Boston, 1903), 68–72; Plan of the Battle of Saratoga by Gen. Rufus Putnam, New-York Historical Society.

8. Burgoyne, *Expedition,* 130; Phillips to Henry Clinton, Oct. 25, 1777, Clinton Papers.

9. Burgoyne, *Expedition,* 32; Frederika von Riedesel, *Baroness von Riedesel,* 58.

10. Stark, *Stark,* 74; Howard P. Moore, *Life of General John Stark* (New York, 1949), 382–84; Stone, *Campaign of Burgoyne,* 92; Riedesel, *Memoirs* 1:173–74.

11. Riedesel, *Memoirs* 1:175–79; minutes of a council of war Oct. 12 and 13, 1777, *DAR* 14:212–14; Frederika von Riedesel, *Letters and Journals Relating to the War of the American Revolution, and the Capture of the German Troops at Saratoga, By Mrs. General Riedesel,* trans. William L. Stone (Albany, 1867), 112; Burgoyne, *Expedition,* 83, 129; Riedesel, *Memoirs* 1:179–81; Burgoyne to Gates, Oct. 13, 1777, Gates Papers.

12. Wilkinson, *Memoirs* 1:299–303.

13. Minutes of a council of war, Oct. 14, 1777, *DAR* 14:214–15; Burgoyne to Gates, Oct. 14, 1777, Gates Papers.

14. George Clinton to Gates, Oct 15, 1777, and Gates to Burgoyne, Oct. 15, 1777, Gates Papers; Wilkinson, *Memoirs* 1:309.

15. Minutes of a council of war, Oct. 15, 1777, *DAR* 14:215; Burgoyne to Gates, Oct. 15, 1777, Gates Papers; Wilkinson, *Memoirs* 1:309–11.

16. Burgoyne, *Expedition,* 32–33, 38–39; Riedesel, *Memoirs* 1:183–84; Frederika von Riedesel, *Journals,* 108–10; Burgoyne to Gates, Oct. 16, 1777, Gates Papers.

17. Wilkinson, *Memoirs* 1:311–16; Oliver Boardman, "Journal," *Collections of the Connecticut Historical Society* 7 (1899); 231.

18. Frederika von Riedesel, *Journals,* 110–11; Frederika von Riedesel, *Baroness von Riedesel,* 60; Riedesel, *Memoirs,* 1:183–84, 188n; Burgoyne to Col. Phillipson, Oct. 20, 1777, Fonblanque, *Episodes,* 315; Burgoyne, *Expedition,* 83, lx; Joshua Pell, "Diary of Joshua Pell, Junior," *Magazine of American History* 2 (Feb. 1878):111.

19. Gordon, *History,* 1:573–74. I have preferred this version of the signing to Wilkinson's claim that he produced a previous letter to himself from Captain Craig, promising Burgoyne's compliance, which, when brought to Burgoyne, persuaded him to sign. Wilkinson, *Memoirs* 1:316–17.

20. Digby, *Journal,* 321; Riedesel, *Memoirs* 1:187, 188.

21. Stone, *Campaign of Burgoyne,* 129n.

22. Digby, *Journal,* 321; Riedesel, *Memoirs* 1:189n.

23. Neilson, *Burgoyne's Campaign,* 219; letter of a German officer, Nov. 15, 1777 to [?], Pettengill, *Letters from America,* 112–13.

24. Ebenezer Mattoon to Philip Schuyler, Oct. 7, 1835, Stone, *Campaign of Burgoyne,* 121, 379–80; Neilson, *Burgoyne's Campaign,* 219–20; Riedesel, *Memoirs* 1:189–90.

25. Snell, "Strength of the British Army," 87–91.

26. Glover to Gates, Nov. 16 and Dec. 4, 1777, Gates Papers; Gates to Lord Thanet, Oct. 26, 1777, "The Trumbull Papers," 174–76; Gates to Burgoyne, Mar. 2, 1778, Sparks, *Corr. Amer. Revolution* 2:532.

20. The Victor and the Vanquished

1. Gates to Timothy Bedel, Oct. 4, 1777, Gates Papers; Max M. Mintz, "Horatio Gates, George Washington's Rival," *History Today* 26 (July 1976): 420–28; Nelson, *Gates,* 171–77, 197–202; Greene, *Papers* 2:28–31.

2. Washington to Gates, Jan. 4, 1778, Washington, *Writings,* 10:263; Graydon, *Memoirs,* 300; Benjamin Rush to John Adams, Feb. 12, 1812, Rush, *Letters* 2:1, 120; Washington to Henry Laurens, Jan. 31, 1778, Washington, *Writings* 10:410.

3. Gates to Bedel, Sept. 14 and Nov. 15, 1777, and paper by Gates, "Troops at Albany, 1777," Gates Papers.

4. *JCC* 9:959, 971; Lafayette to Gates, Oct. 14, 1777, Marquis de Lafayette, *Lafayette in the Age of the American Revolution,* ed. Stanley J. Izerda (Ithaca, N.Y., 1977–79), 1:121; Gates, Instructions for the Marquis de Lafayette, [Jan. 31, 1778], ibid., 263–67.

5. Lafayette to Washington, Feb. 10, 1778, 295–96; Lafayette to Henry Laurens, Feb. 19, 1778, ibid., 299–301.

6. Hazen to Lafayette, Feb. 18, 1777, ibid., 289–90; Hazen to Gates, Feb. 20, 1778, Gates Papers; Allan S. Everest, *Moses Hazen and the Canadian Refugees in the American Revolution* (Syracuse, N.Y., 1976), 58.

7. Lafayette, *Lafayette in the American Revolution* 2:192n.

8. Washington to President of Congress, Nov. 11, 1777, and to Henry Laurens, Nov. 14, 1778, Washington, *Writings* 13:223–44 and 254–57; *JCC* 13:12–13.

9. Gates to Jay, Mar. 15, 1779, and Jay to Washington, Apr. 6 and 21, 1779, Jay, *John Jay* 1:576–77, 577n, 585; Washington to Jay, Apr. 14, 1779, Washington, *Writings* 14:381–86.

10. Richard H. Kohn, "The Inside History of the Newburgh Conspiracy: America and the Coup d'Etat," *William and Mary Quarterly* 27 (Apr. 1970): 187–213.

11. *Parl. Register,* 3 [vol. 20, 1781]: 556, and 5 [vol. 22, 1781]: 138.

12. Hargrove, *Burgoyne,* 221–32.

13. *Parl. Register* 11:154, and 3 [vol. 20, 1781]: 554, and 5 [vol. 22, 1781]: 138–39.

14. *Ibid.* 7 [vol. 14]: 175–76; Maurice R. O'Connell, *Irish Politics and Social Conflict in the Age of the American Revolution* (Philadelphia, 1965), 330–31, 343, 356, 358; Hargrove, *Burgoyne,* 247–50. For a listing of Burgoyne's votes in Parlia-

ment in support of Fox, see Leslie G. Mitchell, *Charles James Fox and the Disintegration of the Whig Party, 1782–1794* (London, 1971), 274.

15. Howson, *Burgoyne,* 283–84.

16. *London Times,* Oct. 26, 1790, cited in Carl B. Cone, *Burke and the Nature of Politics: The Age of the French Revolution* (Lexington, Ky., 1964), 348.

Epilogue. The Turn of the Scale

1. Silas Deane, *The Deane Papers, Collections of the New-York Historical Society,* ed. Charles Isham (New York, 1890), 5:445–46.

2. Jonathan R. Dull, *A Diplomatic History of the American Revolution* (New Haven, Conn., 1985), 80–88.

3. William Temple Franklin, ed., *Memoirs of the Life and Writings of Benjamin Franklin* (London, 1833), 2:59; Jonathan R. Dull, *The French Navy and American Independence: A Study of Arms and Diplomacy, 1774–1787* (Princeton, N.J., 1975), 67–68, 90–93; Gérard to the American Commissioners, Dec. 5, 1777, Franklin, *Papers,* 25:246; Benjamin Franklin, Silas Deane, and Arthur Lee to the Committee for Foreign Affairs, Dec. 18, 1777, ibid., 306; Edward E. Hale and Edward E. Hale, Jr., *Franklin in France, from Original Documents* (Boston, 1887–88), 1:176.

4. Mackesy, *War for America,* 154–59.

5. Dearborn, *Journals,* 106.

Index